TO WHOM DO YOU BELONG?

(An Owner's Manual)

William D. Grebe

PRESS

www.xulonpress.com

This is Book # <u>**ONE**</u>, the First of an
Anticipated Twelve (12) Volumes.

For Information and Copies of this Book, contact:
New Life In Christ Foundation,
<u>P. O. Box 2124, Castle Rock, CO 80104</u>

TABLE OF CONTENTS

Preface. vii

Introduction. xi

Chapter 1:   The Trinity 17

Chapter 2:   God, The Father. 30

Chapter 3:   God, The Son (Jesus Christ) 45

Chapter 4:   God, The Holy Spirit 63

Chapter 5:   Salvation 79

Chapter 6:   Security Of The Believer/Assurance/Confidence 105

Chapter 7:   Word Of God (All Powerful And Imperishable) 120

Chapter 8:   "Lord" Jesus Christ 136

Chapter 9:   Prayer. 152

Chapter 10: Walking With God 196

Chapter 11: Marriage (Separate But Equal Roles) 213

Chapter 12: Husbands 233

Chapter 13: Wives 240

Chapter 14: Fatherhood. 257

Chapter 15: Mothers (Godly Mothers) 276

Chapter 16: Riches, Material Wealth. 298

Chapter 17: God's Conclusion (To All Matters) 365

PREFACE

For most people that have ever worked on appliances, equipment or a vehicle, it is helpful and most often absolutely necessary to have an "Owner's Manual". The Manual contains descriptions, pictures, drawings and schematics of the particular appliance, equipment or vehicle being described. The manual is authored by the "Maker" of the appliance, equipment or vehicle and the "Maker" is therefore the authority on that product.

The "Maker" has an intimate and detailed knowledge of the intricate working of the item(s) being so featured. You as a "Born Again Believer" need such a manual. God is your "Maker", He knows you intimately, He can provide the pictures, the details, the drawings and the best way to fix and cause you to run smoothly. For this God has provided His Word—The Holy Bible. The compilation of Scripture from His Word and thoughts related thereto, which you are about to read, is centered on God's Word as it applies to your everyday life. This book is in no way intended to add anything to His Word or leave out anything from His Word (see the warnings in Matthew and Revelations). It does not pretend to be completely exhaustive on any of the subjects addressed, but is here to help you apply what the "Maker" has already designed.

My prayer is that God will use this subject type of an approach, to meet our needs in times of hope, fears, aspirations, directions, depressions, corrections and all other considerations, by instilling His principles, His Doctrines, His Word, in His Children. That He will build you up in order that you may operate at maximum efficiency while going through this short journey (we call life) (a vapor) here on earth. *(James 4:14) Yet you do not know what your life will be like tomorrow. You are just a vapor that appears for a little while and then vanishes away.*

We as His Children need to function properly when faced with the difficulties of being human and living in a world that is so dominated by non-Godly values. We are in this world, but not of this world.

(John 15:19) "If you were of the world, the world would love its own; but because you are not of the world, but I chose you out of the world, because of this the world hates you. (John 17:15-18)(vs 15) "I do not ask You to take them out of the world, but to keep them from the evil one. (vs 16) "They are not of the world, even as I am not of the world. (vs 17) "Sanctify them in the truth; Your word is truth. (vs 18) "As You sent Me into the world, I also have sent them into the world.

This book, with its subject type of an approach, is intended to be an abbreviated manual to go to for help, as a quick reference, to the specific problems and opportunities that so often and in very real ways confront us on a daily basis. In no way would I presume that this manual would have any ability to help you, except for the truths already found in God's Word. After much agony and desire to run from this project, I compile this only by God's direction and by His allowing me to be a part of what He wants to accomplish. Thanks be to God, that He has directed this to be a part of His Eternal Plan, this compilation of various subject matters already addressed in His Word.

The comments in each Chapter are only to help relate personal experiences or give examples that might help you relate to the principles that God has previously taught. If this manual can only spur you on in considering the Scriptures as it pertains to your everyday life and the interactions we are faced with in relationships, jobs, stewardship and all other matters covered herein, then it will have been a stepping stone in the right direction. The success of this book will not be measured by the number of copies bought and read, but rather by the number of hearts and lives changed eternally by the power of God's Word. If anything changes your heart, and that change has a lasting eternal value, it can only come from the Word of God, by the revelation of the Holy Spirit.

Everything that is eternal and of eternal value, only comes from God. "Except the house be built by God, he who labors, labors in vain".

(Psalms 127:1) A Song of Ascents, of Solomon. Unless the LORD builds the house, They labor in vain who build it;

May God richly bless you as you consider His word as it pertains to your daily life. We are human, yet God's Word is applicable to us while we are here on earth, ... let us get to know It and live It. *(** **Ecclesiastes 12:13) The conclusion, when all has been heard, is: fear God and keep His commandments, because this applies to every person.***

You can't keep His commandments unless you know them. Ignorance of the law is not a defense in our country and it is the same with God.

(1 John 2:15-16)(vs 15) Do not love the world nor the things in the world. If anyone loves the world, the love of the Father is not in him. (vs 16) For all that is in the world, the lust of the flesh and the lust of the eyes and the boastful pride of life, is not from the Father, but is from the world.

If we do not "Belong To The World", then we "Belong To God"!!! "To Whom Do You Belong" (?), and what is your "Owner's Manual"?

INTRODUCTION

As we look at the different things to which we belong or have belonged, we see a little glimpse of the meaning of belonging to something.

As a Child you belonged to your parents. You had certain legal rights as well as did your parents. Each party could be held accountable by the law to fulfill those responsibilities and not violate their authority.

As a Parent you belong to your spouse, your household and again there are certain legal rights and responsibilities attached. Just look at the divorce courts to see what some of these are.

As a Club Member we have rules, by-laws and authority attached which makes us responsible to our fellow members.

As a Team member we need to respect the other members and the coach of the team, all the while having a moral commitment if not a legal responsibility.

As an Employee/Employer we are to obey the applicable rules which involves our bosses, our fellow employees and labor laws as well as numerous other considerations.

The above are but a few brief examples of what we are obligated to in our everyday life. Hopefully this gives you some food for thought as we get into the most important aspect of belonging.

As a Christian we "Belong to God" and therefore also to your fellow "believer". *(Matthew 22:36-40)(vs 36) "Teacher, which is the great commandment in the Law?" (vs 37) And He said to him, " 'YOU SHALL LOVE THE LORD YOUR GOD WITH ALL YOUR HEART, AND WITH ALL YOUR SOUL, AND WITH ALL YOUR MIND.' (vs 38) "This is the great and foremost commandment. (vs 39) "The second is like it, 'YOU SHALL LOVE YOUR NEIGHBOR AS YOURSELF.' (vs 40) "On these two commandments depend the whole Law and the Prophets."*

We do not have a legal requirement to adhere to the above, but a higher calling than any law any nation has ever enacted, implemented or attempted to enforce. Our calling is to the Almighty God, the One "To Whom We Belong"!!!

The Apostle Paul was so filled with the presence of God that he penned the words in *(Acts 27:23-25)(vs 23) "For this very night an angel of the God* **to whom I belong and whom I serve** *stood before me, (vs 24) saying, 'Do not be afraid, Paul; you must stand before Caesar; and behold, God has granted you all those who are sailing with you.' (vs 25) "Therefore, keep up your courage, men, for I believe God that it will turn out exactly as I have been told.*

Paul was a prisoner, being transported by ship to be tried by Caesar himself, when the storms at sea were so severe (14 days and nights in a mighty storm) they were threatening the lives of all on board (276 men). Paul was calm, he had the assurance from God for his protection and all those on the ship. Paul by his own words spoke to all mankind, for all eternity, ... **"The God To Whom I Belong"** ... , stating that he was truly a **"Prisoner"** of God.

The question that must be asked from our inner soul is
" To Whom Do You or I Belong" (?):

1) You cannot serve two (2) masters- *(Matthew 6:24) "No one can serve two masters; for either he will hate the one and love the other, or he will be devoted to one and despise the other. You cannot serve God and wealth.*

We cannot serve God and wealth (defined in the original Greek as mammon or avarice). Wealth or Mammon has the connotation of being an avarice deified. In each and every case it is contrary to trusting God;

2) You must choose "To Whom You Belong"!!!- *(Joshua 24:14-15) (vs 14) "Now, therefore, fear the LORD and serve Him in sincerity and truth; and put away the gods which your fathers served beyond the River and in Egypt, and serve the LORD. (vs 15) "If it is disagreeable in your sight to serve the LORD, choose for yourselves today whom you will serve: whether*

the gods which your fathers served which were beyond the River, or the gods of the Amorites in whose land you are living; but as for me and my house, we will serve the LORD."

Joshua chose to serve the "Most High God" therefore he and his family chose to "Belong To God"!!!;

3) If you choose God, life consists of serving Him- *(Luke 12:15) Then He said to them, "Beware, and be on your guard against every form of greed; for not even when one has an abundance does his life consist of his possessions."*

Life does not consist of our possessions of bank accounts, land, cars, houses, fine garments, yachts or other play toys, but rather in our relationship to God through Faith and Trust in Jesus Christ; and

4) If you choose God, you must recognize that He dwells within you- *(1 Corinthians 6:19-20)(vs 19) Or do you not know that your body is a temple of the Holy Spirit who is in you, whom you have from God, and that you are not your own? (vs 20) For you have been bought with a price: therefore glorify God in your body.*

These verses say it all, we are not our own, we "Belong To God! The last word in verse 20 above (body) indicates a whole, therefore establishing that our Body and Spirit "Belong To Him"!!!. Our physical and spiritual life both need to answer to His Word.

The verses above will truly be our underlying premise or theme throughout the book.

If you "Belong To God":

1) Decide to Serve Him- *(Psalms 100:2-5)(vs 2) Serve the LORD with gladness; Come before Him with joyful singing. (vs 3) Know that the LORD Himself is God; It is He who has made us, and not we ourselves; We are His people and the sheep of His pasture. (vs 4) Enter His gates with thanksgiving And His courts with praise. Give thanks to Him, bless His name. (vs 5) For the LORD is good; His lovingkindness is everlasting And His faithfulness to all generations.*;

2) <u>Seek to Delight yourself in Him</u>- *(Psalms 37:4) Delight your-self in the LORD; And He will give you the desires of your heart.*; and

3) <u>Commit and Subject yourself to Him and His Word</u>- *(Psalms 37:5-9) (vs 5) Commit your way to the LORD, Trust also in Him, and He will do it. (vs 6) He will bring forth your righteousness as the light And your judgment as the noonday. (vs 7) Rest in the LORD and wait patiently for Him; Do not fret because of him who prospers in his way, Because of the man who carries out wicked schemes. (vs 8) Cease from anger and forsake wrath; Do not fret; it leads only to evildoing. (vs 9) For evildoers will be cut off, But those who wait for the LORD, they will inherit the land.*

If you "Belong To Self":

1) <u>Seek Him in order that you might be Born Again</u>- *(John 3:3-8) (vs 3) Jesus answered and said to him, "Truly, truly, I say to you, unless one is born again he cannot see the kingdom of God." (vs 4) Nicodemus *said to Him, "How can a man be born when he is old? He cannot enter a second time into his mother's womb and be born, can he?" (vs 5) Jesus answered, "Truly, truly, I say to you, unless one is born of water and the Spirit he cannot enter into the kingdom of God. (vs 6) "That which is born of the flesh is flesh, and that which is born of the Spirit is spirit. (vs 7) "Do not be amazed that I said to you, 'You must be born again.' (vs 8) "The wind blows where it wishes and you hear the sound of it, but do not know where it comes from and where it is going; so is everyone who is born of the Spirit." (Matthew 7:7-8)(vs 7) "Ask, and it will be given to you; seek, and you will find; knock, and it will be opened to you. (vs 8) "For everyone who asks receives, and he who seeks finds, and to him who knocks it will be opened.*; and

2) <u>Salvation is an act of God</u>- *(Ephesians 2:8-9)(vs 8) For by grace you have been saved through faith; and that not of yourselves, it is the gift of God; (vs 9) not as a result of works, so that no one may boast.*
(Revelation 3:20) 'Behold, I stand at the door and knock; if anyone hears My voice and opens the door, I will come in to him and will dine with him, and he with Me.

Call upon the Lord, Confess that you are a sinner, Trust in the saving grace of Jesus Christ and you will go from "Belonging To Self" to "Belonging to Him", this has eternal consequences.

<u>The Conclusion of This Introduction is this</u>- *(Ecclesiastes 12:13) The conclusion, when all has been heard, is: fear God and keep His commandments, because this applies to every person.*

If "We Belong To Him"!!!, we must reverence Him and keep His commandments, we must know and apply His word! You cannot **apply** His Word until you **<u>know</u>** His Word! May the Holy Word of God be your "Owner's Manual", and may this Book emphasize Such!

CHAPTER 1

THE TRINITY

INTRODUCTION:

It truly is humbling to be found writing about those things which we cannot comprehend or fully and completely describe, the One God, yet Triune in His Three Persons. With the knowledge and agreement of the finite mind being unable to comprehend the Trinity of, God the Father, God the Son and God the Holy Spirit, I will now attempt to make this Doctrine of the Trinity as understandable as possible. I claim minimal ability to do this and therefore much of the following has been researched from the writings of authoritative sources, with proper credit being given. The main documentation for this abbreviated synopsis of the Trinity (or the absolute certainty of our Triune God) is the writings found in "The Trinity Systematic Theology" of Entrust Ministries. I have been given full permission to use direct quotes from their writings as necessary. With this introduction of the source of much of the following information, I can now try to give to the layperson, a brief, yet hopefully an understandable dissertation, of this subject — **THE TRINITY**.

A. THE DOCTRINE OF THE TRINITY:

1. Definitions of the Trinity:
a) Wayne Grudem in his systematic theology defines the doctrine of the Trinity as follows: *"God eternally exists as three persons, Father, Son and Holy Spirit, and each person is fully God, and there is one God." (Wayne Grudem's Systematic Theology* p. 226)

b) James White defines the Trinity this way, **"Within the one being that is God, there exist eternally three coequal and coeternal** persons, namely, the Father, the Son, and the Holy Spirit." (*The Forgotten Trinity* p. 26)

These definitions of the Trinity may be broken down into three precise statements as follows: **# 1** — God is three persons; **# 2** — Each person is fully God; and **# 3** — There is one God. (*Wayne Grudem's Systematic Theology* p. 231) We will look at each of these statements in more detail below.

Statement # 1 — Three Persons: — God is three persons (The Father, the Son, and the Holy Spirit).
  a) The Father and the Son identified:
  (John 1:1-2 & 14)(vs 1) In the beginning was the Word, and the Word was with God, and the Word was God. (vs 2) He was in the beginning with God. (vs 14) And the Word became flesh, and dwelt among us, and we saw His glory, glory as of the only begotten from the Father, full of grace and truth.

Here we have testimony of God the Son eternally existing from the beginning. I know of no one who can explain whenever that was, but certainly it was before time ever existed. We also have in these verses both God the Son and God the Father being identified and manifested in Their separate and distinct roles as God. God the Son was sent in human form by God the Father, to witness to all of man.

Another testimony of the two roles and the distinction between Father and Son is found in. ... *(John 17:24) "Father, I desire that they also, whom You have given Me, be with Me where I am, so that they may see My glory which You have given Me, for You loved Me before the foundation of the world.*

Our God the Father and our God the Son existed before the foundation of the world. The definition of foundation: It is defined in the original Greek as a deposition, that is; founding, or figuratively conception, or to conceive (in other words the beginning of life).

Our Triune God not only existed at the time of the foundation of the world (the beginning of life), but before the foundation of the world, for He (They) spoke it into existence. Jesus and the Father are separate persons. Jesus is found in this verse to be clearly seen, functioning in

His role in human form, while being in obedience to the Father. Jesus and the Father are easily seen as being two separate "Persons".

The following additional verses not only identify God the Son as a separate Godhead person, but in detailed form, give an account of the specific role to be carried out between God the Father and God the Son (Jesus Christ). ... ***(Philippians 2:5-9)(vs 5) Have this attitude in yourselves which was also in Christ Jesus, (vs 6) who, although He existed in the form of God, did not regard equality with God a thing to be grasped, (vs 7) but emptied Himself, taking the form of a bond-servant, and being made in the likeness of men. (vs 8) Being found in appearance as a man, He humbled Himself by becoming obedient to the point of death, even death on a cross. (vs 9) For this reason also, God highly exalted Him, and bestowed on Him the name which is above every name,***

The above Scriptures not only confirm that the Son is a distinct person from the Father but they also confirm the truth that the Father has eternally been a distinct person from the Son. In the beginning the Word was present with God the Father and the Father loved the Son before the foundation of the world. Let us now turn our attention to God the Holy Spirit as a separate part of the Triune Godhead.

b) The Holy Spirit identified:

(John 14:26) "But the Helper, the Holy Spirit, whom the Father will send in My name, He will teach you all things, and bring to your remembrance all that I said to you.

Jesus with His own words is announcing the coming of the Helper (intercessor, consoler, comforter and advocate) or the Holy Spirit, who is being sent by the Father. We see here the separate identity of the Holy Spirit with His distinct and separate function from the Father and The Son.

(John 16:13-14)(vs 13) "But when He, the Spirit of truth, comes, He will guide you into all the truth; for He will not speak on His own initiative, but whatever He hears, He will speak; and He will disclose to you what is to come. (vs 14) "He will glorify Me, for He will take of Mine and will disclose it to you.

Again we see the words of Jesus proclaiming the distinct separate identity of the Holy Spirit and His purposes. Jesus speaks of the Holy Spirit taking the things of God and disclosing them to all of us. The Holy Spirit has this individualized and distinct teacher role as one of His defined purposes, and stands ready and available to carry this out in each of our lives today. He is separate, with many unique functions, yet all the time He is part of the Triune Godhead.

(Romans 8:26-27)(vs 26) In the same way the Spirit also helps our weakness; for we do not know how to pray as we should, but the Spirit Himself intercedes for us with groanings too deep for words; (vs 27) and He who searches the hearts knows what the mind of the Spirit is, because He intercedes for the saints according to the will of God.

Here we find the Apostle Paul teaching to the Romans one of the principle distinct functions of the Holy Spirit. As mentioned above the Holy Spirit is synonymous with intercession. He is truly an individual part of the Triune Godhead.

(1 Corinthians 6:19-20)(vs 19) Or do you not know that your body is a temple of the Holy Spirit who is in you, whom you have from God, and that you are not your own? (vs 20) For you have been bought with a price: therefore glorify God in your body.

As mentioned above the Holy Spirit indwells every "faith believer". This is literally the presence of our Holy God in possession of body, mind and soul, for all of our days upon this earth and until we are resurrected with our new bodies. Truly if we are "born again" or have been "regenerated" by our Holy God, we have this separate yet wholly God (the Holy Spirit) carrying out His separate function in and with us daily.

God's presence is found in and through three distinct persons, God the Father, God the Son and God the Holy Spirit. Let's now look at Statement **# 2**, with the Biblical demonstrations that each of the three Godhead persons is fully God.

Statement # 2 — Each person of the Trinity is fully God: — The three persons of the Triune Godhead eternally exist as coequal and coeternal.

a) References of the Triune Godhead in the same Scripture:

(Matthew 28:19) Go therefore and make disciples of all the nations, baptizing them in the name of the Father and the Son and the Holy Spirit,

This verse is generally known by all Christians and is more commonly known to each of us as the "Great Commission". The main **"Charge"** in this "Great Commission" is that we are instructed to go, **knowing that each of the Persons of the Godhead**, are our resource and authority. While we find them here to be distinctly separate by reference, we are going to find them to be ONE in authority.

(John 10:30) "I and the Father are one."

Admittedly the Holy Spirit is not included in this verse, but The Son and the Father are linked together as One. Jesus is referring to our, God the Father and Himself, as being One. One in this verse is defined in the Greek as a primary numeral one, what more can it mean.

(1 Corinthians 12:4-6)(vs 4) Now there are varieties of gifts, but the same Spirit. (vs 5) And there are varieties of ministries, and the same Lord. (vs 6) There are varieties of effects, but the same God who works all things in all persons.

Even though all of us have different characteristics, desires, looks, talents and abilities, and while God may appear to have multiple characteristics in His three different roles, there is still only one God. He is found in His human role (the Son), His spiritual "Presence" in our lives (the Holy Spirit) and The Almighty God role, (the Father). The function of each is different and unique, but He is the ... *"same God who works all things in all persons"*. Each role of God works in a unique way in our lives, while all Godhead Persons remain fully God.

(2 Corinthians 13:14) The grace of the Lord Jesus Christ, and the love of God, and the fellowship of the Holy Spirit, be with you all.

The Apostle Paul, as he writes his second letter to the church in Corinth, gives us additional insight into the Triune Godhead being **One**. Paul recognizes the Trinity and gives each Person within the Trinity equality, by specifically making reference to each defined Godhead role. Jesus is associated with salvation through **"grace"**, God the Father is associated with **"love"** and The Holy Spirit is associated with **"fellowship"**. We know that all of these attributes or characteristics (a very short list) are common to our **ONE God**. Paul then closes with a blessing from all the Persons of the Godhead. That blessing is summed up as, may God be found present ***"with"*** all "believers". This "Triune Blessing" is extended to all of us as if **One** person is sending it, even though Paul specifically mentions it coming from all three, the Son, the Father and the Holy Spirit.

This common thread, which can be found throughout the Bible, that God has given us **"grace"**, He **"loves"** us, and He desires **"fellowship"** with us, magnificently demonstrates His character of being **ONE God**.

(Ephesians 4:4-6)(vs 4) There is one body and one Spirit, just as also you were called in one hope of your calling; (vs 5) one Lord, one faith, one baptism, (vs 6) one God and Father of all who is over all and through all and in all.

The Apostle Paul as he writes to the Ephesians again gives co-equality to all Persons of the Trinity.

b) **The Father is fully God:**

(Genesis 1:1) In the beginning God created the heavens and the earth.

(John 6:27) "Do not work for the food which perishes, but for the food which endures to eternal life, which the Son of Man will give to you, for on Him the Father, God, has set His seal."

(1 Peter 1:1-2)(vs 1) Peter, an apostle of Jesus Christ, To those who reside as aliens, scattered throughout Pontus, Galatia, Cappadocia, Asia, and Bithynia, who are chosen (vs 2) according to the foreknowledge of God the Father, by the sanctifying work of the Spirit, to obey Jesus Christ and be sprinkled with His blood: May grace and peace be yours in the fullest measure.

Each verse confirms God the Father as being fully God. These verses include references to the three persons of God (The Trinity), but all speak of the Father to be **One** with the supreme God of the Universe.

c) **The Son is fully God:**

(John 1:1-2)(vs 1) In the beginning was the Word, and the Word was with God, and the Word was God. (vs 2) He was in the beginning with God.

John so beautifully refers to Jesus as the Word. He refers to Jesus as being God and was in existence in the beginning, and for emphasis he does it twice. Jesus Christ, the only begotten Son of God, is fully God from the "beginning".

(Colossians 1:15) He is the image of the invisible God, the firstborn of all creation., and *(Colossians 2:9) For in Him all the fullness of Deity dwells in bodily form,*

In each verse above, the one referred to is Jesus Christ the Son of God. In each case the Son is identified and described as the very image of God and in every respect the fullness of Deity, respectively. These proclamations are being made about the Son being fully God, while Jesus was here on this earth in human, bodily form. There is no question that Jesus (the Son), even in His human/bodily form, is fully God.

d) **The Holy Spirit is fully God:**

(Acts 5:3-4)(vs 3) But Peter said, "Ananias, why has Satan filled your heart to lie to the Holy Spirit and to keep back some of the price of the land? (vs 4) "While it remained unsold, did it not remain your own? And after it was sold, was it not under your control? Why is it that you have conceived this deed in your heart? You have not lied to men but to God."

The point here is not to witness the dastardly deed that was done by lying to men, but to point out that when Ananias lied to the Holy Spirit he was at the same time lying to God. The Holy Spirit is fully God.

Statement # 3 – There is One and Only One God:

There are many scriptures throughout both the Old and the New Testament that confirm and re-confirm there is only One God. In fact there are over 1,500 scriptures in the Holy Bible that use the words LORD GOD in the same verse. The three distinctively different Persons of the Trinity are one in purpose and agreement, in thoughts, teachings and all relationships with man, yet there is only One God!!! Please consider the few scriptures listed below, and their dynamic confirmation of our One and Only God.

a) **Old Testament confirmations:**

(Genesis 2:7) Then the LORD God formed man of dust from the ground, and breathed into his nostrils the breath of life; and man became a living being.

Going all the way back to Genesis we find that our very creator is **THE LORD GOD**. He formed us from dust and breathed life into our earthly bodies. He is Jehovah God, the Supreme God. No one else is mentioned in this original act of creation. There is no other, **HE** is one!!!

(Deuteronomy 6:4-5)(vs 4) "Hear, O Israel! The LORD is our God, the LORD is one! (vs 5) "You shall love the LORD your God with all your heart and with all your soul and with all your might.

We are to *"Hear"* (this means to hear intelligently, to understand and to be a witness) that our LORD is One. Our eternal being is to be devoted, with all of our strength, energies and resources, to the One God!!!

(Psalms 18:31) For who is God, but the LORD? And who is a rock, except our God,

(Psalms 31:14) But as for me, I trust in You, O LORD, I say, "You are my God."

(Psalms 50:1) A Psalm of Asaph. The Mighty One, God, the LORD, has spoken, And summoned the earth from the rising of the sun to its setting.

(Psalms 72:18) Blessed be the LORD God, the God of Israel, Who alone works wonders.

The Old Testament Psalms strongly state, by calling our LORD, The Mighty One, that He is the One and Only God. While this Chapter is about establishing the Trinity, we necessarily establish that God the Father, God the Son and God the Holy Spirit are bound miraculously into One God, the Mighty One!!! For He ... *"alone works wonders"*.

(Isaiah 45:5-8)(vs 4) "I am the LORD, and there is no other; Besides Me there is no God. I will gird you, though you have not known Me; (vs 6) That men may know from the rising to the setting of the sun That there is no one besides Me. I am the LORD, and there is no other, (vs 7) The One forming light and creating darkness, Causing well-being and creating calamity; I am the LORD who does all these. (vs 8) "Drip down, O heavens, from above, And let the clouds pour down righteousness; Let the earth open up and salvation bear fruit, And righteousness spring up with it. I, the LORD, have created it.

(Malachi 2:10 partial) "Do we not all have one father? Has not one God created us?

With the absolute statements from the Old Testament verses of His Oneness, and with the magnitude of the above establishments of **HIS** authority, omniscience, omnipotence and being The Creator of all things, these verses confirm **HIS Oneness**.

b) **New Testament confirmations:**

(Mark 12:29) Jesus answered, "The foremost is, 'HEAR, O ISRAEL! THE LORD OUR GOD IS ONE LORD;

(James 2:19) You believe that God is one. You do well; the demons also believe, and shudder.

The demons of hell recognize the One and Only God of the Universe and shudder, but we who have a "faith believing" relationship of knowing Him as Savior and Lord, will look upon Him in peace, for we have been bought with a price and have been adopted into His family. All, both demons and "believers", will one day fully recognize Him as the **One** true God. This day of judgment is coming, where all will bow and confess **this truth**, in His Holy presence!!!

(1 Timothy 2:5) For there is one God, and one mediator also between God and men, the man Christ Jesus,

This verse could be used to show the distinct roles of both God the Father and God the Son, in this case it is being used to reinforce the Oneness of our Almighty God. YES!, there is only **ONE** God, but it is also appropriate to point out that there is only **ONE** way to that **ONE** God and that is through the **ONE** mediator, *"the man Christ Jesus"*!!! ONE God, **ONE** mediator, **ONE** way!!!

(Romans 3:29-30)(vs 29) Or is God the God of Jews only? Is He not the God of Gentiles also? Yes, of Gentiles also, (vs 30) since indeed God who will justify the circumcised by faith and the uncircumcised through faith is one.

If only all of our Jewish brethren could understand that their Messiah has come and they didn't crucify Jesus, but according to God's plan He was placed upon that Cross. Our God is the **ONE** God of all mankind, it matters not whether we are Jews or whether we are Gentiles. It matters not whether God came in the role of Jesus as the Messiah, or whether He has shown Himself as God the Father, He is **ONE** God!!!

(Jude 1:24-25)(vs 24) Now to Him who is able to keep you from stumbling, and to make you stand in the presence of His glory blameless with great joy, (vs 25) to the only God our Savior, through Jesus Christ our Lord, be glory, majesty, dominion and authority, before all time and now and forever. Amen.

The One and Only God of the Universe is also ... *"our Savior, through Jesus Christ our Lord,"*. To our **ONE** God be all Glory .... Before, Now and Forever!

(Revelation 1:8) "I am the Alpha and the Omega," says the Lord God, "who is and who was and who is to come, the Almighty."

(Revelation 4:8) And the four living creatures, each one of them having six wings, are full of eyes around and within; and day and night they do not cease to say, "HOLY, HOLY, HOLY is THE LORD GOD, THE ALMIGHTY, WHO WAS AND WHO IS AND WHO IS TO COME."

Behold, and be thankful all men in all nations, for we find in the Book of Revelations, the prophesies of God the Father, revealing God the Son, through the power of God the Holy Spirit (by the use of His angelic messengers). The above two verses, and many more, were penned by the Apostle John, having been given these final revelations of God's Word. Our **ONE**, personal, Almighty God of the Universe, is the Beginning and the End of ALL MATTERS!!! His purposes, in His revelations to man, required the Triune Godhead, while still being the **ONE** and **ONLY GOD**!!!

B. CONCLUSION TO THE CHAPTER OF THE TRINITY:

A conclusion by this writer would be fragmented and incoherent, so I will take this page to write about a personal experience, which I pray, you find both interesting and helpful in understanding **"THE TRINITY"**.

God through His creation ... *(Romans 1:20) For since the creation of the world His invisible attributes, His eternal power and divine nature, have been clearly seen, being understood through what has been made, so that they are without*

excuse. ... has allowed me to personally witness, in the wilderness of Colorado, a living example of His Trinity. The following will not do complete justice to the Trinity, but might just give each of us a glimpse of how we earthlings may visualize, and for our sakes understand the Trinity, yet the One God.

My family and I were invited to an outdoor worship service on a Sunday morning, just west of Granby, Colorado. We had driven in to the point where we couldn't see any power poles, highways or man-made fixtures, or for that matter any other reminders of civilization. Even our automobiles were parked out of our sight.

The site selected for our service was one located high in this virtual wilderness, with a large meadow interspersed with evergreens. I think this spot on the sloping mountainside was near perfect. It had its close up beauty while still having the distant view of mountain ranges that divide our continent. All in all, the setting would be considered by anyone to be spiritually uplifting. With the surroundings being so visually spectacular and the scene quietly speaking volumes about our Almighty God, a Gospel service here would be easy to pull off.

Colorado, as most of you already know, has forests full of evergreen trees from the spruce and fir families. These trees, with their green needles year around, tend to stand out regardless of the season and are found to be attractive whether in the midst of the many colorful wildflowers of the summer, or in the winter with its predominately white background of deep snow. This was early summer and I can remember the beauty of the wildflowers and green grasses in the meadow, with a few of these evergreens interspersed throughout, making the immediate scene quite awe inspiring. This setting was something special as the dense forest became our background walls as it took over the edges of the meadow and framed this natural amphitheater. I can only praise God as one very unique tree stood, I will call it the "Trinity Tree".

As I sat there listening to the message from the community pastor my eyes caught an appropriate scene right in from of me. It had been there all along, but at the right time God revealed a living example of His Trinity. It was one of these stately evergreens which had been set apart from the dense forest. It was one tree, with a 12-14 inch circumference trunk and three distinct trees (not branches), all about equal size, growing from the main trunk. These three trees were all nourished by the one distinctly, individual base of about 18 inches in height, and had become three separate fully grown trees arising as if they had been meticulously grafted in. As I studied this example of the Trinity right before my eyes I was thankful to God for His revelation to me for this beautiful, worshipful experience. It was as if God had personally planted this tree, the "Trinity Tree", (some 60-80 years before), for me to see this day. He grew this unique tree to be a special witness of Himself and His three Godhead Persons. I can't help but believe He grew this tree just for me (and now for each of you), in order to personalize Himself and visually disclose Himself in this way. It has been a special blessing, how He has demonstrated His Trinity Oneness through the creation.

While on the subject of God growing trees, and I pray this is appropriate to be included, I am also reminded of another tree He grew two thousand years ago. That one, which produced two pieces of hewed wood, became "The Old Rugged Cross". The "Old Rugged Cross" tree has been immortalized in the words of a Christian song, with one verse going like this ... "He grew the tree that He knew would be, used to become the "Old Rugged Cross". Maybe someday, someone will write a song about God's "Trinity Tree" and give praise to His divine purposes of visually disclosing to all of us His Trinity.

He is truly **ONE**, while showing Himself in the roles of the Triune Godhead. Our **ONE** Almighty God of the Universe continually amazes us every day, by personally reaching down to us and loving us. We live in a sea of six (6) billion people, yet the **ONE God of the Universe** reaches down to us, through **God the Father**, by sending **God the Son** (in human form), while leaving **God the Holy Spirit** (to dwell within us). It is these three persons of the Godhead in the form of **"The Trinity"** that have so wonderfully transformed our lives. We do not fully understand all of this, but we trust this **ONE GOD**, and we accept His ways.

I will close with this verse found in Revelations.

(Revelation 19:6) Then I heard something like the voice of a great multitude and like the sound of many waters and like the sound of mighty peals of thunder, saying, "Hallelujah! For the Lord our God, the Almighty, reigns.

He *"reigns"* and always will "reign" as our **ONE LORD GOD**. His eternal reign will be unmistakable, for He plans to come soon with the sounds of deafening waterfalls, surrounded by the never before heard, claps of thunder, and with great voices shouting "Hallelujah". YES, the **ONE GOD,** who has visited us in the past in the form of the Triune Godhead, YES, the **ONE AND ONLY LORD GOD** is returning soon for all of those "Who Belong To Him", YES, even though we now see dimly, as peering through a mist, upon His return we will see through the glass clearly, we will understand this **"TRINITY"** this **"ONE GOD"**!!!

SPECIAL NOTE:

I know many of you may have a special verse or verses regarding this Chapter's subject matter. This special verse or these verses may not have been mentioned due to my ignorance or because of brevity. I apologize for either of these reasons. Please feel free to write any special verse or verses in the space below. This will add your personal touch, and will serve to call to each person's mind their individual "experience of trust", in God's Holy Word.

For to each of us "Who belong To Him", His Holy Word can be truly recognized and relied upon as our **"Owner's Manual"**!!!

_____

_____

_____

_____

_____

_____

CHAPTER 2

GOD, THE FATHER

INTRODUCTORY VERSES:

(Genesis 1:1-5) In the beginning God created the heavens and the earth. (vs 2) The earth was formless and void, and darkness was over the surface of the deep, and the Spirit of God was moving over the surface of the waters. (vs 3) Then God said, "Let there be light"; and there was light. (vs 4) God saw that the light was good; and God separated the light from the darkness. (vs 5) God called the light day, and the darkness He called night. And there was evening and there was morning, one day.

The very first verse in the Bible speaks of **God**, with its Hebrew definition being the **"supreme" God**. The Hebrew word for *beginning* means the first, in place, time, order or rank. There can be no confusion in this verse; **THE ETERNAL, LIVING, GOD OF THE UNIVERSE** is the **"supreme"** beginning of all things and is first in order and rank while creating and established all authority over **EVERYTHING ....** **TO HIM BE ALL GLORY AND WORSHIP**!!!

(Genesis 1:6-25)

In these twenty (20) verses, which are not printed here, we find that God has in His vast knowledge and omnipotence created the entire workings of the entire world, and He did so by **speaking it into being**. This is incomprehensible, yet it speaks of His **"supreme"** authority over all matter, life and everything in-between.

(Genesis 1:26-27 & 31) (vs 26) Then God said, "Let Us make man in Our image, according to Our likeness; and let them rule over the fish of the sea and over the birds of the sky and over the cattle and over all the earth, and over every

creeping thing that creeps on the earth." (vs 27) God created man in His own image, in the image of God He created him; male and female He created them. (vs 31) God saw all that He had made, and behold, it was very good. And there was evening and there was morning, the sixth day.

God created "MAN" in His image, male and female He created them. Both man and woman were created in the image of God. Neither is superior to the other, but they have been assigned different roles in this life. As each of us seeks to perfect and carry out our Biblically defined roles, we need to recognize the absolute importance and significance of the role of our **"MOST HIGH GOD"**, our **GOD, THE FATHER!!!**

INTRODUCTION:

The importance of this Chapter, along with Chapter One **(THE TRINITY),** Chapter Three **(GOD, THE SON)**, and Chapter Four **(GOD, THE HOLY SPIRIT)** are without measure in significance and authority. All of God's Words, as found from cover-to-cover within the entire Bible, have as their basis and foundation the "Truths" found within these four Chapters. All "truth" comes from the Mind of God and we will find these revelations of His Mind, encompassed throughout the Bible, as they pertain to the Father, the Son and the Holy Spirit. We truly find in all matters, His Holy Word to be our "Owner's Manual"!!!

Let us "respectfully" search a relatively few verses in order to establish the **OMNIPOTENCE** and **OMNISCIENCE** of our **GOD**. This is for everyone's enlightenment and benefit, and especially to those of us, "Who Belong To Him"!!! Please be ever knowledgeable and forgiving, and fully recognize this Chapter as inadequate and incomplete when it comes to properly stating or even trying to discuss the full and complete attributes, disclosures and acts of our **GOD, THE FATHER!!!**

This Chapter regarding **GOD, THE FATHER** is written after much research of theological writings. Beware or be aware, it is with all humbleness and a sense of absolute inadequacy that I approach these relatively few, yet most significant truths, regarding the **"MOST HIGH GOD"**, the **"GREAT I AM"**!!! … *(Exodus 3:13-14)(vs 13) Then Moses said to God, "Behold, I am going to the sons of Israel, and I will say to them, 'The God of your fathers has sent me* *to you.' Now they may say to me, 'What is His name?' What shall I say to them?" (vs 14) God said to Moses, "I AM WHO I AM"; and He said, "Thus you shall say to the sons of Israel, 'I AM has sent me to you.'"*

Please read with all humbleness the following.

A. A SELECTED FEW VERSES REGARDING THE ATTRIBUTES, DISCLOSURES AND ACTS OF OUR GOD, THE FATHER :

1. Who Is He?

It is so well stated in Genesis that He is the creator of all universes, all life, all matter, the inter-relationships of all mankind with these things, as well as everything imaginable in-between. *(Genesis 1:1) In the beginning God created the heavens and the earth.*

He is the Alpha and the Omega, the "Only Beginning" and the "Final Authority". There never has been, there presently is not, and there never will be any greater "Authority" in all the heavens and the earth. He is surely the **"Almighty God of the Universe"**, the **"Great I AM"**!!!

2. What might we say about His power?

a) Our "Owner's Manual" makes it clear He can create from "Nothing"! *(Genesis 1:2-3)(vs 2) The earth was formless and void, and darkness was over the surface of the deep, and the Spirit of God was moving over the surface of the waters. (vs 3) Then God said, "Let there be light"; and there was light.*

He spoke all things into being! We find His indefinable and unexplainable powers to speak all things into being not only in verse three above, but as well in multiple additional verses: i) *(Genesis 1:6, 9, 11, 14, 20, 24, 26 & 29)*; ii) In the Book of Romans the Bible has this to say about Him. ... *(Romans 4:17) (as it is written, "A FATHER OF MANY NATIONS HAVE I MADE YOU") in the presence of Him whom he believed, even God, who gives life to the dead and calls into being that which does not exist.*

b) He is "Omnipotent"! The Book of Revelations speaks of His "Omnipotence" ... *(Revelation 19:6) Then I heard something like the voice of a great multitude and like the sound of many waters and like the sound of mighty peals of thunder, saying, "Hallelujah! For the Lord our God, the Almighty, reigns.*

The word "Almighty" as used here is also defined in the Greek as "all ruling, that is God (as absolute and universal sovereign)". "Almighty" and "Omnipotent" are interchangeable.

3. He gave us the Old Testament Ten Commandments:

Everyone is familiar with the Ten Commandments. *(Exodus 34:27-28)(vs 27) Then the LORD said to Moses, "Write down these words, for in accordance with these words I have made a covenant with you and with Israel." (vs 28) So he was there with the LORD forty days and forty nights; he did not eat bread or drink water. And he wrote on the tablets the words of the covenant, the Ten Commandments.*

These were the basis of the Jewish Law for years. They were used as the covenant between **GOD, THE FATHER** and the Israelites. This Old Covenant was the forerunner of our New Covenant, which all in accordance with God's "Master Plan", has allowed the Gentiles to be included into His fold (much detail regarding the importance of this has been covered in other Chapters, beginning with the Chapter on Salvation). It is this New Covenant, which is in force today and will be in force until the end of time, whereby we are allowed the right to become "Born Again", through the completed work of Jesus on the Cross at Calvary. I say this is absolutely important to be mentioned, as **GOD, THE FATHER** orchestrated this "Master Plan" in order for sinful man to be able to come into the presence of our **"MOST HOLY GOD"**. I don't understand why God had to devise His plan in this way, but I can only know and assure you that the God of the Universe, in His "Omnipotence" and "Omniscience", did it for us! His rule and authority could be said to have started with the "Ten Commandments".

4. He expects and requires one hundred percent (100%) allegiance:

(Exodus 34:12-14)(vs 12) "Watch yourself that you make no covenant with the inhabitants of the land into which you are going, or it will become a snare in your midst. (vs 13) "But rather, you are to tear down their altars and smash their sacred pillars and cut down their Asherim (vs 14)—for

you shall not worship any other god, for the LORD, whose name is Jealous, is a jealous God—

Don't try to serve both our **GOD, THE FATHER** and man's fleshly desires, it cannot work. Don't waste 40 years of your life finding out, in a multitude of the most difficult of ways imaginable, that His Word is eternally true. His motivation in being

a jealous God is because He loves us beyond comprehension and desires the best for our earthly lives.

(Joshua 24:15) "If it is disagreeable in your sight to serve the LORD, choose for yourselves today whom you will serve: whether the gods which your fathers served which were beyond the River, or the gods of the Amorites in whose land you are living; but as for me and my house, we will serve the LORD."

This is a strong statement by Joshua, one or our Old Testament pillars of Biblical faith. We can't go wrong by standing shoulder-to-shoulder with Joshua. 100% allegiance will not only bless us immensely, but will answer the prayers of our entire household.

5. GOD, THE FATHER cannot be instructed:

(Job 38:1-5) (vs 1) Then the LORD answered Job out of the whirlwind and said, (vs 2) "Who is this that darkens counsel By words without knowledge? (vs 3) "Now gird up your loins like a man, And I will ask you, and you instruct Me! (vs 4) "Where were you when I laid the foundation of the earth? Tell Me, if you have understanding, (vs 5) Who set its measurements? Since you know. Or who stretched the line on it?

The **LORD GOD , ALMIGHTY,** asked Job questions found in the forty-one (41) verses in Chapter 38 and the thirty (30) verses in Chapter 39 of the Book of Job, none of which Job could answer. Finally Job got the message and answered as follows ... *(Job 40:3-4)(vs 3) Then Job answered the LORD and said, (vs 4) "Behold, I am insignificant; what can I reply to You? I lay my hand on my mouth.*

What great advice, when it comes to instructing God, we need to lay both of our hands across our mouth and keep eternally silent.

6. Examples of GOD, THE FATHER demonstrating His personal touch in everyday life:

Well you may not consider the following two (2) examples to be in the fashion of everyday life in our world today, but it was assuredly so in the Biblical days for the life of certain God fearing, Jewish young men by the names of Shadrach, Meshach and Abed-nego, and the Prophet Daniel. While these selected acts of our Almighty God only allow for a glimpse of the incomprehensibleness of our Heavenly **FATHER**, the glimpse they share is certainly powerful:

a) *(Daniel 3:16-18)(vs 16) Shadrach, Meshach and Abed-nego replied to the king, "O Nebuchadnezzar, we do not need to give you an answer concerning this matter. (vs 17) "If it be so, our God whom we serve is able to deliver us from the furnace of blazing fire; and He will deliver us out of your hand, O king. (vs 18) "But even if He does not, let it be known to you, O king, that we are not going to serve your gods or worship the golden image that you have set up."*

(Daniel 3:27-28) The satraps, the prefects, the governors and the king's high officials gathered around and saw in regard to these men that the fire had no effect on the bodies of these men nor was the hair of their head singed, nor were their trousers damaged, nor had the smell of fire even come upon them. (vs 28) Nebuchadnezzar responded and said, "Blessed be the God of Shadrach, Meshach and Abed-nego, who has sent His angel and delivered His servants who put their trust in Him, violating the king's command, and yielded up their bodies so as not to serve or worship any god except their own God.

In this abbreviated account we see God's personal involvement and His hand directly affecting the outcome and the sparing of the lives of these young men. The circumstances were such that if He hadn't intervened, the young men would have certainly been consumed by the fire. Regardless of the outcome, these young men gave our **GOD, THE FATHER** all the Glory; and

b) God also reached His loving and attentive hand down and touched the life of the Prophet Daniel as he faced certain death from the powerful jaws of hungry lions. *(Daniel 6:22-23)(vs 22) "My*

God sent His angel and shut the lions' mouths and they have not harmed me, inasmuch as I was found innocent before Him; and also toward you, O king, I have committed no crime." (vs 23) Then the king was very pleased and gave orders for Daniel to be taken up out of the den. So Daniel was taken up out of the den and no injury whatever was found on him, because he had trusted in his God.

Again we see the personal hand of God reaching down (through His angel) and literally shutting the vicious jaws of the lions, which would have otherwise been certain death to the Prophet Daniel. We also witness Daniel's trust in **GOD, THE FATHER** regardless of the outcome. Ordinary life back then was certainly different than everyday life today.

You may not feel that our God of today would so dramatically deliver you from the mouth of a hungry lion or from the heat of a furnace (so hot it destroyed those who opened the furnace doors), but I can tell you with complete certainty that the God of Shadrach, Meshach and Abed-nego and the Prophet Daniel, is alive and well today. He neither sleeps nor slumbers and is actively about the business of protecting those "Who Belong to Him".

I have no reason to be alive today, except for the hand of God reaching down and touching my life, including the guiding of the minds and hands of the surgeons and other Doctor/Nurse caregivers as I faced 100% certainty of death. I am not anything special, yet God has something for me to do and answered my prayers, and the prayers of friends and loved ones, to allow me to continue to get in on what He is doing. I was diagnosed with "Boerhaave Syndrome". This is an infection of such magnitude that if it is not found within 48 hours it is 100% fatal. Mine was not diagnosed for five (5) days. That is one-hundred and twenty (120) hours. I am alive today only by the grace of God (see Prayer Chapter for more details).

He truly does demonstrate His power in this present age and is available to administer His personal touch in our everyday life. His demonstrations today, in the real lives of those around us can be for multiple reasons, but certainly in all cases will include comfort, encouragement and inspiration. For all of us who "Belong To Him", we find Him every day to be our **GOD, THE FATHER**.

7. GOD, THE FATHER, creator of all of mankind:

(Malachi 2:10) "Do we not all have one father? Has not one God created us? Why do we deal treacherously each against his brother so as to profane the covenant of our fathers?

We would not be witness to the "ethnic cleansing", the "murder of millions", if all nations recognized **GOD, THE FATHER** as being the creator of all life, the creator of all of mankind. Every life in every continent and in all nations, has been created by **GOD, THE FATHER**.

8. GOD, THE FATHER, directed His Son's (Jesus Christ) work while here on earth:

Even though **GOD, THE FATHER** and Jesus Christ are both One, yet separate in the Trinity, they have identifiably, individual roles regarding the redemption and perfection of man. This has been especially documented while Jesus was here on this earth. The following multiple verses demonstrate the **FATHER** and the Son are One, yet the Son is found submissively carrying out the will of the **FATHER**. More often than not these verses need no comment, for their clarity and understanding is direct and straightforward.

a) *(John 3:35-36)(vs 35) "The Father loves the Son and has given all things into His hand. (vs 36) "He who believes in the Son has eternal life; but he who does not obey the Son will not see life, but the wrath of God abides on him."*

b) *(John 5:19, 26-27, 33-36)(vs 19) Therefore Jesus answered and was saying to them, "Truly, truly, I say to you, the Son can do nothing of Himself, unless it is something He sees the Father doing; for whatever the Father does, these things the Son also does in like manner. (vs 26) "For just as the Father has life in Himself, even so He gave to the Son also to have life in Himself; (vs 27) and He gave Him authority to execute judgment, because He is the Son of Man. (vs 33) "You have sent to John, and he has testified to the truth. (vs 34) "But the testimony which I receive is not from man, but I say these things so that you may be saved. (vs 35) "He was the lamp that was burning and was shining and you were willing to rejoice for a while in his light. (vs 36) "But the testimony which I have is greater than the* *testimony of John; for the works which the Father has given Me to accomplish—the very works that I do—testify about Me, that the Father has sent Me.*

John the Baptist spoke truth while being a forerunner of Jesus Christ. The testimony of Jesus was even greater than that of John's, and He spoke clearly that He was in submission to the Father's will and directives. ... *(Luke 3:16) John answered and said to them all, "As for me, I baptize you with water; but One is coming who is mightier than I, and I am not fit to untie the thong of His sandals; He will baptize you with the Holy Spirit and fire.*

<u>c)</u> *(John 6:39-40)(vs 39) "This is the will of Him who sent Me, that of all that He has given Me I lose nothing, but raise it up on the last day. (vs 40) "For this is the will of My Father, that everyone who beholds the Son and believes in Him will have eternal life, and I Myself will raise him up on the last day."*

We see the will of the FATHER being carried out by the actions of the Son.

<u>d)</u> *(John 10:30) "I and the Father are one."*

<u>e)</u> *(John 12:49-50)(vs 49) "For I did not speak on My own initiative, but the Father Himself who sent Me has given Me a commandment as to what to say and what to speak. (vs 50) "I know that His commandment is eternal life; therefore the things I speak, I speak just as the Father has told Me."*

These are direct quotes from Jesus Christ, the Son of our Living, **GOD, THE FATHER**.

<u>f)</u> Jesus and GOD, THE FATHER are One, and He returns to HIM.

(John 16:28) "I came forth from the Father and have come into the world; I am leaving the world again and going to the Father."

(John 17:1, 5, 11, & 24-26)(vs 1) Jesus spoke these things; and lifting up His eyes to heaven, He said, "Father, the hour has come; glorify Your Son, that the Son may glorify You, (vs 5) "Now, Father, glorify Me together with Yourself, with the glory which I had with You before the world was. (vs 11) "I am no longer in the world; and yet they themselves are in the world, and I come to You. Holy Father, keep them in

Your name, the name which You have given Me, that they may be one even as We are. (vs 24) "Father, I desire that they also, whom You have given Me, be with Me where I am, so that they may see My glory which You have given Me, for You loved Me before the foundation of the world. (vs 25) "O righteous Father, although the world has not known You, yet I have known You; and these have known that You sent Me; (vs 26) and I have made Your name known to them, and will make it known, so that the love with which You loved Me may be in them, and I in them."

Please just meditate on these Words as they can teach us more than any man can hope to be able to teach and/or communicate. Jesus, having completed His work here on earth, returns to the FATHER and is re-established to His original place and status of equality with **GOD, THE FATHER**.

9. GOD, THE FATHER, we exist "for" Him:

(1 Corinthians 8:5-6)(vs 5) For even if there are so-called gods whether in heaven or on earth, as indeed there are many gods and many lords, (vs 6) yet for us there is but one God, the Father, from whom are all things and we exist for Him; and one Lord, Jesus Christ, by whom are all things, and we exist through Him.

We exist "for" ... *God, the Father* ... "through" Jesus Christ and their combined marvelous plan of redemption, which was culminated upon the Cross of Calvary.

Don't ask "how" or "why". Our finite minds cannot handle it.

10. GOD, THE FATHER, has not provided for shifting/moving/portable standards:

(James 1:17) Every good thing given and every perfect gift is from above, coming down from the Father of lights, with whom there is no variation or shifting shadow.

His standards were established once in the Heavens, before the foundation of the world, and will never change. His Word, which is our "Owner's Manual", is as true, exciting and applicable today, as it was before the beginning of time.

11. GOD, THE FATHER, Omnipotent and Omniscient, there is no other!!!

(Isaiah 45:18-22)(vs 18) For thus says the LORD, who created the heavens (He is the God who formed the earth and made it, He established it and did not create it a waste place, but formed it to be inhabited), "I am the LORD, and there is none else. (vs 19) "I have not spoken in secret, In some dark land; I did not say to the offspring of Jacob, 'Seek Me in a waste place'; I, the LORD, speak righteousness, Declaring things that are upright. (vs 20) "Gather yourselves and come; Draw near together, you fugitives of the nations; They have no knowledge, Who carry about their wooden idol And pray to a god who cannot save. (vs 21) "Declare and set forth your case; Indeed, let them consult together. Who has announced this from of old? Who has long since declared it? Is it not I, the LORD? And there is no other God besides Me, A righteous God and a Savior; There is none except Me. (vs 22) "Turn to Me and be saved, all the ends of the earth; For I am God, and there is no other.

The Old Testament powerfully speaks of His being all powerful and all present, He created the heavens and the earth, He is singularly Almighty (there or no other <u>gods</u> to be considered), He is Outspoken to all the earth, He is totally Righteous, He declares "worthless" the wooden idol and the dead gods, He is a Savior (or the Salvation) to all those who Confess Him, and He concludes His case by authoritatively stating ... *For I am God, and there is no other*.

12. GOD, THE FATHER, Worthy of all Glory and Praise, while Demanding our accountability:

(Philippians 2:5-11)(vs 5) Have this attitude in yourselves which was also in Christ Jesus, (vs 6) who, although He existed in the form of God, did not regard equality with God a thing to be grasped, (vs 7) but emptied Himself, taking the form of a bond-servant, and being made in the likeness of men. (vs 8) Being found in appearance as a man, He humbled Himself by becoming obedient to the point of death, even death on a cross. (vs 9) For this reason also, God

highly exalted Him, and bestowed on Him the name which is above every name, (vs 10) so that at the name of Jesus EVERY KNEE WILL BOW, of those who are in heaven and on earth and under the earth, (vs 11) and that every tongue will confess that Jesus Christ is Lord, to the glory of God the Father.

(Philippians 4:20) Now to our God and Father be the glory forever and ever. Amen.

(Romans 14:10-12)(vs 10) But you, why do you judge your brother? Or you again, why do you regard your brother with contempt? For we will all stand before the judgment seat of God. (vs 11) For it is written, "AS I LIVE, SAYS THE LORD, EVERY KNEE SHALL BOW TO ME, AND EVERY TONGUE SHALL GIVE PRAISE TO GOD." (vs 12) So then each one of us will give an account of himself to God.

13. GOD, THE FATHER, and His Imperishable/Eternal WORD:

(1 Peter 1:22 partial, 23-25)(vs 22 partial) Since you have in obedience to the truth purified your souls for a sincere love of the brethren, fervently love one another from the heart, (vs 23) for you have been born again not of seed which is perishable but imperishable, that is, through the living and enduring word of God. (vs 24) For, "ALL FLESH IS LIKE GRASS, AND ALL ITS GLORY LIKE THE FLOWER OF GRASS. THE GRASS WITHERS, AND THE FLOWER FALLS OFF, (vs 25) BUT THE WORD OF THE LORD ENDURES FOREVER." And this is the word which was preached to you.

GOD, THE FATHER, encompassed in His Holy Word, has given us the only thing to be found upon this earth which is Imperishable and Eternal. It seems to me that we should seek the things that … **ENDURES FOREVER** … rather than the things that … **WITHERS** … , dies and falls to the ground. **GOD, THE FATHER**, He is Almighty and Eternal and has given us His Imperishable Word.

14. GOD, THE FATHER – His Revelation "TO" us and "IN" us:

(1 John 3:1-2)(vs 1) See how great a love the Father has bestowed on us, that we would be called children of God;

and such we are. For this reason the world does not know us, because it did not know Him. (vs 2) Beloved, now we are children of God, and it has not appeared as yet what we will be. We know that when He appears, we will be like Him, because we will see Him just as He is.

God has revealed Himself **"TO"** us, through His Son — Jesus Christ, and soon He will reveal Himself **"IN"** us, through His Holy Heavenly Plan. This revelation will not be of any earthly, temporal values, but will be an "Eternity" of eternal values and riches. These values and riches will be of such magnitude they will place the "wealth of this world" in the category of poverty. This world's wealth will be considered nothing more than such as is found in an open, septic gutter. All scales will fall from our eyes, and as the Children of a King, His promises will be revealed and will be lived out **"IN"** each of us who "Belong To Him", in His Holy Magnificent Kingdom.

15. All Praise is to our LORD:

In the light of the times before Jesus Christ and the revelation of the Holy Spirit, such as are found in Psalms 148 of the Old Testament, we have all Praise being directed to our **LORD**. The Hebrew definition for LORD is Jehovah, the Lord, or the Jewish national name for God. Please in no way think this diminishes the Trinity. The point here is that THE FATHER, THE SON and THE HOLY SPIRIT are all to be praised as our Triune God, and in the following verses the Triune God was referred as our **LORD.**

(Psalms 148:1-13)(vs 1) Praise the LORD! Praise the LORD from the heavens; Praise Him in the heights! (vs 2) Praise Him, all His angels; Praise Him, all His hosts! (vs 3) Praise Him, sun and moon; Praise Him, all stars of light! (vs 4) Praise Him, highest heavens, And the waters that are above the heavens! (vs 5) Let them praise the name of the LORD, For He commanded and they were created. (vs 6) He has also established them forever and ever; He has made a decree which will not pass away. (vs 7) Praise the LORD from the earth, Sea monsters and all deeps; (vs 8) Fire and hail, snow and clouds; Stormy wind, fulfilling His word; (vs 9) Mountains and all hills; Fruit trees and all cedars; (vs 10)

Beasts and all cattle; Creeping things and winged fowl; (vs 11) Kings of the earth and all peoples; Princes and all judges of the earth; (vs 12) Both young men and virgins; Old men and children. (vs 13) Let them praise the name of the LORD, For His name alone is exalted; His glory is above earth and heaven.

The magnificence here is that all Praise from all locations, from angels and all of mankind, from the elements, from all creeping things, and even the trees, is to ring out to glorify our **"LORD"**. What more can be said, NOTHING!!!

B. CONCLUSION to GOD THE FATHER:

The above ramblings should give each of us a minute recognition of our **GOD, THE FATHER.** Even with this feeble attempt to give application to only a few of His attributes, hopefully we can each have a more **HIGH** understanding of our **GOD, THE FATHER.** We cannot in any way define Him, and there is no conclusion for He is the **"GREAT I AM",** forever and ever. There is no higher **"Authority"**!!!

Any attempted explanation by man of our **"MOST HIGH AND HOLY GOD",** is totally lacking and is to be judged completely inadequate!!! **His "Word",** the **Mind** of our **Holy God,** can be the only thing man has that can speak for **Him**.

The following verses allow **Him** to speak for **Himself**!!!

(Revelation 1:8) "I am the Alpha and the Omega," says the Lord God, "who is and who was and who is to come, the Almighty."

(Revelation 21:6) Then He said to me, "It is done. I am the Alpha and the Omega, the beginning and the end. I will give to the one who thirsts from the spring of the water of life without cost.

(Revelation 22:13) "I am the Alpha and the Omega, the first and the last, the beginning and the end."

Alpha, as we all know, is the first letter of the Greek alphabet while Omega is the last letter in said alphabet. **HE** is the beginning of the beginning and **HE** is the end of the end, **HE** is incomprehensible, yet it is what **GOD, THE FATHER** is!!!

We can't put **HIM** in a box, **HE** has no limits!!!

SPECIAL NOTE:

I know many of you may have a special verse or verses regarding this Chapter's subject matter. This special verse or these verses may not have been mentioned due to my ignorance or because of brevity. I apologize for either of these reasons. Please feel free to write any special verse or verses in the space below. This will add your personal touch, and will serve to call to each person's mind their individual "experience of trust", in God's Holy Word.

For to each of us "Who belong To Him", His Holy Word can be truly recognized and relied upon as our **"Owner's Manual"**!!!

_____

_____

_____

_____

_____

_____

_____

_____

CHAPTER 3

GOD, THE SON (JESUS CHRIST)

INTRODUCTORY VERSES:

(John 1:1-5)(vs 1) In the beginning was the Word, and the Word was with God, and the Word was God. (vs 2) He was in the beginning with God. (vs 3) All things came into being through Him, and apart from Him nothing came into being that has come into being. (vs 4) In Him was life, and the life was the Light of men. (vs 5) The Light shines in the darkness, and the darkness did not comprehend it.

These verses encompass the full purpose and history of Jesus, the Son of God. He has always been with God, He is God, and His purpose and role was and is, to give "light" to all of man. He is the Savior that man needed. His role in the Triune Godhead was to become human, while still being God, in order to communicate with man. He is to those of us, "Who Belong To Him", the light of Salvation that … **"shines in the darkness"**, meeting this need of ours for a Savior. The "light" He gives, is to make known the Eternal, Almighty God of the Universe, in order that we might know Him in a very personal relationship.

INTRODUCTION:

We will find that Jesus Christ (God the Son) was both fully God and fully human. This Chapter is not written to prove that He was, is, and always will be fully God, but to let the Scriptures highlight His God appointed, earthly role, while also emphasizing the many wonderful and critical facets of His divine life. The Scriptures give us a multitude of examples, as it speaks of Jesus' heavenly appointed position, regarding the teaching and presentation of the Gospel (the history of the birth, life, actions, death, resurrection, ascension and doctrines of Jesus Christ). You will find herein only a small recap of the history of Jesus Christ (God the Son), for the world could not contain the books of all of His deeds. ... *(John 21:25) And there are also many other things which Jesus did, which if they *were written in detail, I suppose that even the world itself *would not contain the books that *would be written.* ...

Jesus was, is, and will be all of the following: a) He was with God from the Beginning; b) He was "incarnate" or, God "clothed or embodied in the fleshly body of man"; c) His virgin birth was miraculous and was announced by an Heavenly Angel; d) He and the Father were ONE and all of His earthly ministries were coordinated and approved by the Father; e) His temptations by the devil were real and all inclusive; f) The final victory over Death was won for all of man and for all of time; g) The grave could not hold Him; h) His ascension was to His proper place with the Father; i) His leaving the earth ushered in the Age of the Holy Spirit; and j) He has promised to return!!!

Jesus Christ is all of the above, with His purposes and role as a part of the Triune Godhead being cemented upon our minds, through the use of the following Scriptures. His life as both human yet fully God, allows for a multitude of encouragements and instructions, as we consider many of His attributes and some of the most significant events of His life.

A. HE EXISTED BEFOE TIME:

(John 1:1-2)(vs 1) In the beginning was the Word, and the Word was with God, and the Word was God. (vs 2) He was in the beginning with God.

B. HE WAS "INCARNATE":

(John 1:14) And the Word became flesh, and dwelt among us, and we saw His glory, glory as of the only begotten from the Father, full of grace and truth.

Jesus was God and was sent into this world as the incarnation of God. The word "incarnation" is defined by Webster as the act of assuming flesh, or of taking a human body and the nature of man; as the incarnation of the Son of God. Webster also defines the word "incarnate" as invested with flesh; embodied in flesh; as the "incarnate" Son of God.

(2 Corinthians 8:9) For you know the grace of our Lord Jesus Christ, that though He was rich, yet for your sake He became poor, so that you through His poverty might become rich.

Jesus came down from the heavens, leaving the true riches that are only known by God, and experienced the poverty of this earth in the form of a man, in order that we might experience the true riches of an eternal presence with Him.

(John 10:30) "I and the Father are one."

Jesus while ministering in human bodily form, was still ONE with God.

C. HIS BIRTH WAS MIRACULOUS:

(Luke 1:26-35)(vs26) Now in the sixth month the angel Gabriel was sent from God to a city in Galilee called Nazareth, (vs 27) to a virgin engaged to a man whose name was Joseph, of the descendants of David; and the virgin's name was Mary. (vs 28) And coming in, he said to her, "Greetings, favored one! The Lord is with you." (vs 29) But she was very perplexed at this statement, and kept pondering what kind of salutation this was. (vs 30) The angel said to her, "Do not be afraid, Mary; for you have found favor with God. (vs 31) "And behold, you will conceive in your womb and bear a son, and you shall name Him Jesus. (vs 32) "He will be great and will be called the Son of the Most High; and the Lord God will give Him the throne of His father David; (vs 33) and He will reign over the house of Jacob forever, and His kingdom will have no end." (vs 34) Mary said to the angel, "How can this be, since I am a virgin?" (vs 35) The angel answered and said to her, "The Holy Spirit will come upon you, and the power of the Most High will overshadow you; and for that reason the holy Child shall be called the Son of God.

(Matthew 1:20-25)(vs 20) But when he had considered this, behold, an angel of the Lord appeared to him in a dream, saying, "Joseph, son of David, do not be afraid to take Mary as your wife; for the Child who has been conceived in her is of the Holy Spirit. (vs 21) "She will bear a Son; and you shall call His name Jesus, for He will save His people from their sins." (vs 22) Now all this took place to fulfill what was spoken by the Lord through the prophet: (vs 23) "BEHOLD, THE VIRGIN SHALL BE WITH CHILD AND SHALL BEAR A SON, AND THEY SHALL CALL HIS NAME IMMANUEL," which translated means, "GOD WITH US." (vs 24) And Joseph awoke from his sleep and did as the angel of the Lord commanded him, and took Mary as his wife, (vs 25) but kept her a virgin until she gave birth to a Son; and he called His name Jesus.

These multiple verses say it so completely and accurately. Jesus' birth and life was miraculous, it was "an Act of God".

D. HE WAS SENT BY GOD THE FATHER AND THEY ARE ONE:

Jesus Christ was sent by God the Father to carry out a master plan for the forgiveness of man's sinful nature and to provide a redemption that man couldn't accomplish alone. Along with this, God the Son, accomplished Teachings, Instructions, Healing, Compassion, Serving Others and so many other things, they are too voluminous to relate in this account. While accomplishing the myriad of things above, He was at all times living and acting as One with the Father.

(Luke 4:18) "THE SPIRIT OF THE LORD IS UPON ME, BECAUSE HE ANOINTED ME TO PREACH THE GOSPEL TO THE POOR. HE HAS SENT ME TO PROCLAIM RELEASE TO THE CAPTIVES, AND RECOVERY OF SIGHT TO THE BLIND, TO SET FREE THOSE WHO ARE OPPRESSED,

As Isaiah foretold in the Old Testament and Luke reiterates in the New Testament, Jesus has been **anointed and sent** by God the Father to preach the Gospel, offering freedom to all who are captive to sin and blinded by the devil.

(John 5:24 & 30)(vs 24) "Truly, truly, I say to you, he who hears My word, and believes Him who sent Me, has eternal life, and does not come into judgment, but has passed out of death into life. (vs 30) "I can do nothing on My own initiative. As I hear, I judge; and My judgment is just, because I do not seek My own will, but the will of Him who sent Me.

Jesus continues to teach and offer eternal life to those who hear His message, while all the time exalting God the Father. Jesus is God, yet is found faithful in his submissive role, while here on earth.

(John 5:36 & 37 partial)(vs 36) "But the testimony which I have is greater than the testimony of John; for the works which the Father has given Me to accomplish—the very works that I do—testify about Me, that the Father has sent Me. (vs 37 partial) "And the Father who sent Me, He has testified of Me.

Jesus is saying that John the Baptist had testified about Him, but the greater testimony is from God the Father. John the Baptist **told** of Jesus and His mighty Gospel plan, God the Father and God the Son jointly **lived and carried out** those things foretold by John. John was a **forerunner**, Jesus was **the real thing**. He and the Father brought forth much more than John could ever have imagined, therefore verifying the Son and the Father as the Heavenly/Human team.

(John 6:38) "For I have come down from heaven, not to do My own will, but the will of Him who sent Me.

(John 8:42) Jesus said to them, "If God were your Father, you would love Me, for I proceeded forth and have come from God, for I have not even come on My own initiative, but He sent Me.

(John 12:49-50)(vs 49) "For I did not speak on My own initiative, but the Father Himself who sent Me has given Me a commandment as to what to say and what to speak. (vs 50) "I know that His commandment is eternal life; therefore the things I speak, I speak just as the Father has told Me."

These are Jesus' own words testifying of the One who sent Him to earth. Jesus testifies of this Heavenly relationship with the Father, while recognizing His subservient role in His witness to man.

(John 17:21-25)(vs 21) that they may all be one; even as You, Father, are in Me and I in You, that they also may be in Us, so that the world may believe that You sent Me. (vs 22) "The glory which You have given Me I have given to them, that they may be one, just as We are one; (vs 23) I in them and You in Me, that they may be perfected in unity, so that the world may know that You sent Me, and loved them, even as You have loved Me. (vs 24) "Father, I desire that they also, whom You have given Me, be with Me where I am, so that they may see My glory which You have given Me, for You loved Me before the foundation of the world. (vs 25) "O righteous Father, although the world has not known You, yet I have known You; and these have known that You sent Me;

We, as adopted children of the Living God, are all witnesses to the most magnificent gift ever offered, and that is eternal life with God the Father and God the Son. Our God the Father and God the Son, as coequals, have a coordinated master plan, to offer the God of the Universe to all of mankind. God's wonderful master plan, as being carried out by **the Son who was sent** into the world, provides an opportunity for all of us to be with Him for all of eternity.

E. HE WAS TEMPTED IN ALL THINGS:

(Mark 1:12-13)(vs 12) Immediately the Spirit *impelled Him to go out into the wilderness. (vs 13) And He was in the wilderness forty days being tempted by Satan; and He was with the wild beasts, and the angels were ministering to Him.

Jesus was tempted in all things as we are. He answered His temptations with Scripture and steadfast confidence in God the Father. (See the full Chapter on Temptation with its more complete details)

(Hebrews 2:18) For since He Himself was tempted in that which He has suffered, He is able to come to the aid of those who are tempted.

(Hebrews 4:15) For we do not have a high priest who cannot sympathize with our weaknesses, but One who has been tempted in all things as we are, yet without sin.

Because of the temptations Jesus endured, He is able to come to our aid in all times of trials. He is fully God, while being available to each of us on a personal, one-on-one relationship.

F. HIS FINAL VICTORY WAS OVER DEATH:

The final victory which God needed to win was the victory over death, and that was won through Jesus Christ at the Cross of Calvary. The needed victory over death could not be accomplished by man.

1. Sin leads to "Death"; Man cannot cope:

(Romans 6:23) For the wages of sin is death, but the free gift of God is eternal life in Christ Jesus our Lord.

(Romans 7:24) Wretched man that I am! Who will set me free from the body of this death?

(James 1:15) Then when lust has conceived, it gives birth to sin; and when sin is accomplished, it brings forth death.

The ultimate purpose for God the Son, was to accomplish what man most desperately needed, yet had no power to conquer. This death and the victory over death, which the Apostle's Paul and James were speaking of, had to be conquered and were completed by Jesus, the Son of God, on the Cross at Calvary.

2. Word of God establishes there is an enemy called "Death":

(1 Corinthians 15:25-26)(vs 25) For He must reign until He has put all His enemies under His feet. (vs 26) The last enemy that will be abolished is death.

3. Word of God establishes the "Victory" over "Death" was won by Jesus Christ:

The victory on the Cross at Calvary was the victory that put "death" in its final resting place, with no authority over those of us "Who Belong To Him"!!! Jesus Christ, God the Son, won this final victory.

(Matthew 26:1-2)(vs 1) When Jesus had finished all these words, He said to His disciples, (vs 2) "You know that after two days the Passover is coming, and the Son of Man is to be handed over for crucifixion."

(1 Corinthians 15:54-57)(vs 54) But when this perishable will have put on the imperishable, and this mortal will have put on immortality, then will come about the saying that

is written, *"DEATH IS SWALLOWED UP in victory. (vs 55) "O DEATH, WHERE IS YOUR VICTORY? O DEATH, WHERE IS YOUR STING?" (vs 56) The sting of death is sin, and the power of sin is the law; (vs 57) but thanks be to God, who gives us the victory through our Lord Jesus Christ.*

God the Father, through His orchestrated master plan which included God the Son, conquered "death" for all of us who are "faith believing", for all time. For further proof please look at these three additional verses.

(2 Timothy 1:10) but now has been revealed by the appearing of our Savior Christ Jesus, who abolished death and brought life and immortality to light through the gospel,

(Hebrews 2:14) Therefore, since the children share in flesh and blood, He Himself likewise also partook of the same, that through death He might render powerless him who had the power of death, that is, the devil,

(Revelation 1:17 partial & 18)(17 partial) "Do not be afraid; I am the first and the last, (vs 18) and the living One; and I was dead, and behold, I am alive forevermore, and I have the keys of death and of Hades.

The revelation that was made directly to the Apostle John in a vision, proclaims the words of Jesus Christ, that He is the Living God who has … *"the keys of death and of Hades"*.

This victory over "death" also accomplished the propitiation (the sacrifice that appeased the wrath of God towards sinners) for the sins of man. God the Son, with His victory over "death" also accomplished the "Gift of Salvation", the two are wonderfully linked.

G. HE AROSE FROM THE GRAVE:

Jesus arose from the grave and appeared to Mary, also to two men on the road to Emmaus and to His disciples. It is so important to know that Jesus arose from the grave just as He predicted. Without His victory over death, we would not be serving and worshiping a Living God. Our God is alive and well, He is not dead, nor does He slumber or sleep. Jesus, God the Son, arose and we will see later He is united with God the Father, for all of eternity.

1. His appearance to Mary Magdalene:

John 20:1, 11-17)(vs 1) Now on the first day of the week Mary Magdalene *came early to the tomb, while it *was still dark, and *saw the stone already taken away from the tomb. (vs 11) But Mary was standing outside the tomb weeping; and so, as she wept, she stooped and looked into the tomb; (vs 12) and she *saw two angels in white sitting, one at the head and one at the feet, where the body of Jesus had been lying. (vs 13) And they *said to her, "Woman, why are you weeping?" She *said to them, "Because they have taken away my Lord, and I do not know where they have laid Him." (vs 14) When she had said this, she turned around and *saw Jesus standing there, and did not know that it was Jesus. (vs 15)

Jesus *said to her, "Woman, why are you weeping? Whom are you seeking?" Supposing Him to be the gardener, she *said to Him, "Sir, if you have carried Him away, tell me where you have laid Him, and I will take Him away." (vs 16) Jesus *said to her, "Mary!" She turned and *said to Him in Hebrew, "Rabboni!" (which means, Teacher). (vs 17) Jesus *said to her, "Stop clinging to Me, for I have not yet ascended to the Father; but go to My brethren and say to them, 'I ascend to My Father and your Father, and My God and your God.'"

This is the abbreviated account of Mary Magdalene seeing firsthand the resurrected presence of Jesus.

2. His appearance on an isolated road between Jerusalem and Emmaus:

Jesus appeared to two men walking on the road to Emmaus, about a seven mile journey from Jerusalem. This appearance has been recorded in the following transcript by the Apostle Luke.

(Luke 24:33-48)(vs 33) And they got up that very hour and returned to Jerusalem, and found gathered together the eleven and those who were with them, (vs 34) saying, "The Lord has really risen and has appeared to Simon." (vs 35) They began to relate their experiences on the road and how He was recognized by them in the breaking of the bread. (vs

36) While they were telling these things, He Himself stood in their midst and *said to them, "Peace be to you." (vs 37) But they were startled and frightened and thought that they were seeing a spirit. (vs 38) And He said to them, "Why are you troubled, and why do doubts arise in your hearts? (vs 39) "See My hands and My feet, that it is I Myself; touch Me and see, for a spirit does not have flesh and bones as you see that I have." (vs 40) And when He had said this, He showed them His hands and His feet. (vs 41) While they still could not believe it because of their joy and amazement, He said to them, "Have you anything here to eat?" (vs 42) They gave Him a piece of a broiled fish; (vs 43) and He took it and ate it before them. (vs 44) Now He said to them, "These are My words which I spoke to you while I was still with you, that all things which are written about Me in the Law of Moses and the Prophets and the Psalms must be fulfilled." (vs 45) Then He opened their minds to understand the Scriptures, (vs 46) and He said to them, "Thus it is written, that the Christ would suffer and rise again from the dead the third day, (vs 47) and that repentance for forgiveness of sins would be proclaimed in His name to all the nations, beginning from Jerusalem. (vs 48) "You are witnesses of these things.

3. His appearance to His Disciples:

We find here Jesus' appearance to His Disciples on two very dramatic occasions:

(John 20:19-20)(vs 19) So when it was evening on that day, the first day of the week, and when the doors were shut where the disciples were, for fear of the Jews, Jesus came and stood in their midst and *said to them, "Peace be with you." (vs 20) And when He had said this, He showed them both His hands and His side. The disciples then rejoiced when they saw the Lord.; and

(John 20:24-28)(vs 24) But Thomas, one of the twelve, called Didymus, was not with them when Jesus came. (vs 25) So the other disciples were saying to him, "We have seen the Lord!" But he said to them, "Unless I see in His hands the imprint of the nails, and put my finger into the place of

*the nails, and put my hand into His side, I will not believe."
(vs 26) After eight days His disciples were again inside, and
Thomas with them. Jesus *came, the doors having been shut,
and stood in their midst and said, "Peace be with you." (vs
27) Then He *said to Thomas, "Reach here with your finger,
and see My hands; and reach here your hand and put it into
My side; and do not be unbelieving, but believing." (vs 28)
Thomas answered and said to Him, "My Lord and my God!"*

Should there be any doubt that Jesus arose from the grave, study the
whole New Testament and register your proof. Jesus' personal relationship with millions of people around the world is proof enough to know
that He no longer remains in the grave, and He is actively serving as the
fully resurrected God.

H. HE ASCENDED TO THE RIGHT HAND OF GOD THE FATHER:

Jesus, as planned before the beginning of time, arose from the grave
and ascended to rule co-equally with God the Father.

1. His Ascension was planned and foretold:

*(John 14:12) "Truly, truly, I say to you, he who believes
in Me, the works that I do, he will do also; and greater works
than these he will do; because I go to the Father.*

*(John 16:28) "I came forth from the Father and have
come into the world; I am leaving the world again and going
to the Father."*

*(John 17:11) "I am no longer in the world; and yet they
themselves are in the world, and I come to You. Holy Father,
keep them in Your name, the name which You have given
Me, that they may be one even as We are.*

*(John 20:17) Jesus *said to her, "Stop clinging to Me, for
I have not yet ascended to the Father; but go to My brethren
and say to them, 'I ascend to My Father and your Father,
and My God and your God.'"*

Jesus made multiple references to His planned return to God the
Father. When Jesus had completed His earthly work He had always
planned to rule from on High, alongside God the Father, as ONE!!!

2. The Testimony of His Ascension comes from many of the New Testament Writers:

(Mark 16:19) So then, when the Lord Jesus had spoken to them, He was received up into heaven and sat down at the right hand of God.

(Luke 22:69) "But from now on THE SON OF MAN WILL BE SEATED AT THE RIGHT HAND of the power OF GOD."

(Luke 24:50-51)(vs 50) And He led them out as far as Bethany, and He lifted up His hands and blessed them. (vs 51) While He was blessing them, He parted from them and was carried up into heaven.

(Acts 2:32-33 partial)(vs 32) "This Jesus God raised up again, to which we are all witnesses. (vs 33 partial) "Therefore having been exalted to the right hand of God,

In the Gospels written by both Mark and Luke, we see they boldly state the ascension of Jesus. This was again reiterated by Luke in the Book of Acts. Their testimony was written independently from each other yet clearly comes to the identical conclusion. It cannot be questioned, Jesus has ascended to God the Father.

(Acts 7:55-56)(vs 55) But being full of the Holy Spirit, he gazed intently into heaven and saw the glory of God, and Jesus standing at the right hand of God; (vs56) and he said, "Behold, I see the heavens opened up and the Son of Man standing at the right hand of God."

These particular verses are loaded with dramatic testimony of Jesus' ascension. We have here in the seventh Chapter of the Book of Acts, as recorded by the Gospel writer Luke, Stephen's very words just shortly before he was stoned to death. Stephen was given the opportunity to testify of the authority of God the Father and Jesus, God the Son. This testimony was from the days of Abraham right up to the present days of Jesus' ascension. His testimony was so direct and cutting that he incited the ire of the Jewish religious leaders and their followers. He had incited them to the point they were furious and they drove him out of the city where they began stoning him. Stephen while being stoned, having been filled with God the Holy Spirit, told his accusers that the heavens were opened and that he could see Jesus standing at the right hand of God. This was his testimony even though he knew he would soon be stoned to death by the hands of those who hated the thought of Jesus being coequal with God. His testimony was unwavering even in the light of his certain death. Stephen as he looked into the heavens and saw Jesus standing there next to God, called directly to Jesus to receive his spirit. Stephen's testimony of Jesus being ascended to God the Father is both pure and true, and stands with no possibility of any selfish motives.

(Romans 8:34 partial) Christ Jesus is He who died, yes, rather who was raised, who is at the right hand of God, who also intercedes for us.

(Hebrews 10:12) but He, having offered one sacrifice for sins for all time, SAT DOWN AT THE RIGHT HAND OF GOD,

(Hebrews 12:2) fixing our eyes on Jesus, the author and perfecter of faith, who for the joy set before Him endured the cross, despising the shame, and has sat down at the right hand of the throne of God.

The most interesting FACT here, and it is found in all three verses above, couple the life of Jesus, emphasizing the fulfillment of His purpose and mission upon the Cross, and His planned return to the Father. He ascended to His coequal place in the heavens as fully God, and now is the intercessor, for all of us "Who Belong To Him"!!!

I. HIS ASCENSION USHERED IN THE PRESENCE OF THE HOLY SPIRIT:

The Holy Spirit was ushered into our presence by the ascension of Jesus Christ. Upon Jesus' return to the Father the Holy Spirit became available to indwell all of those "Who Belong To Him"!!!

1. Jesus must leave in order for the Holy Spirit to come:

a) *(John 14:16-17)(vs 16) "I will ask the Father, and He will give you another Helper, that He may be with you forever; (vs 17) that is the Spirit of truth, whom the world cannot receive, because it does not see Him or know Him, but you know Him because He abides with you and will be in you.*

(John 14:26) "But the Helper, the Holy Spirit, whom the Father will send in My name, He will teach you all things, and bring to your remembrance all that I said to you.

Jesus is explaining to His Disciples that He must go and return to the Father, but the "Comforter', the Holy Spirit will be left with them. The Holy Spirit is to abide in them and literally be the presence of God indwelling each of His Disciples. He is also available as the constant, "presence of God", to each of us who are "Born Again".

b) *(John 16:5-7)(vs 5) "But now I am going to Him who sent Me; and none of you asks Me, 'Where are You going?' (vs 6) "But because I have said these things to you, sorrow has filled your heart. (vs 7) "But I tell you the truth, it is to your advantage that I go away; for if I do not go away, the Helper will not come to you; but if I go, I will send Him to you.*

In God's mighty plan Jesus must return to the Father, and to our advantage the Holy Spirit is now ushered in to fill that gap. The Holy Spirit more than fills this grand canyon left by Jesus' departure, as He indwells us 24/7/365.

c) *(Acts 2:32-33)(vs 32) "This Jesus God raised up again, to which we are all witnesses. (vs 33) "Therefore having been exalted to the right hand of God, and having received from the Father the promise of the Holy Spirit, He has poured forth this which you both see and hear.*

Here we have Luke's confirmation of the presence of the Holy Spirit being made available to all "believers". This was at the time of Jesus' return to the Father and continues today, and will continue until Jesus' "Second Coming".

2. We are Indwelled by God the Holy Spirit:

As a result of Jesus' return to the Father, we as "faith believers" have become the earthly "Temple of God"! Because "We Belong To Him", we are literally a walking presence of God. That brings upon us a responsibility of actions that is impossible to uphold, therefore the reason for the "Indwelling" of the Holy Spirit.

(1 Corinthians 6:19-20)(vs 19) Or do you not know that your body is a temple of the Holy Spirit who is in you, whom you have from God, and that you are not your own? (vs 20) For you have been bought with a price: therefore glorify God in your body.

Jesus had to return to the Father, but He didn't leave us defenseless and alone, the Holy Spirit (the presence of God) is alive and well, and is our daily companion and "Helper".

J. JESUS PROMISES TO RETURN:

There have been many highly important people down throughout the ages that have gone away leaving the people with the promise of returning, but the most anticipated return in all of history is the expected return of Jesus Christ. Jesus foretold of His return and that return will come with a mighty SHOUT (most theological scholars expect that to be soon), AND ALL WILL KNOW THAT IT IS HIS DAY!!!

1. The words of Jesus as He "Promises to Return":

(John 14:2-3)(vs 2) "In My Father's house are many dwelling places; if it were not so, I would have told you; for I go to prepare a place for you. (vs 3) "If I go and prepare a place for you, I will come again and receive you to Myself, that where I am, there you may be also.

2. The "Scene" upon His return:

<u>a)</u> *(Matthew 26:63-64)(vs 63) But Jesus kept silent. And the high priest said to Him, "I adjure You by the living God, that You tell us whether You are the Christ, the Son of God." (vs 64) Jesus *said to him, "You have said it yourself; nevertheless I tell you, hereafter you will see THE SON OF MAN SITTING AT THE RIGHT HAND OF POWER, and COMING ON THE CLOUDS OF HEAVEN."*

<u>b)</u> *(Mark 13:21-26)(vs 21) "And then if anyone says to you, 'Behold, here is the Christ'; or, 'Behold, He is there'; do not believe him; (vs 22) for false Christs and false prophets will arise, and will show signs and wonders, in order to lead astray, if possible, the elect. (vs 23) "But take heed; behold, I have told you everything in advance. (vs 24) "But in those days, after that tribulation, THE SUN WILL BE DARKENED AND THE MOON WILL NOT GIVE ITS LIGHT, (vs 25) AND THE STARS WILL BE FALLING from heaven, and the powers that are in the heavens will be shaken. (vs 26) "Then they*

will see THE SON OF MAN COMING IN CLOUDS with great power and glory.

c) (1 Thessalonians 4:16-17)(vs 16) For the Lord Himself will descend from heaven with a shout, with the voice of the archangel and with the trumpet of God, and the dead in Christ will rise first. (vs 17) Then we who are alive and remain will be caught up together with them in the clouds to meet the Lord in the air, and so we shall always be with the Lord.

The "Second Coming" of Jesus or His "Return" will be super majestic. His "Return" will be accompanied with our seeing Jesus: ... *"THE SON OF MAN COMING IN CLOUDS with great power and glory"* ; with a **"SHOUT"** directed by God Himself; by those "Who Belong To Him" hearing the voice of the archangel; and the unmistakably beautiful sound of the ... *"trumpet of God"* .

Both the dead in Christ and those who are alive will both meet Him in the air as we all ascend to heaven. There will be no misunderstanding, or mistakenly following the false prophets of the world, at Jesus' "Second Coming". We will undeniably know it is the God of the Universe, The GREAT I AM, who is calling this show to a halt. The "Return" of Jesus is **certain**, for His **Word** has announced it!!!

K. CONCLUSION to GOD THE SON:

In conclusion, without in anyway minimizing the magnitude of all of the words reported above about Jesus' purposes and accomplishments, let's look at two (2) last verses.
1. This God/man Jesus, His life and His purposes are summarized by the Apostle Paul in his first letter to Timothy.
(1 Timothy 3:16) By common confession, great is the mystery of godliness: He who was revealed in the flesh, Was vindicated in the Spirit, Seen by angels, Proclaimed among the nations, Believed on in the world, Taken up in glory.

Paul writes with all authority regarding Jesus, the Christ. Paul introduces this verse by stating ... *"great is the mystery of godliness (:)"*. Please note the punctuation here of the colon (:). Godliness here is defined in the original Greek to mean, "specifically the gospel scheme". In other words Paul is confirming that all of Jesus' life was and is the fulfillment of God's mysterious plan to bring "salvation" to a Godless people. He writes a beautiful summary and concludes that after Jesus was finished with His work here on earth, He was ... ***"Taken up in glory"***. Jesus was ... ***"revealed in the flesh"*** ... ***"vindicated in the Spirit"*** ... ***"Seen by angels"*** ... ***"Proclaimed among the nations"*** ... ***"Believed on in the world"*** ... and returned as "Fully God" to reign with God the Father!!!

2. Paul again so appropriately writes of Jesus being both God and man. Here we find as he writes to the Philippians how Jesus left His riches in glory and came to this earth to experience poverty, while offering to make us rich (spiritually-the only lasting riches). It Was through His humbling attitude of selflessness that He performed the greatest work that man could ever imagine, the **WORK** which will bring every knee to bow and every tongue to **"CONFESS"** that Jesus is **GOD!!!**

(Philippians 2:5-11)(vs 5) Have this attitude in yourselves which was also in Christ Jesus, (vs 6) who, although He existed in the form of God, did not regard equality with God a thing to be grasped, (vs 7) but emptied Himself, taking the form of a bond-servant, and being made in the likeness of men. (vs 8) Being found in appearance as a man, He humbled Himself by becoming obedient to the point of death, even death on a cross. (vs 9) For this reason also, God highly exalted Him, and bestowed on Him the name which is above every name, (vs 10) so that at the name of Jesus EVERY KNEE WILL BOW, of those who are in heaven and on earth and under the earth, (vs 11) and that every tongue will confess that Jesus Christ is Lord, to the glory of God the Father.

Jesus was God, yet He took on the likeness of man and became a servant of God the Father, with His ensuing attitude of serving, even to the point of death through the completed work on the Cross at Calvary. There has been discussion that the Jews crucified Jesus, but the truth is that God allowed the Jews of that day, to be a part of the Plan of the Almighty God, to complete the reconciliation of man from his sins or "offenses" against God, and to free man from those sins in the eyes and heart of God. This servant's task included the horrible death upon a cross, taking the burdens from others upon His own life, and doing so while being fully innocent of those burdens and sins, which He both bore and absorbed.

This righteousness created by Jesus, the Son of God, can now be "Imputed" to the life of those who by "faith", "believe" upon Him as God!!!

We can see from the above two (2) passages that Jesus, God the Son, had many roles. He was with God the Father from the beginning, He lived a sinless life while ministering here on earth, and He has returned to continue to rule and intercede at the right hand of God. He was human, yet "Fully God". I know this is incomprehensible, but we must trust that one day we will see it all clearly. **"To Whom Do You Belong (?)"**

SPECIAL NOTE:

I know many of you may have a special verse or verses regarding this Chapter's subject matter. This special verse or these verses may not have been mentioned due to my ignorance or because of brevity. I apologize for either of these reasons. Please feel free to write any special verse or verses in the space below. This will add your personal touch, and will serve to call to each person's mind their individual "experience of trust", in God's Holy Word.

For to each of us "Who belong To Him", His Holy Word can be truly recognized and relied upon as our **"Owner's Manual"**!!!

_____

_____

_____

_____

_____

_____

_____

CHAPTER 4

GOD, THE HOLY SPIRIT

INTRODUCTORY VERSE:

(John 14:16-17)(vs 16) "I will ask the Father, and He will give you another Helper, that He may be with you forever; (vs 17) that is the Spirit of truth, whom the world cannot receive, because it does not see Him or know Him, but you know Him because He abides with you and will be in you.

The "Helper" is the Holy Spirit. He is the "Presence" of God abiding in us until Jesus' Return".

INTRODUCTION:

To those of us "Who Belong To Him", God the Father, upon the request of God the Son, has "forever" made His "Presence" available to us through God the Holy Spirit. The Holy Spirit literally indwells us at all times as we abide in God and His Holy Word. Therefore the "Presence" of God is available daily (24/7) to convict, teach, comfort, witness, minister, and strengthen (along with a multitude of other attributes and purposes) each "Born Again" believer. The Holy Spirit is always available as the "Presence" of God, ministering daily, to and through each "believer".

A. GOD THE HOLY SPIRIT AND HIS DIETY OR ONENESS, IN THE TRIUNE GODHEAD:

God the Holy Spirit existed before time. His place and His value will be shown throughout the Old Testament, while His most predominant and noticeable roles, in our personal lives, are confirmed in the New Testament.

1. Old Testament Verses:

(Genesis 1:2) The earth was formless and void, and darkness was over the surface of the deep, and the Spirit of God was moving over the surface of the waters.

The Spirit of God has always existed, even before God formed the foundations of this and all universes.

(Psalms 51:9-12)(vs 9) Hide Your face from my sins And blot out all my iniquities. (vs 10) Create in me a clean heart, O God, And renew a steadfast spirit within me. (vs 11) Do not cast me away from Your presence And do not take Your Holy Spirit from me. (vs 12) Restore to me the joy of Your salvation And sustain me with a willing spirit.

There are multiple lessons to be learned from these verses. King David is openly repenting of his sin with Bathsheba. This sin was graphically called out to David by Nathan. Upon David's realization that he had sinned against God, he wanted nothing more than to not have the "Presence" of God (God the Holy Spirit) removed from his life. David was truly repentant and pleaded with God to not remove His Spirit, but to restore that daily, living, "sustaining", relationship with his God. The Holy Spirit, as we know Him today, was alive and real in King David's life some four to five thousand years ago. The Holy Spirit has, is, and always will exhibit His being God, and His part in the Triune Godhead.

(Daniel 4:4-9)(vs 4) "I, Nebuchadnezzar, was at ease in my house and flourishing in my palace. (vs 5) "I saw a dream and it made me fearful; and these fantasies as I lay on my bed and the visions in my mind kept alarming me. (vs 6) "So I gave orders to bring into my presence all the wise men of Babylon, that they might make known to me the interpretation of the dream. (vs 7) "Then the magicians, the conjurers, the Chaldeans and the diviners came in and I related the dream to them, but they could not make its interpretation known to me. (vs 8) "But finally Daniel came in before me, whose name is Belteshazzar according to the name of my god, and in whom is a spirit of the holy gods; and I related the dream to him, saying, (vs 9) 'O Belteshazzar, chief of the

magicians, since I know that a spirit of the holy gods is in you and no mystery baffles you, tell me the visions of my dream which I have seen, along with its interpretation.

Daniel, the same one who was cast into the hungry lion's den, was so filled with the Spirit of God that he was the only one able to interrupt Nebuchadnezzar's dreams. It was the "Presence" of God in Daniel's life that gave him this non-human ability. The "Presence" of God the Holy Spirit was alive back then and He is alive and available today, to preside in the lives of those "Who Belong To Him"!!! The Holy Spirit is GOD!!!

2. New Testament Verses:

(John 16:7 & 13-15)(vs 7) "But I tell you the truth, it is to your advantage that I go away; for if I do not go away, the Helper will not come to you; but if I go, I will send Him to you. (vs 13) "But when He, the Spirit of truth, comes, He will guide you into all the truth; for He will not speak on His own initiative, but whatever He hears, He will speak; and He will disclose to you what is to come. (vs 14) "He will glorify Me, for He will take of Mine and will disclose it to you. (vs 15) "All things that the Father has are Mine; therefore I said that He takes of Mine and will disclose it to you.

Jesus, God the Son, tells us here about the "Helper", God the Holy Spirit, and leads us through the link of the Father, the Son, and the Holy Spirit. The Holy Spirit is being emphasized in these verses by Jesus' explanation that the Holy Spirit has been sent to replace the presence of Jesus, and has now become (among His many roles) our guide in regards to understanding the Word. The Holy Spirit will take all thoughts and teachings from Jesus, who has taken these things from God the Father, thereby making the circle of the Triune Godhead complete. We have already seen that the Holy Spirit has existed with the Father before time, and now we have revealed His "Presence" and the magnificent, vital role that He is to play in our everyday life. Praise God that we who are in this world, but not of this world ("Those Who belong To Him"), are not left alone to fend off the fiery darts of the devil.

(2 Peter 1:20-21)(vs 20) But know this first of all, that no prophecy of Scripture is a matter of one's own interpretation, (vs 21) for no prophecy was ever made by an act of human will, but men moved by the Holy Spirit spoke from God.

Here we find another conclusive link that the power of the Holy Spirit, as reflected in the hearts, minds and mouths of man, is from God. The Holy Spirit only speaks that which has been approved by God. God the Holy Spirit and God are "ONE".

B. THE HOLY SPIRIT'S MOST CLOSELY HELD ATTRIBUTES:

The Holy Spirit has multiple Roles and Attributes that are reflected in our lives today. The identification of some of these is not intended to make little of those not mentioned, and it is fully recognized that much, much more could be said about this part of the Trinity of God. Let us look at a selected few of the more well-known attributes of God the Holy Spirit.

1. The Holy Spirit's Job of "Conviction":

It is not man's responsibility to be the convicting conscience of those around us. We often would like to tell others of their sins and wrong doings. God has placed His "Presence", in the form of the Holy Spirit, here on earth to do this distasteful job. The Holy Spirit along with the Holy Bible (our "Owner's Manual") is here to competently fulfill the conviction of all of man's sins. If God's Word says it, as it does in ... *(Proverbs 6:16-19)(vs 16) There are six things which the LORD hates, Yes, seven which are an abomination to Him: (vs 17) Haughty eyes, a lying tongue, And hands that shed innocent blood, (vs 18) A heart that devises wicked plans, Feet that run rapidly to evil, (vs 19) A false witness who utters lies, And one who spreads strife among brothers. ...,* then it is God's responsibility to impress upon all sinners their wayward ways. The sins listed above are not in any way all-inclusive of the sins that man commits against God, but are shown here as an example of what God hates. These verses in Proverbs were used to make the point that God hates all sin and will deal with each person on a personal, individual level. We are not the convicting agent, but we will see in both the Old and New Testament that God the Holy Spirit is that One. In accordance with His "Master Plan", the Holy Spirit will convict those who indulge in things contrary to His Word. It is God the Holy Spirit, who has the power and authority of calling to attention the mighty, awesome, powerful hand of God, as it applies to each individual's life. It is time to quit talking and time to look at God's Word.

(Psalms 40:12)
For evils beyond number have surrounded me; My iniquities have overtaken me, so that I am not able to see; They are more numerous than the hairs of my head, And my heart has failed me.

(Isaiah 64:6)
For all of us have become like one who is unclean, And all our righteous deeds are like a filthy garment; And all of us wither like a leaf, And our iniquities, like the wind, take us away.

(Romans 1:18-32)(vs 18) For the wrath of God is revealed from heaven against all ungodliness and unrighteousness of men who suppress the truth in unrighteousness, (vs 19) because that which is known about God is evident within them; for God made it evident to them. (vs 20) For since the creation of the world His invisible attributes, His eternal power and divine nature, have been clearly seen, being understood through what has been made, so that they are without excuse. (vs 21) For even though they knew God, they did not honor Him as God or give thanks, but they became futile in their speculations, and their foolish heart was darkened. (vs 22) Professing to be wise, they became fools, (vs 23) and exchanged the glory of the incorruptible God for an image in the form of corruptible man and of birds and four-footed animals and crawling creatures. (vs 24) Therefore God gave them over in the lusts of their hearts to impurity, so that their bodies would be dishonored among them. (vs 25) For they exchanged the truth of God for a lie, and worshiped and served the creature rather than the Creator, who is blessed forever. Amen. (vs 26) For this reason God gave them over to degrading passions; for their women exchanged the natural function for that which is unnatural, (vs 27) and in the same way also the men abandoned the natural function of the woman and burned in their desire toward one another, men with men committing indecent acts and receiving in their own persons

the due penalty of their error. (vs 28) And just as they did not see fit to acknowledge God any longer, God gave them over to a depraved mind, to do those things which are not proper, (vs 29) being filled with all unrighteousness, wickedness, greed, evil; full of envy, murder, strife, deceit, malice; they are gossips, (vs 30) slanderers, haters of God, insolent, arrogant, boastful, inventors of evil, disobedient to parents, (vs 31) without understanding, untrustworthy, unloving, unmerciful; (vs 32) and although they know the ordinance of God, that those who practice such things are worthy of death, they not only do the same, but also give hearty approval to those who practice them.

You may be wondering how the above verses tie into God the Holy Spirit. Well, these three Biblical passages are used to demonstrate the depravity of man and are used to set up the solution that man cannot resolve himself. Even though man daily and clearly sees God's Creation, which speaks of Him (Romans vs 20 above) we still disobey. Man's depravity takes on many forms and progresses to every sort of evil (Romans vs's 26-31 above) imaginable. Depravity as we can see in its many forms as described above, cannot be combated by ourselves and this is where God the Holy Spirit comes into play. We need the hand of God, and it is the hand of God reaching down to us in the form of God the Holy Spirit that convicts us of our wrong-doings. Just as He convicted the Old Testament character of King David, He just assuredly convicts us today. This conviction is the first step in our salvation and the Holy Spirit's involvement is confirmed in John 16: 7-8 as we see below.

(John 16:7-8)(vs 7) "But I tell you the truth, it is to your advantage that I go away; for if I do not go away, the Helper will not come to you; but if I go, I will send Him to you. (vs 8) "And He, when He comes, will convict the world concerning sin and righteousness and judgment;

The Spirit of God, literally the very "Presence" of the "Most Holy God", will convict the whole world, and all 6 billion people living today, concerning sin. This is part of God's "Master Plan" and it will be carried out without His needing or requiring our help. God the Holy Spirit is the "Convictor"!!!

2. The Holy Spirit is every "Believers Teacher":

We will see that it is the work of God the Holy Spirit to teach or make known the ways, the paths, and the truth of the God of our salvation. King David of the Old Testament introduces the Biblical fact that God is our "Teacher". We will look at several other verses, primarily in the New Testament, confirming this truth to be God the Holy Spirit (our Teacher).

(Psalms 25:4-5)(vs 4) Make me know Your ways, O LORD; Teach me Your paths. (vs 5) Lead me in Your truth and teach me, For You are the God of my salvation; For You I wait all the day.

(Psalms 119:33-35)(vs 33) Teach me, O LORD, the way of Your statutes, And I shall observe it to the end. (vs 34) Give me understanding, that I may observe Your law And keep it with all my heart. (vs 35) Make me walk in the path of Your commandments, For I delight in it.

In David's desire to be "a man after God's own heart", he lays the foundation for knowing God's way, how to search out God's paths, and clarifies who is the "Teacher" of God's truths. Literally the Holy Spirit is the one being discussed here, even though He isn't called by name.

(John 14:26) "But the Helper, the Holy Spirit, whom the Father will send in My name, He will teach you all things, and bring to your remembrance all that I said to you.

(John 16:13) "But when He, the Spirit of truth, comes, He will guide you into all the truth; for He will not speak on His own initiative, but whatever He hears, He will speak; and He will disclose to you what is to come.

God the Holy Spirit is our teacher, reminder, guide, and the discloser of all the spiritual truth we will ever need. God the Holy Spirit is One with the Father and the Son, and when He speaks it is the truth from our Most High God. He is the "Teacher" of the Triune Godhead.

(1 Corinthians 2:9-13)(vs 9) but just as it is written, "THINGS WHICH EYE HAS NOT SEEN AND EAR HAS NOT HEARD, AND which HAVE NOT ENTERED THE HEART OF MAN, ALL THAT GOD HAS PREPARED FOR THOSE WHO LOVE HIM." (vs 10) For to us God revealed them through the Spirit; for the Spirit searches all things, even the depths of God. (vs 11) For who among men knows the thoughts of a

man except the spirit of the man which is in him? Even so the thoughts of God no one knows except the Spirit of God. (vs 12) Now we have received, not the spirit of the world, but the Spirit who is from God, so that we may know the things freely given to us by God, (vs 13) which things we also speak, not in words taught by human wisdom, but in those taught by the Spirit, combining spiritual thoughts with spiritual words.

No one can know your personal thoughts but yourself. No one can know the thoughts of God but Himself. To those of us "Who Belong To Him", we now have available through God the Holy Spirit, the "Teachings" of spiritual wisdom. Our heavenly "Teacher" is God the Holy Spirit and He is willing to "Teach" each of us the very mind (including the depths of God's thoughts) of our Eternal God!!! This is both a FACT and a PRIVILEGE, and MUST NOT be taken lightly. God's Holy Word, the Holy Bible, will come alive in your hands through the power of God the Holy Spirit.

3. The Holy Spirit is our "Comforter":

Life as a "believer" can be difficult and may at times be very trying, but life without the Holy Spirit as our "Comforter" is unimaginable. God has sent to dwell within us His Spirit, who is available 24 hours per day to help each of us as we deal with the many sorrows, disappointments, illnesses, death of friends, loved ones, and associates, and difficulties beyond description. Let's look at His word regarding this Holy "Comforter".

(Psalms 25:6) Remember, O LORD, Your compassion and Your lovingkindnesses, For they have been from of old.

King David is so thoughtful to remind us of the Lord's compassion and lovingkindnesses. These attributes of God have been with us since the beginning of time. God is so faithful to leave us with His "Presence" in the form of the Holy Spirit as our "Comforter".

(Matthew 10:16-20)(vs 16) "Behold, I send you out as sheep in the midst of wolves; so be shrewd as serpents and innocent as doves. (vs 17) "But beware of men, for they will hand you over to the courts and scourge you in their synagogues; (vs 18) and you will even be brought before governors and kings for My sake, as a testimony to them and to the Gentiles. (vs 19) "But when they hand you over,

do not worry about how or what you are to say; for it will be given you in that hour what you are to say. (vs 20) "For it is not you who speak, but it is the Spirit of your Father who speaks in you.

The words of Jesus warn us that we are in a foreign land. We are in as much danger as a sheep in the presence of a wolf. Without the protection of the shepherd, the sheep are defenseless. So are we without the protection of the Holy Spirit of God. We are to use the defense that He has provided to calm ourselves in these times of stress. We are to use the Holy Spirit to "Comfort" us in the difficult situations. He is our Shepherd and the wolf/wolves of this world cannot harm us. God always stands ready to "Comfort" and calm us in any and all storms, by His Spirit.

(John 14:16) "I will ask the Father, and He will give you another Helper, that He may be with you forever;

(John 14:26) "But the Helper, the Holy Spirit, whom the Father will send in My name, He will teach you all things, and bring to your remembrance all that I said to you.

(John 15:26) "When the Helper comes, whom I will send to you from the Father, that is the Spirit of truth who proceeds from the Father, He will testify about Me,

(John 16:7) "But I tell you the truth, it is to your advantage that I go away; for if I do not go away, the Helper will not come to you; but if I go, I will send Him to you.

In each case where the word "Helper" is used above, it can be defined in the original Greek as intercessor, consoler, advocate and "Comforter". Each of those definitions powerfully indicates the "Helper" is not only on our side, but is actively seeking to be of "Help". God has sent His "Comforter", God the Holy Spirit, to actively support, console, and to be our forerunner of intercession and advocacy, as we deal with this life. The Holy Spirit is our shepherd when the wolves come to the door.

4. The Holy Spirit is our "Witness" of the Living Lord:

God the Holy Spirit will "Witness", through us, to all of those around us.

(2 Corinthians 3:1-3)(vs 1) Are we beginning to commend ourselves again? Or do we need, as some, letters of commendation to you or from you? (vs 2) You are our letter, written

in our hearts, known and read by all men; (vs 3) being manifested that you are a letter of Christ, cared for by us, written not with ink but with the Spirit of the living God, not on tablets of stone but on tablets of human hearts.

The Apostle Paul is writing to the saints at Corinth. He adamantly states that it is the Spirit of the Living God that will be read and heard by all men. This Spirit is demonstrated daily in our actions of love, compassion, concern and friendship. It is not us, but rather the "Spirit of the Living Lord", that causes someone to look at our lives and say "there is something about that person that I would like to have in my life". What is in the heart will come out of the heart. If the Spirit of God is within you, the Spirit of God will come out from you. It is God the Holy Spirit that witnesses of Himself through our lives. Our "Witness" is ... *"written not with ink but with the Spirit of the living God, not on tablets of stone but on tablets of human hearts".* May the testimony of the "Holy Spirit of God" be the only testimony proclaimed, by all of those "Who Profess To Belong To Him"!!!

5. The Holy Spirit "Indwells" all "faith believers":

There are many New Testament verses that tell us about the "Presence" of God in our lives through the "Indwelling" of the Holy Spirit. These should give us hope and strength to live the Christian life while in this earthly body. The "Presence" of the Holy Spirit is available to minister, strengthen and supernaturally defeat the fiery darts of the devil. A great Biblical example of this is vividly portrayed in the scripture as found written by the Apostles Peter and James. ... *(1 Peter 5:8) Be of sober spirit, be on the alert. Your adversary, the devil, prowls around like a roaring lion, seeking someone to devour. (James 4:7) Submit therefore to God. Resist the devil and he will flee from you.* ... The devil is like a roaring lion, prowling around seeking someone to devour, but with the power of the Holy Spirit we can cause him to flee as if he were a rabbit being chased by a dog. Can you imagine a roaring lion fleeing from a man? Not at all!!!, but With God that roaring lion becomes as a kitten.

Let's look at the following verses and glean all that God has for us in regard to the "Indwelling" of God the Holy Spirit.

<u>a)</u> *(1 Corinthians 6:15-20)(vs 15) Do you not know that your bodies are members of Christ? Shall I then take away*

the members of Christ and make them members of a pros-
titute? May it never be! (vs 16) Or do you not know that the
one who joins himself to a prostitute is one body with her?
For He says, "THE TWO SHALL BECOME ONE FLESH." (vs
17) But the one who joins himself to the Lord is one spirit
with Him. (vs 18) Flee immorality. Every other sin that a
man commits is outside the body, but the immoral man sins
against his own body. (vs 19) Or do you not know that your
body is a temple of the Holy Spirit who is in you, whom you
have from God, and that you are not your own? (vs 20) For
you have been bought with a price: therefore glorify God in
your body.

Even though the Apostle Paul is warning Christians here about the detestable act of joining oneself to a prostitute, and the disaster that it creates in our relationship with our Lord, his main message is clearly that of being one with God, through the "Indwelling" of the "Presence" of God. As God the Holy Spirit "Indwells" us, He is able to **minister to us** and **strengthen us**, whereby we are able to resist the devil and not prostitute, in any way, our relationship with Him.

b) *(Romans 8:9) However, you are not in the flesh but*
in the Spirit, if indeed the Spirit of God dwells in you. But
if anyone does not have the Spirit of Christ, he does not
belong to Him.

"To Whom Do You Belong" (?). Give yourself a self-test. Is the Spirit of God "Indwelling" you? As a "Born Again", "faith believer" you have no choice but to be possessed by the Spirit of God. If His Spirit is not in you, "You Do Not Belong To Him". I didn't make this up, but the Holy Word of God is the absolute, final authority, regarding this issue.

c) *(1 Corinthians 3:16) Do you not know that you are a*
temple of God and that the Spirit of God dwells in you?

(Galatians 4:6) Because you are sons, God has sent forth
the Spirit of His Son into our hearts, crying, "Abba! Father!"

(2 Timothy 1:13-14)(vs 13) Retain the standard of sound
words which you have heard from me, in the faith and
love which are in Christ Jesus. (vs 14) Guard, through the

Holy Spirit who dwells in us, the treasure which has been entrusted to you.

(1 John 4:12-13)(vs 12) No one has seen God at any time; if we love one another, God abides in us, and His love is perfected in us. (vs 13) By this we know that we abide in Him and He in us, because He has given us of His Spirit.

The above scriptures, along with numerous others, are conclusive evidence of the "Indwelling" of the Holy Spirit in the lives of those "Who Belong To Him"!!! We are the temple of the Living God with the Spirit of God residing within us. God has granted to all of those "Who Have Been Adopted Into His Family", the "Indwelling" of the Holy Spirit!!! We have not seen God, but others may see Him through the "Indwelling" of His Spirit, as He shines like the noon day sun in our daily lives. A lamp on a hill cannot be hid, and the Spirit of God in each "Born Again Believer" is a treasure that cannot be mistaken.

d) ***(Ephesians 1:13-14)(vs 13) In Him, you also, after listening to the message of truth, the gospel of your salvation—having also believed, you were sealed in Him with the Holy Spirit of promise, (vs 14) who is given as a pledge of our inheritance, with a view to the redemption of God's own possession, to the praise of His glory.***

The definition of a pledge as recorded in verse 14 above is this: part of the purchase money or property given in advance as security for the rest or balance due.

This security of the "Indwelling Spirit of the Living God" gives us a living/daily hope for the future that God's final payment, of eternal life in His presence, will be paid "ON TIME". As the security of our "Future Inheritance", we have been granted the "Earnest Money" in the form of "God the Holy Spirit", with final payment due when we meet Jesus in the air.

C. THE "FRUITS" OF THE HOLY SPIRIT:

There are certain "things" called "Spiritual Fruits" that can only come from the Holy Spirit. These "Fruits" of the Holy Spirit, as found in the lives of "believers", are not something that each of us can manufacture. They are here because of the indwelling of the Spirit of the Living

God. They are here in order to be a blessing to others. They should be ripe and delicious, and they should be available to be picked by those around us. While they are produced by God, they are only available through those "Who Belong To Him"!!! May the Holy Spirit of God be allowed to grow ripe and delicious "Fruit" in each of our lives.

(Galatians 5:22-25)(vs 22) But the fruit of the Spirit is love, joy, peace, patience, kindness, goodness, faithfulness, (vs 23) gentleness, self-control; against such things there is no law. (vs 24) Now those who belong to Christ Jesus have crucified the flesh with its passions and desires. (vs 25) If we live by the Spirit, let us also walk by the Spirit.

Each of these individual "Fruits" of the Spirit will be addressed in detail in Volume Two (2) of "To Whom Do You Belong" (?).

D. THE "GREAT COMMISSION" AND THE HOLY SPIRIT:

The "Great Commission" is not a term that is used in the Bible. It is a description of the challenge left each of us to fulfill God's plan of bringing His love, His teaching, His truths and His salvation, through all means possible, to all people of all the nations. This challenge has been authorized and is supported by God the Father, God the Son and God the Holy Spirit. Since the Holy Spirit of God is the One who remains and dwells among us and in us, it is the Holy Spirit who is to be our source of power. He remains with us and will empower us in all endeavors ....
"even to the end of the age."

(Matthew 28:18-20)(vs 18) And Jesus came up and spoke to them, saying, "All authority has been given to Me in heaven and on earth. (vs 19) "Go therefore and make disciples of all the nations, baptizing them in the name of the Father and the Son and the Holy Spirit, (vs 20) teaching them to observe all that I commanded you; and lo, I am with you always, even to the end of the age."

The Holy Spirit that God has sent to indwell us will be with us until we die, and will be with those who follow us for all time to come. His "Presence" and power will be available to accomplish anything and everything that God sees fit to do. We will lack for nothing in physical, spiritual, financial and mental requirements in order to be able to accomplish the "Great Commission". God is not bankrupt and His Holy Spirit will provide all of our needs.

E. CONCLUSION TO GOD THE HOLY SPIRIT:

God the Holy Spirit is to be taken seriously and is to become a part of our daily lives. We are to understand Him, get acquainted with Him, rely upon Him, utilize His "Presence" and thrive upon His powers. It is my conclusion that He can keep us from all evil and keep us unto all good as we learn to trust Him. We are commanded to … *"be filled with the Spirit" (vs 18 below).*

(Ephesians 5:11-20)(vs 11) Do not participate in the unfruitful deeds of darkness, but instead even expose them; (vs 12) for it is disgraceful even to speak of the things which are done by them in secret. (vs 13) But all things become visible when they are exposed by the light, for everything that becomes visible is light. (vs 14) For this reason it says, "Awake, sleeper, And arise from the dead, And Christ will shine on you." (vs 15) Therefore be careful how you walk, not as unwise men but as wise, (vs 16) making the most of your time, because the days are evil. (vs 17) So then do not be foolish, but understand what the will of the Lord is. (vs 18) And do not get drunk with wine, for that is dissipation, but be filled with the Spirit, (vs 19) speaking to one another in psalms and hymns and spiritual songs, singing and making melody with your heart to the Lord; (vs 20) always giving thanks for all things in the name of our Lord Jesus Christ to God, even the Father;

We are to … *"Awake, sleeper, And arise from the dead"*. This is defined in the original Greek as being asleep and being dead and in need of standing up and being conscious. Therefore in the context here we are to stop living this earthly life as if we were a corpse. We are to be that bright light on the hill, the salt that flavors all that is around it, thereby allowing God to be lifted up to all of those in our community of family, friends and associates.

In an age where the Holy Spirit is being passed over, ignored and left out of our lives, we need this "Presence" of God more than at any other time. Our lives are being filled with pleasures of the world like never before. The availability of things to fulfill our fleshly desires has never been so prevalent to so many. The verses above may look so small and insignificant. They can be pushed aside so easily and rationalized as to being applicable to someone else. We can even go so far as to say these verses are for the "sinners", the "down and out", those who are "Godless". I believe it would bless all of us to return and concentrate upon allowing the Holy Spirit to revive our everyday life and see to it that the "Presence" of the Holy Spirit is allowed to rule and correct our lives. This is a must if our world is to see a revival of people "Walking with God".

The Holy Spirit is available to fill all of us "Who Belong To Him"!!! The Holy Spirit is a part of the Triune Godhead. Even though He is unseen, He is literally the power of the Almighty God, and we could literally "walk on water" if needed. The Holy Spirit is fully God, with God the Father, God the Son and God the Holy Spirit being ONE.

(2 Corinthians 13:14) The grace of the Lord Jesus Christ, and the love of God, and the fellowship of the Holy Spirit, be with you all.

God blesses our lives, through the **"Grace"** afforded us by **Jesus**, because of the **"Love"** bestowed upon us from **God the Father**, and all the while adorning us in **"Fellowship"** with the daily "Presence" of the **Holy Spirit**.

SPECIAL NOTE:

I know many of you may have a special verse or verses regarding this Chapter's subject matter. This special verse or these verses may not have been mentioned due to my ignorance or because of brevity. I apologize for either of these reasons. Please feel free to write any special verse or verses in the space below. This will add your personal touch, and will serve to call to each person's mind their individual "experience of trust", in God's Holy Word.

For to each of us "Who belong To Him", His Holy Word can be truly recognized and relied upon as our **"Owner's Manual"**!!!

CHAPTER 5

SALVATION

INTRODUCTORY VERSES:

(Galatians 2:20) "I have been crucified with Christ; and it is no longer I who live, but Christ lives in me; and the life which I now live in the flesh I live by faith in the Son of God, who loved me and gave Himself up for me.

Paul, through his new found faith in Jesus Christ, was daily experiencing his spiritual crucifixion. Paul was dead to himself and his old ways and it was Christ who was living in him. What he is speaking of here is his "Salvation" experience which can also be described as being "Born Again" or "Regenerated". This is an "Act of God", for it is Christ who will stand before a Holy God on that judgment day and say, Father forgive him for he is one of mine. This same "Salvation" experience is available, and is just as true for you and I today, as it was for the Apostle Paul.

AND

(Acts 4:12) "And there is salvation in no one else; for there is no other name under heaven that has been given among men by which we must be saved."

The Apostle Peter was speaking of Jesus Christ, the Son of God, when he penned these words.

What wonderful verses to know that God provided His sacrificial lamb, His Son, and "We Can Be His"!!! Truly we can "Belong To Him". Our "Salvation", being "Born Again", or being "Regenerated" is obtained in no other way than through God's marvelous plan.

INTRODUCTION:

As one of 6 billion people born and alive today on this earth, we may seem rather insignificant. Even as a part of this giant number, while being a small part of the universe, we find that God in His Almighty Way has provided, through His Holy Word, a simple plan that is available specifically for each of us. This plan is for each of us to be "Born Again" or "Regenerated". Being "Born Again" **is not** based upon belonging to a certain **Religion** or belonging to a **Church Denomination**, but **it is** based upon a **Personal Relationship** with the Almighty God, and **it is an "Act of God"** through a **"believing faith" in Jesus Christ**. *(John 3:5) Jesus answered, "Truly, truly, I say to you, unless one is born of water and the Spirit he cannot enter into the kingdom of God.*

We were all born a physical birth (of water), now we must be "Born Again" through a spiritual birth (the Spirit). This is something we need to recognize and deal with in accordance with the scriptures found in God's Holy Word. If we are to be **"Born Again"**, **"Regenerated"**, become a **"New Creation"** or to be **"Saved"**, it must be according to God's plan, which is only possible through a "believing faith" in Jesus Christ.

(Luke 18:25-27)(vs 25) "For it is easier for a camel to go through the eye of a needle than for a rich man to enter the kingdom of God." (vs 26) They who heard it said, "Then who can be saved?" (vs 27) But He said, "The things that are impossible with people are possible with God."

We all know it is impossible for a camel to pass through the eye of a needle, yet the Bible says "**the things which are impossible with men are possible with God**". Except for an Act of God and the Grace of God, no one would be saved!

The complexity of the human being is beyond our understanding. Psychology today has studied man until it seems to be exhaustive, yet those studies are still baffling to the professor(s) as to what makes us tick. Our complex nature is made up (to only mention a few parts) of emotions, feelings, fears, happiness, and relationships with family, friends, and God. Yet with all this potential complexity in our lives, The Almighty God (Yahweh) (The Great I Am), has provided the most simple, yet narrow way to Him. *(Mark 10:14-15)(vs 14) But when*

Jesus saw this, He was indignant and said to them, "Permit the children to come to Me; do not hinder them; for the kingdom of God belongs to such as these. (vs 15) "Truly I say to you, whoever does not receive the kingdom of God like a child will not enter it at all."

Unless we come as a little child with childlike faith, we cannot enter the Kingdom of Heaven. It is all so simple, but we must trust with "child-like", "believing faith", the Jesus of the Bible.

Please bear with me through the many words and scriptures that follows, for "Salvation" is the **most important thing** a person can consider in one's lifetime. My Prayer is that through the many scriptures, comments, examples and testimonies, everyone will come to know the Jesus of the Bible in this new **"PERSONAL RELATIONSHIP"**.

A. GOD'S PLAN FOR SALVATION:

The following are three serious considerations to be made in regard to God's plan for man:

1) We must know that we need God;

We need to consider the world and its current depravity, as well as the following scriptures, in order to completely understand Man's need for God. We cannot right our own ship. Please consider the following scriptures as they emphasize our need for God. *(Genesis 4:8) And it came about when they were in the field, that Cain rose up against Abel his brother and killed him.*

(Genesis 6:5) Then the LORD saw that the wickedness of man was great on the earth, and that every intent of the thoughts of his heart was only evil continually.

(Genesis 8:21) The LORD smelled the soothing aroma; and the LORD said to Himself, "I will never again curse the ground on account of man, for the intent of man's heart is evil from his youth; and I will never again destroy every living thing, as I have done.

(Isaiah 64:6) For all of us have become like one who is unclean, And all our righteous deeds are like a filthy

garment; And all of us wither like a leaf, And our iniquities, like the wind, take us away.

(Jeremiah 17:9) "The heart is more deceitful than all else And is desperately sick; Who can understand it?

(John 7:7) "The world cannot hate you, but it hates Me because I testify of it, that its deeds are evil.

(Romans 3:9-12)(vs 9) What then? Are we better than they? Not at all; for we have already charged that both Jews and Greeks are all under sin; (vs 10) as it is written, "THERE IS NONE RIGHTEOUS, NOT EVEN ONE; (vs 11) THERE IS NONE WHO UNDERSTANDS, THERE IS NONE WHO SEEKS FOR GOD; (vs 12) ALL HAVE TURNED ASIDE, TOGETHER THEY HAVE BECOME USELESS; THERE IS NONE WHO DOES GOOD, THERE IS NOT EVEN ONE."

(Romans 5:12) Therefore, just as through one man sin entered into the world, and death through sin, and so death spread to all men, because all sinned—

(Romans 6:23) For the wages of sin is death, but the free gift of God is eternal life in Christ Jesus our Lord.

(1 John 1:8) If we say that we have no sin, we are deceiving ourselves and the truth is not in us.

(1 John 1:10) If we say that we have not sinned, we make Him a liar and His word is not in us.

Can't argue with God's Word, we need Him!

2) We must know that God has provided for that need;

We must recognize that God's plan, through Jesus on the cross, is the only way to salvation and it is only as a Gift of God. The following multiple passages from the Bible clearly state and express this gift from God.

(Ephesians 2:8-9)(vs 8) For by grace you have been saved through faith; and that not of yourselves, it is the gift of God; (vs 9) not as a result of works, so that no one may boast.

(Galatians 2:16) nevertheless knowing that a man is not justified by the works of the Law but through faith in Christ Jesus, even we have believed in Christ Jesus, so that we may

be justified by faith in Christ and not by the works of the Law; since by the works of the Law no flesh will be justified.

It was God's plan … *(Acts 2:22-24)(vs 22) "Men of Israel, listen to these words: Jesus the Nazarene, a man attested to you by God with miracles and wonders and signs which God performed through Him in your midst, just as you yourselves know— (vs 23) this Man, delivered over by the predetermined plan and foreknowledge of God, you nailed to a cross by the hands of godless men and put Him to death. (vs 24) "But God raised Him up again, putting an end to the agony of death, since it was impossible for Him to be held in its power.* … to send Jesus (His only begotten Son) to the cross. It was through this shed blood as a sacrifice for our sins (and this sacrifice was not required to be repeated as those in the Old Testament days) that we through "believing faith" are "**Saved**" or "**Counted Righteous**" in the sight of God. God secured this final victory, the victory over death and Satan, by the Cross, and this is for all of eternity and available to all mankind.

*(John 14:6) Jesus *said to him, "I am the way, and the truth, and the life; no one comes to the Father but through Me.*

The following verses continue to establish God's plan through His Son Jesus Christ. We see that it is God's only plan and it is through this "believing faith" in Jesus that we find redemption.

(Acts 4:8-12)(vs 8) Then Peter, filled with the Holy Spirit, said to them, "Rulers and elders of the people, (vs 9) if we are on trial today for a benefit done to a sick man, as to how this man has been made well, (vs 10) let it be known to all of you and to all the people of Israel, that by the name of Jesus Christ the Nazarene, whom you crucified, whom God raised from the dead—by this name this man stands here before you in good health. (vs 11) "He is the STONE WHICH WAS REJECTED by you, THE BUILDERS, but WHICH BECAME THE CHIEF CORNER stone. (vs 12) "And there is salvation in no one else; for there is no other name under heaven that has been given among men by which we must be saved."

(John 3:16-18)(vs 16) "For God so loved the world, that He gave His only begotten Son, that whoever believes in Him shall not perish, but have eternal life. (vs 17) "For God did not send the Son into the world to judge the world, but that the world might be saved through Him. (vs 18) "He who believes in Him is not judged; he who does not believe has been judged already, because he has not believed in the name of the only begotten Son of God.

It matters not the type or the quantity of man's sins, for the only sin that can't be forgiven and the one that condemns a man to eternal separation from God, is the sin of "unbelief". God can and will forgive all sins, no matter the amount or their severity, except the sin of "unbelief".

(John 3:36) "He who believes in the Son has eternal life; but he who does not obey the Son will not see life, but the wrath of God abides on him." (Romans 6:23) For the wages of sin is death, but the free gift of God is eternal life in Christ Jesus our Lord.

(Acts 13:37-39)(vs 37) but He (Jesus) *whom God raised did not undergo decay. (vs 38) "Therefore let it be known to you, brethren, that through Him forgiveness of sins is proclaimed to you, (vs 39) and through Him everyone who believes is freed from all things, from which you could not be freed through the Law of Moses.*

(1 John 1:6-7)(vs 6) If we say that we have fellowship with Him and yet walk in the darkness, we lie and do not practice the truth; (vs 7) but if we walk in the Light as He Himself is in the Light, we have fellowship with one another, and the blood of Jesus His Son cleanses us from all sin.

(1 John 1:9-10)(vs 9) If we confess our sins, He is faithful and righteous to forgive us our sins and to cleanse us from all unrighteousness. (vs 10) If we say that we have not sinned, we make Him a liar and His word is not in us.

(Romans 10:9-13)(vs 9) that if you confess with your mouth Jesus as Lord, and believe in your heart that God raised Him from the dead, you will be saved; (vs 10) for with the heart a person believes, resulting in righteousness, and with the mouth he confesses, resulting in salvation.

(vs 11) For the Scripture says, "WHOEVER BELIEVES IN HIM WILL NOT BE DISAPPOINTED." (vs 12) For there is no distinction between Jew and Greek; for the same Lord is Lord of all, abounding in riches for all who call on Him; (vs 13) for "WHOEVER WILL CALL ON THE NAME OF THE LORD WILL BE SAVED."

God has miraculously provided for our need of a "Savior".

3) and, We must now respond to that need.

We as individuals are a complex being, yet we need God. Our only hope is to now look to God's Word as the solution to our needs. We must respond to Him!

(John 1:12-13) But as many as received Him, to them He gave the right to become children of God, even to those who believe in His name, who were born, not of blood nor of the will of the flesh nor of the will of man, but of God.

(2 Corinthians 5:17-21) Therefore if anyone is in Christ, he is a new creature; the old things passed away; behold, new things have come. Now all these things are from God, who reconciled us to Himself through Christ and gave us the ministry of reconciliation, namely, that God was in Christ reconciling the world to Himself, not counting their trespasses against them, and He has committed to us the word of reconciliation. Therefore, we are ambassadors for Christ, as though God were making an appeal through us; we beg you on behalf of Christ, be reconciled to God. He made Him who knew no sin to be sin on our behalf, so that we might become the righteousness of God in Him.

(2 Corinthians 8:9) For you know the grace of our Lord Jesus Christ, that though He was rich, yet for your sake He became poor, so that you through His poverty might become rich.

If we have become a "New Creation" or "Born Again", and now have the "Riches of Jesus", it is all in knowing Christ as our personal Savior. Jesus went to the Cross and took on the sins of the world.

(Luke 22:41-44) And He withdrew from them about a stone's throw, and He knelt down and began to pray, saying,

"Father, if You are willing, remove this cup from Me; yet not My will, but Yours be done." Now an angel from heaven appeared to Him, strengthening Him. And being in agony He was praying very fervently; and His sweat became like drops of blood, falling down upon the ground.

(Luke 23:33) When they came to the place called The Skull, there they crucified Him and the criminals, one on the right and the other on the left.

(Luke 24:1-7) But on the first day of the week, at early dawn, they came to the tomb bringing the spices which they had prepared. And they found the stone rolled away from the tomb, but when they entered, they did not find the body of the Lord Jesus. While they were perplexed about this, behold, two men suddenly stood near them in dazzling clothing; and as the women were terrified and bowed their faces to the ground, the men said to them, "Why do you seek the living One among the dead? "He is not here, but He has risen. Remember how He spoke to you while He was still in Galilee, saying that the Son of Man must be delivered into the hands of sinful men, and be crucified, and the third day rise again."

(Luke 24:46-51) and He said to them, "Thus it is written, that the Christ would suffer and rise again from the dead the third day, and that repentance for forgiveness of sins would be proclaimed in His name to all the nations, beginning from Jerusalem. "You are witnesses of these things. "And behold, I am sending forth the promise of My Father upon you; but you are to stay in the city until you are clothed with power from on high." And He led them out as far as Bethany, and He lifted up His hands and blessed them. While He was blessing them, He parted from them and was carried up into heaven.

(Romans 14:11-12) For it is written, "AS I LIVE, SAYS THE LORD, EVERY KNEE SHALL BOW TO ME, AND EVERY TONGUE SHALL GIVE PRAISE TO GOD." So then each one of us will give an account of himself to God.

If **you** understand and have responded in a positive manner to the above verses, you are a new Christian, a Child of God. As you proceed through the rest of this book, I pray that you will look at all scripture from the stand point of "To Whom Do I Belong (?)". Understanding that you "Belong to Jesus" and that He has become your "Lord Jesus Christ", will give you an exciting new thirst for His Word. I pray that this thirst, from this day forward, will be guided by His "Owner's Manual". God Almighty's **Holy** and most precious **Word**, is our "Owner's Manual"!!!

B. BIBLICAL EXAMPLES OF THOSE SAVED:

I want to look now at some of the Bible's examples of God's saving grace in the lives of each of these different Biblical characters. They range from the Saints, to thieves, to tax collectors, to harlots, to the Apostle Paul and everything in between. It is also clear, that profession and/or age are not factors.

Abel — *(Hebrews 11:4) By faith Abel offered to God a better sacrifice than Cain, through which he obtained the testimony that he was righteous, God testifying about his gifts, and through faith, though he is dead, he still speaks.*

Enoch — *(Hebrews 11:5-6) By faith Enoch was taken up so that he would not see death; AND HE WAS NOT FOUND BECAUSE GOD TOOK HIM UP; for he obtained the witness that before his being taken up he was pleasing to God. And without faith it is impossible to please Him, for he who comes to God must believe that He is and that He is a rewarder of those who seek Him.*

Noah — *(Hebrews 11:7) By faith Noah, being warned by God about things not yet seen, in reverence prepared an ark for the salvation of his household, by which he condemned the world, and became an heir of the righteousness which is according to faith.*

Abraham — *(Hebrews 11:8) By faith Abraham, when he was called, obeyed by going out to a place which he was to receive for an inheritance; and he went out, not knowing where he was going.*

<u>Rahab</u> — *(Hebrews 11:31) By faith Rahab the harlot did not perish along with those who were disobedient, after she had welcomed the spies in peace. (Joshua 6:25) However, Rahab the harlot and her father's household and all she had, Joshua spared; and she has lived in the midst of Israel to this day, for she hid the messengers whom Joshua sent to spy out Jericho.*

<u>Gideon, Barak, Samson, Jephthah, David and Samuel</u> — *(Hebrews 11:32-34)*
And what more shall I say? For time will fail me if I tell of Gideon, Barak, Samson, Jephthah, of David and Samuel and the prophets, who by faith conquered kingdoms, performed acts of righteousness, obtained promises, shut the mouths of lions, quenched the power of fire, escaped the edge of the sword, from weakness were made strong, became mighty in war, put foreign armies to flight.

<u>Religious Leaders</u> — *(Acts 9:1-6) Now Saul, still breathing threats and murder against the disciples of the Lord, went to the high priest, and asked for letters from him to the synagogues at Damascus, so that if he found any belonging to the Way, both men and women, he might bring them bound to Jerusalem. As he was traveling, it happened that he was approaching Damascus, and suddenly a light from heaven flashed around him; and he fell to the ground and heard a voice saying to him, "Saul, Saul, why are you persecuting Me?" And he said, "Who are You, Lord?" And He said, "I am Jesus whom you are persecuting, but get up and enter the city, and it will be told you what you must do."* The Apostle Paul, formerly known as Saul, states the following: *(1 Timothy 1:12-17) I thank Christ Jesus our Lord, who has strengthened me, because He considered me faithful, putting me into service, even though I was formerly a blasphemer and a persecutor*

and a violent aggressor. Yet I was shown mercy because I acted ignorantly in unbelief; and the grace of our Lord was more than abundant, with the faith and love which are found in Christ Jesus. It is a trustworthy statement, deserving full acceptance, that Christ Jesus came into the world to save sinners, among whom I am foremost of all. Yet for this reason I found mercy, so that in me as the foremost, Jesus Christ might demonstrate His perfect patience as an example for those who would believe in Him for eternal life. Now to the King eternal, immortal, invisible, the only God, be honor and glory forever and ever. Amen.

Blind/Lame/Sick/Deaf/Poor — *(Matthew 11:5) the BLIND RECEIVE SIGHT and the lame walk, the lepers are cleansed and the deaf hear, the dead are raised up, and the POOR HAVE THE GOSPEL PREACHED TO THEM. (Luke 4:18) "THE SPIRIT OF THE LORD IS UPON ME, BECAUSE HE ANOINTED ME TO PREACH THE GOSPEL TO THE POOR. HE HAS SENT ME TO PROCLAIM RELEASE TO THE CAPTIVES, AND RECOVERY OF SIGHT TO THE BLIND, TO SET FREE THOSE WHO ARE OPPRESSED, (Luke 14:21) "And the slave came back and reported this to his master. Then the head of the household became angry and said to his slave, 'Go out at once into the streets and lanes of the city and bring in here the poor and crippled and blind and lame.'*
(James 2:5) Listen, my beloved brethren: did not God choose the poor of this world to be rich in faith and heirs of the kingdom which He promised to those who love Him?

Thief — The thief on the cross next to Jesus had these words to say and his words were followed by the words of Jesus. *(Luke 23:41-43) "And we indeed are suffering justly, for we are receiving what we deserve for our deeds; but this man has done nothing wrong." And he was saying, "Jesus, remember me when You come in Your kingdom!" And He said to him, "Truly I say to you, today you shall be with Me in Paradise."*

Fisherman — *(Matthew 4:17-20) From that time Jesus began to preach and say, "Repent, for the kingdom of heaven is at hand." Now as Jesus was walking by the Sea of Galilee, He saw two brothers, Simon who was called Peter, and Andrew his brother, casting a net into the sea; for they were fishermen. And He *said to them, "Follow Me, and I will make you fishers of men." Immediately they left their nets and followed Him.*

Shepherd/King (David) — *(1 Samuel 17:37) And David said, "The LORD who delivered me from the paw of the lion and from the paw of the bear, He will deliver me from the hand of this Philistine." And Saul said to David, "Go, and may the LORD be with you." (1 Samuel 17:45) Then David said to the Philistine, "You come to me with a sword, a spear, and a javelin, but I come to you in the name of the LORD of hosts, the God of the armies of Israel, whom you have taunted.*

Tax Collector (a legalized thief in that society) — *(Luke 5:27-28) After that He went out and noticed a tax collector named Levi sitting in the tax booth, and He said to him, "Follow Me." And he left everything behind, and got up and began to follow Him.*

Military Leader — *(Matthew 8:8) But the centurion said, "Lord, I am not worthy for You to come under my roof, but just say the word, and my servant will be healed. (Matthew 8:10) Now when Jesus heard this, He marveled and said to those who were following, "Truly I say to you, I have not found such great faith with anyone in Israel. (Matthew 8:13) And Jesus said to the centurion, "Go; it shall be done for you as you have believed." And the servant was healed that very moment.*

Business Executive (Zaccheus) — *(Luke 19:2-3) And there was a man called by the name of Zaccheus; he was a chief tax collector and he was rich. Zaccheus was trying to see who*

Jesus was, and was unable because of the crowd, for he was small in stature. (Luke 19:8-10) Zaccheus stopped and said to the Lord, "Behold, Lord, half of my possessions I will give to the poor, and if I have defrauded anyone of anything, I will give back four times as much." And Jesus said to him, "Today salvation has come to this house, because he, too, is a son of Abraham. "For the Son of Man has come to seek and to save that which was lost."

<u>Jews and Gentiles</u> — The Apostle Paul states: *(Acts 11:17-18) "Therefore if God gave to them the same gift as He gave to us* (THE JEWS) *also after believing in the Lord Jesus Christ, who was I that I could stand in God's way?" When they heard this, they quieted down and glorified God, saying, "Well then, God has granted to the Gentiles also the repentance that leads to life."*

<u>Children</u> — *(Luke 18:16-17) But Jesus called for them, saying, "Permit the children to come to Me, and do not hinder them, for the kingdom of God belongs to such as these. "Truly I say to you, whoever does not receive the kingdom of God like a child will not enter it at all."*

<u>Rich In This World's Wealth</u> — *(Job 1:1-3) There was a man in the land of Uz whose name was Job; and that man was blameless, upright, fearing God and turning away from evil. Seven sons and three daughters were born to him. His possessions also were 7,000 sheep, 3,000 camels, 500 yoke of oxen, 500 female donkeys, and very many servants; and that man was the greatest of all the men of the east.*

<u>Sick/Crippled or with Illness</u> — *(Matthew 8:2-4) And a leper came to Him and bowed down before Him, and said, "Lord, if You are willing, You can make me clean." Jesus stretched out His hand and touched him, saying, "I am willing; be cleansed." And immediately his leprosy was cleansed. And Jesus *said to him, "See that you tell no one; but go, show*

yourself to the priest and present the offering that Moses commanded, as a testimony to them." (Mark 2:4-5) Being unable to get to Him because of the crowd, they removed the roof above Him; and when they had dug an opening, they let down the pallet on which the paralytic was lying. And Jesus seeing their faith *said to the paralytic, "Son, your sins are forgiven." (Luke 16:20-22) "And a poor man named Lazarus was laid at his gate, covered with sores, and longing to be fed with the crumbs which were falling from the rich man's table; besides, even the dogs were coming and licking his sores.
"Now the poor man died and was carried away by the angels to Abraham's bosom;

Prison Guard — *(Acts 16:27-31) When the jailer awoke and saw the prison doors opened, he drew his sword and was about to kill himself, supposing that the prisoners had escaped. But Paul cried out with a loud voice, saying, "Do not harm yourself, for we are all here!" And he called for lights and rushed in, and trembling with fear he fell down before Paul and Silas, and after he brought them out, he said, "Sirs, what must I do to be saved?" They said, "Believe in the Lord Jesus, and you will be saved, you and your household." (Acts 16:34) And he brought them into his house and set food before them, and rejoiced greatly, having believed in God with his whole household.*

Crowds Of Ordinary People – Jews & Gentiles — *(Acts 2:40-41) And with many other words he solemnly testified and kept on exhorting them, saying, "Be saved from this perverse generation!" So then, those who had received his word were baptized; and that day there were added about three thousand souls. (Acts 4:4) But many of those who had heard the message believed; and the number of the men came to be about five thousand. (Acts 13:47-48) "For so the Lord has commanded us, 'I HAVE PLACED YOU AS A LIGHT FOR THE GENTILES, THAT YOU MAY BRING SALVATION TO THE*

END OF THE EARTH.'" When the Gentiles heard this, they began rejoicing and glorifying the word of the Lord; and as many as had been appointed to eternal life believed.

Demon Possessed Or Possibly Mentally Ill — *(Luke 8:33) And the demons came out of the man and entered the swine; and the herd rushed down the steep bank into the lake and was drowned. (Luke 8:38-39) But the man from whom the demons had gone out was begging Him that he might accompany Him; but He sent him away, saying, "Return to your house and describe what great things God has done for you." So he went away, proclaiming throughout the whole city what great things Jesus had done for him.*

Everyone Or As The Bible States It (The Gentiles) — *(Galatians 3:13-14) Christ redeemed us from the curse of the Law, having become a curse for us—for it is written, "CURSED IS EVERYONE WHO HANGS ON A TREE"— in order that in Christ Jesus the blessing of Abraham might come to the Gentiles, so that we would receive the promise of the Spirit through faith. (Galatians 3:28) There is neither Jew nor Greek, there is neither slave nor free man, there is neither male nor female; for you are all one in Christ Jesus. (Acts 11:18) When they heard this, they quieted down and glorified God, saying, "Well then, God has granted to the Gentiles also the repentance that leads to life."*

C. ADDITIONAL SCRIPTURES ABOUT SALVATION:

The word "**REDEEMED**", what a beautiful word it is! For you to be redeemed means you owed a debt you couldn't pay, and someone else paid that debt for you. God through His Son Jesus Christ paid your debt, *(Romans 3:10) as it is written, "THERE IS NONE RIGHTEOUS, NOT EVEN ONE;* and this paid debt was presented to you marked "Paid In Full" as a gift from God.

(Ephesians 2:8-9) For by grace you have been saved through faith; and that not of yourselves, it is the gift of God; not as a result of works, so that no one may boast.

Thanks be to God, we are now a living miracle of His grace. Yes by God's power "it is possible for a camel to go through the eye of a needle". Thank you Lord, I now "Belong To You"!!!

The following scripture verses are fully explanatory and need no comment by this hand.

(Isaiah 1:18-20) "Come now, and let us reason together," Says the LORD, "Though your sins are as scarlet, They will be as white as snow; Though they are red like crimson, They will be like wool. "If you consent and obey, You will eat the best of the land; "But if you refuse and rebel, You will be devoured by the sword." Truly, the mouth of the LORD has spoken.

(Matthew 4:4) But He answered and said, "It is written, 'MAN SHALL NOT LIVE ON BREAD ALONE, BUT ON EVERY WORD THAT PROCEEDS OUT OF THE MOUTH OF GOD.'"

(John 1:12-13) But as many as received Him, to them He gave the right to become children of God, even to those who believe in His name, who were born, not of blood nor of the will of the flesh nor of the will of man, but of God.

(John 3:5) Jesus answered, "Truly, truly, I say to you, unless one is born of water and the Spirit he cannot enter into the kingdom of God.

(John 5:24) "Truly, truly, I say to you, he who hears My word, and believes Him who sent Me, has eternal life, and does not come into judgment, but has passed out of death into life.

(John 6:47) "Truly, truly, I say to you, he who believes has eternal life.

(John 6:51) "I am the living bread that came down out of heaven; if anyone eats of this bread, he will live forever;

(John 14:23) Jesus answered and said to him, "If anyone loves Me, he will keep My word; and My Father will love him, and We will come to him and make Our abode with him.

(Acts 2:21) 'AND IT SHALL BE THAT EVERYONE WHO CALLS ON THE NAME OF THE LORD WILL BE SAVED.'

(Acts 2:38-41) Peter said to them, "Repent, and each of you be baptized in the name of Jesus Christ for the forgiveness of your sins; and you will receive the gift of the Holy Spirit. "For the promise is for you and your children and for all who are far off, as many as the Lord our God will call to Himself." And with many other words he solemnly testified and kept on exhorting them, saying, "Be saved from this perverse generation!" So then, those who had received his word were baptized; and that day there were added about three thousand souls.

(Acts 4:10-12) let it be known to all of you and to all the people of Israel, that by the name of Jesus Christ the Nazarene, whom you crucified, whom God raised from the dead—by this name this man stands here before you in good health. "He is the STONE WHICH WAS REJECTED by you, THE BUILDERS, but WHICH BECAME THE CHIEF CORNER stone. "And there is salvation in no one else; for there is no other name under heaven that has been given among men by which we must be saved."

(Acts 9:22) But Saul kept increasing in strength and confounding the Jews who lived at Damascus by proving that this Jesus is the Christ.

(Acts 10:38-43) "You know of Jesus of Nazareth, how God anointed Him with the Holy Spirit and with power, and how He went about doing good and healing all who were oppressed by the devil, for God was with Him. "We are witnesses of all the things He did both in the land of the Jews and in Jerusalem. They also put Him to death by hanging Him on a cross.

"God raised Him up on the third day and granted that He become visible, not to all the people, but to witnesses who were chosen beforehand by God, that is, to us who ate and drank with Him after He arose from the dead. "And He ordered us to preach to the people, and solemnly to testify that this is the One who has been appointed by God as Judge

of the living and the dead. "Of Him all the prophets bear witness that through His name everyone who believes in Him receives forgiveness of sins."

(Romans 1:20) For since the creation of the world His invisible attributes, His eternal power and divine nature, have been clearly seen, being understood through what has been made, so that they are without excuse.

(Romans 10:18) But I say, surely they have never heard, have they? Indeed they have; "THEIR VOICE HAS GONE OUT INTO ALL THE EARTH, AND THEIR WORDS TO THE ENDS OF THE WORLD."

(Romans 10:12-13) For there is no distinction between Jew and Greek; for the same Lord is Lord of all, abounding in riches for all who call on Him; for "WHOEVER WILL CALL ON THE NAME OF THE LORD WILL BE SAVED."

(1 Timothy 2:3-6) This is good and acceptable in the sight of God our Savior, who desires all men to be saved and to come to the knowledge of the truth. For there is one God, and one mediator also between God and men, the man Christ Jesus, who gave Himself as a ransom for all, the testimony given at the proper time.

(Titus 3:3-7) For we also once were foolish ourselves, disobedient, deceived, enslaved to various lusts and pleasures, spending our life in malice and envy, hateful, hating one another. But when the kindness of God our Savior and His love for mankind appeared, He saved us, not on the basis of deeds which we have done in righteousness, but according to His mercy, by the washing of regeneration and renewing by the Holy Spirit, whom He poured out upon us richly through Jesus Christ our Savior, so that being justified by His grace we would be made heirs according to the hope of eternal life.

(1 Peter 1:7-9) so that the proof of your faith, being more precious than gold which is perishable, even though tested by fire, may be found to result in praise and glory and honor at the revelation of Jesus Christ; and though you have not seen Him, you love Him, and though you do not see Him now, but believe in Him, you greatly rejoice with joy inexpressible

and full of glory, obtaining as the outcome of your faith the salvation of your souls.

(1 Peter 1:18-19) knowing that you were not redeemed with perishable things like silver or gold from your futile way of life inherited from your forefathers, but with precious blood, as of a lamb unblemished and spotless, the blood of Christ.

(1 Peter 1:25) BUT THE WORD OF THE LORD ENDURES FOREVER." And this is the word which was preached to you.

(John 10:27-29) "My sheep hear My voice, and I know them, and they follow Me; and I give eternal life to them, and they will never perish; and no one will snatch them out of My hand. "My Father, who has given them to Me, is greater than all; and no one is able to snatch them out of the Father's hand.

(Romans 8:38-39) For I am convinced that neither death, nor life, nor angels, nor principalities, nor things present, nor things to come, nor powers, nor height, nor depth, nor any other created thing, will be able to separate us from the love of God, which is in Christ Jesus our Lord.

D. BEFORE AND AFTER:

We all like to see a good picture of "Before" and "After". This may take the form of a person "Before" and "After", in a weight loss or exercise program. These can be pretty dramatic and wouldn't be shown if they weren't very complimentary.

Most of us have seen the photographer's books where they have revisited certain scenes or places and re-photographed these same scenes or places many years later. These can be very impressive as to the changes in vegetation or the changes in modern buildings or urban growth.

I recently accompanied my brother, who restores old classic cars, to an exhibit in Branson, MO, where we found displayed all the U. S. made 1957 automobiles. This was most impressive, as the average cost to restore was estimated at $100,000 each. The transformation of each of these cars was amazing as their new condition, "After", was pristine to the minutest detail. We could only imagine what their "Before" was like.

In light of the most impressive things we have seen or done, none tops the transformation of a "changed life" because of what happens when we put our trust in Jesus Christ. It truly is the difference of "night" and "day". It is a full 180 degree turn around from the "Before", to the "After".

Please consider the following "Before" and "After" from the scriptures.

"BEFORE"
***(John 3:3)* (You must be "Born Again")**
Jesus answered and said to him, "Truly, truly, I say to you, unless one is born again he cannot see the kingdom of God."
***(John 3:5)* (Physical Birth—Water)**
Jesus answered, "Truly, truly, I say to you, unless one is born of water ...

"AFTER"
***(John 3:5)* (Spiritual Birth—Spirit—"Born Again")** *... and the Spirit he cannot enter into the kingdom of God.*

"BEFORE"
***(John 3:6)* (Physical Birth—Flesh)**
"That which is born of the flesh is flesh,

"AFTER"
***(John 3:6-7)* (Spiritual Birth—Spirit—"Born Again")**
and that which is born of the Spirit is spirit. "Do not be amazed that I said to you, 'You must be born again.'

"BEFORE"
***(John 3:18)* (Not Believing)**
he who does not believe has been judged already, because he has not believed in the name of the only begotten Son of God.

"AFTER"
(John 3:16) (Believing)
"For God so loved the world, that He gave His only begotten Son, that whoever believes in Him shall not perish, but have eternal life.

"BEFORE"
(Acts 15:10) (Old Law)
"Now therefore why do you put God to the test by placing upon the neck of the disciples a yoke which neither our fathers nor we have been able to bear?

"AFTER"
(Acts 15:11) (New Covenant)
"But we believe that we are saved through the grace of the Lord Jesus, in the same way as they also are."

"BEFORE"
(Acts 26:14) (Saul before Conversion) (Persecuting the Christians)
"And when we had all fallen to the ground, I heard a voice saying to me in the Hebrew dialect, 'Saul, Saul, why are you persecuting Me? It is hard for you to kick against the goads.'

"AFTER"
(Acts 26:15-16) (Saul's Conversion-he is now Paul) (Now a Minister of Jesus)
"And I said, 'Who are You, Lord?' And the Lord said, 'I am Jesus whom you are persecuting. 'But get up and stand on your feet; for this purpose I have appeared to you, to appoint you a minister and a witness not only to the things which you have seen, but also to the things in which I will appear to you;

"BEFORE"
(Acts 26:18) (From Darkness/Controlled by Satan)
to open their eyes so that they may turn from darkness to light and from the dominion of Satan to God,

"AFTER"
(Acts 26:18) (To Light/Inheritance from God)
to open their eyes so that they may turn from darkness to light and from the dominion of Satan to God, that they may receive forgiveness of sins and an inheritance among those who have been sanctified by faith in Me.'

"BEFORE"
(Romans 3:23) (All have sinned/doomed)
for all have sinned and fall short of the glory of God,

"AFTER"
(Romans 3:24) (Justified by His grace)
being justified as a gift by His grace through the redemption which is in Christ Jesus;

"BEFORE"
(Romans 6:23) (Death Sentence/We are all on Death Row)
For the wages of sin is death,

"AFTER"
(Romans 6:23) (God's gift is a Pardon/Stand aside Governor)
but the free gift of God is eternal life in Christ Jesus our Lord.

"BEFORE"
(Romans 5:17) (Death begin with Adam)
For if by the transgression of the one, death reigned through the one,

"AFTER"
(Romans 5:17) (Life begins with Jesus)
much more those who receive the abundance of grace and of the gift of righteousness will reign in life through the One, Jesus Christ.

"BEFORE"
(Romans 5:18) (Condemnation from Adam to All Men)
So then as through one transgression there resulted condemnation to all men,

"AFTER"
(Romans 5:18) (Justification from Jesus to All Men)
even so through one act of righteousness there resulted justification of life to all men.

"BEFORE"
(Romans 5:19) (Adam's Disobedience made many Sinners)
For as through the one man's disobedience the many were made sinners,

"AFTER"
(Romans 5:19-21) (Obedience of Jesus to God has made many Righteous)
even so through the obedience of the One the many will be made righteous.
The Law came in so that the transgression would increase; but where sin increased, grace abounded all the more, so that, as sin reigned in death, even so grace would reign through righteousness to eternal life through Jesus Christ our Lord.

"BEFORE"
(Titus 3:3) (We were Foolish, Disobedient, Deceived, and Enslaved)
For we also once were foolish ourselves, disobedient, deceived, enslaved to various lusts and pleasures, spending our life in malice and envy, hateful, hating one another.

"AFTER"
(Titus 3:4-7) (We are NOW saved and made Heirs to the Hope of Eternal Life by His Kindness, His Mercy and His Grace/We are Free!)
But when the kindness of God our Savior and His love for mankind appeared, He saved us, not on the basis of deeds which we have done in righteousness, but according to His mercy, by the washing of regeneration and renewing by the Holy Spirit, whom He poured out upon us richly through Jesus Christ our Savior, so that being justified by His grace we would be made heirs according to the hope of eternal life.

"BEFORE"
(1 John 1:6) (Darkness)
If we say that we have fellowship with Him and yet walk in the darkness, we lie and do not practice the truth;

"AFTER"
(1 John 1:7) (Light)
but if we walk in the Light as He Himself is in the Light, we have fellowship with one another, and the blood of Jesus His Son cleanses us from all sin.

"BEFORE"
(1 John 1:8) (Deceiving ourselves/Unforgiven)
If we say that we have no sin, we are deceiving ourselves and the truth is not in us.

"AFTER"
(1 John 1:9) Cleansed from Unrighteousness/Forgiven)
If we confess our sins, He is faithful and righteous to forgive
us our sins
and to cleanse us from all unrighteousness.

E. CONCLUSION to SALVATION:

(Matthew 7:24-27) "Therefore everyone who hears these words of Mine and acts on them, may be compared to a wise man who built his house on the rock. "And the rain fell, and the floods came, and the winds blew and slammed against that house; and yet it did not fall, for it had been founded on the rock. "Everyone who hears these words of Mine and does not act on them, will be like a foolish man who built his house on the sand. "The rain fell, and the floods came, and the winds blew and slammed against that house; and it fell—and great was its fall."
Please don't be found without a Foundation built upon The Rock!

(Joshua 24:15) "If it is disagreeable in your sight to serve the LORD, choose for yourselves today whom you will serve: whether the gods which your fathers served which were beyond the River, or the gods of the Amorites in whose land you are living; but as for me and my house, we will serve the LORD."
Choose today whom you will serve ("To Whom Do You Belong") (?), "As for Me and My House We will serve the Lord"!!! He that believes on Him (Jesus) is not condemned. Simple yet Profound!!! Trust right now that the Jesus of the Bible will plead your individual case before God on that **judgment day**.
(Isaiah 45:21-23) "Declare and set forth your case; Indeed, let them consult together. Who has announced this from of old? Who has long since declared it? Is it not I, the LORD? And there is no other God besides Me, A righteous God and a Savior; There is none except Me. "Turn to Me and be saved,

all the ends of the earth; For I am God, and there is no other. "I have sworn by Myself, The word has gone forth from My mouth in righteousness And will not turn back, That to Me every knee will bow, every tongue will swear allegiance.

(Romans 14:11) For it is written, "AS I LIVE, SAYS THE LORD, EVERY KNEE SHALL BOW TO ME, AND EVERY TONGUE SHALL GIVE PRAISE TO GOD."

(Philippians 2:9-11) For this reason also, God highly exalted Him, and bestowed on Him the name which is above every name, so that at the name of Jesus EVERY KNEE WILL BOW, of those who are in heaven and on earth and under the earth, and that every tongue will confess that Jesus Christ is Lord, to the glory of God the Father.

You simply go to Him, put your trust in **Him (Jesus)**, and all of this with child-like Faith. AMEN!!! A prayer might go like this, "Jesus on that great judgment day, I'm trusting you, to plead my case before God the Father, the Great I AM"!!!

As for me and my house I truly desire to "Belong To Jesus"!!! "To Whom Do You Belong" (???)

SPECIAL NOTE:

I know many of you may have a special verse or verses regarding this Chapter's subject matter. This special verse or these verses may not have been mentioned due to my ignorance or because of brevity. I apologize for either of these reasons. Please feel free to write any special verse or verses in the space below. This will add your personal touch, and will serve to call to each person's mind their individual "experience of trust", in God's Holy Word.

For to each of us "Who belong To Him", His Holy Word can be truly recognized and relied upon as our **"Owner's Manual"**!!!

CHAPTER 6

SECURITY OF THE BELIEVER/ ASSURANCE/CONFIDENCE

INTRODUCTORY VERSES:

<u>1.</u> *(Romans 8:11-14)(vs 11) But if the Spirit of Him who raised Jesus from the dead dwells in you, He who raised Christ Jesus from the dead will also give life to your mortal bodies through His Spirit who dwells in you. (vs 12) So then, brethren, we are under obligation, not to the flesh, to live according to the flesh—(vs 13) for if you are living according to the flesh, you must die; but if by the Spirit you are putting to death the deeds of the body, you will live. (vs 14) For all who are being led by the Spirit of God, these are sons of God.*

Our belief in the Son of God grants us the indwelling of the Holy Spirit. Since we are now considered to be the sons of God, we "Belong To Him", therefore our reasonable obligation to the One who has given us this hope of eternal life, is to rely on His "Owner's Manual" (His Holy Word). This should be done on a consistent daily basis! The Spirit of the Living God, living in us, gives us assurance and confidence of our eternal salvation. Nothing can take us out of the hands of the One who has purchased us. He does not lose any of His sheep. We "Securely", "Belong To Him", for eternity.

<u>2.</u> *(John 10:27-30)(vs 27) "My sheep hear My voice, and I know them, and they follow Me; (vs 28) and I give eternal life to them, and they will never perish; and no one will snatch them out of My hand. (vs 29) "My Father, who has given them to Me, is greater than all; and no one is able to snatch them out of the Father's hand. (vs 30) "I and the Father are one."*

We are likened to being sheep which hears the Shepherd's voice and follows him. We are also assured the Father is greater than all and no one can take us from the Father's hand. As a believer in Jesus, and in the hands of the Father, "We Belong To Him"!!! "Jesus and the Father are one". The definition of "No one", as found in *vs 28,* is clearly defined in the Greek as "not even one man, women or thing, none, nobody, nothing". It is clear that nothing, not even yourself, can take you out of the hand of God, we truly "Belong To Him". As a believer, we are **in** God's possession, and we are a part **of** God's possessions!!!

INTRODUCTION:

Is there such a thing as "Perfect Security"? When we think of "Security" today what might come to mind are terms like "Homeland Security", "Security of our Personal Identity", "Security of our Finances", "Security of Health" and many other personal issues.

"Homeland Security" programs have cost billions of government dollars (actually these are your dollars), spent on sophisticated programs, yet it is as if we are living in a house without locks, with cracks and openings for whomever to come through, whenever they desire. This isn't even close to "Perfect Security".

Our "Personal Identity" can be stolen and is done so daily through thieves who physically break-in, or can even electronically steal from us, even while we are asleep. Most of us don't even comprehend the ingenious electronic methods of burglary. Our Social Security numbers, our driver's license and other personal records have been, are being, and will continue to be stolen and used illegally. Our "Identity" and 'Personal Privacy" is violated without our being able to protect ourselves or in any way prevent this intrusion. Our banking, credit card companies and other financial institutions spend millions to protect us, and do a great job, but at times have failed. This is certainly not a "Perfect portrait of Security".

"Health Security" is what everyone would love to be able to control. On the mind of every individual is "what will tomorrow bring". With all the various cancers and heart problems, we all are left with uncertainty and absolutely no security. From our history books we read about Ponce De Leon actually spending a good part of his life, along with a cadre of men, looking for the "Fountain of Youth". Some rulers as well as the common man have gone to extremes to try to figure a way to live forever. These incredulous schemes include things like we find in a neighboring county. There is actually someone packed in dry ice to be preserved until some new, advanced methods of perpetual health can be guaranteed. This family is hoping for some new technology to be developed in order to bring this person back to life. Our health will decline and it is not secure. It will eventually fail. No "Perfect Security" here.

This brings us to the only absolute "Perfect Security" known to man today, and that is the "Security" of being held firmly in the hands of God. As a "Born Again" believer, trusting in … ***(Ephesians 2:8-9)(vs 8) For by grace you have been saved through faith; and that not of yourselves, it is the gift of God; (vs 9) not as a result of works, so that no one may boast.*** … we find eternal salvation by grace alone. We are "Eternally Secure" in the unshakeable arms of our Most High God. We have been "Born Again", "Regenerated", "Born of the Spirit" through His power. It is an "Act of God", which no created thing can alter. It is an "Act of God" based upon the absolute truth found in His Word. ***(John 3:16-18)(vs 16) "For God so loved the world, that He gave His only begotten Son, that whoever believes in Him shall not perish, but have eternal life. (vs 17) "For God did not send the Son into the world to judge the world, but that the world might be saved through Him. (vs 18) "He who believes in Him is not judged; he who does not believe has been judged already, because he has not believed in the name of the only begotten Son of God.*** Simply put, God cannot lie. The only "Perfect Security" to be found anywhere in this world, is our "Eternal Security". This "Eternal Security" is to know and trust our Living Savior. This can only be found by "believing faith" in Jesus Christ. This Biblical plan can only be found and defined in our "Owner's Manual", God's Holy Word.

A. THE "KEY" TO HAVING "SECURITY" AS A "BELIEVER":

Security of the believer has been debated for many years by many people. If Salvation is by Faith and not of any additions by man, then there is no debate. It is a wonderful thing to be held firmly and securely in the hands and arms of Our Most High God.

The whole discussion regarding our security as a believer or as more commonly put, "once saved always saved", centers around and is underlined in the person's beliefs. If one is fully trusting God's plan of salvation through the completion of Jesus' accomplishments on the Cross, as the sole power of our "New birth", then we can never be taken from God's hand. If one is trusting in Jesus' work on the Cross as a part of this salvation experience, plus some additional man-made works of their own or some added man-made requirements, then it is clear throughout the Bible this one has not accepted Ephesians 2: 8 & 9. *(Ephesians 2:8-9)(vs 8) For by grace you have been saved through faith; and that not of yourselves, it is the gift of God; (vs 9) not as a result of works, so that no one may boast.*

Any person who has attached some laws, or works to their salvation experience has nullified God's plan and have centered their beliefs in man's plan. Therefore it is no wonder this person thinks he or she can be lost from God's grip. This person has not been "Born Again' or "Regenerated" by an Act of God, and will come to God's judgment day and will be found lacking. This person was never a child of God and therefore could not lose what he never had. It may look like a simple difference, but we cannot alter God's plan in any way. What might look insignificant is not acceptable in the Holy eyes of God. We cannot attach any man-made requirements of any kind to the Holy plan of God. It is through "believing faith" in Jesus alone, we come to Him. God does the rest!

Unless you come unto Him, by His way only, with no laws , works or personal righteous deeds, through "believing faith", accepting his mercy and grace, you never knew Him. That which was never in His hand is not what is spoken about through the scriptures when we discuss security, assurance and confidence. I must re-emphasize ... *(Ephesians 2:8-9)(vs 8) For by grace you have been saved through faith; and that not of yourselves, it is the gift of God; (vs 9) not as a result of works, so that no one may boast.* ... it is not as a result of works!

We will all stand naked before God (figuratively speaking) on His judgment day. Our hope and confidence will be according to God's Holy Word. That hope, which will be our ONLY HOPE, is that Jesus will answer for us by saying, "Father he is one of ours". Our nakedness means we have absolutely nothing with which to persuade God, we have done absolutely nothing to help plead or insure our case, in fact we won't even be able to speak. Our judgment will be decided by our 'believing faith", and Jesus will intercede for us.

The following could be a prayer that might be appropriate now. Jesus, I know that I am a sinner, I am fully trusting that you as the Only Begotten Son of the Most High God will plead my case as I stand in judgment. I bring absolutely nothing to this judgment day for my defense. Jesus, it is in You and Your Word that I trust! With these thoughts becoming the sincere desire of your heart, you are now a "Born Again", "Regenerated", "Adopted" child of the Living God. You have been bought with a price, paid in full, by God, Himself. *(1 Corinthians 6:19-20)(vs 19) Or do you not know that your body is a temple of the Holy Spirit who is in you, whom you have from God, and that you are not your own? (vs 20) For you have been bought with a price: therefore glorify God in your body.* It is ... *by grace you have been saved through faith* ... you have been brought into His kingdom by this miraculous Act of God!!! You can never lose this God granted relationship.

Since it wasn't you who saved yourself, you or anything else cannot undo this Act of God!!! *(Romans 8:38-39)(vs 38) For I am convinced that neither death, nor life, nor angels, nor principalities, nor things present, nor things to come, nor powers, (vs 39) nor height, nor depth, nor any other created thing, will be able to separate us from the love of God, which is in Christ Jesus our Lord.* I once heard of a High School teacher, in a Bible class at a Christian school, try to tell his students that this verse didn't say that you couldn't take yourself out from the hands of God. Oh, but YES it did! This verse is absolutely clear, unless you are something that has arrived on this earth, but has not been created, you can't touch yourself or any of God's children. There is ABSOLUTELY NOTHING on this earth that hasn't been created by God, therefore NOTHING can separate you from the love of God—NOTHING!!!

B. BIBLICAL VERSES CONCERNING "SECURITY", "ASSURANCE" AND "CONFIDENCE", FOR THE BELIEVER IN JESUS CHRIST:

<u>1</u>. *(John 10:27-30)(vs 27) "My sheep hear My voice, and I know them, and they follow Me; (vs 28) and I give eternal life to them, and they will never perish; and no one will snatch them out of My hand. (vs 29) "My Father, who has given them to Me, is greater than all; and no one is able to snatch them out of the Father's hand. (vs 30) "I and the Father are one."*

Our Almighty God is greater than all. Our "Eternal Security" is absolute in the hands of the only One that can and will prevent a breach. Praise God we "Belong To Him"!!!

<u>2</u>. *(John 6:37-40)(vs 37) "All that the Father gives Me will come to Me, and the one who comes to Me I will certainly not cast out. (vs 38) "For I have come down from heaven, not to do My own will, but the will of Him who sent Me. (vs 39) "This is the will of Him who sent Me, that of all that He has given Me I lose nothing, but raise it up on the last day. (vs 40) "For this is the will of My Father, that everyone who beholds the Son and believes in Him will have eternal life, and I Myself will raise him up on the last day."*

Jesus loses none (NOTHING) of those who have come to Him. At the judgment day, God will personally raise up those who have come to Him. Jesus the Son and God the Father are one. Don't be confused by these references to the Father and the Son. All who have believed with their heart and confessed with their mouth will be raised with a new body to live eternally in heaven with God. Our "Absolute Security" is found in the authority of God, Himself. His "Security" will not be compromised or usurped.

<u>3</u>. *(1 Corinthians 6:19-20)(VS 19) Or do you not know that your body is a temple of the Holy Spirit who is in you, whom you have from God, and that you are not your own? (vs 20) For you have been bought with a price: therefore glorify God in your body.*

You are not your own! Isn't there great comfort from the scriptures that state you have been bought with a price! That price was found on the Cross of Calvary. Jesus paid it in full for you and I. We cannot pay a co-pay, we cannot pay any interest, we cannot pay one monthly premium or payment, we cannot pay any sales taxes, we cannot even contribute the tip, for **Jesus Paid It All**. If you are relying on any partial payment by yourself for your salvation, then you "Don't Belong To Him"!!!

You have been bought with a price. The price was paid by God Himself, through His Son Jesus Christ on the Cross. All of our sins were placed upon Him. There is no wonder that as Jesus prayed in the Garden of Gethsemane, before His crucifixion, He sweat drops of blood. He was God yet also man. We "Belong To Him". We cannot remove ourselves from Him as we don't have ownership of our "Born Again" being. It was an "Act of God" to save us, it would take an "Act of God" to dump us. Thank God that our 'Eternal Security" is not in man's hands.

<u>4.</u> (Philippians 1:6) For I am confident of this very thing, that He who began a good work in you will perfect it until the day of Christ Jesus.

The Apostle Paul writing to the Philippians expresses his confidence in the One to whom "He Belongs". Paul expects his salvation, as experienced on this earth, to include Jesus Christ from the beginning and to conclude with the glorification on that judgment day. The day of Jesus Christ as referred to in this verse can be reasonably concluded to be that final judgment day. Paul is confident Jesus will "perfect" our salvation from beginning to end. There is "Perfect Security", "Assurance" and "Confidence" expressed in this verse.

<u>5.</u> (Colossians 2:1-14)(vs 1) For I want you to know how great a struggle I have on your behalf and for those who are at Laodicea, and for all those who have not personally seen my face, (vs 2) that their hearts may be encouraged, having been knit together in love, and attaining to all the wealth that comes from the full assurance of understanding, resulting in a true knowledge of God's mystery, that is, Christ Himself, (vs 3) in whom are hidden all the treasures of wisdom and knowledge. (vs 4) I say this so that no one will delude you with persuasive argument. (vs 5) For even though I am absent in body, nevertheless I am with you in

spirit, rejoicing to see your good discipline and the stability of your faith in Christ. (vs 6) Therefore as you have received Christ Jesus the Lord, so walk in Him, (vs 7) having been firmly rooted and now being built up in Him and established in your faith, just as you were instructed, and overflowing with gratitude. (vs 8) See to it that no one takes you captive through philosophy and empty deception, according to the tradition of men, according to the elementary principles of the world, rather than according to Christ. (vs 9) For in Him all the fullness of Deity dwells in bodily form, (vs 10) and in Him you have been made complete, and He is the head over all rule and authority; (vs 11) and in Him you were also circumcised with a circumcision made without hands, in the removal of the body of the flesh by the circumcision of Christ; (vs 12) having been buried with Him in baptism, in which you were also raised up with Him through faith in the working of God, who raised Him from the dead. (vs 13) When you were dead in your transgressions and the uncircumcision of your flesh, He made you alive together with Him, having forgiven us all our transgressions, (vs 14) having canceled out the certificate of debt consisting of decrees against us, which was hostile to us; and He has taken it out of the way, having nailed it to the cross.

I know this is a long passage, but it is so encouraging it just couldn't be left out. At this time God has, through His the Son, Jesus Christ, taken all our sins. He has canceled the certificate of our debt and has nailed it all to the cross. This means that God has done all the work for our salvation. Upon our accepting this completed work of God through Christ, we through our "believing faith" are trusting Jesus for our new "Regeneration". No one plucks any believer from God's hands, and of all of those whom He has given "New Birth", He loses NONE—ZERO!!!

6. (1 Timothy 1:12-15) & (2 Timothy 1:12) (1 Timothy 1:12) I thank Christ Jesus our Lord, who has strengthened me, because He considered me faithful, putting me into service, (vs 13) even though I was formerly a blasphemer and a persecutor and a violent aggressor. Yet I was shown mercy

because I acted ignorantly in unbelief; (vs 14) and the grace of our Lord was more than abundant, with the faith and love which are found in Christ Jesus. (vs 15) It is a trustworthy statement, deserving full acceptance, that Christ Jesus came into the world to save sinners, among whom I am foremost of all. (2 Timothy 1:12) For this reason I also suffer these things, but I am not ashamed; for I know whom I have believed and I am convinced that He is able to guard what I have entrusted to Him until that day.

The Apostle Paul is an example of God's saving grace (through Jesus Christ), even of the most vile of sinners. Paul was a blasphemer, a persecutor of the Saints, and even a murderer. Paul, by his own confession was the foremost of sinners, yet God can and did save him. Paul's conclusion is that what God has made possible, even for the most vile of sinners, God will guard and keep until "that day". "That day" is understood to be the "great day of judgment". It will all end for all of us who "Belong To Him" with the "Perfect Security", and that is, He is faithful to care for that which has been … *"entrusted to Him"*. This includes all sinners who have been "saved" by grace, even if you consider yourself as the Apostle Paul has done, to be the chief of sinners.

7. *(2 Timothy 4:18) The Lord will rescue me from every evil deed, and will bring me safely to His heavenly kingdom; to Him be the glory forever and ever. Amen.*

There is no "if" here. There is no "exception" here. God will bring each of His, to safety in His heavenly kingdom.

8. *(Titus 3:5-7)(vs 5) He saved us, not on the basis of deeds which we have done in righteousness, but according to His mercy, by the washing of regeneration and renewing by the Holy Spirit, (vs 6) whom He poured out upon us richly through Jesus Christ our Savior, (vs 7) so that being justified by His grace we would be made heirs according to the hope of eternal life.*

He saved us not because of our deeds or good works, but by His grace and mercy. He has poured out upon us the riches found through Jesus Christ our Savior. We have been made heirs for eternity. This is "Perfect Security" and our inheritance is eternal life!!!

9a. *(Hebrews 7:25) Therefore He is able also to save forever those who draw near to God through Him, since He always lives to make intercession for them.*

"Forever", as I understand it, is only understood by God. "Forever" is beyond our human understanding and can only be thought of with incompletion. This much we can comprehend, "forever" can be described as never ending.

9b. *(Hebrews 7:26-28)(vs 26) For it was fitting for us to have such a high priest, holy, innocent, undefiled, separated from sinners and exalted above the heavens; (vs 27) who does not need daily, like those high priests, to offer up sacrifices, first for His own sins and then for the sins of the people, because this He did once for all when He offered up Himself. (vs 28) For the Law appoints men as high priests who are weak, but the word of the oath, which came after the Law, appoints a Son, made perfect forever.*

Our high priest who grants this forever salvation, is not one appointed by the order of man. Jesus is the High Priest who was appointed in the order of Melchizedek, not appointed by man but appointed directly by God, and He does not need to offer daily sacrifices for Himself or the people. He is God! It is He who was sacrificed upon the Cross, ONCE ONLY, for all time and for all who will believe in Him!!! It is He, who was made perfect "forever", who has the authority to save us and to keep us "forever"!!!

10a. *(Hebrews 10:1-17)(vs 1) For the Law, since it has only a shadow of the good things to come and not the very form of things, can never, by the same sacrifices which they offer continually year by year, make perfect those who draw near. (vs 2) Otherwise, would they not have ceased to be offered, because the worshipers, having once been cleansed, would no longer have had consciousness of sins? (vs 3) But in those sacrifices there is a reminder of sins year by year. (vs 4) For it is impossible for the blood of bulls and goats to take away sins. (vs 5) Therefore, when He comes into the world, He says, "SACRIFICE AND OFFERING YOU HAVE NOT DESIRED, BUT A BODY YOU HAVE PREPARED FOR ME; (vs 6) IN WHOLE BURNT OFFERINGS AND sacrifices FOR*

SIN YOU HAVE TAKEN NO PLEASURE. (vs 7) "THEN I SAID, 'BEHOLD, I HAVE COME (IN THE SCROLL OF THE BOOK IT IS WRITTEN OF ME) TO DO YOUR WILL, O GOD.'" (vs 8) After saying above, "SACRIFICES AND OFFERINGS AND WHOLE BURNT OFFERINGS AND sacrifices FOR SIN YOU HAVE NOT DESIRED, NOR HAVE YOU TAKEN PLEASURE in them" (which are offered according to the Law), (vs 9) then He said, "BEHOLD, I HAVE COME TO DO YOUR WILL." He takes away the first in order to establish the second.

(vs 10) By this will we have been sanctified through the offering of the body of Jesus Christ once for all. (vs 11) Every priest stands daily ministering and offering time after time the same sacrifices, which can never take away sins; (vs 12) but He, having offered one sacrifice for sins for all time, SAT DOWN AT THE RIGHT HAND OF GOD, (vs 13) waiting from that time onward UNTIL HIS ENEMIES BE MADE A FOOTSTOOL FOR HIS FEET. (vs 14) For by one offering He has perfected for all time those who are sanctified. (vs 15) And the Holy Spirit also testifies to us; for after saying, (vs 16) "THIS IS THE COVENANT THAT I WILL MAKE WITH THEM AFTER THOSE DAYS, SAYS THE LORD: I WILL PUT MY LAWS UPON THEIR HEART, AND ON THEIR MIND I WILL WRITE THEM," He then says, (vs 17) "AND THEIR SINS AND THEIR LAWLESS DEEDS I WILL REMEMBER NO MORE."

There is much theology in this passage. It could be summarized by saying it is the complete discussion of salvation by grace and mercy, with NO works added. As it pertains to the "Security" of the believer I would like to point out its major contributions.

The sacrifice of Jesus on the cross is complete, it is … *"once for all"*, … there is no need of any additional sacrifices for our sins. This one offering has … *"perfected for all time those who are sancti-fied"*. Jesus Christ, for all of those who "Belong To Him", has perfected within you this salvation experience, for all time. Our … *"LAWLESS DEEDS I WILL REMEMBER NO MORE"*. The thing that is "perfected" here is our "Perfect Security". We are "Secure" in Christ, not because of our behavior, but because of the completed work on the Cross by Jesus Christ, the only begotten Son of God.

10b. *(Hebrews 10:23) Let us hold fast the confession of our hope without wavering, for He who promised is faithful;*

This is a continuation of the above passage, and it reinforces our hope in the One … *"who promised is faithful"*. There is no higher authority in which we can put our trust. He is faithful!!!

10c. *(Hebrews 10:39) But we are not of those who shrink back to destruction, but of those who have faith to the preserving of the soul.*

This is another continuation of the lengthy passage above. It is our faith in Jesus Christ that initiates our salvation. It is an Act of God that completes our becoming 'Born Again" of the Spirit. Neither our faith can be recanted, nor can this Act of God be overturned. Our souls are preserved by the highest authority in the universe, it is none other than the great I AM, the Most High God.

11a. *(1 Peter 1:3-5)(vs 3) Blessed be the God and Father of our Lord Jesus Christ, who according to His great mercy has caused us to be born again to a living hope through the resurrection of Jesus Christ from the dead, (vs 4) to obtain an inheritance which is imperishable and undefiled and will not fade away, reserved in heaven for you, (vs 5) who are protected by the power of God through faith for a salvation ready to be revealed in the last time.*

"protected by the power of God" … As for me and my house we can't buy a better security system. My salvation and inheritance is imperishable and reserved in heaven by the only "Perfect Security" system. I am trusting the One who wrote our "Owner's Manual", for He is able to keep me for all of eternity!!!

11b. *(1 Peter 1:24-25)(vs 24) For, "ALL FLESH IS LIKE GRASS, AND ALL ITS GLORY LIKE THE FLOWER OF GRASS. THE GRASS WITHERS, AND THE FLOWER FALLS OFF, (vs 25) BUT THE WORD OF THE LORD ENDURES FOREVER." And this is the word which was preached to you.*

You may not think this is proof of the "security" of the believer, but look at the words … *"WORD OF THE LORD ENDURES FOREVER"*. This is proof of the proof.

12. *(1 John 4:15-17)(vs 15) Whoever confesses that Jesus is the Son of God, God abides in him, and he in God. (vs 16)*

We have come to know and have believed the love which God has for us. God is love, and the one who abides in love abides in God, and God abides in him. (vs 17) By this, love is perfected with us, so that we may have confidence in the day of judgment; because as He is, so also are we in this world.

If you have confessed that Jesus is the Son of God, God abides in you and you in Him. With this interwoven relationship, we ... *"have confidence in the day of judgment"*. This love is "perfected" in us and we have "confidence" in Jesus that He will intercede our case before the Holy God. I know of no better "Security". The God given Living Water, of which we will never thirst, is "protected" until judgment day and after that, will last forever.

13. *(Ephesians 1:13-14)(vs 13) In Him, you also, after listening to the message of truth, the gospel of your salvation—having also believed, you were sealed in Him with the Holy Spirit of promise, (vs 14) who is given as a pledge of our inheritance, with a view to the redemption of God's own possession, to the praise of His glory.*

It is so beautiful to conclude this section with these verses. The last is certainly not always the least. More often than not the best is saved for the last. These verses have so much of the power of God in them, we could stand alone on these writings of Paul, as we understand our assurance that God will never abandon our "Born Again" status. God has made the "Down Payment" and has put us in lay-a-way. He will make the "Final Payment" on judgment day and will redeem us from the "shelves" of this life, for we are "His Possession"!!!

Verses 13-14 have several key parts. We listen to the message of the truth (the Gospel), we embrace this Gospel through believing faith which grants us the same relationship to God as Jesus Christ has with the Father, and as proof of our "Belonging To Him", we are "sealed" in Him. When we are "sealed" in Him, which means we are stamped as with a signet or a private mark by one in authority, we are given the daily presence of the Holy Spirit as a down payment or pledge (partial payment) towards our ultimate reward. The full payment or completion or our ultimate reward will be paid upon the death of this temporary body. This final inheritance will come upon the judgment day when God redeems us as "His possession" ... *to the praise of His glory*.

Our down payment while in this earthly life is His Holy Spirit. His payment in full, or as people call it in the real estate world, the "Balloon Payment" is our eternal life, living with Him, in the mansions He has prepared for us.

C. CONCLUSION TO SECURITY/ASSURANCE/CONFIDENCE OF THE BELIEVER:

"S O S", what do these letters mean in this world? I believe they mean some sort of trouble or distress is happening to, or being incurred by, the person sending the message. In our Chapter the S. O. S. means Security Of Salvation.

If you "Belong To Him", due to an Act of God, without any works, deeds or help by man, then the God who saved you has already provided the "Perfect Security".

(Ephesians 2:8-9)(vs 8) For by grace you have been saved through faith; and that not of yourselves, it is the gift of God; (vs 9) not as a result of works, so that no one may boast.

(John 10:27-30)(vs 27) "My sheep hear My voice, and I know them, and they follow Me; (vs 28) and I give eternal life to them, and they will never perish; and no one will snatch them out of My hand. (vs 29) "My Father, who has given them to Me, is greater than all; and no one is able to snatch them out of the Father's hand. (vs 30) "I and the Father are one."

(Romans 8:38-39)(vs 38) For I am convinced that neither death, nor life, nor angels, nor principalities, nor things present, nor things to come, nor powers, (vs 39) nor height, nor depth, nor any other created thing, will be able to separate us from the love of God, which is in Christ Jesus our Lord.

What could possibly be added. Our **S. O. S.** is Security Of Salvation. Security Of Salvation is the only **"Perfect Security"** that anyone can ever experience.

SPECIAL NOTE:

I know many of you may have a special verse or verses regarding this Chapter's subject matter. This special verse or these verses may not have been mentioned due to my ignorance or because of brevity. I apologize for either of these reasons. Please feel free to write any special verse or verses in the space below. This will add your personal touch, and will serve to call to each person's mind their individual "experience of trust", in God's Holy Word.

For to each of us "Who belong To Him", His Holy Word can be truly recognized and relied upon as our **"Owner's Manual"**!!!

_____

_____

_____

_____

_____

_____

_____

_____

CHAPTER 7

WORD OF GOD (ALL POWERFUL AND IMPERISHABLE)

INTRODUCTORY VERSES:

1. *(Deuteronomy 4:2) "You shall not add to the word which I am commanding you, nor take away from it, that you may keep the commandments of the LORD your God which I command you.*

2. *(Psalms 18:30) As for God, His way is blameless; The word of the LORD is tried; He is a shield to all who take refuge in Him.*

3. *(Proverbs 30:4-6)(vs 4) Who has ascended into heaven and descended? Who has gathered the wind in His fists? Who has wrapped the waters in His garment? Who has established all the ends of the earth? What is His name or His son's name? Surely you know! (vs 5) Every word of God is tested; He is a shield to those who take refuge in Him. (vs 6) Do not add to His words Or He will reprove you, and you will be proved a liar.*

4. *(Isaiah 40:8) The grass withers, the flower fades, But the word of our God stands forever.*

5. *(Matthew 4:4) But He answered and said, "It is written, 'MAN SHALL NOT LIVE ON BREAD ALONE, BUT ON EVERY WORD THAT PROCEEDS OUT OF THE MOUTH OF GOD.'"*

6. *(Hebrews 4:12) For the word of God is living and active and sharper than any two-edged sword, and piercing as far as the division of soul and spirit, of both joints and marrow, and able to judge the thoughts and intentions of the heart.*

What wonderful verses to know that God loves us enough to give us His Holy, **"IMPERISHABLE"** Word! Truly we can "Belong to Him" all the time being thankful for this wonderful guide, **His "Owner's Manual"**!!!

INTRODUCTION:

WORD OF GOD—THE ONLY "IMPERISHABLE" IN OUR LIFE :

The Word of God is "IMPERISHABLE", it is alive, real, inspiring, it is eternal, it is living and active, it is indescribable, it is Holy, it is not just words on a page, but it is the Mind of God. It is found to be eternally alive, it imparts wisdom, love, kindness, direction, hope, and absolute truth (there are no sliding scales of standards for different ages or times in history). It is sharper than a two-edged sword, it divides or separates the truth even when the world has confused the truth. The Bible in its entirety is beyond the comprehension of the MOST INTELLIGENT minds mankind has ever known, yet it is so simple that unless we have the faith as a little child, we cannot know the Jesus of this Bible. The Word of God is the most exciting thing that can happen in anyone's life. It is fulfilling, brings peace, teaches a love for others, teaches "it is more blessed to give than receive" and a wealth of other things. The wealth of the Bible cannot be measured in man's financial terms. The one who knows God's Word is undeniably more wealthy than the Walton's of Wal-Mart fame, or the Bill Gates and the Warren Buffets of the world.

We all know about rust, mold, rot and other forms of decay. Rust attacks metals, objects in some cases so hard we can't dent them with a hammer. It tarnishes them as well as literally destroys them. Rot or mold attacks organic matter such as vegetables. We have all seen the results of rot or mold. In fact we have a family joke that has been a source of fun and laughter for many years. If you go to the refrigerator and find a moldy bag or container of food, you ask the one closest to you "Is this one ready?". The meaning is a little sarcastic, but we all do it to each other in fun. God's Word does not rust, mold, rot or is it found in any other form of decay. God's Word, we will find as we explore the following valuable Biblical verses, is truly **"ETERNALLY IMPERISHABLE"**.

A. FAMILIAR BIBLICAL VERSES REGARDING THE "IMPERISHABLE" WORD OF GOD:

(Hebrews 13:7-9)(vs 7) Remember those who led you, who spoke the word of God to you; and considering the result of their conduct, imitate their faith. (vs 8) Jesus Christ is the same yesterday and today and forever. (vs 9) Do not be carried away by varied and strange teachings; for it is good for the heart to be strengthened by grace, not by foods, through which those who were so occupied were not benefited.

Those Godly people who spoke the Word of God to us should be imitated as to their faith. We are strengthened by the Word of God for eternity, not like the daily physical foods which soon pass away with no lasting benefits.

(Hebrews 4:12) For the word of God is living and active and sharper than any two-edged sword, and piercing as far as the division of soul and spirit, of both joints and marrow, and able to judge the thoughts and intentions of the heart.

God's Word is living and produces miraculous results, which are beyond our comprehension or our comparison with anything here on this earth. There is not a surgeon that has lived, that is alive today or will be alive in the future, that can divide the body and spirit. God's Living Word can direct itself, as we see in (vs 12) above, to differentiate between the physical, the spiritual, the joints and marrow of the bone, as well as literally judge the silent thoughts and intentions of the heart. God's Word is more powerful than any thought, fact or event. Remember that God spoke the earth and its parts into being, He did not rely on evolution, a Big Bang or any little creeping things. He made it all by His Word!!! He made it from nothing!!!

(Isaiah 40:6-8)(vs 6) A voice says, "Call out." Then he answered, "What shall I call out?" All flesh is grass, and all its loveliness is like the flower of the field. (vs 7) The grass withers, the flower fades, When the breath of the LORD blows

upon it; Surely the people are grass. (vs 8) The grass withers, the flower fades, But the word of our God stands forever.

(1 Peter 1:23) for you have been born again not of seed which is perishable but imperishable, that is, through the living and enduring word of God

God's Word is truly "IMPERISHABLE". We mortals or humans, made of flesh, are like the grass which in its season withers and dies. Not so with God's Word, It is "EVERLASTING".

(1 Peter 1:3-7)(vs 3) Blessed be the God and Father of our Lord Jesus Christ, who according to His great mercy has caused us to be born again to a living hope through the resurrection of Jesus Christ from the dead, (vs 4) to obtain an inheritance which is imperishable and undefiled and will not fade away, reserved in heaven for you, (vs 5) who are protected by the power of God through faith for a salvation ready to be revealed in the last time. (vs 6) In this you greatly rejoice, even though now for a little while, if necessary, you have been distressed by various trials, (vs 7) so that the proof of your faith, being more precious than gold which is perishable, even though tested by fire, may be found to result in praise and glory and honor at the revelation of Jesus Christ;

There is nothing more valuable than the Word of God. It is our only "NON-PERISHABLE" in this world. The Word of God is the mind of God, the revelation of Jesus Christ, the spiritual food that sustains us from morning until night. We must read it, meditate upon it, and apply it. Anything else will rot, be moth eaten, rust, or is subject to being stolen.

These verses are our hope even though we have not seen God or Jesus, but because of the Word of God we can love Him, believe in Him and be reassured that God through faith will reveal Himself in the last time (**vs 5**). God will take this mortal, perishing body and grant us an imperishable one, one of eternal immortality, one that is more precious than gold. Our inheritance is imperishable, laid up for ourselves in Heaven, where we will be spending an eternity. Any inheritance here on earth can only be enjoyed, and hopefully properly used, for maybe eighty years. Eighty years is a fleeting, disappearing vapor as compared with eternity. It just makes tremendous sense for us to...*(Matthew 6:19-21)(vs 19) "Do not store up for yourselves treasures on earth, where moth and rust destroy, and where thieves break in and steal. (vs 20) "But store up for yourselves treasures in heaven, where neither moth nor rust destroys, and where thieves do not break in or steal; (vs 21) for where your treasure is, there your heart will be also.*...put all our efforts into something that will last an eternity versus a fleeting, disappearing vapor. There is no comparison! Besides being the practical thing to do, we are commanded **by JESUS** (see His very words above) to lay up "Imperishable" treasures in Heaven!

B. ADDITIONAL BIBLICAL VERSES REGARDING THE "IMPERISHABLE" WORD OF GOD, AND THE WISDOM AND INSTRUCTION THEY PROCLAIM:

The following familiar verses are to be considered, meditated upon and put into practice in our daily life. These are not in any way all inclusive, and may not include your favorite verse. They were selected to clearly demonstrate that God wants us to know His mind and live an abundant life of service to Him, which will be a blessing to ourselves as well as others. Consider these verses and their powerful wisdom, they are all the **"Word of God"**, and they are **"All Imperishable"**!!!

(Psalms 1:1-6) (vs 1) How blessed is the man who does not walk in the counsel of the wicked, Nor stand in the path of sinners, Nor sit in the seat of scoffers! (vs 2) But his delight is in the law of the LORD, And in His law he meditates day and night. (vs 3) He will be like a tree firmly planted by streams of water, Which yields its fruit in its season And its leaf does not wither; And in whatever he does, he prospers. (vs 4) The wicked are not so, But they are like chaff which the wind drives away. (vs 5) Therefore the wicked will not stand in the judgment, Nor sinners in the assembly of the righteous. (vs 6) For the LORD knows the way of the righteous, But the way of the wicked will perish.

Our charge is to walk, stand and sit in the counsel of the Almighty, by delighting (delighting is defined as pleasure, desire, concretely a valuable thing) in His Word and meditating (meditating is defined as speak, study, talk, utter, by implication to ponder) on His Word day and night.

Our promise is that we will be firmly planted and whatever we do will prosper. Remember that prosperity is being blessed by God, for service to Him and others, and not for a selfish mis-use of that prosperity. Regardless of the form of the prosperity, be in the form of material wealth, intelligence, powerful position or other abilities, it comes hand in hand with the responsibility of Godly "stewardship". With Godly "stewardship" comes the opportunity to lay up, "Imperishable" treasures for eternity, ... *"For the LORD knows the way of the righteous"*.

(Proverbs 3:5-7)(vs 5) Trust in the LORD with all your heart And do not lean on your own understanding. (vs 6) In all your ways acknowledge Him, And He will make your paths straight. (vs 7) Do not be wise in your own eyes; Fear the LORD and turn away from evil.

These are verses many of us have committed to memory. We need to call them to mind each day and apply them accordingly. There is not a day that goes by whereby we wouldn't be better off if we were standing on these principles and trusting in these promises. The above, "Imperishable" Word of God, has probably been called upon by more people in more circumstances than any other scripture.

(Psalms 24:1) A Psalm of David. The earth is the LORD'S, and all it contains, The world, and those who dwell in it.

(Psalms 37:3-5)(vs 3) Trust in the LORD and do good; Dwell in the land and cultivate faithfulness. (vs 4) Delight yourself in the LORD; And He will give you the desires of your heart. (vs 5) Commit your way to the LORD, Trust also in Him, and He will do it.

(Psalms 118:24) This is the day which the LORD has made; Let us rejoice and be glad in it.

The above verses all speak to God's authority and ownership. His desire is to give those who delight in Him the desires of their heart. His blessings are on us as we commit to this knowledge, trust in this knowledge and actively participate with Him, as He brings it all to pass. These "Imperishable" words of God are enough to last us and direct us for a lifetime, even if this is all we had ever known of the Bible.

(Matthew 6:33-34)(vs 33) "But seek first His kingdom and His righteousness, and all these things will be added to you. (vs 34) "So do not worry about tomorrow; for tomorrow will care for itself. Each day has enough trouble of its own.

In Matthew we witness the very "Words of Jesus"! These verses are a direct quote from God! He didn't audibly speak to us, but He might as well have been across our desk or sitting in our living room, as He spoke these direct instructions. We have here both a command and a promise. The application is "do not worry or fret" as we seek His ways. He will take care of all the details. I know many of you already apply these verses, but if you haven't, start TODAY! The "Imperishable" words of God teach us to "Trust" in Him.

(Ecclesiastes 12:13-14)(vs 13) The conclusion, when all has been heard, is: fear God and keep His commandments, because this applies to every person. (vs 14) For God will bring every act to judgment, everything which is hidden, whether it is good or evil.

Reverence God and keep His commandments (keep "The Word of God"). You can't possibly keep His commandments unless you know them. You can't possibly know them unless you are exposed to them. The most common methods of exposure are to read His Word, attend a quality Bible Study group, and regularly attend a Church with sound Bible teaching. You won't get God's Word by putting a Bible under your pillow each night! "That" Bible and "that" pillow will both "Perish", but putting God's Word into your heart and soul will last an "eternity".

The above verses are only a few of the examples of the "Word of God". There are so many more you would have to re-print the entire Holy Bible. Thank you Lord, for sharing your Word with us.

C. OTHER BIBLICAL VERSES REGARDING THE "IMPERISHABLE" WORD OF GOD:

I am violating one of my decisions for this book. I had decided to not reference a verse without printing that verse. This decision was made in order to aid the reader by not having to look up the referenced scriptures. There are so many references to the "Word of God", I will not print each scripture, but will in some cases print the reference and a brief comment as to that scripture's content. Please forgive me and take the time to locate and read as many of these references (in their entirety) as you desire.

(Deuteronomy 4:2) "You shall not add to the word which I am commanding you, nor take away from it, that you may keep the commandments of the LORD your God which I command you.

"Don't add to or take away from God's Word".

(Joshua 23:14) "Now behold, today I am going the way of all the earth, and you know in all your hearts and in all your souls that not one word of all the good words which the LORD your God spoke concerning you has failed; all have been fulfilled for you, not one of them has failed.

"Not one of God's words has failed and all have been fulfilled".

(1 Samuel 9:27) ... "Samuel proclaims the Word of God to Saul"...

(2 Samuel 22:31) "As for God, His way is blameless; The word of the LORD is tested; He is a shield to all who take refuge in Him.

"The Word of the Lord is tested, it has been refined, it is pure".

(1 Kings 12:22-24) ... "The Word of God was spoken, the people listened and obeyed" ...

(1 Kings 13:26) ... "A severe warning if we disobey the Word of God" ...

(2 Kings 1:16) ... "a warning unto death to heed God's Word" ...

(2 Kings 5:1-19, key vs 14) … "Naaman, a captain of an army, was cleansed of leprosy by being <u>obedient to the word of God</u>" …

(Psalms 18:30) As for God, His way is blameless; The word of the LORD is tried; He is a shield to all who take refuge in Him.

(Proverbs 30:5) Every word of God is tested; He is a shield to those who take refuge in Him.

(Isaiah 40:8) The grass withers, the flower fades, But the word of our God stands forever.

(Luke 5:1-10, key vs(s) 4 & 5) (vs 4) When He had finished speaking, He said to Simon, "Put out into the deep water and let down your nets for a catch." (vs 5) Simon answered and said, "Master, we worked hard all night and caught nothing, but I will do as You say and let down the nets."

"Jesus spoke, Simon Peter said it doesn't make any sense, but <u>I will do as You say</u>".

What a life lesson to be learned and applied! We are to <u>follow the Words of God,</u> even when we don't understand, and in fact even when we have proof that He surely is wrong! The results will be a catch we can't contain! Trust and Obey—for we find the "Imperishable" Word of God to be faithful always!!!

(Luke 11:27-28) … "Blessed are those who hear the Word of God and obey it" …

(Acts 20:32) "And now I commend you to God and to the word of His grace, which is able to build you up and to give you the inheritance among all those who are sanctified.

"Our inheritance is not in this world and it is not of this world. We are in this world but we are not of this world".

(John 15:19) "If you were of the world, the world would love its own; but because you are not of the world, but I chose you out of the world, because of this the world hates you.

"Our inheritance and reward is being in the presence of God for eternity, all else will **Perish**".

(1 Corinthians 1:18) For the word of the cross is foolishness to those who are perishing, but to us who are being saved it is the power of God.

(1 Thessalonians 2:13) For this reason we also constantly thank God that when you received the word of God which you heard from us, you accepted it not as the word of men, but for what it really is, the word of God, which also performs its work in you who believe.

(Hebrews 4:12) ... "The Word of God is able to judge the thoughts and intentions of the heart" ...

(Hebrews 11:3) By faith we understand that the worlds were prepared by the word of God, so that what is seen was not made out of things which are visible.

"God's verbal words literally spoke everything into existence".

(1 Peter 1:23) for you have been born again not of seed which is perishable but imperishable, that is, through the living and enduring word of God.

"Further proof of the "**Imperishable**" Word of God".

(Revelation 1:1-3) (vs 1) The Revelation of Jesus Christ, which God gave Him to show to His bond-servants, the things which must soon take place; and He sent and communicated it by His angel to His bond-servant John, (vs 2) who testified to the word of God and to the testimony of Jesus Christ, even to all that he saw. (vs 3) Blessed is he who reads and those who hear the words of the prophecy, and heed the things which are written in it; for the time is near.

"Read, hear and heed".

(Revelation 19:13) He is clothed with a robe dipped in blood, and His name is called The Word of God.

"John penned the Book of The Revelation of Jesus Christ, as God through His angel, spoke it to him". The Word of God! The Word of God! The Word of God! It is a thread woven throughout the entire Bible. The Word of God is the Mind of God, it is to be sought after, acquired and valued above all else. It is truly the only thing "Imperishable" in our lives, and we are to seek it with all of our hearts.

D. CONCLUSION TO THE WORD OF GOD (IMPERISHABLE)

I hope the individual meanings of all the verses written above, their Warnings, their Encouragements, their Instructions and their Promises will not be lost in this large number of verses about the "Word of God", but that each will be meditated upon and applied as needed in each specific life. If only one verse above hits your need or hot button, then grab it and ride it for all the value God has for you. Let God impress you with "His Word" to meet your need(s) and to encourage you to serve Him and others. *(Colossians 3:16) Let the word of Christ richly dwell within you, with all wisdom teaching and admonishing one another with psalms and hymns and spiritual songs, singing with thankfulness in your hearts to God.*

The following analogy may be a bit frivolous, but on the other hand may cause us to think. The Word of God is more powerful than Superman! We all know the comic character of Superman is not real, yet we have read about him, seen movies about him and watched TV series about him to the point he is imprinted upon our minds. Superman is not real, but we refer to him as if in some distant place or land he really exists. He is touted to be more powerful than a locomotive and faster than a speeding bullet. God's Word has no comparison or comparable in reality or fantasy! God's Word is the only "IMPERISHABLE" thing on this earth!

God's Word is the final say about anything and everything! God's Word is truly more powerful than anything this world has seen or will see until the end of time. Just look at a very small number of the things God's Word can accomplish.

1. God's Word is LIVING and ACTIVE and can discern the thoughts and intentions of the heart!!!

(Hebrews 4:12) For the word of God is living and active and sharper than any two-edged sword, and piercing as far as the division of soul and spirit, of both joints and marrow, and able to judge the thoughts and intentions of the heart.

2. God's Word says that no one will be able to stand in His presence and all will confess that Jesus Christ is Lord!!!

(Philippians 2:8-11) (vs 8) Being found in appearance as a man, He humbled Himself by becoming obedient to the point

of death, even death on a cross. (vs 9) For this reason also, God highly exalted Him, and bestowed on Him the name which is above every name, (vs 10) so that at the name of Jesus EVERY KNEE WILL BOW, of those who are in heaven and on earth and under the earth, (vs 11) and that every tongue will confess that Jesus Christ is Lord, to the glory of God the Father.

3. The Word of God can move mountains!!!

*(Genesis 1:9-10) (vs 9) Then God said, "Let the waters below the heavens be gathered into one place, and let the dry land appear"; and it was so. (vs 10) God called the dry land earth, and the gathering of the waters He called seas; and God saw that it was good. ... (Zechariah 14:4) In that day His feet will stand on the Mount of Olives, which is in front of Jerusalem on the east; and the Mount of Olives will be split in its middle from east to west by a very large valley, so that half of the mountain will move toward the north and the other half toward the south. ... (Matthew 17:20) And He *said to them, "Because of the littleness of your faith; for truly I say to you, if you have faith the size of a mustard seed, you will say to this mountain, 'Move from here to there,' and it will move; and nothing will be impossible to you.*

4. The Word of God can lay down snow without destroying the landscape!!! *(Job 38:22) "Have you entered the storehouses of the snow, Or have you seen the storehouses of the hail, ...* Man at several of our Ski resorts is in the snow making business. We find him tearing up the terrain with tracks, ditches, hoses, heavy equipment and water supplies. With all this he can still only cover a few square feet as he still must still rely on God to provide the proper weather conditions. When God makes snow He doesn't leave a track and covers hundreds of thousands of acres in whatever depths He chooses, all with one storm. Try to beat that even with Superman's help. God through His Word, does all things, to the astonishment of man.

5. In God's Word we find that He has "Wonderfully" made us, while numbering our days!!!

(Psalms 139:13-16) (vs 13) For You formed my inward parts; You wove me in my mother's womb. (vs 14) I will give

thanks to You, for I am fearfully and wonderfully made; Wonderful are Your works, And my soul knows it very well. (vs 15) My frame was not hidden from You, When I was made in secret, And skillfully wrought in the depths of the earth; (vs 16) Your eyes have seen my unformed substance; And in Your book were all written The days that were ordained for me, When as yet there was not one of them.

6. The Word of God not only can form us in the womb, but can create a second birth!!!

(John 3:1-7) (vs 1) Now there was a man of the Pharisees, named Nicodemus, a ruler of the Jews; (vs 2) this man came to Jesus by night and said to Him, "Rabbi, we know that You have come from God as a teacher; for no one can do these signs that You do unless God is with him." (vs 3) Jesus answered and said to him, "Truly, truly, I say to you, unless one is born again he cannot see the kingdom of God." (vs 4) Nicodemus *said to Him, "How can a man be born when he is old? He cannot enter a second time into his mother's womb and be born, can he?" (vs 5) Jesus answered, "Truly, truly, I say to you, unless one is born of water and the Spirit he cannot enter into the kingdom of God. (vs 6 "That which is born of the flesh is flesh, and that which is born of the Spirit is spirit. (vs 7) "Do not be amazed that I said to you, 'You must be born again.' ... (1 Peter 1:3-5) (vs 3) Blessed be the God and Father of our Lord Jesus Christ, who according to His great mercy has caused us to be born again to a living hope through the resurrection of Jesus Christ from the dead, (vs 4) to obtain an inheritance which is imperishable and undefiled and will not fade away, reserved in heaven for you, (vs 5) who are protected by the power of God through faith for a salvation ready to be revealed in the last time.

7. The Word of God can regenerate one heart!!!

(Luke 19:5-10) (vs 5) When Jesus came to the place, He looked up and said to him, "Zaccheus, hurry and come down, for today I must stay at your house." (vs 6) And he hurried and came down and received Him gladly. (vs 7) When they saw it, they all began to grumble, saying, "He has gone to be

the guest of a man who is a sinner." (vs 8) Zaccheus stopped and said to the Lord, "Behold, Lord, half of my possessions I will give to the poor, and if I have defrauded anyone of anything, I will give back four times as much." (vs 9) And Jesus said to him, "Today salvation has come to this house, because he, too, is a son of Abraham. (vs 10) "For the Son of Man has come to seek and to save that which was lost."

8. The Word of God can regenerate thousands of hearts!!!

(Acts 4:4) But many of those who had heard the message believed; and the number of the men came to be about five thousand. ... (Acts 2:38-41) (vs 38) Peter said to them, "Repent, and each of you be baptized in the name of Jesus Christ for the forgiveness of your sins; and you will receive the gift of the Holy Spirit. (vs 39) "For the promise is for you and your children and for all who are far off, as many as the Lord our God will call to Himself." (vs 40) And with many other words he solemnly testified and kept on exhorting them, saying, "Be saved from this perverse generation!" (vs 41) So then, those who had received his word were baptized; and that day there were added about three thousand souls.

9. The Word of God can make a man speechless!!!

(Matthew 22:46) No one was able to answer Him a word, nor did anyone dare from that day on to ask Him another question.

10. The Word of God can humble anyone and everyone, including the greatest men and minds that have ever existed!!!

(Job 38:1-12) (vs 1) Then the LORD answered Job out of the whirlwind and said, (vs 2) "Who is this that darkens counsel By words without knowledge? (vs 3) "Now gird up your loins like a man, And I will ask you, and you instruct Me! (vs 4) "Where were you when I laid the foundation of the earth? Tell Me, if you have understanding, (vs 5) Who set its measurements? Since you know. Or who stretched the line on it? (vs 6) "On what were its bases sunk? Or who laid its cornerstone, (vs 7) When the morning stars sang together And all the sons of God shouted for joy? (vs 8) "Or who enclosed the sea with doors When, bursting forth, it

*went out from the womb; (vs 9) When I made a cloud its gar-
ment And thick darkness its swaddling band, (vs 10) And I
placed boundaries on it And set a bolt and doors, (vs 11) And
I said, 'Thus far you shall come, but no farther; And here
shall your proud waves stop'? (vs 12)"Have you ever in your
life commanded the morning, And caused the dawn to know
its place,*

*(Ecclesiastes 12:10-11)(vs 10) The Preacher sought to find
delightful words and to write words of truth correctly. (vs
11) The words of wise men are like goads, and masters of
these collections are like well-driven nails; they are given
by one Shepherd.*

The two men, Job and Solomon, were both humbled by the
Word of God.

11. The Word of God is to be Obeyed with a "Promise" given!!!

*(Deuteronomy 11:13-15)(vs 13) "It shall come about, if
you listen obediently to my commandments which I am
commanding you today, to love the LORD your God and to
serve Him with all your heart and all your soul, (vs 14) that
He will give the rain for your land in its season, the early
and late rain, that you may gather in your grain and your
new wine and your oil. (vs 15) "He will give grass in your
fields for your cattle, and you will eat and be satisfied.*

12. The Word of God must be taught to your Children (The Sunday School and Christian School teachers can do their part, but the ultimate responsibility is YOURS)!!!

*(Deuteronomy 11:18-19)(vs 18) "You shall therefore
impress these words of mine on your heart and on your
soul; and you shall bind them as a sign on your hand, and
they shall be as frontals on your forehead. (vs 19) "You shall
teach them to your sons, talking of them when you sit in
your house and when you walk along the road and when
you lie down and when you rise up.*

13. The Word of God will fight all your "Battles"!!!

*(Deuteronomy 11:22-25)(vs 22) "For if you are careful to
keep all this commandment which I am commanding you
to do, to love the LORD your God, to walk in all His ways*

and hold fast to Him, (vs 23) then the LORD will drive out all these nations from before you, and you will dispossess nations greater and mightier than you. (vs 24) "Every place on which the sole of your foot treads shall be yours; your border will be from the wilderness to Lebanon, and from the river, the river Euphrates, as far as the western sea. (vs 25) "No man will be able to stand before you; the LORD your God will lay the dread of you and the fear of you on all the land on which you set foot, as He has spoken to you.

God and His Word are "Omnipotent" and "Omniscience"!!! We can do no better in this life than to Read It, Study It, Memorize It, Meditate upon It, Act in accordance with It and Make It a Part of Our Minds. His "Imperishable" Word is the "Final" say about everything!!!

With all the things that God's Word can accomplish, we would be wise to "Know" **IT** as much as is possible, and "Heed" **IT** in all matters before us. For **IT** is truly as "Powerful" in its actions, as **IT** is "Imperishable" in its endurance!!!

SPECIAL NOTE:

I know many of you may have a special verse or verses regarding this Chapter's subject matter. This special verse or these verses may not have been mentioned due to my ignorance or because of brevity. I apologize for either of these reasons. Please feel free to write any special verse or verses in the space below. This will add your personal touch, and will serve to call to each person's mind their individual "experience of trust", in God's Holy Word.

For to each of us "Who belong To Him", His Holy Word can be truly recognized and relied upon as our **"Owner's Manual"**!!!

_____

_____

_____

_____

_____

_____

CHAPTER 8

"LORD" JESUS CHRIST

INTRODUCTORY VERSES:

(Matthew 26:38-39) Then He *said to them, "My soul is deeply grieved, to the point of death; remain here and keep watch with Me." (vs 39) And He went a little beyond them, and fell on His face and prayed, saying, "My Father, if it is possible, let this cup pass from Me; yet not as I will, but as You will." ... (Luke 22:44) And being in agony He was praying very fervently; and His sweat became like drops of blood, falling down upon the ground.

Jesus was agonizing over our very souls. You don't suppose He only had a plan to save us from eternal separation from God, but couldn't address the life we live here on earth, do you?

INTRODUCTION:

It is with both inadequacy and certainty that I write this Chapter. My convictions are strong regarding that JESUS must be LORD in order to be our SAVIOR. Even though I feel this Chapter could be written more conclusively by a scholarly theologian, I will nevertheless attempt to expose what God's Word says about JESUS being both LORD and SAVIOR.

Since we can never argue with His Word, and there are certainly many verses that are applicable to this subject, let's let the Word of God speak and convict. The statement, "What is in your heart is what will come out", is the basis of my conclusion, and that is if JESUS is our SAVIOR, He must be LORD!

The definition of "JESUS is LORD" can be summed up in the following verses.

The negative being ... *(Matthew 15:18-19)(vs 18) "But the things that proceed out of the mouth come from the heart, and those defile the man. (vs 19) "For out of the heart come evil thoughts, murders, adulteries, fornications, thefts, false witness, slanders.* ... with the contrary being ... *(1 Corinthians 6:17 & 19-20)(vs 17) But the one who joins himself to the Lord is one spirit with Him. (vs 19) Or do you not know that your body is a temple of the Holy Spirit who is in you, whom you have from God, and that you are not your own? (vs 20) For you have been bought with a price: therefore glorify God in your body.*

No one can possibly read the above scriptures and declare that JESUS is my "fire insurance", now I can live any way I please!!! If JESUS is truly our SAVIOR, he is truly our LORD!!!

A. 85 NEW TESTAMENT VERSES THAT PROCLAIM THE "LORD" JESUS CHRIST:

Yes, there are eighty-five (85) New Testament verses that use the "Lord Jesus Christ" in their content. No, we will not look at every one of these. It seems right to me to now address the definition of each of these words. It is also worthy of note that in each of the 85 verses the root word s used for Lord, Jesus and Christ, are the same respectively. In other words the following definitions will apply universally to each of the scriptures highlighted below. I believe it is also fitting and appropriate at this time to include the Biblical definition of Savior. The definitions are as follows:

a) **"LORD"** — The original Greek defines this to mean: supremacy; supreme in authority; controller; and titles would include God, Lord and master. Thayer's dictionary definition stated Lord to mean "he to whom a person or thing belongs". In other words if Jesus is our Lord, "We Belong to Him"!!! Thayer further states in his definition that Lord means "the owner, one who has control of the person, master".

Since I am taking the position that Jesus Christ is our Lord, the One who lovingly looks after us, and since He has left His Word in the form of the Holy Bible and that we can rely upon the Holy Spirit to be our instructor, we can be certain His Word is our "Owner's Manual"!!! As we look further into our "Owner's Manual" regarding this subject, I think all will conclude and agree, that "Jesus Is Lord" as defined above, and He is to be magnified, as we will see below!!!;

b) "**JESUS**" — of Hebrew origin, Jesus (that is Jehoshua), the name of our Lord. There is no question who this was referring to in each and every one of the 85 New Testament verses. We can be certain when Jesus is used in any/all of the verses below, the reference is to Jesus, the Son of God;

c) "**CHRIST**" – anointed, that is, the Messiah, an epithet of Jesus; and

d) "**SAVIOR**" – the New Testament definition is a deliverer, that is, God or Christ.

With our definitions in place we can now look at individual and multiple verses, and how they speak to us, proving that **JESUS CHRIST** our **SAVIOR**, is **LORD**!!! Please read the following selected passages as they confirm the fact that **JESUS CHRIST** is **LORD**!!!

1. *(Acts 2:36) "Therefore let all the house of Israel know for certain that God has made Him both Lord and Christ— this Jesus whom you crucified."*

How appropriate for the first verse in the New Testament, using all three of the words defined above, to be so direct. It firmly states that God has made Jesus both our Lord and Christ. Re-read the definitions supplied above. If you have accepted the work accomplished upon the Cross, Jesus crucified, then He is your Lord and Master and Supreme in authority.

2. *(Acts 15:25-27)(vs 25) it seemed good to us, having become of one mind, to select men to send to you with our beloved Barnabas and Paul, (vs 26) men who have risked their lives for the name of our Lord Jesus Christ. (vs 27) "Therefore we have sent Judas and Silas, who themselves will also report the same things by word of mouth.*

These men, Judas and Silas, were men that have risked their lives for their **LORD JESUS CHRIST**. What is coming out of their hearts, and therefore what comes from their everyday life, is an expression of the appreciation of what the **LORD JESUS CHRIST** has done for them. He is the One who not only risked His life for them, but **gave** His life for them.

<u>3.</u> *(Romans 13:12-14)(vs 12) The night is almost gone, and the day is near. Therefore let us lay aside the deeds of darkness and put on the armor of light. (vs 13) Let us behave properly as in the day, not in carousing and drunkenness, not in sexual promiscuity and sensuality, not in strife and jealousy. (vs 14) But put on the Lord Jesus Christ, and make no provision for the flesh in regard to its lusts.*

Jesus is returning soon. We are to come to Christ for forgiveness, receiving His act of "regeneration", and use this new life of being "born of the spirit", for the things of God. We are commanded to abstain from the lusts of the flesh, as so vividly described above, and are to put on the *"armor of light"*, as made available to us through our *"Lord Jesus Christ"*.

<u>4.</u> *(1 Corinthians 1:1-3)(vs 1) Paul, called as an apostle of Jesus Christ by the will of God, and Sosthenes our brother, (vs 2) To the church of God which is at Corinth, to those who have been sanctified in Christ Jesus, saints by calling, with all who in every place call on the name of our Lord Jesus Christ, their Lord and ours: (vs 3) Grace to you and peace from God our Father and the Lord Jesus Christ.*

The Apostle Paul is addressing the Christian believers of the church at Corinth. He emphatically states on two occasions, to those who are believers and referred to here as saints by calling, that they come under the authority of the **LORD JESUS CHRIST**. Paul, without amplification of the subject, has taken a stand that **JESUS CHRIST** is **LORD** of every believer at Corinth, as well as every believer today.

<u>5.</u> *(2 Corinthians 8:9) For you know the grace of our Lord Jesus Christ, that though He was rich, yet for your sake He became poor, so that you through His poverty might become rich.*

This verse is so "rich" in truths that a book could be written to tell of its values and still not cover the subject exhaustively. One truth is clear, the same Son of God who gave up the "riches" He found in heaven, came here to earth and experienced poverty (the **BEST** this earth has to offer is considered poverty through heavenly eyes) in order that we might become "rich". Becoming **"Rich"** is personally knowing the **LORD JESUS CHRIST**. 85 times Jesus Christ is referred to as **LORD**! "Riches" are personally knowing **JESUS,** and serving Him as **LORD**!

6. *(Ephesians 6:23-24)(vs 23) Peace be to the brethren, and love with faith, from God the Father and the Lord Jesus Christ. (vs 24) Grace be with all those who love our Lord Jesus Christ with incorruptible love.*

Do we love Him with *"incorruptible love"* (unending existence, genuineness, and sincerity)? If so He is **LORD**!!!

7. *(Philippians 2:9-11)(vs 9) For this reason also, God highly exalted Him, and bestowed on Him the name which is above every name, (vs 10) so that at the name of Jesus EVERY KNEE WILL BOW, of those who are in heaven and on earth and under the earth, (vs 11) and that every tongue will confess that Jesus Christ is Lord, to the glory of God the Father.*

Our judgment day is coming. With man the two things that are certain are "death" and "taxes". With God the two things of certainty are, "every knee will bow at the name of Jesus", and "every tongue will confess that Jesus Christ is **LORD**"!!!

8. *(Colossians 2:6-8 & 13-14)(vs 6) Therefore as you have received Christ Jesus the Lord, so walk in Him, (vs 7) having been firmly rooted and now being built up in Him and established in your faith, just as you were instructed, and overflowing with gratitude. (vs 8) See to it that no one takes you captive through philosophy and empty deception, according to the tradition of men, according to the elementary principles of the world, rather than according to Christ. (vs13) When you were dead in your transgressions and the uncircumcision of your flesh, He made you alive together with Him, having forgiven us all our transgressions, (vs 14) having canceled out the certificate of debt consisting of decrees against us, which was hostile to us; and He has taken it out of the way, having nailed it to the cross.*

We were dead and He made us alive. Let us walk in Him, seeing that no philosophies, empty deception and traditions of men, block our paths. We are to live according to Christ for He has forgiven us, cancelled our debts and has nailed our sins to the Cross. He has truly earned the name and position of **LORD JESUS CHRIST**!!!

9. *(2 Thessalonians 3:4-6)(vs 3) We have confidence in the Lord concerning you, that you are doing and will continue to do what we command. (vs 5) May the Lord direct your hearts into the love of God and into the steadfastness of Christ. (vs 6) Now we command you, brethren, in the name of our Lord Jesus Christ, that you keep away from every brother who leads an unruly life and not according to the tradition which you received from us.*

After looking at these verses you may call them rather obscure. I cannot recall ever having someone quote or read to me these scriptures. Look closer, the word command is used in verses three (3) and six (6). We are commanded in the name of the **LORD JESUS CHRIST** to stay away from those who are unruly or disorderly. The definition and connotation of an unruly brother is one who is morally suspect or disorderly. The word brother as used in verse six (6) is not referring to a "Christian Brother", but a brother by natural birth, such as a neighbor, acquaintance or an associate. To elaborate, this means we are not warned to stay away from our "Christian Brothers", but we are warned to stay apart and not associate and participate with the people of the world who are known to be Godless and trouble makers. The trouble these people are into is not defined here, but it is alluded to and refers to those who are morally suspect. This may encompass anything including morality issues to bank robbery. You fill in the blanks. Regardless of the specifics of the degradation, we as "faith believers" cannot be associated with anything that is contrary to the Biblical standards and the teachings of the Apostle Paul, and his fellow teachers and leaders of the Christian Faith. As one who "Belongs To God", we need to call upon the Holy Spirit who is within us, to open our eyes to those things which might fall under the category of morally suspect.

What Paul is talking about here is we are to act as if Jesus were our daily companion and is in our presence at all of our work and play. If He is **SAVIOR**, He is **LORD**!!! If **LORD**, go back to the introduction and find we are joined with God and the Holy Spirit resides in us. We are not our own, but we have been bought with a price, therefore He is Master and Supreme in authority. It is because of the Cross and His forgiveness that we should delight in living our daily lifestyle for Him. It must be emphasized that His control is not externally imposed, but comes from within, for only the Love of God can come out from one who truly "Belongs To Him"!!! If He is **SAVIOR**, He is **LORD**!!!

We are commanded in the name of the **LORD JESUS CHRIST** to keep away from and not participate with those, *"who leads an unruly life"* (morally suspect and disorderly).

10. *(1 Timothy 6:3-5)(vs 3) If anyone advocates a different doctrine and does not agree with sound words, those of our Lord Jesus Christ, and with the doctrine conforming to godliness, (vs 4) he is conceited and understands nothing; but he has a morbid interest in controversial questions and disputes about words, out of which arise envy, strife, abusive language, evil suspicions, (vs 5) and constant friction between men of depraved mind and deprived of the truth, who suppose that godliness is a means of gain.*

If the things described above come out of us (things which are opposite to the "Fruits of the Spirit"), the Love of God cannot be in us. This person is trying to "use" God for personal gain, instead of "submitting" to Him!

11. *(2 Peter 1:5-11)(vs 5) Now for this very reason also, applying all diligence, in your faith supply moral excellence, and in your moral excellence, knowledge, (vs 6) and in your knowledge, self-control, and in your self-control, perseverance, and in your perseverance, godliness, (vs 7) and in your godliness, brotherly kindness, and in your brotherly kindness, love. (vs 8) For if these qualities are yours and are increasing, they render you neither useless nor unfruitful in the true knowledge of our Lord Jesus Christ. (vs 9) For he who lacks these qualities is blind or short-sighted, having forgotten his purification from his former sins. (vs 10) Therefore, brethren, be all the more diligent to make certain about His calling and choosing you; for as long as you practice these things, you will never stumble; (vs 11) for in this way the entrance into the eternal kingdom of our Lord and Savior Jesus Christ will be abundantly supplied to you.*

AND

(2 Peter 2:20-22)(vs 20) For if, after they have escaped the defilements of the world by the knowledge of the Lord and Savior Jesus Christ, they are again entangled in them and are overcome, the last state has become worse for them than the first. (vs 21) For it would be better for them not to have known the way of righteousness, than having known it, to turn away from the holy commandment handed on to them. (vs 22) It has happened to them according to the true proverb, "A DOG RETURNS TO ITS OWN VOMIT," and, "A sow, after washing, returns to wallowing in the mire."

The Almighty God of Heaven is our judge! No man is our judge! The words above are overwhelmingly to the point. We can consider these to be a test of our faith! Please seriously read them and answer the question "To Whom Do You Belong?"!!!

12. *(2 Peter 3:17-18)(vs 17) You therefore, beloved, knowing this beforehand, be on your guard so that you are not carried away by the error of unprincipled men and fall from your own steadfastness, (vs 18) but grow in the grace and knowledge of our Lord and Savior Jesus Christ. To Him be the glory, both now and to the day of eternity. Amen.*

We are encouraged to *"grow in the grace and knowledge of our Lord and Savior Jesus Christ"*. This blesses us both NOW and FOREVER, and is a living testimony that **"JESUS our SAVIOR is LORD"**.

13. *(Jude 1:4, 21 & 24-25)(vs 4) For certain persons have crept in unnoticed, those who were long beforehand marked out for this condemnation, ungodly persons who turn the grace of our God into licentiousness and deny our only Master and Lord, Jesus Christ. (vs 21) keep yourselves in the love of God, waiting anxiously for the mercy of our Lord Jesus Christ to eternal life. (vs 24) Now to Him who is able to keep you from stumbling, and to make you stand in the presence of His glory blameless with great joy, (vs 25) to the only God our Savior, through Jesus Christ our Lord, be glory, majesty, dominion and authority, before all time and now and forever. Amen.*

There are wolves who disguise themselves in sheep's clothing. We are to be diligently on guard against this intrusion. We are to keep our eyes, our hearts, our hands and our legs *"in the love of God"* . Our thoughts, our actions, and our praise, are only reserved for **THE LORD JESUS CHRIST**!!!

B. THE "LORD" JESUS CHRIST – ANYTHING ELSE – "MAY IT NEVER BE":

"May It Never Be" is a biblical phrase used quite often, generally in reference to the sins of man. It is especially used to caution Christians to avoid sinning, knowing that the Grace and Mercy of God will forgive.

When "May It Never Be" is used, it adamantly says we are to never be caught up in taking advantage of the situation, by selfishly indulging in the pleasures of the flesh. The Biblical use of "May It Never Be" is definitely a caution to never prostitute our behavior at the expense of our relationship with our **LORD JESUS CHRIST**.

"May It Never Be" is affirmative in the negative sense as something that should never take the place for what is **IN US** (our love and respect for the One who gave His life for us). We should never allow our fleshly desires to surface and degrade His wondrously, unselfish action upon the Cross.

The phrase "May It Never Be" is used fifteen (15) times in the New Testament. Each time it is defined as an absolute denial, God forbid, neither, never, no, none, not and nothing. All of these make it certain that where "May It Never Be" is used, God has condemned the preceding statement(s). Let's look at a few of these examples of God's strict caution as they apply to **JESUS CHRIST** being **LORD**.

1. *(Romans 3:5-6)(vs 5) But if our unrighteousness demonstrates the righteousness of God, what shall we say? The God who inflicts wrath is not unrighteous, is He? (I am speaking in human terms.) (vs 6) May it never be! For otherwise, how will God judge the world?*

This is a difficult verse, but as I see it, the unrighteousness of man can never be transposed to place this unrighteousness upon our righteous God. Always remember to throw my opinion in the trash, and allow the Holy Spirit of God and His Holy Scriptures, to teach you the truth.

2. *(Romans 6:1-7)(vs 1) What shall we say then? Are we to continue in sin so that grace may increase? (vs 2) May it never be! How shall we who died to sin still live in it? (vs 3) Or do you not know that all of us who have been baptized into Christ Jesus have been baptized into His death? (vs 4) Therefore we have been buried with Him through baptism into death, so that as Christ was raised from the dead through the glory of the Father, so we too might walk in newness of life. (vs 5) For if we have become united with Him in the likeness of His death, certainly we shall also be in the likeness of His resurrection, (vs 6) knowing this, that our old self was crucified with Him, in order that our body of sin might be done away with, so that we would no longer be slaves to sin; (vs 7) for he who has died is freed from sin.*

This is probably the most direct command from our **LORD JESUS CHRIST,** that we are not to continue in sin. We have died to our old life and have been raised into a new life (in these verses we find the symbolism of physical immersion by water baptism). Yes, the temptation of the flesh still wars in our physical bodies, and that subject is covered in other Scriptures where God lovingly shows us an **"OUT"** for every temptation encountered ... *(1 Corinthians 10:13) No temptation has overtaken you but such as is common to man; and God is faithful, who will not allow you to be tempted beyond what you are able, but with the temptation will provide the way of escape also, so that you will be able to endure it.* The "truth" of God's Word is that we have been "freed from sin", and "May It Never Be" that we "excuse and accept sin" while never looking for the "way out".

"May It Never Be" that we use the **Grace of God** as an excuse to continue in sin!!!

(Romans 6:12-15)(vs 12) Therefore do not let sin reign in your mortal body so that you obey its lusts, (vs 13) and do not go on presenting the members of your body to sin as instruments of unrighteousness; but present yourselves to God as those alive from the dead, and your members as instruments of righteousness to God. (vs 14) For sin shall not be master over you, for you are not under law but under

grace. (vs 15) What then? Shall we sin because we are not under law but under grace? May it never be!

"May It Never Be" – If you would like to refresh your mind, re-read the definition (it is defined as: an absolute denial, God forbid, neither, never, no, none, not and nothing)!

3. *(1 Corinthians 6:15-17)(vs 15) Do you not know that your bodies are members of Christ? Shall I then take away the members of Christ and make them members of a prostitute? May it never be! (vs 16) Or do you not know that the one who joins himself to a prostitute is one body with her? For He says, "THE TWO SHALL BECOME ONE FLESH." (vs 17) But the one who joins himself to the Lord is one spirit with Him.*

Do you not know that anything we entertain in place of what God had provided for us is wrong? As a believer, it is idolatry for us to join ourselves to any substitute of what God can do for us. Therefore, if we substitute anything in the place of God's provisions, it is considered prostitution. This can pertain to mind altering drinks or substances taking into our bodies, to pastimes that massage our mind and cause us to forget about our SAVIOR, and to any other deliberate indulgences that satisfy the flesh, all to the exclusion of God's Word and provisions.

"May It Never Be" that we should do so!!!

C. AS A BELIEVER OUR THOUGHTS AND ACTIONS ARE GOVERNED BY THE "LORD" JESUS CHRIST:

(Philippians 4:8-9)(vs 8) Finally, brethren, whatever is true, whatever is honorable, whatever is right, whatever is pure, whatever is lovely, whatever is of good repute, if there is any excellence and if anything worthy of praise, dwell on these things. (vs 9) The things you have learned and received and heard and seen in me, practice these things, and the God of peace will be with you.

This passage in Philippians points out to us, as "faith believers", we need to seal our relationship with the **LORD JESUS CHRIST.** It is with honorable, pure thoughts and actions, we are to dwell with our minds and do with our hands, these things as so instructed. If we "Belong To Him", our thoughts as well as our actions (in parallel), will cause the fulfilling of these concepts. I tried for many years to ignore this verse, but finally I am attempting to commit this into my daily lifestyle. I would suggest you do the same, including memorization if possible.

<u>a)</u> **"Whatever is true"** – true is defined as: that not concealed, or truth. "True" in God's standard never fluctuates. His "truth" has never changed and will never change for all of eternity. His entire Holy Word is "Truth".

<u>b)</u> **"Whatever is honorable"** – honorable means: venerable, grave or honest. Is it "honorable" to play with controlling substances that put you in a state of uncontrol? Is it "honorable" to be so close to the worldly things that if you went to court, you couldn't gather enough evidence to prove you were a Christian? In your mind, if something is suspect, it probably is not "honorable".

<u>c)</u> **"Whatever is right"** – right is: equitable, by implication innocent or holy, just or righteous. God's standards are proclaimed throughout the Bible and His standards of "right" and wrong are undeniably clear. It is man who wants to bend and rationalize for the sake of a few moments of fleshly pleasure. If **JESUS** is both **SAVIOR** and <u>**LORD**</u>, we need not worry what is "right" or wrong, because that which flows out from our decisions will be inclined to be what is considered "righteous".

<u>d)</u> **"Whatever is pure"** – defined as: innocent, modest, perfect, chaste and clean. The water in a clear glass may appear to be clean if it is transparent. The life of a person can only be judged to be "pure" by the heart of that person, which may not be so transparent. We certainly don't know the heart, the intentions or the mind of someone else. "Purity" is between you and God. He knows our hearts, and secrets cannot be hidden from Him.

<u>e)</u> **"Whatever is lovely"** – "lovely means: friendly towards, that which is acceptable. "Lovely" stands alone as a beautiful word. It can be used to describe many people, events or situations. If a person is described as "lovely" they are truly acceptable and proper in their care and concern for others. "Lovely" is a delicate word, used only when the person is deserving.

<u>f)</u> **"Whatever is of good repute"** — well-spoken of, that is, reputable, of good report. We are to cleanse our minds and our hearts. Our instructions are to think upon the good things which have been provided to us by God. On the contrary we are to do away with negative thoughts

and those things which can cause hurt and be debilitating, always concentrating on those things which are of "good repute".

g) "Dwell on the things worthy of praise" – laudation, concretely a commendable thing. This is not the "power of positive thinking", but the power of God injected into our lives as we dwell on commendable things. If our thoughts dwell on commendable things, our hands will be involved with the production of commendable deeds.

All of these attitudes and actions will bring Glory to God and will leave a peace in our hearts that is beyond measure and beyond understanding. The **LORD JESUS CHRIST** has planned our path. As a "born again believer" **JESUS** our **SAVIOR** is **"LORD"**!

D. MISCELLANEOUS VERSES REGARDING THE "LORD" JESUS CHRIST:

1. *(Matthew 15:16-20)(vs 16) Jesus said, "Are you still lacking in understanding also? (vs 17) "Do you not understand that everything that goes into the mouth passes into the stomach, and is eliminated? (vs 18) "But the things that proceed out of the mouth come from the heart, and those defile the man. (vs 19) "For out of the heart come evil thoughts, murders, adulteries, fornications, thefts, false witness, slanders. (vs 20) "These are the things which defile the man; but to eat with unwashed hands does not defile the man."*

AND

(1 Corinthians 6:9-11)(vs 9) Or do you not know that the unrighteous will not inherit the kingdom of God? Do not be deceived; neither fornicators, nor idolaters, nor adulterers, nor effeminate, nor homosexuals, (vs 10) nor thieves, nor the covetous, nor drunkards, nor revilers, nor swindlers, will inherit the kingdom of God. (vs 11) Such were some of you; but you were washed, but you were sanctified, but you were justified in the name of the Lord Jesus Christ and in the Spirit of our God.

Man is defiled by his depraved condition from birth. The only way it can change is to be "born again" by the Spirit of God. Until that happens, the **"LORD" JESUS CHRIST** has no authority over us . What is in us will come out, and as detailed above it will be very unpleasant and vile.

The only way to change what is within us is through the **"LORD" JESUS CHRIST** and His completed work upon the Cross. Praise God that **JESUS CHRIST** can be our **SAVIOR,** and therefore be our **"LORD"** (Master and Authority)!!!

2. (Galatians 5:18-25)(vs 18) But if you are led by the Spirit, you are not under the Law. (vs 19) Now the deeds of the flesh are evident, which are: immorality, impurity, sensuality, (vs 20) idolatry, sorcery, enmities, strife, jealousy, outbursts of anger, disputes, dissensions, factions, (vs 21) envying, drunkenness, carousing, and things like these, of which I forewarn you, just as I have forewarned you, that those who practice such things will not inherit the kingdom of God. (vs 22) But the fruit of the Spirit is love, joy, peace, patience, kindness, goodness, faithfulness, (vs 23) gentleness, self-control; against such things there is no law. (vs 24) Now those who belong to Christ Jesus have crucified the flesh with its passions and desires. (vs 25) If we live by the Spirit, let us also walk by the Spirit.

Contrasted above are the deeds of the flesh and the fruits of the Spirit. A self-diagnosis will reveal if we are in "need of a **SAVIOR**", or if we "Belong To Him"!!! If we "Belong To Him" we will practice the things of God and demonstrate that **JESUS CHRIST** is **"LORD"**. If we are in "need of a **SAVIOR**", the deeds of the flesh and their easily identified depravity, will be apparent. The convicting factor was true, is true and will forever be true … "what is in us will come out of us".

E. CONCLUSION TO "LORD" JESUS CHRIST:

Many church members in today's age are looking for ways to rationalize their sins. They want to, let's say "play on both sides of the fence". They want their "fire insurance" for their entry to heaven, but want to exercise the fleshly desires of the world. This is all in association with not wanting to have the feelings of guilt. This requires us to look within and establish if we have been "born again" or are we on the outside looking in. Are we like King Agrippa (?) and almost persuaded as in … *(Acts 26:25-29)(vs 25) But Paul *said, "I am not out of my mind, most excellent Festus, but I utter words of sober truth. (vs 26) "For the king knows about these matters, and I speak to him also with confidence, since I am persuaded that none of these things escape his notice; for this has not been done in a corner. (vs 27) "King Agrippa, do you believe the Prophets? I know that you do." (vs 28) Agrippa replied to Paul, "In a short time you will persuade me to become a Christian." (vs 29) And Paul said, "I would wish to God, that whether in a short or long time, not only you, but also all who hear me this day, might become such as I am, except for these chains."*

Don't come to the door, knock and just look in. Man cannot serve two masters … *(Matthew 6:24) "No one can serve two masters; for either he will hate the one and love the other, or he will be devoted to one and despise the other. You cannot serve God and wealth.* It has been said "JESUS is either LORD of all, or not LORD at all".

AND

God cannot be divided against Himself … *(Matthew 12:24-26) (vs 24) But when the Pharisees heard this, they said, "This man casts out demons only by Beelzebul the ruler of the demons." (vs 25) And knowing their thoughts Jesus said to them, "Any kingdom divided against itself is laid waste; and any city or house divided against itself will not stand. (vs 26) "If Satan casts out Satan, he is divided against himself; how then will his kingdom stand?* … Do you find yourself being "divided" against yourself? Do you hope in JESUS, while still pursuing all fleshly desires?

Find the verses in the Bible that you resist the most and commit these to memory. Quote them to yourself each time you are tempted to do anything your conscience tells you is wrong. Believe me from experience, those verses will start to be meaningful and will have become such a part of you, that your inner self will find it very difficult to disobey what you know is God's Word and His desires for your life.

When you find you have failed Him, your remorse will be like Peter when he sinned and went out of the presence of those he had just cursed and into God's presence, and wept bitterly.

You will find that "what is in you will come out", and if **JESUS** is **"LORD"** it will show. While walking with our **"LORD"**, should we find anything in our lifestyle contrary to His Word, it should cause remorse. This should be followed by repentance, thus activating forgiveness by God, and restoration of our relationship with Him.

There is no question in my mind that the Bible teaches, **JESUS** is **"LORD",** Supreme in authority, Controller and Master. If we "Belong To Him", He is our **"LORD"**. **"TO WHOM DO YOU BELONG"?**

SPECIAL NOTE:

I know many of you may have a special verse or verses regarding this Chapter's subject matter. This special verse or these verses may not have been mentioned due to my ignorance or because of brevity. I apologize for either of these reasons. Please feel free to write any special verse or verses in the space below. This will add your personal touch, and will serve to call to each person's mind their individual "experience of trust", in God's Holy Word.

For to each of us "Who belong To Him", His Holy Word can be truly recognized and relied upon as our **"Owner's Manual"**!!!

_____

_____

_____

_____

_____

_____

_____

_____

CHAPTER 9

PRAYER

INTRODUCTORY VERSE:

(Romans 1:9-10)(vs 9) For God, whom I serve in my spirit in the preaching of the gospel of His Son, is my witness as to how unceasingly I make mention of you, (vs 10) always in my prayers making request, if perhaps now at last by the will of God I may succeed in coming to you.

The Apostle Paul knows "To Whom He Belongs" for he has again stated, that it is God "Whom he Serves". One thing that is found in this desire to serve is his teaching about Prayer. Paul is so intense in his confession of prayer and concern for the Gentiles, he makes the point that his prayers are unceasing and without intermission. Paul "Belongs To Him" and his prayers are always for the Gospel to reach "hearing" ears. Prayer to Paul was a PRIORITY, let us consider his example as we read this Chapter.

INTRODUCTION:

Prayer has been written on so many times I tend to think we have become desensitized. My prayer life has never been what it should have been, and I confess there are many who know so very much more about the subject than I do. This should not keep us from exploring the scriptures from a fresh start and see firsthand what God's Word says about this most important relationship with the One to "Whom We Belong"!!! We will look at this subject from a fresh, unbiased position, and without a predetermined point of view. This will allow God to work His miracles of divine revelation to our souls, as we consider His Word regarding Prayer. As always you will find this subject has not been exhausted from what the Bible contains, but as always you will find what is contained herein is God's Holy Word and therefore cannot be refuted or ignored. You will have a basis to build upon and strengthen yourself in the subject of your personal prayer life. Let us look with joy towards what God has in store for us. Our "Owner's Manual", as found in the Holy Scriptures, has all the ingredients, the directions for life, the design of our being, and all things necessary to understand our relationship with the Most Holy God. Prayer is one part of this relationship.

A. PRAYER AND ITS IMPORTANCE AS TO WHOM IT IS DIRECTED:

1. Prayers are to be made to God Almighty – no one else:

Prayer is only as good as the one to whom it is directed. If we pray to some wooden, earthen or metallic god, we can expect no response and our time is wasted. If we pray to the Only Living God, the Almighty God of the Universe, the One who has provided for our salvation, we have substantial hope of being heard. The scriptures bear out that our prayers need to be in accordance to His will and not selfishly minded. Let's look at in whose name we are to pray.

a) *(Matthew 6:9-10)(vs 9) "Pray, then, in this way: 'Our Father who is in heaven, Hallowed be Your name. (vs 10) 'Your kingdom come. Your will be done, On earth as it is in heaven.*

To pray, means to supplicate or to worship God, to Pray to Him! We are instructed by Jesus' very words to call upon … *'Our Father who is in heaven* … . Our prayers, our requests, our worship needs go only to the Father of the Universe. There is no other name or deity for us to call upon. It is clear we are to call upon the Lord our God only, and it is equally clear we are to reverence His Holy name … *Hallowed be Your name*, as we begin our prayers. This stage is set in concrete, we are to reverentially call upon the Only True God, and while calling upon His presence in our lives, we are to also recognize His will and His plans, not our will and our plans.

Joined with, to whom we pray to, is the recognition of His Kingdom, His Will and His Plans, all surrounding the context of our prayer life. We are to call upon Him only for all the events here on earth to be as if they were operating in heaven. We are to "get in on what God is doing rather start something and then try to get God in on what we are doing". As we are found bowing before God, there is no other name under heaven with the authority to command our knees to bow and our hearts to confess, other than the "Most High God", our "God Almighty".

b) *(Acts 4:10-12)(vs 10) let it be known to all of you and to all the people of Israel, that by the name of Jesus Christ the Nazarene, whom you crucified, whom God raised from the dead—by this name this man stands here before you in good health. (vs 11) "He is the STONE WHICH WAS REJECTED by you, THE BUILDERS, but WHICH BECAME THE CHIEF CORNER stone. (vs 12) "And there is salvation in no one else; for there is no other name under heaven that has been given among men by which we must be saved."*

The most important and significant keys to our eternal being are emphatically stated here. We are not to call upon (pray to) any other than the Living Lord Jesus Christ and God the Father **(for they are ONE)**, for our salvation!!!

c) *(Psalms 4:1) A Psalm of David. Answer me when I call, O God of my righteousness! You have relieved me in my distress; Be gracious to me and hear my prayer.*

When we pray we are to call upon the God of our righteousness. The God of our righteousness, is the One who has provided His Son, Jesus Christ as the propitiation for our sins and the One to "Whom We Belong" and the One in which there is no other name under heaven that establishes our eternal salvation.

d) *(Psalms 5:1-2)(vs 1) A Psalm of David. Give ear to my words, O LORD, Consider my groaning. (vs 2) Heed the sound of my cry for help, my King and my God, For to You I pray.*

Our prayers, our words, our groaning are to be to none other than our ... **LORD** ... (in Hebrew this is the Jewish national name of God, or Jehovah, the Lord). Our prayers and our ... **cry for help** ... are only to be to <u>our King</u> and <u>our God</u>, ... **For to You I pray**.

e) *(Psalms 65:1-2)(vs 1) There will be silence before You, and praise in Zion, O God, And to You the vow will be performed. (vs 2) O You who hear prayer, To You all men come.*

A *"vow"* as used above, and described in the original Hebrew, is a "concretely promise to God". Our prayers are to be to none other than to the Almighty God of the Holy Bible. There will be "silence" and "reverence" when we come and bow before The Holy God of Heaven.

f) *(Psalms 69:13) But as for me, my prayer is to You, O LORD, at an acceptable time; O God, in the greatness of Your lovingkindness, Answer me with Your saving truth.*

Our prayers are to be to God alone and we are to pray unselfishly, with the expectation that His loving kindness will answer us with ... *"Your saving truth"* ... .

It must be noted that there are multiple verses like the above, that clearly state our prayers are to be to the "Most High God" of the Bible. They will all be found to reinforce the above FACTS!!!

2. Warnings about praying to idols, as opposed to praying to God Almighty:

The following are brief side notes of warning for those who have or may try to call upon their own man-made gods. I may have called these side notes, but the warnings are severe. Take heed, for there is both a **WARNING AND A CALL TO REPENTANCE** in the following Old Testament Verses.

a) *(Isaiah 45:20-22)(vs 20) "Gather yourselves and come; Draw near together, you fugitives of the nations; They have no knowledge, Who carry about their wooden idol And pray to a god who cannot save. (vs 21) "Declare and set forth your case; Indeed, let them consult together. Who has announced this from of old? Who has long since declared it? Is it not I, the LORD? And there is no other God besides Me, A righteous God and a Savior; There is none except Me. (vs 22) "Turn to Me and be saved, all the ends of the earth; For I am God, and there is no other.*

What a powerful passage to proclaim a warning and salvation in only three verses. The Holy Word of God is truly amazing and beyond our imagination or comprehension.

b) *(Deuteronomy 4:15-19)(vs 15) "So watch yourselves carefully, since you did not see any form on the day the LORD spoke to you at Horeb from the midst of the fire, (vs 16) so that you do not act corruptly and make a graven*

image for yourselves in the form of any figure, the likeness of male or female, (vs 17) the likeness of any animal that is on the earth, the likeness of any winged bird that flies in the sky, (vs 18) the likeness of anything that creeps on the ground, the likeness of any fish that is in the water below the earth. (vs 19) "And beware not to lift up your eyes to heaven and see the sun and the moon and the stars, all the host of heaven, and be drawn away and worship them and serve them, those which the LORD your God has allotted to all the peoples under the whole heaven.

c) *(Deuteronomy 29:10-20)(vs 10) "You stand today, all of you, before the LORD your God: your chiefs, your tribes, your elders and your officers, even all the men of Israel, (vs 11) your little ones, your wives, and the alien who is within your camps, from the one who chops your wood to the one who draws your water, (vs 12) that you may enter into the covenant with the LORD your God, and into His oath which the LORD your God is making with you today, (vs 13) in order that He may establish you today as His people and that He may be your God, just as He spoke to you and as He swore to your fathers, to Abraham, Isaac, and Jacob. (vs 14) "Now not with you alone am I making this covenant and this oath, (vs 15) but both with those who stand here with us today in the presence of the LORD our God and with those who are not with us here today (vs 16) (for you know how we lived in the land of Egypt, and how we came through the midst of the nations through which you passed; (vs 17) moreover, you have seen their abominations and their idols of wood, stone, silver, and gold, which they had with them); (vs 18) so that there will not be among you a man or woman, or family or tribe, whose heart turns away today from the LORD our God, to go and serve the gods of those nations; that there will not be among you a root bearing poisonous fruit and wormwood. (vs 19) "It shall be when he hears the words of this curse, that he will boast, saying, 'I have peace though I walk in the stubbornness of my heart in order to destroy the watered land with the dry.' (vs 20) "The LORD*

*shall never be willing to forgive him, but rather the anger of
the LORD and His jealousy will burn against that man, and
every curse which is written in this book will rest on him,
and the LORD will blot out his name from under heaven.*

Our God is a jealous God and will not tolerate our calling upon the
name of any other god or have us to bow before any graven (an idol or
carved) images. You and I cannot imagine the wrath that will be played
out against those who choose to worship any other. Our Prayers, our
devotion, our very being, are to be accountable to our Almighty Father,
our Almighty Loving God, and to Him alone. Hopefully this is the one
"To Whom You Belong"!!!

B. OUR PRAYERS—ARE THEY HEARD OR UNHEARD AND WHY?:

1. Our Prayers are heard for their pure or righteous reasons:

As we Pray we should be motivated by God's plan and purpose, and
not our selfish gain.

a) *(Psalms 17:1)* A Prayer of David. *Hear a just cause, O
LORD, give heed to my cry; Give ear to my prayer, which is
not from deceitful lips.*

David, of Old Testament fame, declares we are to call upon the Lord
with just causes and non-deceitful lips. We are to demonstrate our intentions to be for the advancement of God's kingdom. With these criteria in
the foremost of our minds, we can expect God to **hear** our Prayers and
call upon Him with confidence.

b) *(Psalms 20:6-7)(vs 6) Now I know that the LORD saves
His anointed; He will answer him from His holy heaven With
the saving strength of His right hand. (vs 7) Some boast in
chariots and some in horses, But we will boast in the name
of the LORD, our God.*

God answers not from the strength of your possessions or from the
strength of your position in life, but from and because of His own power
and might. Our only hope or boast of **being heard** is in His Holy name.

c) *(Psalms 21:1-2)(vs 1)* A Psalm of David. *O LORD, in
Your strength the king will be glad, And in Your salvation
how greatly he will rejoice! (vs 2) You have given him his*

heart's desire, And You have not withheld the request of his lips. Selah.

Our heart's desires and the requests of our lips **have been granted (heard)**, it is God's way and His promise to His children. King David experienced this and wrote this truth, which is to be relied upon in this present world, to give us comfort in all things.

d) *(Proverbs 15:8) The sacrifice of the wicked is an abomination to the LORD, But the prayer of the upright is His delight.*

The Prayer of the upright or righteous is delightful **(heard)** in the eyes of our God.

e) *(John 11:21-23 & 11:40-43)(vs 21) Martha then said to Jesus, "Lord, if You had been here, my brother would not have died. (vs 22) "Even now I know that whatever You ask of God, God will give You." (vs 23) Jesus *said to her, "Your brother will rise again." (vs 40) Jesus *said to her, "Did I not say to you that if you believe, you will see the glory of God?" (vs 41) So they removed the stone. Then Jesus raised His eyes, and said, "Father, I thank You that You have heard Me. (vs 42) "I knew that You always hear Me; but because of the people standing around I said it, so that they may believe that You sent Me." (vs 43) When He had said these things, He cried out with a loud voice, "Lazarus, come forth."*

I believe these passages to be some of the most dramatic and far-reaching answer to prayer in the Bible. Jesus raised Lazarus from the grave after he had been there several days (he was reportedly in a decomposing state). Mary, Lazarus' sister, so trusted Jesus that she stated ... ***whatever You ask of God, God will give You*** ... . Jesus was true to His word then and is still today. Jesus called Lazarus froth from his grave. It has been said by many people through the ages that if Jesus had not called Lazarus specifically that all graves would have been emptied by His statement of ... ***come forth*** ... . God answers unselfish prayers and He demonstrated here His victory over all things, including death. No prayer is too small and no prayer is too big for our Savior and Lord. I trust that you "Belong To The One Who Can Answer All Prayers".

f) *(John 15:5-7)(vs 5) "I am the vine, you are the branches; he who abides in Me and I in him, he bears much fruit, for apart from Me you can do nothing. (vs 6) "If anyone does not abide in Me, he is thrown away as a branch and dries up; and they gather them, and cast them into the fire and they are burned. (vs 7) "If you abide in Me, and My words abide in you, ask whatever you wish, and it will be done for you.*

Whatever we wish will be done for us as we "abide in Him and as His words abide in us".

g) *(Romans 8:26-27)(vs 26) In the same way the Spirit also helps our weakness; for we do not know how to pray as we should, but the Spirit Himself intercedes for us with groanings too deep for words; (vs 27) and He who searches the hearts knows what the mind of the Spirit is, because He intercedes for the saints according to the will of God.*

The Holy Spirit is literally available to help us to Pray. He will intercede for us in order to perfect the will of God in our lives. These are Prayers that **are heard**.

h) *(James 5:13-18)(vs 13) Is anyone among you suffering? Then he must pray. Is anyone cheerful? He is to sing praises. (vs 14) Is anyone among you sick? Then he must call for the elders of the church and they are to pray over him, anointing him with oil in the name of the Lord; (vs 15) and the prayer offered in faith will restore the one who is sick, and the Lord will raise him up, and if he has committed sins, they will be forgiven him. (vs 16) Therefore, confess your sins to one another, and pray for one another so that you may be healed. The effective prayer of a righteous man can accomplish much. (vs 17) Elijah was a man with a nature like ours, and he prayed earnestly that it would not rain, and it did not rain on the earth for three years and six months. (vs 18) Then he prayed again, and the sky poured rain and the earth produced its fruit.*

I know these verses may seem to be voluminous, but they are so real, alive and pertinent to our spiritual vitality and our earthly lives that they can't be ignored. We all get sick and we all sin. God has an answer to both of our frailties. He loves us so much He has provided for these human weaknesses and wants us to call upon Him in prayer in order to demonstrate **His timely answers in these critical times of need**! If you are sick and if you have sinned, God has healing and forgiveness available. Please note that sickness and sinning are not necessarily related as James clearly and strategically places the word *"if"* in *verse 15*, to clearly delineate they may or may not be related.

James ends his statements of truths with the real life example from the Old Testament, and it is one of the most God fearing, dramatically penned verses of the Bible. *(vs 17) Elijah was a man with a nature like ours,* ... yet he controlled the rain for three and one-half years. All I can say is to repeat a part of *(vs 16) The effective prayer of a righteous man can accomplish much.* Our righteousness is obviously not found in our unredeemed human nature, but is found in the imputed righteousness of Jesus Christ, which has been made available to us because of His work on the Cross. If a man with a nature like ours can control the rain for three and one-half years, who knows what we can accomplish as we thank God daily, for the One "To Whom We Belong"!!!

   i) *(1 Peter 3:12) "FOR THE EYES OF THE LORD ARE TOWARD THE RIGHTEOUS, AND HIS EARS ATTEND TO THEIR PRAYER, BUT THE FACE OF THE LORD IS AGAINST THOSE WHO DO EVIL."*

The Prayers of a righteous man are **heard**! A righteous man is one who has received the Grace of salvation through Jesus Christ and therefore His imputed righteousness. All thanks and all glory is to the One to "Whom We Belong"!!!

   j) *(1 John 5:14-15)(vs 14) This is the confidence which we have before Him, that, if we ask anything according to His will, He hears us.*

   (vs 15) And if we know that He hears us in whatever we ask, we know that we have the requests which we have asked from Him.

He grants our petitions if He hears us, He hears us if we ask in accordance with His will. His will is defined in the Greek as His desire or pleasure. Therefore as one who abides in the Lord and delights in the Lord God, we are going to seek to pray for His desires and His good pleasure. This unselfish prayer is quite clearly for God's will to be done and we can trust that God will lay on our minds and hearts these supernatural thoughts that become prayers ... *(Matthew 6:10) 'Your kingdom come. Your will be done, On earth as it is in heaven. ... .*

2. Our Prayers are unheard for their selfish and temporal reasons:

When our prayers are motivated for selfish and temporary reasons, with self-gratifying purposes, we can count on them being **unheard** by the only One who can answer prayers and that is the God of the Universe.

a) *(Isaiah 59:1-2)(vs 1) Behold, the LORD'S hand is not so short That it cannot save; Nor is His ear so dull That it cannot hear. (vs 2) But your iniquities have made a separation between you and your God, And your sins have hidden His face from you so that He does not hear.*

You need not be a genius to figure this out. Your prayers are not heard if there is sin in your life, therefore causing a separation between you and God. Go and confess your sins and then He will hear and answer you.

b) One well known verse regarding sin, speaks specifically of the sin of unforgiveness. This sin, although not exclusively this sin, can and will cause our Prayers to remain **unheard**. *(Mark 11:25-26)(vs 25) "Whenever you stand praying, forgive, if you have anything against anyone, so that your Father who is in heaven will also forgive you your transgressions. (vs 26) ["But if you do not forgive, neither will your Father who is in heaven forgive your transgressions."]*

Another passage that ties into the above verses and makes, the sin of not forgiving our brothers absolutely undeniable, is ... *(Matthew 18:21-22)(vs 21) Then Peter came and said to Him, "Lord, how often shall my brother sin against me and I forgive him? Up to seven times?" (vs 22) Jesus *said to him, "I do not say to you, up to seven times, but up to seventy times seven.*

Jesus followed this statement up with a parable telling of a master that forgave his slave a massive amount of debt and sent the slave out debt free. This slave then went out and threw a fellow debtor into prison for a small amount owed to him, the one who had just been forgiven millions. Upon hearing of this the master reconsidered the millions owed and it is reported as follows ... *(Matthew 18:34-35)(vs 34)*

"And his lord, moved with anger, handed him over to the torturers until he should repay all that was owed him. (vs 35) "My heavenly Father will also do the same to you, if each of you does not forgive his brother from your heart." We are to forgive our brothers from our heart, regardless of the repercussions, and certainly if we are to have any hope of having our **Prayers heard**.

c) *(James 4:2-partial & 3)(vs 2-partial) You do not have because you do not ask. (vs 3) You ask and do not receive, because you ask with wrong motives, so that you may spend it on your pleasures.*

Wrong motives and selfish reasons kill the deal every time. God is not our genie and cannot be put in box. We cannot do certain things and because of our actions then require God to perform in a certain way. This is related to selfish motives as well as trying to manipulate God. Our prayers will remain **unheard** as long as our motives are wrong. We must **abide** and **delight** in Him, only then will our thoughts be in accordance with His will.

I believe the following passages are complimentary, descriptive and appropriate to expound upon the theme at hand. *(James 3:16-18)(vs 16) For where jealousy and selfish ambition exist, there is disorder and every evil thing. (vs 17) But the wisdom from above is first pure, then peaceable, gentle, reasonable, full of mercy and good fruits, unwavering, without hypocrisy. (vs 18) And the seed whose fruit is righteousness is sown in peace by those who make peace.*

If our prayers are guided by the above passages we will be found to be **abiding** and **delighting** in our Lord and Savior, Jesus Christ.

d) *(1 Peter 3:7) You husbands in the same way, live with your wives in an understanding way, as with someone weaker, since she is a woman; and show her honor as a fellow heir of the grace of life, so that your prayers will not be hindered.*

All of us have probably been ignorant about the fact that a wrong attitude and treatment of our wives can cause our Prayers to go unattended (**unheard**). Our wives are fellow heirs of the eternal salvation granted by God through grace. As we respect that we can count on our Prayers being **heard**.

C. DO'S AND DON'TS IN PRAYING:

1. The scriptural DO'S regarding PRAYER:
a) *(1 Chronicles 5:19-21)(vs 19) They made war against the Hagrites, Jetur, Naphish and Nodab. (vs 20) They were helped against them, and the Hagrites and all who were with them were given into their hand; for they cried out to God in the battle, and He answered their prayers because they trusted in Him. (vs 21) They took away their cattle: their 50,000 camels, 250,000 sheep, 2,000 donkeys; and 100,000 men.*

The Do's were the Israelites crying out to God in Prayer. The magnificent answer was due to their trusting in Him. I feel certain the Israelites didn't ask for the quantity of spoil they were given. I believe it was God granting this abundant answer to their prayers, by granting the overwhelming spoil, due to their trusting in Him.

b) *(Matthew 5:43-45)(vs 43) "You have heard that it was said, 'YOU SHALL LOVE YOUR NEIGHBOR and hate your enemy.' (vs 44) "But I say to you, love your enemies and pray for those who persecute you, (vs 45) so that you may be sons of your Father who is in heaven; for He causes His sun to rise on the evil and the good, and sends rain on the righteous and the unrighteous.*

Our prayers for those who persecute us are a sign that we respect God way more than our own agenda. It is our commitment to getting in on His plan rather than carrying out our own. When we pray for our enemies, it is submission at its fullest. We are demonstrating our trust in Him, even when we don't seem to understand His purposes.

c) *(Matthew 6:5-7)(vs 5) "When you pray, you are not to be like the hypocrites; for they love to stand and pray in the synagogues and on the street corners so that they may be seen by men. Truly I say to you, they have their reward in full. (vs 6) "But you, when you pray, go into your inner room, close your door and pray to your Father who is in secret, and your Father who sees what is done in secret will reward you. (vs 7) "And when you are praying, do not use meaningless repetition as the Gentiles do, for they suppose that they will be heard for their many words.*

There are both **Do's** and **Don'ts** in these scripture verses. Each point made is powerful and is to be listened to and acted upon.

d) *(Matthew 21:21-22)(vs 21) And Jesus answered and said to them, "Truly I say to you, if you have faith and do not doubt, you will not only do what was done to the fig tree, but even if you say to this mountain, 'Be taken up and cast into the sea,' it will happen. (vs 22) "And all things you ask in prayer, believing, you will receive."*

The key **Do** here is in the word believing. It is defined in the Greek as to entrust (especially one's spiritual wellbeing to Christ), to commit (to trust) and put in trust with. Our commitment to our Heavenly father, when we pray, is to place His causes first in our thoughts and in our heart. Our spiritual wellbeing in Christ is number one in our relationship with the God of our Salvation and should be reflected in all of our prayers.

e) *(Philippians 4:6-7)(vs 6) Be anxious for nothing, but in everything by prayer and supplication with thanksgiving let your requests be made known to God. (vs 7) And the peace of God, which surpasses all comprehension, will guard your hearts and your minds in Christ Jesus.*

The key here is to Pray about everything. We are to bring all things before God, and **Do** so with thanksgiving, all the time maintaining an attitude of non-anxiousness, without fear. The reward is beyond our comprehension, with a peace that can only be found through our Christ Jesus. This kind of Praying will eliminate the need for artificial stimulants, alcohol and drugs that are sometimes used to excite or calm our nerves. You can always look at it like this, it will save you money.

2. The scriptural DON'TS regarding PRAYER:

a) *(Proverbs 21:13) He who shuts his ear to the cry of the poor Will also cry himself and not be answered.*

We will see many needs throughout our lifetime. Some of these needs are placed before us by God in order to give us an opportunity to respond and reflect the love that God has shown to us and placed within us. As we Pray, **DON'T** expect an answer from God if our heart is such that we have refused to see and respond to the true needs that He has brought into our paths.

b) *(Isaiah 1:15) "So when you spread out your hands in prayer, I will hide My eyes from you; Yes, even though you multiply prayers, I will not listen. Your hands are covered with blood.*

This verse was a warning to the people of the time as they were sacrificing animals to God, while their hearts were full of wickedness. God is not fooled by our actions, but He knows our heart. We must first repent with the heart or our Prayers will be an abomination to our Loving God.

c) *(Lamentations 3:42-47 & 55-58)(vs 42) We have transgressed and rebelled, You have not pardoned. (vs 43) You have covered Yourself with anger And pursued us; You have slain and have not spared. (vs 44) You have covered Yourself with a cloud So that no prayer can pass through. (vs 45) You have made us mere offscouring and refuse In the midst of the peoples. (vs 46) All our enemies have opened their mouths against us. (vs 47) Panic and pitfall have befallen us, Devastation and destruction; (vs 55) I called on Your name, O LORD, Out of the lowest pit. (vs 56) You have heard my voice, "Do not hide Your ear from my prayer for relief, From my cry for help." (vs 57) You drew near when I called on You; You said, "Do not fear!" (vs 58) O Lord, You have pleaded my soul's cause; You have redeemed my life.*

This was a Lamentation from the Children of Israel because they had been in sin. We find in the last four verses their confession was answered, and they were vindicated in this time of severe trial. These words are to be trusted today, as if they were written by the very hand of God, and handed to us individually.

d) *(Matthew 23:14) ["Woe to you, scribes and Pharisees, hypocrites, because you devour widows' houses, and for a pretense you make long prayers; therefore you will receive greater condemnation.]*

If you fit the above category you will not only be not heard, but your condemnation will be magnified.

e) *(Luke 18:10-14)(vs 10) "Two men went up into the temple to pray, one a Pharisee and the other a tax collector. (vs 11) "The Pharisee stood and was praying this to himself: 'God, I thank You that I am not like other people: swindlers, unjust, adulterers, or even like this tax collector. (vs 12) 'I fast twice a week; I pay tithes of all that I get.' (vs 13) "But the tax collector, standing some distance away, was even unwilling to lift up his eyes to heaven, but was beating his breast, saying, 'God, be merciful to me, the sinner!' (vs 14) "I tell you, this man went to his house justified rather than the other; for everyone who exalts himself will be humbled, but he who humbles himself will be exalted."*

Jesus has set the standard for Praying. His very words above are our guide! These passages have both a **DON'T** and a **DO**, and we stand to learn from each.

f) *(1 Corinthians 14:14-19)(vs 14) For if I pray in a tongue, my spirit prays, but my mind is unfruitful. (vs 15) What is the outcome then? I will pray with the spirit and I will pray with the mind also; I will sing with the spirit and I will sing with the mind also. (vs 16) Otherwise if you bless in the spirit only, how will the one who fills the place of the ungifted say the "Amen" at your giving of thanks, since he does not know what you are saying? (vs 17) For you are giving thanks well enough, but the other person is not edified. (vs 18) I thank God, I speak in tongues more than you all; (vs19) however, in the church I desire to speak five words with my mind so that I may instruct others also, rather than ten thousand words in a tongue.*

This is not intended to speak for or against "speaking in tongues". It is part of God's word as penned by the Apostle Paul to instruct us in the value of speaking in a language that people can understand. He goes so far as to compare the value by using the number five (5) in comparison to the number ten thousand (10,000). Five (5) words of intelligible instruction of Godly principles, or as a Prayer to our Heavenly Father, are more valuable than ten thousand (10,000) words that are unintelligible. This can be magnified by using a percentage ratio. The percentage ratio of 5 to 10,000 is 5% of 1% or 5/10,000. Another way to put this in perspective is to try to put this in a monetary value. If this were in dollars, Paul would rather have $5 in U. S. currency than $10,000 in monopoly money. Maybe this is a poor example, but Paul is adamant about the importance of Praying or speaking God's instruction in an intelligible language. If God, through Paul, was willing to spend six verses of the Holy Bible to cover this topic, we should be willing to meditate upon and digest His efforts.

D. EXAPMPLES OF PRAYER BY CATEGORY:

1. PRAYERS OF PETITION AND SUPPLICATION:
a) *(Exodus 33:13)* *"Now therefore, I pray You, if I have found favor in Your sight, let me know Your ways that I may know You, so that I may find favor in Your sight. Consider too, that this nation is Your people." (Exodus 34:9) He said, "If now I have found favor in Your sight, O Lord, I pray, let the Lord go along in our midst, even though the people are so obstinate, and pardon our iniquity and our sin, and take us as Your own possession."*

Moses is praying earnestly for the people of Israel. They needed someone to petition God for the return of His favor. God may call any one of us, at any time, into this position of "petitioning" Him for our loved ones, our friends, our fellow man.

b) *(Psalms 142:1-2 & 7)(vs 1) Maskil of David, when he was in the cave. A Prayer. I cry aloud with my voice to the LORD; I make supplication with my voice to the LORD. (vs 2) I pour out my complaint before Him; I declare my trouble before Him. (vs 7) "Bring my soul out of prison, So that I may give thanks to Your name; The righteous will surround me, For You will deal bountifully with me." (Psalms 143:1 & 8-10)(vs 1) A Psalm of David. Hear my prayer, O LORD, Give ear to my supplications! Answer me in Your faithfulness, in Your righteousness! (vs 8) Let me hear Your lovingkindness in the morning; For I trust in You; Teach me the way in which I should walk; For to You I lift up my soul. (vs 9) Deliver me, O LORD, from my enemies; I take refuge in You. (vs 10) Teach me to do Your will, For You are my God; Let Your good Spirit lead me on level ground.*

David has been appointed King, yet he runs for his life and hides in a dark and damp cave. David Prays a prayer of petition rather than taking into his own hands the opportunity to kill Saul. David recognizes it is God's hand that will take care of Saul, and that it is God alone who can establish the timing of his rule. We should often listen to God about His timing of things instead of trying to hurry things along. Our Prayer of petition and supplication should be "not my will, but thine be done".

c) *(Mark 11:22-24)(vs 22) And Jesus *answered saying to them, "Have faith in God. (vs 23) "Truly I say to you, whoever says to this mountain, 'Be taken up and cast into the sea,' and does not doubt in his heart, but believes that what he says is going to happen, it will be granted him. (vs 24) "Therefore I say to you, all things for which you pray and ask, believe that you have received them, and they will be granted you.*

I have not personally seen a mountain removed to the sea. I don't know anyone who has witnessed this type of miracle. What I do know is God's Word says it, and if it is ever needed in our lives, it will happen. Pray for God's will, Pray with faith, and Pray believing that you have received your request. I recently experienced God's sparing of my life in a time of grave sickness, and I am confident the God of our salvation does not have His hands tied behind His back. The One to "Whom We Belong" is **omnipotent**!!!

d) *(Ephesians 1:18-21)(vs 18) I pray that the eyes of your heart may be enlightened, so that you will know what is the hope of His calling, what are the riches of the glory of His inheritance in the saints, (vs 19) and what is the surpassing greatness of His power toward us who believe. These are in accordance with the working of the strength of His might (vs 20) which He brought about in Christ, when He raised Him from the dead and seated Him at His right hand in the heavenly places, (vs 21) far above all rule and authority and power and dominion, and every name that is named, not only in this age but also in the one to come.*

The Apostle Paul petitioned God for the Ephesians. His petition was to the only Living Heavenly Father, the only One who can answer Prayer. Paul Prays that ... *"your heart may be enlightened"*, that we will know ... *"the riches of the glory of His inheritance in the saints"*, and that we may know ... *"the surpassing greatness of His power toward us who believe"*. If "We Belong To Him" we have riches and greatness untold. Our inheritance is immeasurable! Our Prayers are answered by the incomparable God of the Universe! We are to call upon Him with our supplications and pleas, for His will to be done in our lives. Praise God for what He has done through the Cross and the raising of Jesus Christ from the grave! Our petitions will all be accomplished in accordance with His will and for the benefit of mankind.

e) *(Ephesians 6:18-20)(vs 18) With all prayer and petition pray at all times in the Spirit, and with this in view, be on the alert with all perseverance and petition for all the saints, (vs 19) and pray on my behalf, that utterance may be given to me in the opening of my mouth, to make known with boldness the mystery of the gospel, (vs 20) for which I am an ambassador in chains; that in proclaiming it I may speak boldly, as I ought to speak.*

These verses strongly emphasize the importance of Prayer and the high regard with which we should engage our requests. What may seem to be simple requests should be given over to God with the highest regard for His attention. Nothing is too small or too big for Him to consider.

f) *(1 Timothy 2:1-2)(vs 1) First of all, then, I urge that entreaties and prayers, petitions and thanksgivings, be made on behalf of all men, (vs 2) for kings and all who are in authority, so that we may lead a tranquil and quiet life in all godliness and dignity.*

These Prayers of petition for all men, including our authorities, can have added benefits of our leading a tranquil life.

2. PRAYERS OF THANKFULNESS:

a) *(Psalms 69:30-31)(vs 30) I will praise the name of God with song And magnify Him with thanksgiving. (vs 31) And it will please the LORD better than an ox Or a young bull with horns and hoofs.*

(Psalms 95:1-2)(vs 1) O come, let us sing for joy to the LORD, Let us shout joyfully to the rock of our salvation. (vs 2) Let us come before His presence with thanksgiving, Let us shout joyfully to Him with psalms.

(Psalms 100:4) Enter His gates with thanksgiving And His courts with praise. Give thanks to Him, bless His name.

Our words of thanksgiving to God are more pleasing than any animal sacrifices. God appreciates and is tremendously pleased with these verbalizations from our heart.

b) *(Matthew 15:36-37)(vs 36) and He took the seven loaves and the fish; and giving thanks, He broke them and started giving them to the disciples, and the disciples gave them to the people. (vs 37) And they all ate and were satisfied, and they picked up what was left over of the broken pieces, seven large baskets full.*

Here we find an excellent example of Jesus performing a miracle while Praying and giving thanks. This miracle abundantly met the needs of four thousand men plus women and children. As an additional bonus God shows us the food leftover filled a perfect number of seven baskets. God doesn't do anything half-way.

c) *(Matthew 26:26-28))(vs 26) While they were eating, Jesus took some bread, and after a blessing, He broke it and gave it to the disciples, and said, "Take, eat; this is My body." (vs 27) And when He had taken a cup and given thanks, He gave it to them, saying, "Drink from it, all of you; (vs 28) for this is My blood of the covenant, which is poured out for many for forgiveness of sins.*

We should all recognize these verses regarding Jesus with His disciples at the last supper. One of the significant things to point out here is Jesus was true to His Word and gave thanks while Praying with those He so loved.

d) *(Luke 17:15-16)(vs 15) Now one of them, when he saw that he had been healed, turned back, glorifying God with a loud voice, (vs 16) and he fell on his face at His feet, giving thanks to Him. And he was a Samaritan.*

I would consider ... ***glorifying God with a loud voice*** ... to be a form of Praying. This man was so thankful to be healed, he fell at Jesus' feet and praised Him with thanksgiving.

e) *(Philippians 4:6) Be anxious for nothing, but in everything by prayer and supplication with thanksgiving let your requests be made known to God.*

(Colossians 4:2) Devote yourselves to prayer, keeping alert in it with an attitude of thanksgiving;

I would consider these verses to include commands which are directly from God. We are commanded to be thankful in our Prayers. As we study and meditate upon His Word (as found throughout His "Owner's Manual"), God will use these and all passages to properly tune our hearts.

3. PRAYERS OF REPENTANCE LEADING TO FORGIVENESS:

a) *(Daniel 9:3-5)(vs 3) So I gave my attention to the Lord God to seek Him by prayer and supplications, with fasting, sackcloth and ashes. (vs 4) I prayed to the LORD my God and confessed and said, "Alas, O Lord, the great and awesome God, who keeps His covenant and lovingkindness for those who love Him and keep His commandments, (vs 5) we have sinned, committed iniquity, acted wickedly and rebelled, even turning aside from Your commandments and ordinances.*

(Daniel 9:9) "To the Lord our God belong compassion and forgiveness, for we have rebelled against Him;

(Daniel 9:19) "O Lord, hear! O Lord, forgive! O Lord, listen and take action! For Your own sake, O my God, do not delay, because Your city and Your people are called by Your name."

God knows our hearts so our Prayers need to be found to be truthful. These Old Testament passages demonstrate how we are to confess, repent and expect our Lord's forgiveness in these times of need.

b) *(Acts 8:22-23)(vs 22) "Therefore repent of this wickedness of yours, and pray the Lord that, if possible, the intention of your heart may be forgiven you. (vs 23) "For I see that you are in the gall of bitterness and in the bondage of iniquity."*

We are to Pray with a repentant heart and hope for God's forgiveness. This forgiveness is assured as we will see in the next passage.

c) *(1 John 1:9) If we confess our sins, He is faithful and righteous to forgive us our sins and to cleanse us from all unrighteousness.*

This well-known passage has been relied upon by countless thousands of people. It is most precious to all of us for the comfort it gives regarding our prayers of confession and repentance. God forgives our sins and cleanses us as if these sins have never existed. He is our Father and loves us beyond our comprehension.

His compassion is measured as high as the heavens, and He removes our sins as far as the East is from the West. *(Psalms 103:10-13) (vs 10) He has not dealt with us according to our sins, Nor rewarded us according to our iniquities. (vs 11) For as high as the heavens are above the earth, So great is His lovingkindness toward those who fear Him. (vs 12) As far as the east is from the west, So far has He removed our transgressions from us. (vs 13) Just as a father has compassion on his children, So the LORD has compassion on those who fear Him.*

4. PRAYERS OF INTERCESSION:

a) *(Isaiah 65:21-24)(vs 21) "They will build houses and inhabit them; They will also plant vineyards and eat their fruit. (vs 22) "They will not build and another inhabit, They will not plant and another eat; For as the lifetime of a tree, so will be the days of My people, And My chosen ones will wear out the work of their hands. (vs 23) "They will not labor in vain, Or bear children for calamity; For they are the offspring of those blessed by the LORD, And their descendants with them. (vs 24) "It will also come to pass that before they call, I will answer; and while they are still speaking, I will hear.*

Can any of us imagine a God that has our answer ready before we speak and hears us while we are speaking. He did so back in the days of the Prophet Isaiah and stands ready to do so today.

(Daniel 9:20-22)(vs 20) Now while I was speaking and prayinɡ, and confessing my sin and the sin of my people Israel, and presenting my supplication before the LORD my God in behalf of the holy mountain of my God, (vs 21) while I was still speaking in prayer, then the man Gabriel, whom I had seen in the vision previously, came to me in my extreme weariness about the time of the evening offering. (vs 22) He gave me instruction and talked with me and said, "O Daniel, I have now come forth to give you insight with understanding.

Daniel was confessing his own sin as well as interceding for the people of Israel. It was while he was still speaking that God presented into his presence the Angel Gabriel. The subject here is not the answer granted to Daniel's intercessory Prayer (which was an astounding positive), but the fact that God answers quickly and definitively as we intercede for our own causes as well as the causes of others. As we confess and intercede for ourselves and others we can expect the Only True Living God, to hear and answer. He is alive, He neither slumbers nor sleeps!!!

b) *(Acts 12:5-8 & 11)(vs 5) So Peter was kept in the prison, but prayer for him was being made fervently by the church to God. (vs 6) On the very night when Herod was about to bring him forward, Peter was sleeping between two soldiers, bound with two chains, and guards in front of the door were watching over the prison. (vs 7) And behold, an angel of the Lord suddenly appeared and a light shone in the cell; and he struck Peter's side and woke him up, saying, "Get up quickly." And his chains fell off his hands. (vs 8) And the angel said to him, "Gird yourself and put on your sandals." And he did so. And he *said to him, "Wrap your cloak around you and follow me." (vs 11) When Peter came to himself, he said, "Now I know for sure that the Lord has sent forth His angel and rescued me from the hand of Herod and from all that the Jewish people were expecting."*

What a beautiful account of God's people Praying in intercession for Peter. He was miraculously rescued from the hands of Herod. Peter had chains drop from his body and walked through gates, all of which were opened by the will of God. Intersession is a miraculous tool. We should all try to master its use, or at least attempt it, to see what God might do in our lives and the lives of those around us. Of course it will all be done in accordance with His will.

The above is also a demonstration of God's power. We can expect the power of God to intervene when we Pray. His power can and will come in many forms, both spiritual as well as physical.

c) *(Ephesians 1:18) I pray that the eyes of your heart may be enlightened, so that you will know what is the hope of His calling, what are the riches of the glory of His inheritance in the saints,*

Paul is Praying a prayer of intercession for the saints at Ephesus. His Prayer exemplifies his tremendous concern for their spiritual growth, and that they have complete knowledge of the fullness of knowing what Christ has done for them. This Prayer can be translated to us today. We can be assured that Paul was just as concerned for us today, and that we know and live according to the fullness of what Christ has accomplished for us. I am absolutely certain the Apostle Paul was interceding for each Christian that is living today.

d) *(Ephesians 6:18) With all prayer and petition pray at all times in the Spirit, and with this in view, be on the alert with all perseverance and petition for all the saints,*

God's Holy Word, through the hands of the Apostle Paul is commanding us to Pray for all the saints. We need to intercede for all the saints found in our churches, in our family, our friends and our acquaintances.

e) *(Philippians 1:9-10)(vs 9) And this I pray, that your love may abound still more and more in real knowledge and all discernment, (vs 10) so that you may approve the things that are excellent, in order to be sincere and blameless until the day of Christ;*

(Colossians 1:9-10)(vs 9) For this reason also, since the day we heard of it, we have not ceased to pray for you and to ask that you may be filled with the knowledge of His will in all spiritual wisdom and understanding, (vs 10) so that you will walk in a manner worthy of the Lord, to please Him in all respects, bearing fruit in every good work and increasing in the knowledge of God;

(Colossians 4:12) Epaphras, who is one of your number, a bondslave of Jesus Christ, sends you his greetings, always laboring earnestly for you in his prayers, that you may stand perfect and fully assured in all the will of God.

(2 Thessalonians 1:11) To this end also we pray for you always, that our God will count you worthy of your calling, and fulfill every desire for goodness and the work of faith with power,

Paul is again Praying or interceding for the saints. Paul stands with Timothy in the examples above interceding for both those from Philippi and Colossae, as well as the Thessalonians. It seems Paul's examples are deafening as they continue to be repeated, calling upon God for the spiritual growth of **His children**. If "You Belong To Him", you are **His children,** and are included along with the ones Paul was Praying for above.

5. PRAYERS FOR THE SALVATION OF OTHERS:

a) *(Romans 10:1) Brethren, my heart's desire and my prayer to God for them is for their salvation.*

The Apostle Paul is Praying for the salvation of the Jews. If Paul gives us the example of Praying for the salvation of others, we are to follow his example and Pray for the salvation of those we are close to, and especially for our loved ones and friends.

b) *(2 Corinthians 9:13-15)(vs 13) Because of the proof given by this ministry, they will glorify God for your obedience to your confession of the gospel of Christ and for the liberality of your contribution to them and to all, (vs 14) while they also, by prayer on your behalf, yearn for you because of the surpassing grace of God in you. (vs 15) Thanks be to God for His indescribable gift!*

I believe the indescribable gift is the regeneration of Jesus Christ in the lives of those being spoken about in these verses. I am sure the Prayers of those on the behalf of others were for salvation, because those Praying are giving thanks unto God for this indescribable gift being granted.

c) *(Acts 3:6 & 8 & 16)(vs 6) But Peter said, "I do not possess silver and gold, but what I do have I give to you: In the name of Jesus Christ the Nazarene—walk!" (vs 8) With a leap he stood upright and began to walk; and he entered the temple with them, walking and leaping and praising God. (vs 16) "And on the basis of faith in His name, it is the name of Jesus which has strengthened this man whom you see and know; and the faith which comes through Him has given him this perfect health in the presence of you all.*

The Apostle Peter by calling upon the name of Jesus Christ was able to call down an act of God for both physical and spiritual healing. The lame was able to both, physically walk, and most important of all, was able to enjoy this new personal relationship with Jesus Christ. This lame man could now state, "I Belong to God"!!!

6. PRAY WITHOUT CEASING:

a) *(Matthew 26:41) "Keep watching and praying that you may not enter into temptation; the spirit is willing, but the flesh is weak."*

While Jesus was facing the most difficult time of His life, His thoughts of concern were for His followers. Our command from Jesus is to always be on the lookout for the prowling lion, the devil, while staying before Him in Prayer, since our flesh is weak.

b) *(Luke 2:36-37)(vs 36) And there was a prophetess, Anna the daughter of Phanuel, of the tribe of Asher. She was advanced in years and had lived with her husband seven years after her marriage, (vs 37) and then as a widow to the age of eighty-four. She never left the temple, serving night and day with fastings and prayers.*

This Biblical account of a person Praying without ceasing is a challenge to those of us called to this ministry. Anna had received this calling from God, and she was faithful until death, welcoming the fulfillment of this task, which had been assigned to her.

c) *(Acts 1:13-14)(vs 13) When they had entered the city, they went up to the upper room where they were staying; that is, Peter and John and James and Andrew, Philip and Thomas, Bartholomew and Matthew, James the son of Alphaeus, and Simon the Zealot, and Judas the son of James. (vs 14) These all with one mind were continually devoting*

themselves to prayer, along with the women, and Mary the mother of Jesus, and with His brothers.

We have here an example of multiple persons, including Jesus' Disciples, devoting themselves to Prayer. There is a time for us to do the same!

d) (Acts 2:42) They were continually devoting themselves to the apostles' teaching and to fellowship, to the breaking of bread and to prayer.

We find here a great model from the early church that can be used as our pattern today. They devoted themselves to great teaching, to fellowship, to participating in meals together and to Prayer. Prayer was not an afterthought, but an integral part of their worship.

e) (Acts 6:2-4)(vs 2) So the twelve summoned the congregation of the disciples and said, "It is not desirable for us to neglect the word of God in order to serve tables. (vs 3) "Therefore, brethren, select from among you seven men of good reputation, full of the Spirit and of wisdom, whom we may put in charge of this task. (vs 4) "But we will devote ourselves to prayer and to the ministry of the word."

Here we find Jesus' Disciples, assigning to others, the tasks of serving tables and ministering to the physical needs of the people. This was being done in order to allow time to be devoted to the spiritual needs of the congregation. **Prayer and Teaching** were considered a higher calling than serving tables, and as such have been established as an important part of all spiritual ministry, both then and today.

f) (1 Thessalonians 5:16-17)(vs 16) Rejoice always; (vs 17) pray without ceasing;

We are to always be full of cheer. In our attitude of rejoicing, we are to Pray as needed, with this joy in our hearts, that God will answer our unselfish prayers. Ceasing here means uninterruptedly, without omission (on an appropriate occasion). Our Prayers are to be designed by God, and carried out by each of us as an act of obedience.

g) (1 Timothy 5:5) Now she who is a widow indeed and who has been left alone, has fixed her hope on God and continues in entreaties and prayers night and day.

True widows are to be cared for by their family, and if they do not have a family, they are to be cared for by the church. Since they have their physical needs taken care of, they are to devote themselves to the ministry of Prayer. God will direct these Prayer lives.

7. REQUESTED PRAYER:

a) *(1 Thessalonians 5:25) Brethren, pray for us. (2 Thessalonians 3:1) Finally, brethren, pray for us that the word of the Lord will spread rapidly and be glorified, just as it did also with you;*

If the Apostle Paul requests Prayer from the congregation, it would be appropriate for our pastors to request Prayer from their congregations. As these requests are made it would be wise for us to Pray for these, our pastors, our elders and our fellow church members.

b) *(1 Timothy 2:8) Therefore I want the men in every place to pray, lifting up holy hands, without wrath and dissension.*

All of us are called to Pray for and with the saints. We are to Pray without malice or any kind of disharmony. God will direct these requested Prayers.

c) *(Hebrews 13:18-19)(vs 18) Pray for us, for we are sure that we have a good conscience, desiring to conduct our- selves honorably in all things. (vs 19) And I urge you all the more to do this, so that I may be restored to you the sooner.*

Most likely the author of Hebrews is the Apostle Paul. Here we find the writer requesting Prayer to support the good conscience and the conduct of the Apostle's in question. We can take from these verses that we are to Pray specifically for the needs of all of our teachers and leaders.

8. PRAYER FOR TIMES OF SUFFERING OR SICKNESS:

a) *(Psalms 39:12) "Hear my prayer, O LORD, and give ear to my cry; Do not be silent at my tears; For I am a stranger with You, A sojourner like all my fathers. (Psalms 102:1)* A Prayer of the Afflicted when he is faint and pours out his complaint before the LORD. *Hear my prayer, O LORD! And let my cry for help come to You.*

David suffered often, yet he always knew where to go with his Prayers. Our Prayers, born out of suffering, will always be heard as we go before the Lord in the appropriate manner.

b) *(James 5:13) Is anyone among you suffering? Then he must pray. Is anyone cheerful? He is to sing praises.*

We are to Pray and Praise our Lord regardless of our condition. To God be the Glory .... for Everything!!!

c) *(James 5:14-15 partial)(vs 14) Is anyone among you sick? Then he must call for the elders of the church and they are to pray over him, anointing him with oil in the name of the Lord; (vs 15 patrtial) and the prayer offered in faith will restore the one who is sick, and the Lord will raise him up,*

I know these verses were used earlier in this chapter, but the context here is regarding those who are feeble, wearied or diseased. We have specific instructions here to Pray over those in need and we can expect them to be restored.

9. PRAYER RESULTING IN GOD'S DEMONSTRATION OF POWER:

a) *(2 Chronicles 6:40-42)(VS 40) "Now, O my God, I pray, let Your eyes be open and Your ears attentive to the prayer offered in this place. (vs 41) "Now therefore arise, O LORD God, to Your resting place, You and the ark of Your might; let Your priests, O LORD God, be clothed with salvation and let Your godly ones rejoice in what is good. (vs 42) "O LORD God, do not turn away the face of Your anointed; remember Your lovingkindness to Your servant David."*

(2 Chronicles 7:1) Now when Solomon had finished praying, fire came down from heaven and consumed the burnt offering and the sacrifices, and the glory of the LORD filled the house.

Occasionally we need to see the power of God. It bolsters our faith and encourages us in our weaknesses. It is available to us today in many forms and as we Pray unselfishly, we will see His power demonstrated in our lives and the lives of others. It may not be fire from heaven, but I have seen His power come alive in the healing of the young and old, including my children and myself.

b) *(Acts 4:31) And when they had prayed, the place where they had gathered together was shaken, and they were all*

filled with the Holy Spirit and began to speak the word of God with boldness.

Apparently, and without asking, these believers were rewarded with God's demonstration of power. He gave them a physical sign, along with the Holy Spirit, to increase their boldness. It worked then, it will work today! God is unchanging!!!

10. GOD'S CO-ORDINATED PRAYER FROM DIFFERENT PEOPLE AND DIFFERENT PLACES:

It occurs to me that we have all seen business documents that require multiple signatures. These documents provide for individual signatures from each participant from varied locations around the country on separate signature pages, yet the document provides in its legal dictation that all signatures are valid as if they were all signed on one page at the same time and location. God often has us Pray in this fashion. We are at different locations, different times of the day, yet He hears and answers these Prayers as if we were joined in hands, in the same room, calling upon Him for the identical cause. God lays upon our hearts what to Pray, and He is the master of hearing and answering regardless of the logistical environment.

We will see below that the Bible speaks to us by giving us examples of these types of Prayers, assuring us that they were designed and ordained by God, and therefore will be heard and answered by Him. I am sure that everyone out there can recall a real life example of coordinated Prayer. A Prayer that was originated by God's urging, and Prayed by multiple people in different locations at different times of the day, yet was designed to accomplish the same purpose. When this happens we should praise God for allowing us to be used, through Prayer, to further His kingdom.

a) Coordinated Prayer as found in the Book of Acts:
Testimony from Cornelius:
(Acts 10:30-32)(vs 30) Cornelius said, "Four days ago to this hour, I was praying in my house during the ninth hour; and behold, a man stood before me in shining garments, (vs 31) and he *said, 'Cornelius, your prayer has been heard and your alms have been remembered before God. (vs 32) 'Therefore send to Joppa and invite Simon, who is also called

Peter, to come to you; he is staying at the house of Simon the tanner by the sea.'

<u>Testimony from the Apostle Peter:</u>

(Acts 11:5) "I was in the city of Joppa praying; and in a trance I saw a vision, an object coming down like a great sheet lowered by four corners from the sky; and it came right down to me,

(Acts 11:11-13)(vs 11) "And behold, at that moment three men appeared at the house in which we were staying, having been sent to me from Caesarea. (vs 12) "The Spirit told me to go with them without misgivings. These six brethren also went with me and we entered the man's house. (vs 13) "And he reported to us how he had seen the angel standing in his house, and saying, 'Send to Joppa and have Simon, who is also called Peter, brought here;

This coordinated Prayer brought Peter to Cornelius' house and brought the Gospel of Jesus Christ to the Gentiles.

b) <u>Paul and Silas in prison Praying:</u> *(Acts 16:25-26)(vs 25) But about midnight Paul and Silas were praying and singing hymns of praise to God, and the prisoners were listening to them; (vs 26) and suddenly there came a great earthquake, so that the foundations of the prison house were shaken; and immediately all the doors were opened and everyone's chains were unfastened.*

<u>Results of their Prayer:</u> *(Acts 16:34) And he brought them into his house and set food before them, and rejoiced greatly, having believed in God with his whole household.*

The jailer was converted by the actions of Paul and Silas. He was so thankful for this new found faith in Jesus Christ that he bathed them, fed them and brought them into his home. They were released shortly and we find the following account.

(Acts 16:40) They went out of the prison and entered the house of Lydia, and when they saw the brethren, they encouraged them and departed.

It is my belief, along with some Biblical scholars, that the other disciples were very likely at the house of Lydia Praying (in disconnected coordination) for the safety and release of Paul and Silas. The Bible doesn't confirm this, but it is not too much of a stretch to arrive at this conclusion.

11. A PRAYER OF FAREWELL AND CONCERN FOR OTHERS:

(Acts 21:5) When our days there were ended, we left and started on our journey, while they all, with wives and children, escorted us until we were out of the city. After kneeling down on the beach and praying, we said farewell to one another.

Obviously there was great sorrow (as exemplified by the families mentioned in the verse above) as these families experienced the departure of the Disciples from their city. We don't know the exact circumstances, but we can surely surmise that these people had an abundant love for the Disciples, and were grieved by the thought of never seeing them again (we do know that the Apostle Paul's life was being severely and repeatedly threatened), this side of heaven.

This brings to mind a personal remembrance of a farewell of equal sadness. I only relate this (hopefully it will not be boring) to emphasize and drive home a point.

One of the most difficult times of my life was leaving my mother in a nursing home, feeling certain that I could never again regain or replace the beauty of this last visit. Our visits usually included my wife and I, our five children, generally a few in-law spouses and several grandchildren and would be filled with several hours of visiting, recalling old family times (both good and bad) and singing many of my mother's favorite gospel songs. She loved those visits, and was able to recall with us, many happy events from the past. She was thrilled with the presence of this large family group and the joy of having this family fellowship. It brings tears to my eyes today as I recall her watching from her wheel chair as we left this last "good" visit. I think both we and she knew that this visit could never be replicated in the future. It was fairly clear that time was taking its toll, and her mind would not allow her to be as receptive in the future. It broke my heart as I watched her strain to watch us as we went out the glass doors and as we finally disappeared around the buildings. Our family lived about 850 miles away and with the raising of the family, the cost of travel, and work, we were fortunate to see her more than once a year. In these last days of her life she would enjoy our visits but wouldn't even remember that we had been there an hour after we left. This didn't matter, as it was still difficult to leave her without family by her side.

The above verse reminded me of this farewell, and the touching love that transpires among family members and other loved ones. We never know as we say our goodbyes, whether they are for a day, a week or until we meet in eternity, so let us remember to honor those we love, with Prayer.

As you can see this verse has caused me to recall a very touching time in my life. The visualization of these participants, escorting Paul and the others completely out from the city, kneeling down and Praying on the beach before saying their farewells, should stir something in our hearts. This Biblical example is an inspiration to me and hopefully to you, and it is my Prayer that it will cause each of us "Who Belong To Him", to be more diligent in the future, by Praying for and with, those to whom we may need to say goodbye. Prayer can be a "blessing", a "healing" and a "comfort" in any type of situation, and especially so in our most difficult, trying times.

12. A GLIMPSE OF THE PRAYER LIFE OF JESUS:
a) *(Matthew 14:23) After He had sent the crowds away, He went up on the mountain by Himself to pray; and when it was evening, He was there alone.*

Jesus sent the crowd of over five thousand away and sent his disciples to take their boat across the sea while He went and had His quiet time. If Jesus needed time alone while communing with God the Father, how much more do we need this? His quiet time lasted until approximately 3:00 am, and to a sleepyhead like me this is quite impressive. This is not His requirement of us, but it shows His passion and devotion to God's Holy Plan for the salvation of each of us.

b) *(Matthew 19:13-14)(vs 13) Then some children were brought to Him so that He might lay His hands on them and pray; and the disciples rebuked them. (vs 14) But Jesus said, "Let the children alone, and do not hinder them from coming to Me; for the kingdom of heaven belongs to such as these."*

Jesus had compassion for even the children. He said that all of us must come to Him, not as little children, but with the faith as demonstrated by a little child. During Jesus' time here on this earth, He spent much time Praying, including over what was considered at the time, to be this most insignificant people group.

c) *(Mark 1:35) In the early morning, while it was still dark, Jesus got up, left the house, and went away to a secluded place, and was praying there.*

We find here another example of Jesus going away by Himself to Pray, where He was alone and communicating only with God the Father. This example is worthy of note since it was in the early morning hours before the busyness of the day had begun.

d) *(Luke 3:21-22)(vs 21) Now when all the people were baptized, Jesus was also baptized, and while He was praying, heaven was opened, (vs 22) and the Holy Spirit descended upon Him in bodily form like a dove, and a voice came out of heaven, "You are My beloved Son, in You I am well-pleased."*

Jesus was both God and man. He set the examples for us today. He was baptized like the other common people, while giving us the example of Prayer through the power of the Holy Spirit. The huge difference is He was pronounced to be ... ***"You are My beloved Son, in You I am well-pleased".*** His examples of Praying, among all His other attributes, were made known to mankind forever. His attributes, including His need for Praying, should be exemplified by each of us throughout our lifetime.

e) *(Luke 5:16) But Jesus Himself would often slip away to the wilderness and pray.*

We are not sure of the exact number the word often refers to, but we know often means several or many. Jesus Prayed often and usually went to a solitary place. I believe this example is to be taken seriously enough to prompt our minds to duplicate it in both number and location. A solitary or desolate place can leave you with the thoughts counting for Jesus, and those thoughts will not be encumbered or obliterated by the necessary mundane or routine chores of the day. Seek a solitary place and Pray often.

(Luke 6:12) It was at this time that He went off to the mountain to pray, and He spent the whole night in prayer to God.

This is beyond my comprehension how one could spend the whole night in Prayer. I confess that it is not in my character to do such. My eyes close before getting to bed, and I have even fallen asleep standing up. While pursuing big game in both Colorado and Alaska, I have spent two fitful and frightful nights out on a mountain side in freezing cold, snowy weather. Maybe it is to my shame, but my concern was to stay warm and alive, not to be Praying for others. Jesus was obviously **SPECIAL** (He didn't hold any of my selfish traits), while being both God and man. We can only attempt to emulate Him.

f) *(Luke 6:27-30)(vs 27) "But I say to you who hear, love your enemies, do good to those who hate you, (vs 28) bless those who curse you, pray for those who mistreat you. (vs 29) "Whoever hits you on the cheek, offer him the other also; and whoever takes away your coat, do not withhold your shirt from him either. (vs 30) "Give to everyone who asks of you, and whoever takes away what is yours, do not demand it back.*

You get more than a lesson in Prayer from the above verses. Jesus is verbally instructing us in how to act in times of mistreatment. One of the key ingredients is Prayer. Prayer will calm our minds and allow time for Godly thoughts resulting in Godly actions.

g) *(Luke 9:28-29)(vs 28) Some eight days after these sayings, He took along Peter and John and James, and went up on the mountain to pray. (vs 29) And while He was praying, the appearance of His face became different, and His clothing became white and gleaming.*

This is known as Christ's transfiguration. It is not inconsequential that this Glory from God the Father was bestowed upon Him during His Prayers. Jesus and we are closer to our God while in reverential Prayer time.

h) *(Luke 18:1-2 & 6-8 partial))(vs 1) Now He was telling them a parable to show that at all times they ought to pray and not to lose heart, (vs 2) saying, "In a certain city there was a judge who did not fear God and did not respect man. (vs 6) And the Lord said, "Hear what the unrighteous judge *said; (vs 7) now, will not God bring about justice for His elect who cry to Him day and night, and will He delay long* *over them? (vs 8 partial) "I tell you that He will bring about justice for them quickly.*

The unrighteous judge said he will hear those who persist in bringing their case before him. Our righteous Heavenly Father will even more quickly hear those of us who "Belong To Him"!!! He will swiftly bring about justice, according to His will and our Prayers.

i) *(Luke 22:40-44)(vs 40) When He arrived at the place, He said to them, "Pray that you may not enter into temptation." (vs 41) And He withdrew from them about a stone's throw, and He knelt down and began to pray, (vs 42) saying, "Father, if You are willing, remove this cup from Me; yet not My will, but Yours be done." (vs 43) Now an angel from heaven appeared to Him, strengthening Him. (vs 44) And being in agony He was praying very fervently; and His sweat became like drops of blood, falling down upon the ground.*

Never has it been recorded that Jesus Prayed as earnestly as He did this night. He was Praying for things we cannot know about. He was Praying for the souls of all mankind. He was Praying in regard to the powers found only in heavenly places. His will was to do that of the Heavenly Father, not his earthly desires. I leave it to you as to how you may react to this passage, it truly is powerful.

E. MISC. VERSES REGARDING PRAYER AND THE HINDRANCES CAUSED BY IDOLS:

An idol doesn't need to be an image made of metal or wood. It can be people, parents or children, it can be material possessions such as property, homes or cars, or it can be anything you desire more than the pure relationship with Jesus, our Lord and Savior. The following speaks of idols and their hindrance to us if we let them sneak into our homes or our lives. We not only block our **Prayer life**, but we offend God to the limit. See the following for a glimpse of His concern and His wrath.

1. WE CANNOT SERVE THE TRUE GOD WHILE HAVING ALLEGIENCE TO OTHER gods:

a) *(Ezekiel 14:1-8)(vs 1) Then some elders of Israel came to me and sat down before me. (vs 2) And the word of the LORD came to me, saying, (vs 3) "Son of man, these men have set*

up their idols in their hearts and have put right before their faces the stumbling block of their iniquity. Should I be consulted by them at all? (vs 4) "Therefore speak to them and tell them, 'Thus says the Lord GOD, "Any man of the house of Israel who sets up his idols in his heart, puts right before his face the stumbling block of his iniquity, and then comes to the prophet, I the LORD will be brought to give him an answer in the matter in view of the multitude of his idols, (vs 5) in order to lay hold of the hearts of the house of Israel who are estranged from Me through all their idols."' (vs 6) "Therefore say to the house of Israel, 'Thus says the Lord GOD, "Repent and turn away from your idols and turn your faces away from all your abominations. (vs 7) "For anyone of the house of Israel or of the immigrants who stay in Israel who separates himself from Me, sets up his idols in his heart, puts right before his face the stumbling block of his iniquity, and then comes to the prophet to inquire of Me for himself, I the LORD will be brought to answer him in My own person. (vs 8) "I will set My face against that man and make him a sign and a proverb, and I will cut him off from among My people. So you will know that I am the LORD.

The key verses here are underlined. We cannot serve the true God and have our idol gods in our minds or on our shelves in our homes. If we call upon the true God in Prayer while having our idol gods in our lives He will only reject those prayers and reject us for His Word says ... *(Exodus 20:2-6)(vs 2) "I am the LORD your God, who brought you out of the land of Egypt, out of the house of slavery. (vs 3) "You shall have no other gods before Me. (vs 4) "You shall not make for yourself an idol, or any likeness of what is in heaven above or on the earth beneath or in the water under the earth. (vs 5) "You shall not worship them or serve them; for I, the LORD your God, am a jealous God, visiting the iniquity of the fathers on the children, on the third and the fourth generations of those who hate Me, (vs 6) but showing lovingkindness to thousands, to those who love Me and keep My commandments.* ... He truly is a loving

God who protects and cherishes those who love Him. Call upon Him freely in Prayer, but only if you have rejected all idols and earthly gods.

b) *(Nahum 1:14) The LORD has issued a command concerning you: "Your name will no longer be perpetuated. I will cut off idol and image From the house of your gods. I will prepare your grave, For you are contemptible."*

This verse is mentioned and recorded here in case there is any question about our God's concern over idols. If there are idols in our lives He will prepare our grave and find us in "contempt of His court", or find us just plain "contemptible". **The Prayers of the Ungodly will not be heard!**

2. GOD ANSWERS PRAYER WITH AMAZING PURITY:

(Matthew 7:7-11)(vs 7) "Ask, and it will be given to you; seek, and you will find; knock, and it will be opened to you. (vs 8) "For everyone who asks receives, and he who seeks finds, and to him who knocks it will be opened. (vs 9) "Or what man is there among you who, when his son asks for a loaf, will give him a stone? (vs 10) "Or if he asks for a fish, he will not give him a snake, will he? (vs 11) "If you then, being evil, know how to give good gifts to your children, how much more will your Father who is in heaven give what is good to those who ask Him!

This most amazing promise comes from our Father in heaven. He promises to give what is **good** to those who ask of Him.

3. THE LOCATION IS NOT A FACTOR/PURE AND HOLY INTENTIONS ARE REQUIRED:

(1 Timothy 2:8) Therefore I want the men in every place to pray, lifting up holy hands, without wrath and dissension.

The location of where one should Pray is determined by where we are at the time we need to Pray. Any and every place we may be is a place of Prayer. The need dictates the calling upon our Heavenly Father, not the location. This doesn't preclude our seeking a "quiet place" is such is available.

The second part of this verse is full of instruction and commands. We are to lift up holy hands, which means we are to call upon God as if we are a righteous person. This righteousness is available to us and can only be exercised because of our trust in the saving work accomplished upon the Cross by Jesus Christ. The commands part of this verse states we are to do so without wrath and dissension. This means we are to call upon God after having forgiven all others and having reconciled any disputes that may have arisen with those in question. It is with these conditions that we can expect God to hear and answer our Prayers.

F. CONCLUSION TO PRAYER:

Of all the verses about Prayer as found throughout the Bible, there is none that sums it up better than what is known as the Lord's Prayer, as found in Matthew and Luke. We find contained in this Model Prayer all the ingredients necessary to accomplish a healthy and complete Prayer life (communication) with our Lord, or with the one "To Whom We Belong"!!! Let's look at the account given to us by Matthew. These words are directly from the lips of Jesus Christ and are to be respected as if He spoke them directly to our ears.

(Matthew 6:5-13)(vs 5) "When you pray, you are not to be like the hypocrites; for they love to stand and pray in the synagogues and on the street corners so that they may be seen by men. Truly I say to you, they have their reward in full. (vs 6) "But you, when you pray, go into your inner room, close your door and pray to your Father who is in secret, and your Father who sees what is done in secret will reward you. (vs 7) "And when you are praying, do not use meaningless repetition as the Gentiles do, for they suppose that they will be heard for their many words. (vs 8) "So do not be like them; for your Father knows what you need before you ask Him. (vs 9) "Pray, then, in this way: 'Our Father who is in heaven, Hallowed be Your name. (vs 10) 'Your kingdom come. Your will be done, On earth as it is in heaven. (vs 11) 'Give us this day our daily bread. (vs 12) 'And forgive us our debts, as we also have forgiven our debtors. (vs 13) 'And do not lead us into temptation, but deliver us from evil. [For Yours is the kingdom and the power and the glory forever. Amen.]'

Verses 5-8: These are full of instructions regarding the proper attitude and sincerity of heart as we Pray. We are to fully consider the sacred relationship that God has granted and expects from us.

Verse 9: We are to call upon the name of God by fully recognizing His Holiness. We are to have a reverence beyond comparison, as He is absolutely Holy. There is no other name under heaven that we can offer our Prayers up to!

Verse 10: Here we find the most unselfish Prayer one can Pray. This, in effect, is to say "not my will, but Yours be done". This Prayer was Prayed by Jesus in the Garden of Gethsemane, as He was so in earnest over the sins of mankind, that He sweat drops of blood.

Verse 11: We are to ask, even though He already knows our needs, for the necessities of this world. Food, water, clothing, shelter and all the necessities of life are to be Prayed for, and acknowledgement is to be given to God for providing these things.

Verse 12: Our asking for forgiveness is most often a daily thing. For this forgiveness to be granted by the Almighty Heavenly Father, we are to forgive those who may have sinned against us. We are to forgive like the Father forgives, and that is to remove those sins against us as far as the East is from the West and to be remembered no more.

Verse 13: We know according to His Word that God does not tempt anyone. All temptation comes from the human lust, having been born within man … *(James 1:13-14)(vs 13) Let no one say when he is tempted, "I am being tempted by God"; for God cannot be tempted by evil, and He Himself does not tempt anyone. (vs 14) But each one is tempted when he is carried away and enticed by his own lust.*

We also know that God is our protector and deliverer when temptations come. He is to be called upon to be the one to chase and put to route the devil as we resist those temptations. And finally we see we are to close our Prayers the same way they began, and that is to acknowledge the God of the universe, for His Power and His Glory! Amen!

Prayer is a sacred gift granted by God to all of us "Who Belong To Him"!!! Practice it **righteously** and He will be as close as our spoken words, or the thoughts of our minds. To God be the Glory .... For Everything!!!

(John 15:7) "If you abide in Me, and My words abide in you, ask whatever you wish, and it will be done for you.

(*) FOOTNOTE # 1 — TO THIS CHAPTER:

I would like to relate a personal experience regarding recent "Prayers" in my life, and how the Great I AM of the Universe, the One "To Whom I Belong", has answered those "Prayers" to allow me to live. You will see, He must not be through with me yet!!!

During the writing of this Book, I contacted a rare and most normally fatal infection in the area around my left lung. This infection is named by the one who discovered it and it is called "Boerhaave Syndrome". According to the medical journals, that both my wife and I read on-line, this infection is caused by the puncture or a rupture of the esophagus. Subsequent to the puncture or the rupture, acid comes up from the stomach and bacteria comes down with the food from the mouth, and they each leak into the lung cavity thereby creating this deadly infection. One of the medical records we read stated that if this infection is not diagnosed within 24 hours there is 75% mortality and if it isn't diagnosed within 48 hours it is 100% fatal. My diagnosis wasn't made for 5 days or 120 hours. Obviously I'm alive or I wouldn't be writing this, but all medical records and conclusions to be drawn state the opposite. God gave me something so severe and conclusively fatal, that the only conclusion to be drawn upon my survival, is this disease was to bring Glory to Himself.

I am reminded of the following Biblical passage ... *(James 5:16–partial) The effective prayer of a righteous man can accomplish much.*, ... and I know that I have been privileged to have numerous of these qualified persons (men, women and children) "Praying" for me. God allowed the problem and He alone is to be recognized as having allowed me to live. While the previous statement is a fact, I don't want to take away from the Doctors and Nurses and their diligent efforts expended during my Hospital stay. Certainly God blessed all of their hands, minds and efforts and they are to be given earthly credit for saving my life. God knew what He was doing and He used the "Power" of "Prayer", through these numerous *"righteous"* people, to accomplish His purpose.

Even with a timely diagnosis and all of our modern treatments, the patient with "Boerhaave" cannot be guaranteed to live. A Doctor friend of mine, who practices "Family Medicine", has told me that during his practice of thirty-five years, he has seen only one case of this and that person is dead. This account, as related to me by my Doctor friend, further confirms the rarity and severity of this disease, as emphasized above.

I tell you all of this to demonstrate and recount the Power of God, and our part in God's actions, which may be activated by both the opportunity and requirement of "Prayer". My family, my church and many friends, as well as many who only knew of me through one of the above acquaintances, were "Praying" for me. It was God's decision to spare my life and I give Him full Glory for doing so, while at the same time thanking all of those who "Prayed" for me. After nineteen (19) days in the hospital and three weeks of "high powered", IV antibiotics at home (three times per day), I have been given a clean bill of health from this infection. I had two surgeries, eight holes in my stomach and chest area, including two drain hoses, a feeding tube for several weeks, and a five inch incision, plus one additional hole, in my back. I am left with a constant reminder that God is sovereign, He is all powerful, He is the giver of life and He is the **only one** who can take life. I will always be in awe, as I live the rest of my life fully understanding that I "Belong To Him". I am only still here for one purpose and that is to be able to serve His purposes. His "Owner's Manual" (His Holy Word) gives me the guide to accomplish this!!!

My conclusion from this ordeal is that He answered the many "Prayers" that went up for me, all to His Glory, and therefore He is not finished with me yet! God has something for me to do each day that I draw a breath and I am reminded of this with each and every breath I take. God's has left me with a gentle reminder of His omnipotence by allowing the scar tissue in both my chest and back to give me a little twinge with each expansion of the lungs. My "Prayer" is that this twinge will remain with me until the day I die, reminding me daily that the God of the Universe, has allowed me to live, and that my highest calling and response will always be to give Him the Glory, the Honor and the Praise (as much as humanly possible) for the dawning of each new day. Until His plan for our lives is over, we are to seek to "Serve" Him.

Let me tell you that I am not anything special, but after saying goodbye to my wife of 47 years and each of us not knowing whether she would awaken a widow and I in heaven, and having experienced the regret of not being able to say goodbye to my five (5) children and their spouses as well as our seventeen (17) grandchildren, "**I can now say I look forward to getting in on what God is doing**"!!! My wife and I have also experienced His granting us a miraculous peace in this most difficult situation ... *(Philippians 4:6-7)(vs 6) Be anxious for nothing, but in everything by prayer and supplication with thanksgiving let your requests be made known to God. (vs 7) And the peace of God, which surpasses all comprehension, will guard your hearts and your minds in Christ Jesus.* We have experienced His peace, the peace that passes all understanding. As an ordinary person I can personally witness to His involvement in my life, and regardless of the outcome or the difficulty of the situation, I can say without a doubt, you can know you are "Safe" in the clutch of His hand. God deals with ordinary people, and is ready to bring "Peace" into each and everyone's life, if you will only call upon Him!!!

I must confess that for most of my 68 years I have tried to get God in on what I was doing, but not anymore. From now on I am seeking to find out "What God Is Doing", and asking Him to let me be involved!!! I will always have many imperfections, but please listen, as I desire to share with everyone who cares to hear, how He gets the Glory for sparing my life. Even more than the physical extension of my life, I would love to share with anyone who cares to know, how He has granted to me eternal spiritual life. Both my physical life here on this earth, and my eternal spiritual life with Him in the heavens, were given by Him through the "Power" of "Prayer".

The **"Power"** of **"Prayer"** is in your hands and mine and it is available to all of us "Who Belong To Him", we need to use it mightily in all things, and may this use accomplish the "Glory" intended by our **"Almighty Heavenly Father"**!!!

(*) FOOTNOTE # 1a:
As a footnote to this Footnote, I would be remiss if I were to leave out these following details.

After having found out about this "Boerhaave Syndrome" infection, along with only a glimpse of its seriousness and the immediate need for surgery, and as I was lying on the table being prepped for this surgery, I said something which is totally out of my character. I said to Doctor Ram Nene, my surgeon, "I just want you to know that I have an angel on my shoulder". I had no idea where this thought came from, as it is not normally in my personality to blurt out with this type of statement. I often times give God the praise or am conscience of His miraculous powers, but I just don't speak these thoughts out to strangers. Dr. Nene, who is obviously a very intelligent man and is world renown in his surgical abilities, was professional and courteous by not commenting on his thoughts. I believed I could read his mind and to me it said, "hey I'm the intelligent one here and you aren't going to live through the night". This all happened before I was later made aware by Doctor Nene that only 5% of those diagnosed within 48 hours of contacting the "Boerhaave Syndrome" live. **NONE** after 48 hours! Dr. Nene came into my room the next morning about 6 am, which I discovered over the next few weeks to be his routine, saw that I was alive, pointed at me and said, "you certainly do have an angel on your shoulder". This to me confirmed that he had no earthly explanation of my still being alive. Dr. Nene never said much in these patient visits except for a few medical explanations (in medical terms, which I generally didn't understand), and while walking towards the door he would always ask "do you have any questions". That first morning I answered back by saying "are you going to write this up in a Medical Journal". His short answer as he went through the door was "you are not out of the woods yet". As I thought about this statement I realized he was letting me know that he was still not at all sure that I was going to live. We never discussed that again, but as Dr. Nene told me later of the severity of this infection and the mortality rate, I can only know that God has made a statement in both of our lives.

Dr. Nene has since moved to India to practice his surgical skills in the homeland country of his wife. His wife had been the number one actress in that country for many years and wished to return to her profession after having their two children. I give Dr. Nene the credit for saving my life (obviously with God's blessings), and he and his family will always be in my future "Prayers". May, your and my "Prayers", be joined together.

"Prayers" like the example related above will always be answered if we ask with God given motives ... *(James 4:3) You ask and do not receive, because you ask with wrong motives, so that you may spend it on your pleasures. (John 14:13-14)(vs 13) "Whatever you ask in My name, that will I do, so that the Father may be glorified in the Son. (vs 14) "If you ask Me anything in My name, I will do it.* THANK YOU "PRAYER" PARTNERS for asking unselfishly and exercising the true God given motives!!!

I now and finally conclude this Chapter on "Prayer", and say with a resounding shout ... Praise be to our Almighty and Most Holy God for this <u>Gift</u> and <u>Right</u> of proper "Prayer", and the victories we gain as we are **"Able to Move Mountains"**!!!

<u>SPECIAL NOTE:</u>

I know many of you may have a special verse or verses regarding this Chapter's subject matter. This special verse or these verses may not have been mentioned due to my ignorance or because of brevity. I apologize for either of these reasons. Please feel free to write any special verse or verses in the space below. This will add your personal touch, and will serve to call to each person's mind their individual "experience of trust", in God's Holy Word.

For to each of us "Who belong To Him", His Holy Word can be truly recognized and relied upon as our **<u>"Owner's Manual"</u>**!!!

_____

_____

_____

_____

_____

_____

_____

CHAPTER 10

WALKING WITH GOD

INTRODUCTORY VERSE:

(Genesis 5:22-24)(vs 22) Then Enoch walked with God three hundred years after he became the father of Methuselah, and he had other sons and daughters. (vs 23) So all the days of Enoch were three hundred and sixty-five years. (vs 24) Enoch walked with God; and he was not, for God took him.

I don't know of any "believer" who would turn down the opportunity of having God write upon their tombstone, "he spent his life Walking with Me". Enoch set the standard for "Walking with God"!!!

INTRODUCTION:

When a man or a woman has become "born again" by the Spirit of God, this is an Act of God, and he or she has become a new creation … *(Romans 6:4 & 11-13)(vs 4) Therefore we have been buried with Him through baptism into death, so that as Christ was raised from the dead through the glory of the Father, so we too might walk in newness of life. (vs 11) Even so consider yourselves to be dead to sin, but alive to God in Christ Jesus. (vs 12) Therefore do not let sin reign in your mortal body so that you obey its lusts, (vs 13) and do not go on presenting the members of your body to sin as instruments of unrighteousness; but present yourselves to God as those alive from the dead, and your members as instruments of righteousness to God.*

This new creation, having been born originally of water or the physical birth, has now experienced being "born of the Spirit", or the Spiritual Birth. This Act of God has now put us into a new category of "Belonging To Him"!!! Since we now "Belong To God", it is **important,** and we really should describe this as **imperative,** that we know and understand God's "Owner's Manual" and His expectations. His "Owner's Manual", and His expectations included therein, have been provided for us in the form of the Holy Bible. Every verse in the Bible is mighty, powerful and full of instruction. This Holy Word is the mind of God. Within these holy pages we can find what it means to "Walk with God". We find a few verses, in the only Chapter of the Book of Jude, to establish our basis.

The Book of Jude includes much wisdom. I have taken the liberty to separate out a few verses which give us a tidbit, yet mighty revelation, regarding our "Walking with God". *(Jude 1:3 & 20-21) (vs 3) Beloved, while I was making every effort to write you about our common salvation, I felt the necessity to write to you appealing that you contend earnestly for the faith which was once for all handed down to the saints. (vs 20) But you, beloved, building yourselves up on your most holy faith, praying in the Holy Spirit, (vs 21) keep yourselves in the love of God, waiting anxiously for the mercy of our Lord Jesus Christ to eternal life.*

Jude refers to non-believers as being selfishly minded or as he so states in ... *(Jude 1:12 partial & 13 partial) "caring for themselves; clouds without water, autumn trees without fruit"*, and says for them *"the black darkness has been reserved forever"*. Jude develops these elaborate examples of the negative in order to accentuate the positive. He is really most desirous to direct "believers" who will "Walk with God", by emphasizing in his writing, the facts about those who have no clue who God is. We are to constantly and consistently contend for the faith thereby building ourselves up in the holy faith. We are to pray utilizing the Holy Spirit, hold fast to the love of God, and anxiously await with confidence and patience, for the mercy of God, which will cause this earthly life to pale as we compare it to the richness and beauty of eternal glory. This is all to be accomplished under the authority of our "LORD" JESUS CHRIST. He is our supreme authority, He is our master, He is our "LORD"!!! He expects us to "Walk with Him".

Finally we can understand as told in ... *(Jude 1:24-25)(vs 24)* ***Now to Him who is able to keep you from stumbling, and to make you stand in the presence of His glory blameless with great joy, (vs 25) to the only God our Savior, through Jesus Christ our Lord, be glory, majesty, dominion and authority, before all time and now and forever.*** ... "Walking with God" is directed by God, is commanded by God and is a privilege to those who choose to love and "Belong To Him!!! This "Walk" is to be "with" the "One" who has, ***"glory, majesty, dominion and authority, before all time and now and forever"***.

We will look at great historical Biblical men who "Walked with God", look at specific verses that challenge us today to "Walk with Him", and look at the hope and benefits of "Walking with Him". This is not an exhaustive study, but will feature some of God's insights, that if mastered and put into practice, will affect our life beyond measure in a beautiful way, and will cause us to delight in the Lord. We will find that there is no time to argue over or pursue the things of this world. We will find that whatever we do will bring Glory to God ... *(Colossians 3:17)* ***Whatever you do in word or deed, do all in the name of the Lord Jesus, giving thanks through Him to God the Father.*** It is worthy of our time, to consider "Walking with God"!!!

A. MEN OF FAITH WHO "WALKED WITH GOD":

1. Enoch – "Walked with God" — *(Genesis 5:18-24)(vs 18)* ***Jared lived one hundred and sixty-two years, and became the father of Enoch. (vs 19) Then Jared lived eight hundred years after he became the father of Enoch, and he had other sons and daughters. (vs 20) So all the days of Jared were nine hundred and sixty-two years, and he died. (vs 21) Enoch lived sixty-five years, and became the father of Methuselah. (vs 22) Then Enoch walked with God three hundred years after he became the father of Methuselah, and he had other sons and daughters. (vs 23) So all the days of Enoch were***

three hundred and sixty-five years. (vs 24) Enoch walked with God; and he was not, for God took him.

This brief genealogy of Enoch, along with these most favorable comments regarding his character, are all we have to understand Enoch's "Walk with the Lord". The words, "Walked with God", are additionally defined to include in its meaning the thoughts of: keeping pace with and being conversant while walking. This is consistent with the relationship that Enoch had with God as we find him "Walking with God" for over three hundred years. He was found keeping pace with the expectations of God and was conversant as they communicated each day. This brings to mind that they might have taken daily walks in the cool of the day and maybe even through gardens of flowers with the sweet smells and beautiful colors contributing in a positive way to their time together. Their relationship was certainly so special that God took him without earthly death and burial.

The last words regarding Enoch are found in the New Testament and reaffirm this special relationship that Enoch had with the Living God. ... *(Hebrews 11:5) By faith Enoch was taken up so that he would not see death; AND HE WAS NOT FOUND BECAUSE GOD TOOK HIM UP; for he obtained the witness that before his being taken up he was pleasing to God.* It is truly pleasing to God if we are to be found "Walking with Him".

2. Noah – "Walked with God" — *(Genesis 6:8-9)(vs 6) But Noah found favor in the eyes of the LORD. (vs 9) These are the records of the generations of Noah. Noah was a righteous man, blameless in his time; Noah walked with God.*

Much has been written about the life of Noah and his family and his following God's instructions. God started over with man by taking Noah's family and sparing them during the great flood. Noah took on responsibilities which were unheard of at the time and built a huge boat in accordance with God's directions. Noah exercised faith beyond imagination as he literally floated off into "uncharted" waters. Noah's "Walk with God" was termed "blameless". He is truly an example to be modeled and followed as we all attempt to "Walk with our Lord".

Noah was also highlighted in the New Testament in ... *(Hebrews 11:7) By faith Noah, being warned by God about things not yet seen, in reverence prepared an ark for the salvation of his*

household, by which he condemned the world, and became an heir of the righteousness which is according to faith.

This "Walking with God" by Noah, also super emphasizes the "Walking by Faith" principles, which were required of all in the days of old, and are now required of all of us today. Our "Walking with God" is not always on a path that is well defined, but that path may be only revealed with each step we take. Praise God for He is faithful to keep us from stumbling (or drowning as we see in the life of Noah), as we take these steps of faith in our "Walk with Him"!

3. John The Baptist – "Walked with God" — **(Matthew 3:1-6) (vs 1) Now in those days John the Baptist *came, preaching in the wilderness of Judea, saying, (vs 2) "Repent, for the kingdom of heaven is at hand." (vs 3) For this is the one referred to by Isaiah the prophet when he said, "THE VOICE OF ONE CRYING IN THE WILDERNESS, 'MAKE READY THE WAY OF THE LORD, MAKE HIS PATHS STRAIGHT!'" (vs 4) Now John himself had a garment of camel's hair and a leather belt around his waist; and his food was locusts and wild honey. (vs 5) Then Jerusalem was going out to him, and all Judea and all the district around the Jordan; (vs 6) and they were being baptized by him in the Jordan River, as they confessed their sins.**

John the Baptist was special from the time spent in his mother's womb until his untimely death. His entire life was spent "Walking with God". He was called out by God to bring the Good News of the Gospel as the forerunner of Jesus, and he faithfully did so without compromise. Jesus himself, gave John the highest compliment attributable to man ... **(Matthew 11:9-11)(vs 9) "But what did you go out to see? A prophet? Yes, I tell you, and one who is more than a prophet. (vs 10) "This is the one about whom it is written, 'BEHOLD, I SEND MY MESSENGER AHEAD OF YOU, WHO WILL PREPARE YOUR WAY BEFORE YOU.' (vs 11) "Truly I say to you, among those born of women there has not arisen anyone greater than John the Baptist! Yet the one who is least in the kingdom of heaven is greater than he.**

If only each of us could hear these words spoken at our funerals as we go to meet our Savior. "Well done you faithful servant" would be music to our ears as we depart, after having "Walked with Jesus" for our 60-80 years. John the Baptist is a role model and example to be followed in our "Walk with Him". John the Baptist's life is worthy of further study.

B. VERSES ENCOMPASSING GOD'S DESIRE THAT WE "WALK WITH HIM":

It is truly the desire of our Lord Jesus Christ that we "Walk with Him".

1. *(Psalms 15:1-5)(vs 1) A Psalm of David. O LORD, who may abide in Your tent? Who may dwell on Your holy hill? (vs 2) He who walks with integrity, and works righteousness, And speaks truth in his heart. (vs 3) He does not slander with his tongue, Nor does evil to his neighbor, Nor takes up a reproach against his friend; (vs 4) In whose eyes a reprobate is despised, But who honors those who fear the LORD; He swears to his own hurt and does not change; (vs 5) He does not put out his money at interest, Nor does he take a bribe against the innocent. He who does these things will never be shaken.*

We find these instructions in the Old Testament delivered to us from the hand and pen of the Psalmist David. These words of authority do very much encompass our life and affairs, as we go from day to day. The depth of advice and cautions as covered in these five (5) verses are sufficient for our lives from birth until death. Our challenge is to know and apply these Godly thoughts from morning until night of each of our days. They certainly contain a road map to "Walking with God".

Our "Walking with God" may be ordinary or it may someday lead us to a tightrope above the falls of Niagara. In either case, and in all variations between, we are assured by His Word that we ... ***"will never be shaken"***. This promise from God is that we will never be alone regardless of the mundane situations we may find ourselves involved in, or if we are called upon to "Walk" through the valley of the shadow of death. Let me testify, I have been there and I found a peace only explainable by the presence of the Almighty God. We are steadied and held fast by His hands and no one can shake our lives if we are held by Him.

2. *(Philippians 4:6-7)(vs 6) Be anxious for nothing, but in everything by prayer and supplication with thanksgiving let your requests be made known to God. (vs 7) And the peace of God, which surpasses all comprehension, will guard your hearts and your minds in Christ Jesus.*

In the world we live in today, where the news media is current with events from any part of our globe, and is devilishly trying to impose upon us a creation of anxiety, we need this verse more than at any time in history. I don't mean to be simplistic, harsh or seem to come across as out of touch, but we don't need to be giving our kids pills to reduce their natural energies, and we don't need to be modifying our own minds with prescription pills, alcohol or even illegal drugs to calm our nerves. Jesus has provided the answers to all of our anxieties. He is sufficient if we study our "Owner's Manual" and "Abide in Him", or in other words, "Walk with Him"!

3. Colossians 3: 1-17 is the perfect example of many of the details involved in "Walking with God". Because of the length of this passage I believe it would be helpful to break this down and look at these seventeen (17) verses in three smaller parcels. Hopefully this will allow for more consideration of each verse and maybe help to prevent the magnitude of the individual verses from being lost in the volume of the whole. We are amazingly blessed by God's Word being so rich, that we generally can only glean small amounts from each reading. With this in mind, let's glean and absorb what we can, leaving many additional truths and wisdom for future readings.

a. *(Colossians 3:1-3)(vs 1) Therefore if you have been raised up with Christ, keep seeking the things above, where Christ is, seated at the right hand of God. (vs 2) Set your mind on the things above, not on the things that are on earth. (vs 3) For you have died and your life is hidden with Christ in God.*

The Apostle Paul beautifully writes how we Christians are to "Walk with God". Without using those words, he exhorts us to remember where we came from and who it was who raised us up to this new level of life. He encourages us to put our thoughts on the things above and not on earthly, perishable goods. Our old life is dead and we are now engulfed in the life and love of Christ.

b. *(Colossians 3:4-11)(vs 4) When Christ, who is our life, is revealed, then you also will be revealed with Him in glory. (vs 5) Therefore consider the members of your earthly body as dead to immorality, impurity, passion, evil desire, and greed, which amounts to idolatry. (vs 6) For it is because of these things that the wrath of God will come upon the sons of disobedience, (vs 7) and in them you also once walked, when you were living in them. (vs 8) But now you also, put them all aside: anger, wrath, malice, slander, and abusive speech from your mouth. (vs 9) Do not lie to one another, since you laid aside the old self with its evil practices, (vs 10) and have put on the new self who is being renewed to a true knowledge according to the image of the One who created him— (vs 11) a renewal in which there is no distinction between Greek and Jew, circumcised and uncircumcised, barbarian, Scythian, slave and freeman, but Christ is all, and in all.*

We are to put away the old self and "Walk" in our new regeneration, as perfected through Christ and His work on the Cross. We are encouraged, exhorted, and pleaded with to put away the old degenerate ways for the new self, eternally founded in the image of God. We now have no ethnic, cultural or positional backgrounds. We are new creations since we now find that *"Christ is all, and in all"*. These verses deal with the "old" and the "new", the "dead" and the "alive", as we venture out in our new eternal journey of "Walking with Him".

c. *(Colossians 3:12-17)(vs 12) So, as those who have been chosen of God, holy and beloved, put on a heart of compassion, kindness, humility, gentleness and patience; (vs 13) bearing with one another, and forgiving each other, whoever has a complaint against anyone; just as the Lord forgave you, so also should you. (vs 14) Beyond all these things put on love, which is the perfect bond of unity. (vs 15) Let the peace of Christ rule in your hearts, to which indeed you were called in one body; and be thankful. (vs 16) Let the word of Christ richly dwell within you, with all wisdom teaching and admonishing one another with psalms and hymns and spiritual songs, singing with thankfulness in your hearts to God. (vs 17) Whatever you do in word or deed, do all in the*

name of the Lord Jesus, giving thanks through Him to God the Father.

If "We Belong To Him" we are to exemplify Christ in all the ways spoken of in verses 12-17. These verses encompass "Walking with God" more succinctly and completely than anything I could say. "Walking with God" is doing all that we do, in word and deed, ***"in the name of the Lord Jesus",*** while ***"giving thanks through Him to God the Father".***

C. BENEFITS OF "WALKING WITH GOD":

<u>1</u>. (Deuteronomy 5:33) "You shall walk in all the way which the LORD your God has commanded you, that you may live and that it may be well with you, and that you may prolong your days in the land which you will possess.

God's promises are certain, absolute, unchanging and to be relied upon forever. If we will "Walk with the Lord", our paths will be blessed and the possessions He has awarded to us will be used to glorify Him. Our days will be many and our life will be established in contentment, before our God.

<u>2</u>. (Psalms 23:1-6)(vs 1) A Psalm of David. The LORD is my shepherd, I shall not want. (vs 2) He makes me lie down in green pastures; He leads me beside quiet waters. (vs 3) He restores my soul; He guides me in the paths of righteousness For His name's sake. (vs 4) Even though I walk through the valley of the shadow of death, I fear no evil, for You are with me; Your rod and Your staff, they comfort me. (vs 5) You prepare a table before me in the presence of my enemies; You have anointed my head with oil; My cup overflows. (vs 6) Surely goodness and lovingkindness will follow me all the days of my life, And I will dwell in the house of the LORD forever.

Most everyone has heard of or read the 23rd Psalm. It exudes comfort, peacefulness, and assurance, as well as contains many wonderful promises. It is often used in times of trials and is associated with the comforting of the grieving, that is understandably found at funerals.

Without overlooking the blessings of comforts so readily available in these verses, we are to look deeply at the promises and benefits of "Walking with God". These promises and benefits, as only can be found wrapped up in the bountiful treasures of His Word, are readily available in the 23rd Psalm. The Psalmist David writes with authority, that God will keep us from fear, grant us abundance as needed, while all the time we will be protected with His goodness and loving kindness. God's Word promises us that through all circumstances His presence is with us including even in the most extreme times of need, such as walking *"through the valley of the shadow of death"*. My suggestion is that we all, "Walk with" and have as our "constant companion", the Almighty God of Heaven.

There was a popular song recorded by a well-known artist some years ago about two sets of footprints in the sand. The story goes something like this. God and man were walking together through life and it was noted by man that during times of difficulty and trials, there were only one set of footprints. The man asked God, "Why did you abandon me when times were the most difficult". God looked at the man and said, "son I didn't leave you, for when times were at the worse I carried you, that is why there was so often only one set of footprints". This illustrates the benefits of "Walking with God", for He will carry each of us in these times of greatest need.

3. (Proverbs 3:19-26)(vs 19) The LORD by wisdom founded the earth, By understanding He established the heavens. (vs 20) By His knowledge the deeps were broken up And the skies drip with dew. (vs 21) My son, let them not vanish from your sight; Keep sound wisdom and discretion, (vs 22) So they will be life to your soul And adornment to your neck. (vs 23) Then you will walk in your way securely And your foot will not stumble. (vs 24) When you lie down, you will not be afraid; When you lie down, your sleep will be sweet. (vs 25) Do not be afraid of sudden fear Nor of the onslaught of the wicked when it comes; (vs 26) For the LORD will be your confidence And will keep your foot from being caught.

The One who established the heavens and founded the earth is talking. We need to give special attention and listen. He is most knowledgeable and I for one am sure if He were available to speak with us today on a one-to-one basis, He would give us the straight scoop on all current matters. This would include among many topics, the current controversial issue over global warming. After all, He is in control of our universe, which is much bigger than our little speck called planet earth. This much is certain and that is, His plan will not be altered by man's genius or the lack thereof. Now back to the issues at hand.

The benefits detailed in the above scriptures are many. We find wisdom and discretion, with the rights and responsibilities to utilize these life-long, God-given qualities. We find the ability of not stumbling, in other words, as we "Walk with Him", He grants us assurance and security in our personal and business ventures. We are immune to fears or sudden disturbances and when trouble comes (as it most certainly will) we will have the confidence that He is "Walking with us". The *"onslaught of the wicked"* will come, but it will be taken in stride because even though the battle may seem to go against us, we know already the war has been won in our favor. The God who created the universe is willing to "Walk with us"! Let us get into His "Owner's Manual" and learn what it takes to "Walk with Him"!!!

D. BIBLICAL ENCOURAGEMENTS TO "WALK WITH HIM":

1. *(Deuteronomy 10:12-15)(vs 12) "Now, Israel, what does the LORD your God require from you, but to fear the LORD your God, to walk in all His ways and love Him, and to serve the LORD your God with all your heart and with all your soul, (vs 13) and to keep the LORD'S commandments and His statutes which I am commanding you today for your good? (vs 14) "Behold, to the LORD your God belong heaven and the highest heavens, the earth and all that is in it. (vs 15) "Yet on your fathers did the LORD set His affection to love them, and He chose their descendants after them, even you above all peoples, as it is this day.*

As "born again" New Testament believers we are free to apply the Old Testament teachings to our lives. These Old Testament scriptures require of us ... *"to fear the LORD your God, to walk in all His ways and love Him"*. These requirements fulfilled, bring promised blessings that are sooo good that I can't imagine anyone passing on these. God promises to love us and our descendants after us. This love will always be for our good, including our need for times of discipline. Yes! His affection towards us is without bounds and is unsurpassable as we ... *"walk in all His ways and love Him"*.

2. *(Jeremiah 7:23-24)(vs 23) "But this is what I commanded them, saying, 'Obey My voice, and I will be your God, and you will be My people; and you will walk in all the way which I command you, that it may be well with you.' (vs 24) "Yet they did not obey or incline their ear, but walked in their own counsels and in the stubbornness of their evil heart, and went backward and not forward.*

Jeremiah, a God appointed prophet, has declared it will be "well" with those who choose to "Walk with God". "Well" carries a meaning of: thoroughly, or as applied in all areas of our daily lives, we will find contentment in everything we do or attempt to accomplish. Everyone wants to be a success in life and here we find the keys to successful living and that is "Walking with Him". I guess we have no more need of those self-improvement books, just simply apply the "Word of God".

It would not be fair to each of us to not consider the negative or contrary to "Walking with God" since this warning is found in such close proximity to our verse of highlighted consideration. We find this sister verse to be *Jeremiah 7:24*, and it sternly warns us as follows: If we choose to not obey or if we choose not to listen to God's Word, then we can expect to be rewarded with going *"backward"*. This in the original Hebrew is defined as: being "without". As we study and look at what "without" meant to the Children of Israel for their disobedience, we find misery and even death, as God exercised His wrath and justice on a whole generation of disobedient hearts.

As for me and my house, and hopefully and prayerfully for your house, the decision will be made to "Walk with God" instead of "Walking **backward**"!!!

3. *(Philippians 1:27) Only conduct yourselves in a manner worthy of the gospel of Christ, so that whether I come and see you or remain absent, I will hear of you that* *you are standing firm in one spirit, with one mind striving together for the faith of the gospel;*

I consider *"standing firm in one spirit, with one mind striving together for the faith of the gospel"* to be akin to "Walking with God". The Apostle Paul exhorts us to "Stand Firm" or in other words to always be in "Step with our Living Lord".

We can do nothing to persuade someone into the Kingdom of Heaven. We cannot talk people into a salvation experience of becoming a "born-again" believer in Jesus Christ. As one "Who Belongs To Him" we have the responsibility to be the Godly example that will lead those around us to consider Christ. We may be the only example of the Gospel that someone in the world may experience. May our testimony be one that demonstrates His righteousness and not one that tears down the credibility of the word Christian. "Standing Firm" and "Walking with Him" are one and the same.

E. COMMANDMENT TO "WALK WITH THE LORD YOUR GOD":

<u>1.</u> *(Joshua 22:5) "Only be very careful to observe the commandment and the law which Moses the servant of the LORD commanded you, to love the LORD your God and walk in all His ways and keep His commandments and hold fast to Him and serve Him with all your heart and with all your soul."*

Because of what Jesus accomplished upon the Cross and because of His love for us, we are expected and literally commanded to live out the appreciation of His Sacrifice and the resulting unmerited Grace which has been allowed to us. This is not something we do as a required work to earn favor or in any way to earn salvation, but it is something that naturally flows from our inner being, as we recognize and appreciate our "Belonging To Him"!!!

Our lifestyle will daily demonstrate by living out what the Apostle James has so wisely stated in ... *(James 2:18) But someone may well say, "You have faith and I have works; show me your faith without the works, and I will show you my faith by my works."*

208

F. CONCLUSION TO "WALKING WITH GOD":

The Church is a burning flame while it is meeting together. It is when we walk alone, without the fellowship of others, that we tend to lose our candlepower. God desires us to be a dispersed burning flame as we go out into our individual homes and workplaces. It is in this, that we call our daily routine, where we are most challenged to "Walk with Him". The question is, how do we maintain our candlepower and our "Walk with God", seven days a week?

(John 10:10) "The thief comes only to steal and kill and destroy; I came that they may have life, and have it abundantly.

Each individual has the opportunity to allow an ever flowing river of love, joy and peace to pass through their being while serving others. These qualities are available as if there were a direct pipeline from heaven's reservoirs, plugged into our hands and feet. With peace in our minds, love flowing through the actions of our hands and our feet and with a joy in our hearts, we have the opportunity of being gloriously transformed into the image of God. This likeness of Him should then be lived out in our homes and our workplace, all the while being of service to others ... *(Mark 10:45) "For even the Son of Man did not come to be served, but to serve, and to give His life a ransom for many.";* ... *(Acts 20:35) "In everything I showed you that by working hard in this manner you must help the weak and remember the words of the Lord Jesus, that He Himself said, 'It is more blessed to give than to receive.'";* and ... *(Galatians 5:13) For you were called to freedom, brethren; only do not turn your freedom into an opportunity for the flesh, but through love serve one another.* These things will all take place in a natural fashion as we find ourselves abiding in the exciting adventures of "Walking with God".

A person who finds the fruits of the Holy Spirit to be real in their lives, cannot help but to look upon their jobs (lawyer, insurance, surgeon, medical doctor, manufacturer, accountant, clergyman, craftsman, builder, engineer, geologist, businessman, consultant, and so many others) as an opportunity of serving God with all excitement and enthusiasm. If we have failed to experience this type of abundant life, and are only inwardly lying to ourselves by saying we have this "Walk with God", while not feeling or experiencing this joy of service, then it is time to do a check-up on "To Whom Do You Belong" (?).

God has an abundant life plan for each of us and that can be carried out as it lies within the conscientious grasp of each of us. This promise of abundant life is both in knowing Him as well as in serving Him. Any resemblance of carrying on this abundant life of service to Him, will be in direct relationship of the amount of time spent in His Word. The flame and desire to be of service to God, will burn in direct proportion with the amount of feeding and nourishment being taken from His Word. Just as we become weak from lack of daily intake of physical food, we also become malnourished from lack of spiritual food. This condition can come to the point that we leave ourselves open to spiritual disease and subject ourselves to the influence of Satan. In a weakened condition Satan finds it both possible and easy to enter into our lives to create frustration and disappointment with our "Walk with God".

On the other side of this coin, we have the spiritually full person who has eaten daily with their study, reading and meditating upon God's Word, and cannot lose the battle with Satan. As we have the Holy Spirit fed, alive and well within us ... *(1 Corinthians 3:16) Do you not know that you are a temple of God and that the Spirit of God dwells in you? (1 Corinthians 6:19) Or do you not know that your body is a temple of the Holy Spirit who is in you, whom you have from God, and that you are not your own? ... (2 Timothy 1:14) Guard, through the Holy Spirit who dwells in us, the treasure which has been entrusted to you.* ... we have the power to defeat Satan in every battle ... *(1 John 4:4) You are from God, little children, and have overcome them; because greater is He who is in you than he who is in the world.*

The battle that goes on within us is not of flesh and blood, but in principalities and powers and spiritual forces in dark places, of which as man we have no defense ... *(Ephesians 6:12) For our struggle is not against flesh and blood, but against the rulers, against the powers, against the world forces of this darkness, against the spiritual forces of wickedness in the heavenly places.* This is probably the primary reason God has placed into every "born-again" believer the indwelling of His Holy Spirit. Once we realize the above is a fact, and true at all times, not just part of the time, we should be able to effectively overcome all challenges or any thoughts of irrevocable dilemmas. Knowing that we are indwelled by His Holy Spirit, gives us full confidence that we can daily "Walk with Him"!!!

The conditions of maintaining spiritual health, or a real "Walk with God", are not optional, but are **LAWS**. Just as we recognize the laws of gravity, or forces and other universal physical restraints, we must also recognize our spiritual laws cannot be violated. All of the scripture above referring to "Walking with God", are our governing laws, and must be abided by. In abiding in Him and "Walking with Him" we will find an abundant earthly life.

God offers us and has made available to us this abundant life. This is a life filled with the indwelling of the Holy Spirit. The "Fruits of His Spirit" are ... *(Galatians 5:22-23)(vs 22) But the fruit of the Spirit is love, joy, peace, patience, kindness, goodness, faithfulness, (vs 23) gentleness, self-control; against such things there is no law.* Now with this indwelling of the Holy Spirit, and the availability of His "Owner's Manual" as our guide, we have all the necessary tools and ingredients to "Walk with Him", seven days a week. This ability to "Walk with Him" 24/7/365, will bless us beyond measure and will overflow into the lives of those who are around us.

All of those having read the above have now been led into this clear path of "Walking with Him". God has provided an abundant life for us, He indwells the "believer", He gives us the "Fruits of the Spirit", and He is greater than any other power in the universe. All the ingredients are here, we only need to know and be obedient to our "Owner's Manual".

SPECIAL NOTE:

I know many of you may have a special verse or verses regarding this Chapter's subject matter. This special verse or these verses may not have been mentioned due to my ignorance or because of brevity. I apologize for either of these reasons. Please feel free to write any special verse or verses in the space below. This will add your personal touch, and will serve to call to each person's mind their individual "experience of trust", in God's Holy Word.

For to each of us "Who belong To Him", His Holy Word can be truly recognized and relied upon as our **"Owner's Manual"**!!!

_____

_____

_____

_____

_____

_____

_____

CHAPTER 11

MARRIAGE (SEPARATE BUT EQUAL ROLES)

INTRODUCTORY VERSE:

(Romans 16:3-5)(vs 3) Greet Prisca and Aquila, my fellow workers in Christ Jesus, (vs 4) who for my life risked their own necks, to whom not only do I give thanks, but also all the churches of the Gentiles; (vs 5) also greet the church that is in their house.

This wife and husband, as a team, are mentioned several times in the New Testament. They are, in all cases, mentioned as favorable to God's work and as a witness of His Word. The above mentions their dedication to "Whom they Belonged", as they ministered to Paul the Apostle, by taking unknown risks, *"who for my life risked their own necks"*. We are not sure what these risks were, but we are certain they were serious and very real. Paul was eternally thankful to them, and their efforts were a blessing to not only himself, but to all the churches of the Gentiles.

As married couples today, together serving the Lord, we can only hope we are spoken of as favorably as Priscilla and Aquila, and that our lives and all the days given to us by God, will have a positive impact for the One "To Whom We Belong"!!! This couple, along with many others, are "such a beautiful example to model".

INTRODUCTION — The Marriage Relationship Built To Last:

The roles found in the Christian, earthly marriage, to be properly understood and implemented, are best to be compared and modeled after God and His Triune relationship of the Father, the Son and the Holy

Spirit. The Almighty God, Yahweh, has devised an incomprehensible plan of the SEPARATE roles of the Triune Godhead. While each role is decidedly different, the Three are ONE GOD! Not the Father, nor the Son, nor the Holy Spirit have a superior role in God's heavenly plan, but each has delivered and continue to deliver, their specific, respective and SEPARATE part in the reconciliation of MAN. These Godhead roles will continue in their eternally designed fashion until MAN is judged by God on that Final Judgment Day. God the Son, while sitting at the right hand of God the Father, will each administer their EQUAL yet SEPARATE roles, as they usher in our new eternal Kingdom. This mystery is great, but His Word is to be trusted even when we don't fully understand.

The mystery of the earthly marriage is equally as great as the mystery of the Triune Godhead, as we can see through the following words found in our "Owner's Manual". .... *(Eph 5:31-32)(vs 31) FOR THIS REASON A MAN SHALL LEAVE HIS FATHER AND MOTHER AND SHALL BE JOINED TO HIS WIFE, AND THE TWO SHALL BECOME ONE FLESH. (vs 32) This mystery is great; but I am speaking with reference to Christ and the church.* This mysterious relationship of Husband and Wife and their ONENESS, can only be explained throughout the Bible by understanding that neither the Husband nor the Wife, have superior roles. These roles are EQUAL while being SEPARATE and are specifically defined by God, to be answered for by each in Honoring and bring Glory to God in their fulfillment. It cannot be emphasized enough to understand that these roles are EQUAL yet SEPARATE, and cannot be thought of by either party of one being superior over the other. These roles are to be understood and implemented as each of us who "Belong To Him" stand before God in the exercising of this responsibility of loving and caring for our earthly mates

The sooner the Husband and Wife understands this EQUAL while SEPARATE responsibilities in their relationship, the sooner the peace of God can settle over the earthly marriage, thereby creating a ONENESS, modeled after the ONENESS found in the Triune Godhead. With this mystery of <u>man</u> and <u>woman</u> becoming one flesh being grasped, and with God's help in this understanding, we can now implement, demonstrate and therefore receive His blessings, throughout this fleeting stay here on earth.

Man and Woman can now be reconciled to love, cherish, support, respect and enjoy each other in a loving and working relationship, that will Honor God, and will last a life time. This God appointed relationship will now become one to be demonstrated to all the world, that the mystery spoken of by God can work and therefore bring complete (100%) satisfaction of both spouses, all the while bring full Glory to God!!!

While the above principles are the intertwining theme throughout this Chapter there are numerous daily, mundane details in our marriages that need consideration. A few of these daily marriage details are considered in the balance of this introduction. These real life examples of problem areas are not exhaustive, but are here to wake up the marriage partners to the fact that God can work in all "believers" relationships to solve anything!

Our marriages are constantly being bombarded by stress and conflict that can drain the joy out of any marriage relationship and lead to ruin. Christian marriages are as prone to cracking under this daily bombardment as a non-Christian marriage and will do so unless we take action, to allow Christ to seal our marriage in Him. This should take place at the altar, but often does not.

What can we do to be certain Satan will not get his foot in the door and begin the insidious unraveling of what began as the "perfect" romance, the "perfect" marriage, the road to "happy forever after"? How can we be certain that throughout our marriage, no matter what storm clouds gather and gale winds blow, our marriage stands strong?

Perhaps your marriage is just getting started. You are in the honeymoon period and there is not a cloud in the sky. I can only say that the clouds will form and the storms will come. You can count on it. Perhaps you have already encountered issues, differences of opinions on finances, problems with parents or other such skirmishes. Or perhaps your relationship is being strained to the limits by major stressors such as how to raise the children, illness, intimacy issues, death of a child, financial issues. Or perhaps the fire of romance that once burned has been reduced to embers or worse yet has gone out completely and you now see no way out short of separation.

The following Biblical principles can help pull you from the brink, or provide a foundation for a marriage built to last, no matter your stage or circumstance. It is with these basic scriptural principles that we can build our marriages upon to fend off the storms, or if the storms have already been ravaging our lives, we can begin to rebuild our marriage relationship and find joy and romance once again.

A. FOUNDATIONAL SCRIPTURES:

1. One Flesh:

A marriage built to last is a Christ centered marriage with a foundation built on scriptural principles and obedience to God's commands. To set the cornerstone for this foundation we must go literally to the beginning, to the book of Genesis which sets forth the "one flesh" principle.

(Genesis 2:23-24)(vs 23) The man said, "This is now bone of my bones, And flesh of my flesh; She shall be called Woman, Because she was taken out of Man." (vs 24) For this reason a man shall leave his father and his mother, and be joined to his wife; and they shall become one flesh.

This verse describes the creation of marriage prior to sin's entrance into the world and could therefore be considered a part of God's perfect plan.[1]

How would we apply this verse to our marriages today? Does it refer to the breaking away from parental protection or authority to go out on our own? Does it refer to the intimacy of the sexual union? Yes answers can be appropriately inferred, but when examined closely we see it means even more than these thoughts. A man and wife are to lose their identity as individuals, serving their own needs and purposes, and are now to become a new entity we call man and wife. The man, now broken away from his parents, takes on the role of provider, protector and possibly father and the wife, now broken away from her parental shelter, takes on the role as helpmate, homemaker and possibly mother. The two individuals now become "one", physically through sexual intimacy, emotionally or mentally in seeking the mutual best interest of the new entity or family unit and spiritually in their focus and obedience to our God.

---

[1] How Should a Christian View Marriage and Divorce, Amy Desai, J.D. Article for Focus on the Family, *Helping Families Thrive*

It is to show this new special union that, traditionally, the wife gives up her own family name and takes on that of her husband. It is also the reason that in many weddings it is typical to take the flame of two individual candles on the altar that represent the man and the wife and light a new larger candle. This symbolizes the fusion of two individuals into one new unit, and I like to think of it as under one light, the light of Christ.

The two have become "one", a new, mystical unit joined together by God through the marriage vows, and inseparable, never to be taken apart by any man inside or outside the marriage relationship.

2. The Model of the Trinity:

To further illustrate this new union and to guide us as to how it is to function, we have within scripture the model of the Trinity. Marriage has often been referred to as an analogy to the Trinity in efforts to try to explain in human terms how our Triune God functions. This comparison, however, is also beneficial to us in our marriage if we look at it the other way around and see our Triune God as a model for our marriage.

To further examine this let's look at this diagram below used to describe the relationship of God the Father, God the Son and God the Holy Spirit.

The Shield of the Trinity[2]

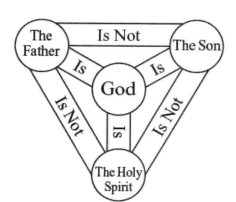

Within the Trinity we have three distinct Persons, coequal, coexistent and coeternal. Yet, all are one Being. James White, in his book, "The

---

2   Shield of the Trinity Graphic from Wikipedia

Forgotten Trinity", puts it this way. "God, though three distinct persons is one indivisible divine essence. Each Person in full and equal participation in the Divine Being. And though each person of the Trinity is fully God, each has separate and distinct roles and yet works in perfect harmony and understanding of the other as one substance".[3]

When we take our marriage vows before God, is this not the type of union He would expect in our marriage relationship. That we should be one in body, mind and spirit, "one flesh", yet, two people coequal in humanity, importance and personhood, working together harmoniously.

What a beautiful picture of how matrimony should be as we walk away from the altar having committed our marriage to God almighty, focused on Jesus Christ and walking in the Spirit.

So our second principle is to model our marriage, through our vows, after the relationship God has shown us between the Father and the Son. We will come back to this illustration as we progress in this chapter.

3. Submit One to the Other:

The third principle is if we submit one to the other we foster marital harmony and accord. The model of the Trinity gives us a picture of the way in which a man and a wife are to be mutually submissive. As God the Father and God the Son have distinctive roles within the Trinity, so do a husband and wife have distinctive roles within the marriage relationship, yet each have equality within the "one flesh" as do God the Father and God the Son within the Trinity.

With this in mind, look at how Paul describes this relationship, comparing the relationship of husband and wife to Christ and the church.

(Ephesians 5:22-31)(vs 22) Wives, be subject to your own husbands, as to the Lord. (vs 23) For the husband is the head of the wife, as Christ also is the head of the church, He Himself being the Savior of the body. (vs 24) But as the church is subject to Christ, so also the wives ought to be to their husbands in everything. (vs 25) Husbands, love your wives, just as Christ also loved the church and gave Himself up for her, (vs 26) so that He might sanctify her, having cleansed her by the washing of water with the word, (vs 27) that He might present to Himself the church in all her glory,

---

3   James White, The Forgotten Trinity

having no spot or wrinkle or any such thing; but that she would be holy and blameless. (vs 28) So husbands ought also to love their own wives as their own bodies. He who loves his own wife loves himself; (vs 29) for no one ever hated his own flesh, but nourishes and cherishes it, just as Christ also does the church, (vs 30) because we are members of His body. (vs 31) FOR THIS REASON A MAN SHALL LEAVE HIS FATHER AND MOTHER AND SHALL BE JOINED TO HIS WIFE, AND THE TWO SHALL BECOME ONE FLESH.

What a beautiful passage and yet so many want to distort it. Many read this and see only a wife kowtowing in temerity to a demanding husband whenever he snaps his fingers. What in fact is portrayed, are the roles and responsibilities that each person has within a beautiful symbiotic relationship of a "one flesh" marriage. So, what do these verses mean?

Husbands are to have the leadership role spiritually. This is an important responsibility with very serious implications. Just as Christ incarnate was in constant communion with the Father, seeking his will at all times, so must a husband be doing the same. And just as Christ was shepherding and protecting his flock of believers, so must a husband be doing the same for his wife.

To get further insight into this responsibility and relationship of husband to wife, such as Christ has with His church, let us look at how Christ related to his disciples.

a. First, Christ loved his disciples completely and unconditionally.

(John 3:16) "For God so loved the world, that He gave His only begotten Son, that whoever believes in Him shall not perish, but have eternal life.

He was willing to give his life for them and for us even though we did not deserve it. And so should a husband be willing to do the same for his wife.

b. Second, Jesus looked after their needs large and small. He turns water into wine.

(John 2:11) This beginning of His signs Jesus did in Cana of Galilee, and manifested His glory, and His disciples believed in Him.

He provides them with a bountiful catch of fish after they had been toiling all day and had come up empty handed after.

(Luke 5:4-11)(vs 4) When He had finished speaking, He said to Simon, "Put out into the deep water and let down your nets for a catch." (vs 5) Simon answered and said, "Master, we worked hard all night and caught nothing, but I will do as You say and let down the nets." (vs 6) When they had done this, they enclosed a great quantity of fish, and their nets began to break; (vs 7) so they signaled to their partners in the other boat for them to come and help them. And they came and filled both of the boats, so that they began to sink. (vs 8) But when Simon Peter saw that, he fell down at Jesus' feet, saying, "Go away from me Lord, for I am a sinful man!" (vs 9) For amazement had seized him and all his companions because of the catch of fish which they had taken; (vs 10) and so also were James and John, sons of Zebedee, who were partners with Simon. And Jesus said to Simon, "Do not fear, from now on you will be catching men." (vs 11) When they had brought their boats to land, they left everything and followed Him.

In ... *(Matthew 8:23-27)(vs 23) When He got into the boat, His disciples followed Him. (vs 24) And behold, there arose a great storm on the sea, so that the boat was being covered with the waves; but Jesus Himself was asleep. (vs 25) And they came to Him and woke Him, saying, "Save us, Lord; we are perishing!" (vs 26) He *said to them, "Why are you afraid, you men of little faith?" Then He got up and rebuked the winds and the sea, and it became perfectly calm. (vs 27) The men were amazed, and said, "What kind of a man is this, that even the winds and the sea obey Him?"* ... He calmed the storm that endangered their lives and again in ... *(Matthew 14:32-33) (vs 32) When they got into the boat, the wind stopped. (vs 33) And those who were in the boat worshiped Him, saying, "You are certainly God's Son!"* ... He calms the strong headwind that was making it difficult to bring their boat to shore.

c. Third, Jesus showed humility in their presence by serving them as He washed their feet.

(Luke 22:27) "For who is greater, the one who reclines at the table or the one who serves? Is it not the one who reclines at the table? But I am among you as the one who serves.

We as husbands are to put our ego and pride aside to be certain that our actions toward our wife are focused on building her esteem, meeting her needs and making her a better person.

d. Fourth, He taught them. This is evident throughout Scripture including the verse above. A husband should be helping his wife grow in her faith and understanding of God's word, facilitating her "walk" and not being an impediment.

e. Fifth, He gave them assurance and provided for them at a time when he would be gone.

An example of this assurance is shown to us in *(John 14:1-4)(vs 1) "Do not let your heart be troubled; believe in God, believe also in Me. (vs 2) "In My Father's house are many dwelling places; if it were not so, I would have told you; for I go to prepare a place for you. (vs 3) "If I go and prepare a place for you, I will come again and receive you to Myself, that where I am, there you may be also. (vs 4) "And you know the way where I am going."*

He provided for them, and for us, when He sent the Holy Spirit upon His departure from earth.

(John 14:16-17)(vs 16) "I will ask the Father, and He will give you another Helper, that He may be with you forever; (vs 17) that is the Spirit of truth, whom the world cannot receive, because it does not see Him or know Him, but you know Him because He abides with you and will be in you.

Husbands are to provide for their wife's security while on this earth and make provisions for her in the event God calls us to glory ahead of her.

f. Sixth, He revealed God to his disciples.

(John 17:3) "This is eternal life, that they may know You, the only true God, and Jesus Christ whom You have sent. Husbands, do you let God's light shine through you in your attitude, speech and actions toward your wife? Is Christ revealed through you to your wife?

g. Seventh, Jesus had a "oneness" with his disciples.

(John 15:7) "If you abide in Me, and My words abide in you, ask whatever you wish, and it will be done for you.

This is a oneness in thought and purpose that translates to the disciples wanting to do that which Jesus wanted done, and Jesus wanting to provide their every need to accomplishing it. Is this the relationship you as a husband are fostering with your wife?

h. Summary of the above seven points:

Nowhere in these seven examples do we get a picture of a man snapping his fingers for "his subject" to do his bidding. Instead, we see a picture of Christ humbling himself to step out of glory to be on a level with man, with a concern so great for his disciples, or church, to teach and protect them and pray for them and ultimately die for them, so as to assure they would be presented as holy and spotless before the Father. Jesus was able to say to the Father, in ... *(John 17:12) "While I was with them, I was keeping them in Your name which You have given Me; and I guarded them and not one of them perished".* Men, is this the attitude we have in our relationship with our wives? It is the model Christ has given us to follow.

Nowhere in these examples do we get a picture of the disciples bowing out of fear for what He might do to them, but rather submitting to the will and word of Christ because of His love and caring for them. And it is this kind of volitional submission or subjection, or yielding of ones rights, that Paul speaks of in Ephesians 5:22 (quoted earlier in this section).

So, how does this play out in the role that a woman has in the marriage relationship? We have a clear model of the role of the husband as "Christ is the head of, and loves, the church", and many examples such as those just mentioned, but what about the wife? In the 24th verse of Ephesians 5, Paul does flip the analogy around stating that wives are to be subject to their husbands as the church is to Christ, or in other words as an act of submission to Christ.

This model of a Godly woman is perhaps best presented in the Epilogue of Proverbs 31.

(Proverbs 31:10)(vs 10) An excellent wife, who can find? For her worth is far above jewels. (vs 11) The heart of her husband trusts in her, And he will have no lack of gain. (vs 12) She does him good and not evil All the days of her life. (vs

13) She looks for wool and flax And works with her hands in delight. (vs 14) She is like merchant ships; She brings her food from afar. (vs 15) She rises also while it is still night And gives food to her household And portions to her maidens. (vs 16) She considers a field and buys it; From her earnings she plants a vineyard. (vs 17) She girds herself with strength And makes her arms strong. (vs 18) She senses that her gain is good; Her lamp does not go out at night. (vs 19) She stretches out her hands to the distaff, And her hands grasp the spindle. (vs 20) She extends her hand to the poor, And she stretches out her hands to the needy. (vs 21) She is not afraid of the snow for her household, For all her household are clothed with scarlet. (vs 22) She makes coverings for herself; Her clothing is fine linen and purple. (vs 23) Her husband is known in the gates, When he sits among the elders of the land. (vs 24) She makes linen garments and sells them, And supplies belts to the tradesmen. (vs 25) Strength and dignity are her clothing, And she smiles at the future. (vs 26) She opens her mouth in wisdom, And the teaching of kindness is on her tongue. (vs 27) She looks well to the ways of her household, And does not eat the bread of idleness. (vs 28) Her children rise up and bless her; Her husband also, and he praises her, saying: (vs 29) "Many daughters have done nobly, But you excel them all." (vs 30) Charm is deceitful and beauty is vain, But a woman who fears the LORD, she shall be praised. (vs 31) Give her the product of her hands, And let her works praise her in the gates.

Proverbs 31 says it about as well as it can be stated. This is not the picture of an unthinking woman who pitter-patters around after her husband, never having a thought or opinion of her own, always listening but never speaking. On the contrary, it is the picture of a woman who is treasured "far above jewels" She is one who thinks for herself, is intelligent, industrious, looks after her household and their needs but does not neglect, and in fact has a heart for, others that are needy. She is strong in spirit, has a positive outlook, free of anxiety and worry, and walks with dignity. And when she speaks, it is with wisdom. She is a wise and loving counselor to her family and her friends. She too, makes certain as best she can, that her husband is viewed with respect by others. And she can do this all, first, because of her love for Christ, and second, because of the environment created by a loving, Godly, husband.

So, the picture we draw from our third principle of submitting one to the other while maintaining distinct and separate roles leads us naturally to our fourth principle that each one belongs to the other.

4. Each Belongs to the Other:

We belong to each other as much as to ourselves. To explore this principle we now turn to ... *(1 Corinthians 7:4) The wife does not have authority over her own body, but the husband does; and likewise also the husband does not have authority over his own body, but the wife does.*

This verse flows naturally from the "one-flesh" principle of *Genesis 2:23-24*, talked about earlier and ties directly also to the verse just discussed, *Ephesians 5:28 and 29*. We now get this picture of a wife having a say over her husband's body and a husband having a say over his wife's body and when combined with a caring, loving respect for one another and a mutual mind-set and purpose within God's will it can only result in something quite beautiful and satisfying to experience.

This principle can be applied in a number of ways, such as in our appearance or in our activities or hygiene, but is especially true in the sense of physical intimacy when put in context with the verses before and after as follows.

(1 Corinthians 7:3-5)(vs 3) The husband must fulfill his duty to his wife, and likewise also the wife to her husband. (vs 4) The wife does not have authority over her own body, but the husband does; and likewise also the husband does not have authority over his own body, but the wife does. (vs 5) Stop depriving one another, except by agreement for a time, so that you may devote yourselves to prayer, and come together again so that Satan will not tempt you because of your lack of self-control.

The principle of belonging one to the other can be abused if not understood within the framework of the other principles, and in that which we are taught throughout scripture, about God's will and purpose for our lives. Also, as with all these principles, we are required to be communicating in a loving way with our wife or husband. How we communicate is the subject of another discussion, but the one thing we know, because we are human, there will always be times of misunderstanding and/or conflict. This takes us to our fifth principle.

5. Deal With Conflict and Anger Immediately:

Conflict will occur within the marriage relationship. It is not a matter of if, but rather when. How we deal with that conflict is crucial to maintaining harmony within our marriage relationship. Too many times the conflict arises, tempers will flare causing things to be said that can hurt deeply and cause wounds that take years to heal, often leaving permanent scars. That healing process is often prolonged by walking away from the conflict or argument which only exacerbates the pain, hides the problem and either festers to the point of boiling up at a later time, or covers over to cause a permanent hindrance in the functioning of the marriage.

There are a number of verses in scripture that provide wise counsel in this area of any relationship and are crucial to the functioning of the marriage relationship. *(Proverbs 14:29, 15:18, 16:32 and 19:11)* all speak to this subject. *(Proverbs 14:29) He who is slow to anger has great understanding, But he who is quick-tempered exalts folly. (Proverbs 15:18) A hot-tempered man stirs up strife, But the slow to anger calms a dispute. (Proverbs 16:32) He who is slow to anger is better than the mighty, And he who rules his spirit, than he who captures a city. (Proverbs 19:11) A man's discretion makes him slow to anger, And it is his glory to overlook a transgression.*

The following three New Testament verses give us particularly sage advice. The first offered by Paul to the Colossians, surfaces the fact that if we could be perfect in our Christian walk, we could avoid the problems that anger brings, before it even arises.

(Colossians 3:8) But now you also, put them all aside: anger, wrath, malice, slander, and abusive speech from your mouth.

As Christians, we should be continually striving to put aside our anger, wrath and abusive speech. If we could put this into practice in resolving disputes within our marriage, we would find conflict resolution to be expedient and constructive.

James also gives us advice to heed that would help provide a smoother, quicker resolution to disputes or conflicts when he says:

(James 1:19) This you know, my beloved brethren. But everyone must be quick to hear, slow to speak and slow to anger;

Take time to listen with interest to what is on our mate's mind, holding our own tongue until they have had time to disclose the entire nature of their concern or issue, and then and only then, offer appropriate and measured comment or, if need be, an apology when warranted.

But, of course, there will always be those times when emotions take over and tempers flare and verbal discourse ceases. In these cases we must heed the advice given to us by Paul when he addressed the Ephesians and said:

(Ephesians 4:26-27)(vs 26) BE ANGRY, AND yet DO NOT SIN; do not let the sun go down on your anger, (vs 27) and do not give the devil an opportunity.

Resolve differences or arguments quickly. Do not let molehills develop into mountains and become an irritation of unknown source by covering an issue over without mutual resolution. Unresolved conflict, can and will, become a drain on romance in the marriage relationship. The converse is also true that conflict resolved brings harmony within the relationship and provides an environment in which love can grow and romance flourish.

6. God Does Not Want Us to Divorce:

Should a couple find themselves in a deteriorating relationship, or in a relationship where the flame of romance has grown cold, it is important that all possible be done by both parties in submission to our Lord, to rehabilitate that relationship. We know, that if both individuals put their desire for reconciliation before the Lord, that He will lead them in the path of reconciliation and restore a vibrant marriage relationship. How do we know this? First, let's look at the Old Testament.

(Malachi 2:15-16)(vs 15) "But not one has done so who has a remnant of the Spirit. And what did that one do while he was seeking a godly offspring? Take heed then to your

spirit, and let no one deal treacherously against the wife of your youth. (vs 16) "For I hate divorce," says the LORD, the God of Israel, "and him who covers his garment with wrong," says the LORD of hosts. "So take heed to your spirit, that you do not deal treacherously."

The Lord makes a very strong statement in verse 16 when He says "For I hate divorce." He is emphatically reinforcing his concept of the "one flesh" principle in Genesis. God's desire is for us to keep our marriage vows, and this principle given us in Genesis is again repeated by Jesus in Matthew.

(Matthew 19:3-6)(vs 3) Some Pharisees came to Jesus, testing Him and asking, "Is it lawful for a man to divorce his wife for any reason at all?" (vs 4) And He answered and said, "Have you not read that He who created them from the beginning MADE THEM MALE AND FEMALE, (vs 5) and said, 'FOR THIS REASON A MAN SHALL LEAVE HIS FATHER AND MOTHER AND BE JOINED TO HIS WIFE, AND THE TWO SHALL BECOME ONE FLESH'? (vs 6) "So they are no longer two, but one flesh. What therefore God has joined together, let no man separate."

Paul then re-states Christ's position when he makes these statements to the Corinthians.

(1 Corinthians 7:10-11)(vs 10) But to the married I give instructions, not I, but the Lord, that the wife should not leave her husband (vs 11) (but if she does leave, she must remain unmarried, or else be reconciled to her husband), and that the husband should not divorce his wife.

You might be asking, "didn't Christ himself allow for divorce in certain circumstances"? In ... *(Matthew 5:31-32)(vs 31) "It was said, 'WHOEVER SENDS HIS WIFE AWAY, LET HIM GIVE HER A CERTIFICATE OF DIVORCE'; (vs 32) but I say to you that everyone who divorces his wife, except for the reason of unchastity, makes her commit adultery; and whoever marries a divorced woman commits adultery.* ... and again in ... *(Matthew 19:9) "And I say to you, whoever divorces his wife, except for immorality, and marries another woman commits adultery."*

Jesus clearly acknowledges permission for divorce in the case of adultery, but it is also clear in the wording of these verses and in the context of those quoted previously, that He does not condone it and that this is not God's desire. Many times, even marriages that have experienced an unfaithful spouse can be repaired and rehabilitated.

Based on the total context of scripture, it is clear that God regards our vows taken before Him as sacred and serious and the marriage relationship as a special one, not to be broken. So it is incumbent upon us to make every effort to repair a damaged marriage no matter the circumstances. We are one flesh with our spouse. This is a very somber relationship. It is worth repeating... *(Matthew 19:5) and said, 'FOR THIS REASON A MAN SHALL LEAVE HIS FATHER AND MOTHER AND BE JOINED TO HIS WIFE, AND THE TWO SHALL BECOME ONE FLESH'?*

Having said this, it is also true that we have a loving and merciful God who forgives our failings and transgressions when brought before Him by a truly contrite heart. So, if you have been a victim of divorce for whatever reason, be assured that a new start is possible by His grace as you turn from your past to His loving arms. If you are contemplating divorce please consider the next section regarding God's plan of forgiveness, reconciliation and restoration.

B. Forgiveness, Reconciliation, and Restoration for Husbands and Wives:

As we consider **Forgiveness**, **Reconciliation**, and **Restoration** we need to focus on each of these subjects, starting here with **Forgiveness**. Let's face it, not all marriages are perfect or even near perfect. **Forgiveness** is in order whether we have, what we might call minor sins against each other, or have what we may have easily determined to be major sins. **Forgiveness** is in order regardless of the degree of sin, and it is absolutely necessary in order to protect the trust, that is so essential to all good marriages. It is a blessing and a great hope to all of us, to realize the Biblical position and guarantee regarding **Forgiveness**.

We are not here to define the many and different marriage relationship sins, but to show the way to God's **Forgiveness**. There can be as many sins against our spouses as there are words in the dictionary, and any of these sins, and certainly all of them put together, can take their toll and cause serious rifts in our relationships. Perhaps the most serious sin against our spouse is the one of infidelity, but be aware that many of the others can and will create equal hatred and distrust. There have been marriage vows broken by so many couples, and with these broken vows and commitments comes unbelievable devastation, hatred and distrust. These broken vows and commitments have produced wounds so deep that they cannot be healed by man. But don't despair, there is hope and subsequent blessings, if both marriage partners as "born again believers", are willing to seek God's Word and therefore find a way to be **Reconciled** and **Restored**.

Any sin against your spouse is a sin against your Heavenly Father. All sins of "believers" are forgivable ... *(1 John 1:9) If we confess our sins, He is faithful and righteous to forgive us our sins and to cleanse us from all unrighteousness.* As God has made provisions to forgive you, He has also made provisions where you can forgive your spouse and your spouse can forgive you. The Lord's Prayer, and it is a very brief prayer, reinforces this two-way forgiveness by including and commanding us to forgive those who have sinned against us. ... *(Matthew 6:12) 'And forgive us our debts, as we also have forgiven our debtors.* The following scriptures contain additional wisdom for the keys to **Forgiveness** from God, as well as the **Forgiveness** of our fellow man. It is important to note this **Forgiveness** of our fellow man is required regarding others, in order to experience God's **Forgiveness** of ourselves. ... *(Matthew 6:14-15) (vs 14) "For if you forgive others for their transgressions, your heavenly Father will also forgive you. (vs 15) "But if you do not forgive others, then your Father will not forgive your transgressions. (Matthew 18:21-22)(vs 21) Then Peter came and said to Him, "Lord, how often shall my brother sin against me and I forgive him? Up to seven times?" (vs 22) Jesus *said to him, "I do not say to you, up to seven times, but up to seventy times seven. (Luke 17:3) "Be on your guard! If your brother sins, rebuke him; and if he repents, forgive him.*

These verses can be accurately imposed into our lives as the situation demands and thus are very applicable to spouses. They must be utilized in order to **Reconcile** our relationship with our spouse. The marriage relationship is like no other relationship on this earth. It is incomparably unique and special. It is the one which God refers to where the two individuals have become as **"ONE FLESH"**. We need to guard this relationship with all the powers and tools available to us, and that includes God's Word as it pertains to **Forgiveness**.

With the establishment of the availability of **Forgiveness** as detailed above, let's now look at how the needs of husband and wife can be blessed by this **Forgiveness** in order to bring about **Reconciliation** and **Restoration**.

Since all men and women answer to the Heavenly Father for their actions, and since all married couples sometimes have areas of failures (including what appears to be devastating and irreconcilable differences), we assume here that every couple has need of confession and repentance to God the Father. There have been and always will be sins of spouse against spouse, and these sins are against the Heavenly Father as well. Therefore we all have need for **Forgiveness** in our marriage relationship, as well as **Forgiveness** by our Heavenly Father. In light of the above verses we are to seek **Forgiveness** by God as well as to grant **Forgiveness** to our spouses.

As this confession, repentance and **Forgiveness** takes place, God can and will renew our earthly love for each other beyond all imagination. This can and will be a true **Reconciliation** and a lasting **Restoration,** of our love for each other. This renewed, God given love for each other, is then to be lived out in the daily lives of each marriage partnership. I can't emphasize enough, if we sin against each other, it is foremost a sin against our Most High God. It is with Him we must start this path of **Restoration** and all the rest will fall in place. ... *(Mark 10:9) "What therefore God has joined together, let no man separate." ... (Ephesians 4:26-27)(vs 26) ..... do not let the sun go down on your anger, (vs 27) and do not give the devil an opportunity.*

Don't let anything stand in the way to **Restoration** of your marriage relationship. God has provided the answer in our "Owner's Manual" for those who "Belong to Him"!!! Seek His answer, apply His truth, and He will give each of us a loving relationship for our spouses. This renewed relationship will heal all wounds, and will gloriously do so, beyond our most vivid imagination. God will restore or ignite a love for each other, which will be one that will be utterly amazing and humanly impossible.

C. Conclusion to Marriage:

We have looked at six fundamental principles that provide a rock solid framework for a strong, vibrant marriage relationship. Together we are "one Flesh", co-equal persons with distinctive, God given roles, submitting one to the other, and belonging each to the other. All of this takes place by allowing the power of the Holy Spirit to work within us and between us, to overcome the trials and tribulations that are sure to beset a union, when the storm winds blow. We have also looked at the reconciliation that can happen given the proper repentance and forgiveness.

How can we know we can not only have a solid marriage relationship but one that grows stronger with each passing day and one which is vibrant and filled with romance even into our later years? Because we know it is the will of God and we know that whatever we pray for, in His will, He will give us.

With Christ in the center of our marriage, though we may sometimes stumble, we will never fall. Our marriages will grow stronger by the day and the romance we enjoyed when we were first joined in marriage will become richer, sweeter and more fulfilled until our final day on earth.

Always remember ... ***(Matthew 19:6) "So they are no longer two, but one flesh. What therefore God has joined together, let no man separate."***

SPECIAL NOTE:

I know many of you may have a special verse or verses regarding this Chapter's subject matter. This special verse or these verses may not have been mentioned due to my ignorance or because of brevity. I apologize for either of these reasons. Please feel free to write any special verse or verses in the space below. This will add your personal touch, and will serve to call to each person's mind their individual "experience of trust", in God's Holy Word.

For to each of us "Who belong To Him", His Holy Word can be truly recognized and relied upon as our **"Owner's Manual"**!!!

_____

_____

_____

_____

_____

_____

CHAPTER 12

HUSBANDS

INTRODUCTORY VERSE:

(Psalms 1:1-3)(vs 1) How blessed is the man who does not walk in the counsel of the wicked, Nor stand in the path of sinners, Nor sit in the seat of scoffers! (vs 2) But his delight is in the law of the LORD, And in His law he meditates day and night. (vs 3) He will be like a tree firmly planted by streams of water, Which yields its fruit in its season And its leaf does not wither; And in whatever he does, he prospers.

We find here, like no other place in the Bible, the blessedness of "Belonging To Him"!!! As we meditate on God's Word day and night, we find our life is blessed beyond measure. We are guaranteed the living water, which is so necessary to our spiritual life. We are guaranteed fruit in our lives and we will never go into dormancy. Our leaf will not turn colors, wither up and drop off. Our prosperity is not "Material Wealth" related, but it is being allowed by the "God of the Universe", to get in on what He is doing, thereby guaranteeing perpetual and absolute success in all that we do. We can truly have our cake and eat it too. This passage is truly the basis, the strength, the foundation of being a Biblical Husband.

INTRODUCTION:

As a Husband we have taken on tremendous responsibility. We will need to perfect our skills in loving our wife, teaching our children, being the bread winner and so many other tasks, they are too numerous to count. ... *(Genesis 2:21-24)(vs 21) So the LORD God caused a deep sleep to fall upon the man, and he slept; then He took one of his ribs and closed up the flesh at that place. (vs 22) The LORD God fashioned into a woman the rib which He had taken from the man, and brought her to the man. (vs 23) The man said, "This is now bone of my bones, And flesh of my flesh; She shall be called Woman, Because she was taken out of Man." (vs 24) For this reason a man shall leave his father and his mother, and be joined to his wife; and they shall become one flesh.* You have just witnessed the first Husband and Wife team, Adam and Eve.

The position of Husband is a position in the family that has been appointed and approved by God. Hopefully it will be honoring to God for each of us who take on this God appointed role. This role is not to be taken frivolously, but with commitment, a mind to learn and a stewardship to bring glory to God. My prayer for each person reading the following is that they will be blessed to learn of their responsibility, and therefore be convicted to fulfill this God given calling.

A. OUR "GREATEST CHALLENGE" AS A HUSBAND:

(Ephesians 5:25-30)(vs 25) Husbands, love your wives, just as Christ also loved the church and gave Himself up for her, (vs 26) so that He might sanctify her, having cleansed her by the washing of water with the word, (vs 27) that He might present to Himself the church in all her glory, having no spot or wrinkle or any such thing; but that she would be holy and blameless. (vs 28) So husbands ought also to love their own wives as their own bodies. He who loves his own wife loves himself; (vs 29) for no one ever hated his own flesh, but nourishes and cherishes it, just as Christ also does the church, (vs 30) because we are members of His body.

As members of Christ's body of believers, the Husband has been given a difficult task. The "greatest challenge" ever put to man, is found in this passage of the Bible. This challenge is to love our wives as Christ loved the Church (the people of God) and gave Himself for it. This could be studied for years and we would still be finding new information as to how Christ spent his days, months and years loving the Church.

(John 21:25) And there are also many other things which Jesus did, which if they *were written in detail, I suppose that even the world itself *would not contain the books that *would be written.

From this perspective I can only conclude that we as Husbands are to continually learn how to love our wives. It should not be assumed that we know how to perfectly love our wives on the day of our marriage. We are to continually learn how to love our wives as a process over each and every year that God has appointed us to be that Husband. I can only testify that I have severely failed in this command, but I will continue to expend the effort to learn and apply what God shows me. This confession and promise is coming from one who is completing our 48th year of marriage. My confession is not alone. If any man states that he has perfectly fulfilled this God given command, then he is either delusional or a liar. The point here, is don't let any past failure(s) stand in the way of our planning for success, for both today and tomorrow. If we "Belong To Him" we are responsible to His Word, and the above verses are not to be ignored, but are to expanded upon and utilized each day.

Our past is forgiven and our joy for the future, is to conscientiously do better. Take one day at a time, and love that bride of one day or 50 years, like you never before have done. Even as I write this, my mind says I will again be a failure to this "most high calling". You may feel the same way. All I can say is just get up every day that God allows you to have breath, and fulfill His desire for your life for that day. I believe it will become easier to comply with this "greatest challenge" of our life, as we see small successes each day. I know for a fact, our earthly reward will be a more loving wife to each of us. The real, eternal blessing, is being found faithful to God.

B. ADDITIONAL BIBLICAL VERSES REGARDING HUSBANDS:

<u>1.</u> *(Ephesians 5:31-33 partial)(vs 31) FOR THIS REASON A MAN SHALL LEAVE HIS FATHER AND MOTHER AND SHALL BE JOINED TO HIS WIFE, AND THE TWO SHALL BECOME ONE FLESH. (vs 32) This mystery is great; but I am speaking with reference to Christ and the church. (partial vs*

33) Nevertheless, each individual among you also is to love his own wife even as himself,

Without getting into a theological discussion (of which I am not capable), these verses demonstrate the relationship of Jesus and the Church. Jesus is often described as the bridegroom and the Church is described as the bride. This is referred to as a great mystery. What we can gather from this is the relationship of protection by Jesus for the Church and our related responsibility, as an earthly Husband, of protecting our bride. As we have become one flesh, we protect our bride as well as ourselves, with every act of kindness and unselfishness.

<u>2</u>. Some very stern warnings and instructions, that all of us and especially Husbands, need to seriously consider are found in Proverbs.

(Proverbs 5:3-5)(vs 3) For the lips of an adulteress drip honey And smoother than oil is her speech; (vs 4) But in the end she is bitter as wormwood, Sharp as a two-edged sword. (vs 5) Her feet go down to death, Her steps take hold of Sheol.

(Proverbs 5:11-19)(vs 11) And you groan at your final end, When your flesh and your body are consumed; (vs 12) And you say, "How I have hated instruction! And my heart spurned reproof! (vs 13) "I have not listened to the voice of my teachers, Nor inclined my ear to my instructors! (vs 14) "I was almost in utter ruin In the midst of the assembly and congregation." (vs 15) Drink water from your own cistern And fresh water from your own well. (vs 16) Should your springs be dispersed abroad, Streams of water in the streets? (vs 17) Let them be yours alone And not for strangers with you. (vs 18) Let your fountain be blessed, And rejoice in the wife of your youth. (vs 19) As a loving hind and a graceful doe, Let her breasts satisfy you at all times; Be exhilarated always with her love.

When we relate the above to Jesus and the Church and the words that we have become as "One Flesh" with our spouse, we see that the sins discussed above are against God, against ourselves and against our mates.

<u>3</u>. **(1 Corinthians 6:15-18)(vs 15) Do you not know that your bodies are members of Christ? Shall I then take away the members of Christ and make them members of a**

prostitute? May it never be! (vs 16) Or do you not know that the one who joins himself to a prostitute is one body with her? For He says, "THE TWO SHALL BECOME ONE FLESH." (vs 17) But the one who joins himself to the Lord is one spirit with Him. (vs 18) Flee immorality. Every other sin that a man commits is outside the body, but the immoral man sins against his own body.

I know we are not supposed to talk about these things in public, but it is so important to know God's Word about sexual immorality and its impact upon ourselves, our family and our friends. Verse eighteen (18) indicates that the immoral man sins against his own body, therefore the connotation is that this sin is more significant than most other sins, because of its effect upon yourself, as well as so many other people. These scriptures must be included, as they are very important and tremendously significant. The conclusion is this ... *"Be exhilarated always with her love"* ... that is the wife of your youth. God isn't trying to destroy your "fun(?)", He is trying to expose His Word as found in our "Owner's Manual"!!! God in His infinite love for each of us, has our best interest in the forefront of His mind.

<u>4.</u> An important word and instruction to Husbands, from the Apostle Peter, to all of us.

(1 Peter 3:7) You husbands in the same way, live with your wives in an understanding way, as with someone weaker, since she is a woman; and show her honor as a fellow heir of the grace of life, so that your prayers will not be hindered.

This passage came out of *(1 Peter 3:1-9)* which primarily instructs the Wife, in a Christian marital relationship, to honor God by respecting the Biblical position to which God has appointed her. Verse seven (7) commands the Husband to also respect God's Biblical calling in our marital relationships by knowing and exercising a "caregiving" attitude towards our wives. As Husbands we are to honor our Wife as an equal *"heir of the grace of life"*, or in God's perspective, protect her, nourish her and fulfill her in her God given role. Neither Husband nor Wife has a superior role in this earthly marital relationship, but **BOTH** stand to answer before the Almighty God for their separate Biblical responsibilities. Neither Husband nor Wife has any rights to any thoughts, that they have a right of superiority, as **BOTH** stand before God, equally responsible for their respective calling.

<u>5.</u> *(Romans 5:8) But God demonstrates His own love toward us, in that while we were yet sinners, Christ died for us.*

Christ loved His Church so much that He died for it while we were yet sinners. Our love for our Wives should be equal to Christ's love for His Church. By living a long life and serving our Wife daily, we are dying for our spouse. Let's figure out by living each day, how we can die for our Wife. This is God's command and it is unconditional, meaning it is to be fulfilled regardless of the response of the recipient. It is truly a supreme command, and difficult to imagine how we can fulfill it. Christ died for us (the Church). He requires that we love our wives as He loved the Church. You write the rest of this paragraph.

<u>6.</u> *(1 Timothy 3:1-4)(vs 1) It is a trustworthy statement: if any man aspires to the office of overseer, it is a fine work he desires to do. (vs 2) An overseer, then, must be above reproach, the husband of one wife, temperate, prudent, respectable, hospitable, able to teach, (vs 3) not addicted to wine or pugnacious, but gentle, peaceable, free from the love of money. (vs 4) He must be one who manages his own household well, keeping his children under control with all dignity*

While recognizing these verses are primarily for the qualifications of an overseer or a deacon, as the guardian of the church, we can glean a few choice morsels of spiritual food regarding Husbands. Obviously we are to have only one wife, but just as important are the other twelve honorable characteristics. A man found keeping or attempting to keep these twelve, will be a great Husband.

Don't overlook these verses and try to say they are not applicable to <u>each</u> of us. Whether an overseer, a church member or a husband, these characteristics are to be tremendously sought after.

C. CONCLUSION TO HUSBANDS:

The conclusion is simple. ... *(Ephesians 5:25) Husbands, love your wives, just as Christ also loved the church and*

gave Himself up for her ... The fulfillment of this conclusion is the tough part. There are numerous other things the Husband does such as being a Father, a Brother, a Grandfather, an Uncle, a Friend, a Business associate, a Teacher, and on-and-on. Hopefully you meet all the requirements, but foremost "love your wife and give yourself for her".

SPECIAL NOTE:

I know many of you may have a special verse or verses regarding this Chapter's subject matter. This special verse or these verses may not have been mentioned due to my ignorance or because of brevity. I apologize for either of these reasons. Please feel free to write any special verse or verses in the space below. This will add your personal touch, and will serve to call to each person's mind their individual "experience of trust", in God's Holy Word.

For to each of us "Who belong To Him", His Holy Word can be truly recognized and relied upon as our **"Owner's Manual"**!!!

_____

_____

_____

_____

_____

_____

_____

CHAPTER 13

WIVES

INTRODUCTORY VERSE:

(Proverbs 18:22) He who finds a wife finds a good thing And obtains favor from the LORD.

We will find out later just what a "GOOD THING" this can be! Favor from the Lord is for those who "Belong To Him"!!!

INTRODUCTION:

(Ephesians 5:22-24)(vs 22) Wives, be subject to your own husbands, as to the Lord. (vs 23) For the husband is the head of the wife, as Christ also is the head of the church, He Himself being the Savior of the body.

(vs 24) But as the church is subject to Christ, so also the wives ought to be to their husbands in everything.

The words "to be subject to" are defined as: to be subordinate; or submit self unto; and this applies to the Wife in relationship to her husband. The husband is to love his Wife as Christ loved the Church. The husband supports the Wife in her role and the Wife supports the husband in his role. Neither is inherently superior or better, but both answer to God in their respective responsibilities to fulfill these separate, yet different roles.

This explanation is not designed to soften the instruction to the Wife, to be submissive to her own husband, but to clarify the God ordained and planned relationship.

Way too often a misled preacher has touted ignorantly and arrogantly, a false teaching that the woman is to be submissive to her downfall. This is not true, but both the roles of Wife and husband are designed by God, and when each answers to God, by fulfilling their God-given tasks, they each experience, as God has designed and intended, a blessed equality and harmony.

We will now look at the "origin" of the "wife" and some of the Biblical Wives, and their roles. You may be surprised at the accomplishments, the significance and the importance played out by these women. Even the world will stand up and applaud.

A. ORGIN OF A WIFE:

(Genesis 2:20-24)(vs 20) The man gave names to all the cattle, and to the birds of the sky, and to every beast of the field, but for Adam there was not found a helper suitable for him. (vs 20) So the LORD God caused a deep sleep to fall upon the man, and he slept; then He took one of his ribs and closed up the flesh at that place. (vs 22) The LORD God fashioned into a woman the rib which He had taken from the man, and brought her to the man. (vs 23) The man said, "This is now bone of my bones, And flesh of my flesh; She shall be called Woman, Because she was taken out of Man." (vs 24) For this reason a man shall leave his father and his mother, and be joined to his wife; and they shall become one flesh.

Woman was not an afterthought by God, but was planned before the beginning of time. She was planned, designed and brought into this world with the same forethought that brought into being the intricacies of the entire universe. Just as God's creation of the universe is overwhelming, so is His creation of the woman. The creation of man and woman certainly is exceedingly more important than any earthly creation.

God tells us that He fashioned woman from the rib He took from the sleeping man. He created woman by molding her into being, with a delicacy and tenderness you can't find anywhere in the physical creation. Woman was created as a help meet for man. Woman was created with the same thoughtfulness and purpose as the universe, but with a purposefulness that cannot be compared to any of God's other creations.

She was taken from man to be a help meet, she is bone of man's bone, and she is one flesh with her husband. This relationship is so full of meaning and complete it is no wonder that God says … *(Matthew*

19:6) "So they are no longer two, but one flesh. What therefore God has joined together, let no man separate."

B. QUALITY AND SUCCESS OF BIBLICAL WIVES:

This paragraph will only discuss a few of the Biblical Wives to whom credit and exposure are due. It is not intended to highlight or leave out any from the standpoint of measuring their quality or success. Certainly, the ones highlighted, are worthy of our discussion, and are great examples from which to glean and learn.

NEW TESTAMENTS EXAMPLES:

1. Mary, Wife of Joseph and mother of Jesus.
(Matthew 1:16) Jacob was the father of Joseph the husband of Mary, by whom Jesus was born, who is called the Messiah. (Luke 1:26-35 & 38 & 46-49)(vs 26) Now in the sixth month the angel Gabriel was sent from God to a city in Galilee called Nazareth, (vs 27) to a virgin engaged to a man whose name was Joseph, of the descendants of David; and the virgin's name was Mary. (vs 28) And coming in, he said to her, "Greetings, favored one! The Lord is with you." (vs 29) But she was very perplexed at this statement, and kept pondering what kind of salutation this was. (vs 30) The angel said to her, "Do not be afraid, Mary; for you have found favor with God. (vs 31) "And behold, you will conceive in your womb and bear a son, and you shall name Him Jesus. (vs 32) "He will be great and will be called the Son of the Most High; and the Lord God will give Him the throne of His father David; (vs 33) and He will reign over the house of Jacob forever, and His kingdom will have no end." (vs 34) Mary said to the angel, "How can this be, since I am a virgin?" (vs 35) The angel answered and said to her, "The Holy Spirit will come upon you, and the power of the Most High will overshadow you; and for that reason the holy Child shall be called the Son of God. (vs 38) And Mary said, "Behold, the bondslave of the Lord; may it be done to

me according to your word." And the angel departed from her. (vs 46) And Mary said: "My soul exalts the Lord, (vs 47) And my spirit has rejoiced in God my Savior. (vs 48) "For He has had regard for the humble state of His bondslave; For behold, from this time on all generations will count me blessed. (vs 49) "For the Mighty One has done great things for me; And holy is His name.

We cannot fathom the scene we have just witnessed from the above scriptures. Mary, the virgin Wife of Joseph was overwhelmed, but called herself a *"bondslave of the Lord"*. As a servant she accepted her role as one in subjection or subserviency to her Lord, the Almighty God. Mary, the mother of the One soon to be called the Son of God, in complete humility stated, *"may it be done to me according to your word"*, ... *"And holy is His name"*. Mary fulfilled her God-given role in this life.

It is important in this section to point out that Mary was human like all of us. Nowhere in any Biblical writings was Mary, the earthly Wife of Joseph, and the biological mother of Jesus, ever stated to be Deity. She was a servant! Yes, to be highly regarded by all of mankind for her subserviency, but NEVER to be worshiped. She was a human Wife and mother, who took on a tremendous "Act of God", and handled it admirably.

2. Elizabeth, Wife of Zacharias, mother of John the Baptist.

(Luke 1:5-7 & 11-17 & 57 & 80)(vs 5) In the days of Herod, king of Judea, there was a priest named Zacharias, of the division of Abijah; and he had a wife from the daughters of Aaron, and her name was Elizabeth. (vs 6) They were both righteous in the sight of God, walking blamelessly in all the commandments and requirements of the Lord. (vs 7) But they had no child, because Elizabeth was barren, and they were both advanced in years. (vs 11) And an angel of the Lord appeared to him, standing to the right of the altar of incense. (vs 12) Zacharias was troubled when he saw the angel, and fear gripped him. (vs 13) But the angel said to him, "Do not be afraid, Zacharias, for your petition has been heard, and your wife Elizabeth will bear you a son, and you will give him the name John. (vs 14) "You will have joy and

gladness, and many will rejoice at his birth. (vs 15) "For he will be great in the sight of the Lord; and he will drink no wine or liquor, and he will be filled with the Holy Spirit while yet in his mother's womb. (vs 16) "And he will turn many of the sons of Israel back to the Lord their God. (vs 17) "It is he who will go as a forerunner before Him in the spirit and power of Elijah, TO TURN THE HEARTS OF THE FATHERS BACK TO THE CHILDREN, and the disobedient to the attitude of the righteous, so as to make ready a people prepared for the Lord." (vs 57) Now the time had come for Elizabeth to give birth, and she gave birth to a son. (vs 80) And the child continued to grow and to become strong in spirit, and he lived in the deserts until the day of his public appearance to Israel.

Elizabeth was the Wife of Zacharias and the mother of John the Baptist. She has earned her respect by being *"righteous in the sight of God, walking blamelessly in all the commandments and requirements of the Lord"*. She trusted God in this miraculous birth. She provided daily care to this child from a baby to adulthood. She undoubtedly provided teaching, training and discipline to this soon to be "Giant of the Faith". This would have come as a natural conveyance of who she was, due to her righteous relationship with the Lord.

We all know that John the Baptist grew up to be a stalwart of the Faith. He was unparalleled in the proclaiming the coming of Jesus. In his popularity as a forerunner of Christ, he was without criticism in his subjection to Jesus. Much can be learned from this Wife and mother as she was found faithful while being entrusted with such an important historical role. Due to her exemplary character and righteous behavior, she is a Godly model for all, and for all of time.

3. Prisca, Wife of Aquila, fellow workers of the Apostle Paul.

(Romans 16:3- part of 5)(vs 3) Greet Prisca and Aquila, my fellow workers in Christ Jesus, (vs 4) who for my life risked their own necks, to whom not only do I give thanks, but also all the churches of the Gentiles; (vs 5) also greet the church that is in their house.

(1 Corinthians 16:19) The churches of Asia greet you. Aquila and Prisca greet you heartily in the Lord, with the church that is in their house.

Prisca was the Wife of Aquila. Not much is known about their lives, but what is known speaks volumes about their character. Prisca is mentioned at all times in association with her husband. She is given equal credit along with her husband, for the sacrifices and dedication of their actions. They are equally credited with literally risking their lives, or the possibility of being executed, for the safety of Paul. They were fellow workers of Paul's and received several commendations for the church in their home. They were respected and given thanks by not only Paul, but all the churches of the Gentiles. They were strong in their knowledge of the Word and demonstrated this by teaching individuals. They took aside a Jew named Apollos and instructed him more accurately in the Word. *(Acts 18:26) and he began to speak out boldly in the synagogue. But when Priscilla and Aquila heard him, they took him aside and explained to him the way of God more accurately.* This team of Wife and husband are to be commended and modeled as examples to each of us. They were truly sold out to the God "To Whom They Belonged"!!!

OLD TESTAMENTS EXAMPLES:

1. The Wives of Noah and his three sons.

(Genesis 7:5-7 & 13)(vs 5) Noah did according to all that the LORD had commanded him. (vs 6) Now Noah was six hundred years old when the flood of water came upon the earth. (vs 7) Then Noah and his sons and his wife and his sons' wives with him entered the ark because of the water of the flood. (vs 13) On the very same day Noah and Shem and Ham and Japheth, the sons of Noah, and Noah's wife and the three wives of his sons with them, entered the ark,

(Genesis 8:15-18)(vs 15) Then God spoke to Noah, saying, (vs 16) "Go out of the ark, you and your wife and your sons and your sons' wives with you. (vs 17) "Bring out with you every living thing of all flesh that is with you, birds and

animals and every creeping thing that creeps on the earth, that they may breed abundantly on the earth, and be fruitful and multiply on the earth." (vs 18) So Noah went out, and his sons and his wife and his sons' wives with him.

(Genesis 9:1) And God blessed Noah and his sons and said to them, "Be fruitful and multiply, and fill the earth.

After Adam and Eve, God in effect started over with Noah's family. His new start was with Noah and his Wife, and their three sons and their Wives. These Wives were found to be faithful. They entered the ark and endured the rain, the animals and the flood and its aftermath. They were called upon to begin the new generation of people. This is no minor calling. They were blessed by God and charged with the task of filling the earth with people. This high calling would not be administrated randomly. God choose those who stood above the crowd and could say without hesitation, "I Belong To Him"!!!

2. Ruth, Wife of Boaz, mother of Obed, ancestor to Joseph (who was the husband to the Virgin Mary, the earthly mother of Jesus).

Ruth was a Moabite woman. Naomi, who was to become Ruth's mother-in-law, was part of a Jewish family. Naomi had two sons to care for because her husband had died. Ruth married into this Jewish family by becoming the wife of one of Naomi's sons. Ruth's husband then dies after only about ten years of marriage. It was at this time Naomi encouraged Ruth to leave her and return to Ruth's own people. We have here Ruth's response. ... *(Ruth 1:16-17)(vs 16) But Ruth said, "Do not urge me to leave you or turn back from following you; for where you go, I will go, and where you lodge, I will lodge. Your people shall be my people, and your God, my God. (Ruth 1:17) "Where you die, I will die, and there I will be buried. Thus may the LORD do to me, and worse, if anything but death parts you and me."* Ruth has now accepted into her life, and confessed with her mouth, her new found faith in the one and only true God ... *"your God, my God"*. This mother-in-law/daughter-in-law combination stayed together and went back into Naomi's homeland, to keep form starving to death. It was during this difficult time that Ruth experienced God's direct hand in her life.

Boaz now enters the picture. He is a relative of Naomi's dead husband. Let's see what Boaz has to say ... *(Ruth 2:8-12)(vs 8) Then*

Boaz said to Ruth, "Listen carefully, my daughter. Do not go to glean in another field; furthermore, do not go on from this one, but stay here with my maids. (vs 9) "Let your eyes be on the field which they reap, and go after them. Indeed, I have commanded the servants not to touch you. When you are thirsty, go to the water jars and drink from what the servants draw." (vs 10) Then she fell on her face, bowing to the ground and said to him, "Why have I found favor in your sight that you should take notice of me, since I am a foreigner?" (vs 11) Boaz replied to her, "All that you have done for your mother-in-law after the death of your husband has been fully reported to me, and how you left your father and your mother and the land of your birth, and came to a people that you did not previously know. (vs 12) "May the LORD reward your work, and your wages be full from the LORD, the God of Israel, under whose wings you have come to seek refuge."

Boaz is responding to the will of God **because of the faith of Ruth**. He is taking her into his personal protection because it is the right thing for him to do. Boaz is living out his accountability before God. As this accountability before God has been carried out by faithful men and women since the beginning of time, it is beautiful to again witness it one more here.

Boaz now adds to his previous statements, by expressing his blessing to Ruth for her demonstration of Godliness. ... *(Ruth 3:10-11)(vs 10) Then he said, "May you be blessed of the LORD, my daughter. You have shown your last kindness to be better than the first by not going after young men, whether poor or rich. (vs 11) "Now, my daughter, do not fear. I will do for you whatever you ask, for all my people in the city know that you are a woman of excellence.*

The next step is marriage. Ruth becomes a Wife for the second time, all of this under the guidance of the direct hand of God. ... *(Ruth 4:13) So Boaz took Ruth, and she became his wife, and he went in to her. And the LORD enabled her to conceive, and she gave birth to a son. (Ruth 4: partial vs 17) So they named him Obed. He is the father of Jesse, the father of David.* By this we see Ruth's position in history. She was obedient and used by God and becomes part of the genealogy of Jesus.

We should now recap the rest of the story in order to magnify the importance of a Godly Wife and her obedience to God. We will never know how God plans to use us today, but as we are found obedient to His direction, time will reveal the miraculous results.

Jesus was born to the Virgin Mary, the Wife of Joseph. Joseph was the earthly father of Jesus. Ruth was part of the historical lineage of Jesus. Ruth, through some most difficult circumstances, including the availability of food from day-to-day, was used mightily by God. She fulfilled her high calling from God in this most important role as a Wife, as she became a part of the genealogy of Jesus the Messiah. ... ***(Matthew 1:1) The record of the genealogy of Jesus the Messiah, the son of David, the son of Abraham: (Matthew 1:5) Salmon was the father of Boaz by Rahab, Boaz was the father of Obed by Ruth, and Obed the father of Jesse.*** (For the record, Jesse's genealogy to Joseph is confirmed in Matthew 1: 6-16) ... ***(Matthew 1:17-18)(vs 17) So all the generations from Abraham to David are fourteen generations; from David to the deportation to Babylon, fourteen generations; and from the deportation to Babylon to the Messiah, fourteen generations. (vs 18) Now the birth of Jesus Christ was as follows: when His mother Mary had been betrothed to Joseph, before they came together she was found to be with child by the Holy Spirit.***

Ruth became a child of God's. She followed His direction in unknown and difficult times. She did all of this, which was absolutely honoring to the Almighty God, while standing firm on her spoken testimony. ... ***(Ruth 1:16) But Ruth said, "Do not urge me to leave you or turn back from following you; for where you go, I will go, and where you lodge, I will lodge. Your people shall be my people, and your God, my God.*** Her living testimony as a God fearing Wife is without flaw, and a blessing to all of us who have read this account.

As we absorb these accounts of a Godly Wives and their living testimonies, we can only rejoice with them and be eternally grateful to the

One to "Whom We Belong"!!! Do you think that it will be neat to meet some of these "Wives" of faith, when we get to Heaven?

C. THE EXPLOITS AND ACCOMPLISHMENTS OF A BIBLICAL WIFE:

(Proverbs 31:10) An excellent wife, who can find? For her worth is far above jewels. Other words for "excellent" are: virtuous; strength; efficiency; capable; and strong. What we find in the following passages are specific qualities and accomplishments of this "excellent" Wife.

A "Proverbs 31" Wife is certainly to be valued far above jewels, she is one of God's greatest gifts to man.

(Proverbs 31:11-28)(vs 11) The heart of her husband trusts in her, And he will have no lack of gain. (vs 12) She does him good and not evil All the days of her life. (vs 13) She looks for wool and flax And works with her hands in delight. (vs 14) She is like merchant ships; She brings her food from afar. (vs 15) She rises also while it is still night And gives food to her household And portions to her maidens. (vs 16) She considers a field and buys it; From her earnings she plants a vineyard. (vs 17) She girds herself with strength And makes her arms strong. (vs 18) She senses that her gain is good; Her lamp does not go out at night. (vs 19) She stretches out her hands to the distaff, And her hands grasp the spindle. (vs 20) She extends her hand to the poor, And she stretches out her hands to the needy. (vs 21) She is not afraid of the snow for her household, For all her household are clothed with scarlet. (vs 22) She makes coverings for herself; Her clothing is fine linen and purple. (vs 23) Her husband is known in the gates, When he sits among the elders of the land. (vs 24) She makes linen garments and sells them, And supplies belts to the tradesmen. (vs 25) Strength and dignity are her clothing, And she smiles at the future. (vs 26) She opens her mouth in wisdom, And the teaching of kindness is on her tongue. (vs 27) She looks well to the ways of her household, And does not eat the bread of idleness. (vs 28)

Her children rise up and bless her; Her husband also, and he praises her, saying:

These 18 verses are so defining they need to be isolated in order that they don't get ignored or minimized by getting caught up with the whole. Yes, they should be considered in many cases in total, but more than that they should be individualized in order to amplify the high characteristics of each one separately. The comments below are minimal and should be expanded upon by the reader, as one sits and meditates upon these verses.

1. Verse 11. This husband has ultimate confidence in his Wife. He has no need of anything beyond her. He has it all!

2. Verse 12. The Wife is a trusted companion to the husband for all the days of his and her life.

3. Verse 13. Wool and flax are both clothing materials and it is with delight the Wife turns these into useful items.

4. Verse 14. She has imagination and is creative to serve foods that are not commonplace.

5. Verse 15. She is not lazy and lovingly serves the whole family and extended family.

6. Verse 16. Wives can be very capable businesswomen. Given the chance they will produce a profit and then use it for the benefit of the whole family. It would be wise if all husbands would consult their Wives in business dealings in order to get their perspective.

7. Verse 17. She surrounds herself with boldness and uses that to attack all family problems and opportunities.

8. Verse 18. She produces good gain for her family and she is diligent about this service, even at the expense of her sleep.

9. Verse 19. This reference is to the Wife's work ethic and most likely refers to the making of garments or household materials. She is serious in her work as she <u>grasps</u> the spindle.

10. Verse 20. As a servant, she includes the poor and needy in addition to her family. This is emphasized by the fact she extends her **hands**, denoting the plural.

11. Verse 21. This Wife is not bothered by the cold weather. She has prepared for this by providing her family with clothing that has the necessary characteristics to ward off the temperatures of the day. She probably invented the forerunner of today's insulated garments.

12. Verse 22. This wife has not forgotten her responsibility to herself. She dresses with the best materials and colors.

13. Verse 23. Her husband is beneficiary of all her attributes. He is well respected in the community, and this is in no small part, due to his Wife.

14. Verse 24. She not only makes the clothing for her family, but has a "home based business" which includes the selling of shirts and belts to the tradesmen or local vendors.

15. Verse 25. She is virtually wrapped in boldness and majesty as she eagerly anticipates the future, for she is prepared.

16. Verse 26. A Wife that knows and loves the Word of God, teaches it everywhere she goes. Her teachings are found to be wise and are grounded in expressible kindness.

17. Verse 27. Her thoughts are always for others. The beneficiaries are those of her household, and you never see her unnecessarily wasting time.

18. Verse 28. The family relationships are filled with blessings because of the Wife's heart for God. Her confident heart full of joy, gives birth to these most beautiful actions. The husband, as an important part of this household, is blessed beyond measure by her Godly actions. This husband can't keep these blessings a secret and he makes them known wherever he goes.

Don't try to emulate these most admirable qualities. Believe in Jesus as the Lord of your life, and you will experience these qualities, as they come forth naturally from your daily living. "What is in you will come out". If you "Belong To Him" what comes out will be a blessing to those around you.

The above are exploits and accomplishments of the Biblical Wife. The following are the praises for these accomplishments. *(Proverbs 31:29-31)(vs 29) "Many daughters have done nobly, But you excel them all." (vs 30) Charm is deceitful and beauty is vain, But a woman who fears the LORD, she shall be praised. (vs 31) Give her the product of her hands, And let her works praise her in the gates.*

The key to these last three verses and all of the above scriptures are *"a woman who fears the LORD"*. A Wife who loves God and has trusted Jesus as her personal Savior, can be found living out these excellent qualities.

D. WIVES YOU CAN WIN YOUR HUSBANDS TO THE LORD:

Wives, did you know, you can be responsible to win your unbelieving husband to the Lord. Are you aware of the only sin that sends a man to hell, and that is the sin of unbelief. … *(John 3:18) "He who believes in Him is not judged; he who does not believe has been judged already, because he has not believed in the name of the only begotten Son of God.* It is true, of all the sins of mankind, the only one that can't be forgiven is the one of unbelief. Take a look at the Biblical answer to that issue. *(1 Peter 3:1-4)(vs 1) In the same way, you wives, be submissive to your own husbands so that even if any of them are disobedient to the word, they may be won without a word by the behavior of their wives,*

(vs 2) as they observe your chaste and respectful behavior. (vs 3) Your adornment must not be merely external—braiding the hair, and wearing gold jewelry, or putting on dresses; (vs 4) but let it be the hidden person of the heart, with the imperishable quality of a gentle and quiet spirit, which is precious in the sight of God.
The imperishable quality of the gentle, quiet spirit of the Godly Wife can and will work miracles. It will always be God's miracles that take place in a man's heart regarding "Salvation", but it is a Wife who has a "Holy Fear" of the Lord, that might be the earthly instrument that God uses.

E. OTHER VERSES REGARDING BIBLICAL WIVES:

1. *(Judges 14:16-17)(vs 16) Samson's wife wept before him and said, "You only hate me, and you do not love me; you have propounded a riddle to the sons of my people, and have not told it to me." And he said to her, "Behold, I have not told it to my father or mother; so should I tell you?" (vs 17) However she wept before him seven days while their feast lasted. And on the seventh day he told her because she* *pressed him so hard. She then told the riddle to the sons of her people.*

This is not the example to follow for being a Godly Wife, however we can all learn from other people's mistakes. Take this lesson and be wiser.

2. *(Psalms 128:3) Your wife shall be like a fruitful vine Within your house, Your children like olive plants Around your table.*

3. *(Proverbs 5:18) Let your fountain be blessed, And rejoice in the wife of your youth.*

4. *(Proverbs 12:4) An excellent wife is the crown of her husband, But she who shames him is like rottenness in his bones.*

5. *(Proverbs 19:14) House and wealth are an inheritance from fathers, But a prudent wife is from the LORD.*

God's greatest gift to man is salvation by Grace through the Lord Jesus Christ. This gift is beyond comparison, and is given as an eternal blessing to those who have accepted it through "believing faith". I believe our second most significant gift from God is a prudent Wife.

This prudent Wife, according to the scriptures is from the Lord. This relationship that He has established should be intensely cared for, as it carries a value more precious than all the silver or gold found in this world. This relationship with a prudent Wife is a gift granted to us directly by God, and He intends for us to respect this gift with utmost value and honor. If we were to compare this relationship with all the earthly material values, including all the silver and gold found in the world, it would be like comparing Mt. Everest to a spec of dirt. All material things of this world will soon be found to be a pile of ashes. Our relationship with our Wives has eternal consequences. The gift of a prudent Wife needs to be found in a place of emphasis, reserved only for those things which are of eternal value. This gift should be respected with utmost consideration, since it is truly a gift, directly given by our Almighty Father!

Prudent Wives, be lifted up and encouraged by your God appointed importance!

6. *(Ecclesiastes 9:9) Enjoy life with the woman whom you love all the days of your fleeting life which He has given to* *you under the sun; for this is your reward in life and in your toil in which you have labored under the sun.*

Our days while on this earth are fleeting. This is confirmed by Solomon's words of wisdom found in the book of Ecclesiastes. Solomon's words are for us to enjoy life with the woman we love. This indicates a mutual relationship of love and admiration, a two way relationship, with, by and to, the Wife of our youth. Both husband and Wife are to be blessed by God in this relationship. This loving relationship is to be recognized as a Godly reward, and it is to be enjoyed each and every day of our fleeting years.

As we each enjoy the pleasures of being husband and Wife, we recognize God's comfort and sustenance given to both married partners. We are to enjoy this life, as we toil and labor together, throughout our earthly experience.

7. (1 Corinthians 7:2-4)(vs 2) But because of immoralities, each man is to have his own wife, and each woman is to have her own husband.

(vs 3) The husband must fulfill his duty to his wife, and likewise also the wife to her husband. (vs 4) The wife does not have authority over her own body, but the husband does; and likewise also the husband does not have authority over his own body, but the wife does.

God's gift to both the Husband and Wife is to respect each other and mutually fulfill each other, and in doing so, it is to be accomplished without selfish purposes or motives.

8. (1 Corinthians 11:3) But I want you to understand that Christ is the head of every man, and the man is the head of a woman, and God is the head of Christ.

This verse could be viewed as the Godly chain of command or His corporate organizational chart. Please note that all power and authority goes back to God the Father.

9. (Ephesians 5:31) FOR THIS REASON A MAN SHALL LEAVE HIS FATHER AND MOTHER AND SHALL BE JOINED TO HIS WIFE, AND THE TWO SHALL BECOME ONE FLESH.

10. (Colossians 3:18) Wives, be subject to your husbands, as is fitting in the Lord.

11. *(1 Corinthians 11:11-12)(vs 11) However, in the Lord, neither is woman independent of man, nor is man independent of woman. (vs 12) For as the woman originates from the man, so also the man has his birth through the woman; and all things originate from God.*

Wives have their roles! Husbands have their roles! Both **"ANSWER"** to God, as *"all things originate from God"*!!!

F. CONCLUSION TO WIVES:

The conclusion about Wives, with much left out, is as follows:

1. The Wife was not an afterthought by God, but was planned before time;

2. The Wife's Biblical role in the marriage relationship is different from the husband, but of equal value as seen in the focus of God's plan;

3. The origin of the Wife (suitable helper for man) was literally a creation by God from the rib of man (Adam). Since the creation by God of both Adam and Eve, every person that is living today and has died in the past, is also a creation by Him. It is of importance to note that each of these creations have been born of a woman. This significant involvement by the woman (Wife) is a reality, for each of these estimated eleven (11) billion births, that is a worthy fact to be noted;

4. Wives have given birth to and helped train-up great Biblical leaders such as Abraham, Moses, David, John the Baptist, the Apostle Paul, and too many others, too numerous to name, in this writing. The Greatest of all mankind, who was both God and man, was born of a woman, this being none other than Jesus Christ, our Lord and Savior, "To Whom We Belong"!!!;

5. *(Proverbs 31:10) An excellent wife, who can find? For her worth is far above jewels.* Wives have accomplished everything from clothing their family, securing the trust of their husband's heart, buying and selling land, rising early and staying up late, extending a helping hand to the poor and needy, and expressing wisdom and the teaching of kindness. This is a most noble and honorable list, but please be aware this is only a short list. ... *(Proverbs 31:30-31) (vs 30) Charm is deceitful and beauty is vain, But a woman who fears the LORD, she shall be praised. (vs 31) Give her* *the product of her hands, And let her works praise her in the gates.* The contributions and accomplishments of Godly Wives, are without measure; and

6. A Godly wife can be responsible for the salvation of an unregenerate husband.

(1 Peter 3:1-2)(vs 1) In the same way, you wives, be submissive to your own husbands so that even if any of them are disobedient to the word, they may be won without a word by the behavior of their wives, (vs 2) as they observe your chaste and respectful behavior.

A Godly Wife has fulfilled her role of being a suitable helper for man. She is found to be unique, invaluable, and a great treasure. *(Proverbs 31:10) An excellent wife, who can find? For her worth is far above jewels. (Proverbs 18:22) He who finds a wife finds a good thing And obtains favor from the LORD.*

Can anyone find anything or anybody, to give more credit and accolades to, than to the Godly Wife!

SPECIAL NOTE:

I know many of you may have a special verse or verses regarding this Chapter's subject matter. This special verse or these verses may not have been mentioned due to my ignorance or because of brevity. I apologize for either of these reasons. Please feel free to write any special verse or verses in the space below. This will add your personal touch, and will serve to call to each person's mind their individual "experience of trust", in God's Holy Word.

For to each of us "Who belong To Him", His Holy Word can be truly recognized and relied upon as our **"Owner's Manual"**!!!

_____

_____

_____

_____

_____

CHAPTER 14

FATHERHOOD

INTRODUCTORY VERSE:

Please bear with me as we consider the subject of being a Biblical Father. The following verse, as an introductory verse, may need some clarification. With the proper forgiving attitude on your part, and a little bit of your imagination, we can put this together. *(Romans 8:15) For you have not received a spirit of slavery leading to fear again, but you have received a spirit of adoption as sons by which we cry out, "Abba! Father!"*

INTRODUCTION:

Found in the above verse are the words **"Abba"** and **"Father"**. Each of these means the same thing — father, but are of two different language origins. Our conclusion here is the Apostle Paul wanted to emphasize the endearment of the term father, as he gives his personal example, by calling out to and acknowledging God as our Heavenly, **"Abba! Father!"**. We can only believe that he repeats himself, due to his thankfulness and endearment, as he openly expresses his joy of being loved and cared for by the Almighty God of the Universe. This was and is truly something to shout about in repetition! Our **"Abba! Father!"**!!!

The first part of this verse where it states, ***"a spirit of slavery leading to fear"***, (fear being defined as: to have exceeding fright, fear or terror) is associated with evil and corruption, promoted by the father of lies, the devil. We haven't received this spirit of slavery, but we have received the spirit of being a son of God, therefore we rejoice and call out to Him ***"Abba! Father!"***. This is a grandiose utterance, to be made by the one "Who Belongs To Him", for we know we are a **"son"** of the **"Most High Father"** not a "slave" of the devil.

When I think about carrying through life the "spirit of being a slave", versus the "joy of knowing that I am a Child of God" (with my **"Father"** being the "Living God of the Universe"), I can't help but be reminded of a poem by William Cullen Bryant, entitled **Thanatopsis**. Please bear with me as we take this short detour from **"Fatherhood"**.

"Thanatopsis" was about dying, and the millions, even the billions of people that have preceded us down that long but certain hallway of death. Those mentioned were described as, "youth in life's fresh spring, matron and maid, speechless babes and gray-headed man". This poem includes all of mankind, as it vividly portrays the two different ways man will enter into his last days, while preparing to exit this earth. The full poem concludes, "it doesn't **matter** a person's status, for all will wind up entombed in this earth". What does **matter** is, "Do We Belong" to the "father of lies", or the **"FATHER OF LIGHT"**???

The last paragraph in this poem is very graphic as to how we approach our mortality and the grave, and I re-print it here for your consideration. The decision to be considered here is, are we going to go as a "dungeon slave" or are we going to leave this life joyously in peace, while trusting Our **"Heavenly Father"**. Trusting the One we can call *"Abba! Father!"*. Please read below the final verses of the poem **Thanatopsis**:

> **"So live, that when thy summons comes to join**
> **The innumerable caravan, which moves**
> **To that mysterious realm, where each shall take**
> **His chamber in the silent halls of death,**
> **Thou go not, like the quarry-slave at night,**
> **Scourged to his dungeon, but, sustained and soothed**
> **By an unfaltering trust, approach thy grave**
> **Like one who wraps the drapery of his couch**
> **About him, and lies down to pleasant dreams".([4])**

---

[4]   From a Poem by William Cullen Bryant

All men are going to die, wouldn't you rather go as an "Adopted Son of God", calling out *"Abba! Father!"*, than as a "quarry-slave scourged to his dungeon".

We haven't received this *"spirit of slavery leading to fear"* but have received *"a spirit of adoption as sons"*—this is one of a bond-servant, whereby we serve the **"Father"** out of love and gratitude, for the unfathomable work He accomplished for us on the Cross some two thousand years ago. We cry out to Him *"Abba! Father!"*, because "We Belong To Him"!!!, in a loving relationship that goes both ways, from the **"Father"** to us and from us back to Him.

God is our model of the absolutely perfect **"Father"**. Please be gracious to me as I struggle through the Biblical instructions, responsibilities, examples and requirements, we find regarding **"Fatherhood"**. Through the words found in our "Owner's Manual", there can be no greater instructor or example of **"Fatherhood"**, than by the one we call *"Abba! Father!"*

A. OUR MOST CRITICAL RESPONSIBILITY AS BIBLICAL FATHERS:

If you are a child of God, if you "Belong To Him", God's Word has commands, directions and instructions that are all worthy of learning about and putting into action. I believe **the worst thing a "father" can do is to neglect the teaching of the Word of God to his children**. Therefore the counter to this, or in the positive sense, our greatest commission and our greatest responsibility, **is to teach or train up a child in the Word of God**. This young generation can be lost to God's powerful salvation if we neglect this most high calling. Let's look at what the scripture has to say.

The first thing we need to consider, as Biblical "fathers", is our concerns and responsibilities are beyond the care of ourselves.

(1 Corinthians 6:19-20)(vs 19) Or do you not know that your body is a temple of the Holy Spirit who is in you, whom you have from God, and that you are not your own? (vs 20) For you have been bought with a price: therefore glorify God in your body.

If you are not your own, and have been bought with a price (Jesus paid this price on the Cross), you have a responsibility and a stewardship to the One to whom you owe this great debt.

The next thing we must learn and apply, are the direct commands by God's Word to teach and train up our children:

a. *(Deuteronomy 4:10) "Remember the day you stood before the LORD your God at Horeb, when the LORD said to me, 'Assemble the people to Me, that I may let them hear My words so they may learn to fear Me all the days they live on the earth, and that they may teach their children.'* ... Moses says revere God, hear His words, and teach your children;

b. *(Deuteronomy 6:6-9)(vs 6) "These words, which I am commanding you today, shall be on your heart. (vs 7) "You shall teach them diligently to your sons and shall talk of them when you sit in your house and when you walk by the way and when you lie down and when you rise up. (vs 8) "You shall bind them as a sign on your hand and they shall be as frontals on your forehead. (vs 9) "You shall write them on the doorposts of your house and on your gates.* ;

c. *(Deuteronomy 11:18-19)(vs 18) "You shall therefore impress these words of mine on your heart and on your soul; and you shall bind them as a sign on your hand, and they shall be as frontals on your forehead. (vs 19) "You shall teach them to your sons, talking of them when you sit in your house and when you walk along the road and when you lie down and when you rise up.* ;

d. *(Psalms 78:5-8)(vs 5) For He established a testimony in Jacob And appointed a law in Israel, Which He commanded our fathers That they should teach them to their children, (vs 6) That the generation to come might know, even the children yet to be born, That they may arise and tell them to their children, (vs 7) That they should put their confidence in God And not forget the works of God, But keep His commandments, (vs 8) And not be like their fathers, A stubborn and rebellious generation, A generation that did not prepare its heart And whose spirit was not faithful to God.* ; and

e. *(Ephesians 6:4) Fathers, do not provoke your children to anger, but bring them up in the discipline and instruction of the Lord.*

As the Bible says, we are to teach and train up our children. It is impossible to add to or amplify anything in the above scriptures. All I can do is encourage every **"father"** to take these Words seriously. The eternal lives of our children are at stake.

B. ADDITIONAL INSTRUCTIONS AND RESPONSIBILITY OF BIBLICAL FATHERHOOD:

1. God the Father, God the Son. I have selected a few of the significant verses regarding this most high relationship. This relationship of God the Father and God the Son gives us "The Most High" example. If only we could apply a part of this to our earthly "father"/ "children" relationships. We can never be expected to be in full compliance with this Heavenly relationship, but perhaps we can glean some valuable tidbits from these most overflowing and overwhelming verses.

a. *(John 5:19-20)(vs 19) Therefore Jesus answered and was saying to them, "Truly, truly, I say to you, the Son can do nothing of Himself, unless it is something He sees the Father doing; for whatever the Father does, these things the Son also does in like manner. (vs 20) "For the Father loves the Son, and shows Him all things that He Himself is doing; and the Father will show Him greater works than these, so that you will marvel.*

b. *(Matthew 11:27) "All things have been handed over to Me by My Father; and no one knows the Son except the Father; nor does anyone know the Father except the Son, and anyone to whom the Son wills to reveal Him.*

c. *(John 10:30) "I and the Father are one."*

d. *(John 3:35-36)(vs 35) "The Father loves the Son and has given all things into His hand. (vs 36) "He who believes in the Son has eternal life; but he who does not obey the Son will not see life, but the wrath of God abides on him."*

I cannot even try to make application, but only have to believe that God will speak to each person's heart and make His application on an individual basis. Seek God's blessings as you read these scriptures, the spiritual lives of your children depend upon it.

2. Instructions are required by earthly "fathers".

a. *(Proverbs 1:8-9)(vs 8) Hear, my son, your father's instruction And do not forsake your mother's teaching; (vs 9) Indeed, they are a graceful wreath to your head And ornaments about your neck.*

(Proverbs 4:1) Hear, O sons, the instruction of a father, And give attention that you may gain understanding,

These verses go both ways. They are instruction to both "fathers" and sons. They can be well received and applied accordingly.

b. *(Ecclesiastes 4:13) A poor yet wise lad is better than an old and foolish king who no longer knows how to receive instruction.*

Monetary wealth, political power and a lofty personal position, cannot even be compared to the wealth of a poor lad who is found to be wise and receiving instruction.

3. Responsibilities of the earthly "fathers".

a. *(Proverbs 22:6) Train up a child in the way he should go, Even when he is old he will not depart from it.*

Fathers, by accepting this commandment and putting it into action, you have just passed on to your children the promise of eternal life. You have just fulfilled your part in the greatest gift and inheritance you can give. While life is so fleeting and frail, you have honored them with the only imperishable gift that can be given. What you have given them will not rot, it will not be stolen and it will not rust. You have given them the opportunity to "Belong To Him"!!!

b. *(Ephesians 6:4) Fathers, do not provoke your children to anger, but bring them up in the discipline and instruction of the Lord.*

As fathers we are not to provoke our children. The Greek meaning found in the New Testament for this word "provoke" is: anger alongside, enrage and provoke to wrath. If we are not to do these things, then on the contrary we must be patient, nurture, cherish, train, educate by disciplinary correction, and teach through other acts of loving kindness.

All of our interactions with them should be of honest intent and should include **"the discipline and instruction of the Lord"**. There can be no higher calling as a "father".

4. Discipline is a Godly requirement, both to and from earthly "fathers".

a. (Job 5:17) "Behold, how happy is the man whom God reproves, So do not despise the discipline of the Almighty.

(Proverbs 3:11-12)(vs 11) My son, do not reject the discipline of the LORD Or loathe His reproof, (vs 12) For whom the LORD loves He reproves, Even as a father corrects the son in whom he delights.

As God the Father disciplines us because He loves us, we should also discipline our children because we love them. If you don't discipline your children, in effect you are telling them and actively demonstrating to them, that you do not care about them.

b. (Proverbs 6:23-24)(vs23) For the commandment is a lamp and the teaching is light; And reproofs for discipline are the way of life (vs 24) To keep you from the evil woman, From the smooth tongue of the adulteress.

(Proverbs 12:1) Whoever loves discipline loves knowledge, But he who hates reproof is stupid.

(Proverbs 13:1) A wise son accepts his father's discipline, But a scoffer does not listen to rebuke.

(Proverbs 19:18) Discipline your son while there is hope, And do not desire his death.

(Proverbs 19:27) Cease listening, my son, to discipline, And you will stray from the words of knowledge.

(Proverbs 22:15) Foolishness is bound up in the heart of a child; The rod of discipline will remove it far from him.

(Proverbs 23:13) Do not hold back discipline from the child, Although you strike him with the rod, he will not die.

You will find in the Proverbs, multiple upon multiple words of instruction and wisdom. These great Proverbs are twofold in their present application. We as 'fathers" need to accept these instructions from God, and as "fathers" we need to apply these to our child rearing. Remember, if you really don't love or have any desire for the good of your children, then don't discipline them. It is interesting that God, through Solomon, has approved discipline by the rod. This doesn't mean you "beat" your children, but when you inflict a physical sting, it causes them to have a better memory.

c. (Hebrews 12:5-11)(vs 5) and you have forgotten the exhortation which is addressed to you as sons, "MY SON, DO NOT REGARD LIGHTLY THE DISCIPLINE OF THE LORD, NOR FAINT WHEN YOU ARE REPROVED BY HIM; (vs 6) FOR THOSE WHOM THE LORD LOVES HE DISCIPLINES, AND HE SCOURGES EVERY SON WHOM HE RECEIVES." (vs 7) It is for discipline that you endure; God deals with you as with sons; for what son is there whom his father does not discipline? (vs 8) But if you are without discipline, of which all have become partakers, then you are illegitimate children and not sons. (vs 9) Furthermore, we had earthly fathers to discipline us, and we respected them; shall we not much rather be subject to the Father of spirits, and live? (vs 10) For they disciplined us for a short time as seemed best to them, but He disciplines us for our good, so that we may share His holiness. (vs 11) All discipline for the moment seems not to be joyful, but sorrowful; yet to those who have been trained by it, afterwards it yields the peaceful fruit of righteousness.

All discipline is for our good. It produces the best thing possible, even though it may hurt for a while, because the end product is **"His holiness"** and **"the peaceful fruit of righteousness"**. It is this **"holiness"** or the **"Imputed Righteousness because of Jesus Christ"**, that we should desire to pass on to our children. The most precious gift or inheritance ever to be granted is the imperishable gift of God in the form of "believing faith" in Jesus Christ. It is this gift that we desire to pass on to our children. As **"fathers"** there can be no higher calling then to **"Teach"** and **"Discipline"** our children in the ways of God.

d. (Revelation 3:19) 'Those whom I love, I reprove and discipline; therefore be zealous and repent.

The words of Jesus as given to John during his exile on the Isle of Patmos.

264

C. EXAMPLES AND MODELS OF BIBLICAL FATHERHOOD:

1. Abraham and Isaac.

The following account of obedience by man is the most powerful demonstration that can be found in the Bible. This is a man, Abraham, who knows "To Whom He Belongs". Abraham was so certain that it was God speaking to him, he was willing to carry out a most difficult command, and that was to sacrifice his son. This is truly a forerunning glimpse of what God did for all of us some four thousand years later, by sacrificing His only Son, Jesus.

(Genesis 22:1-3 & 9-13)(vs 1) Now it came about after these things, that God tested Abraham, and said to him, "Abraham!" And he said, "Here I am." (vs 2) He said, "Take now your son, your only son, whom you love, Isaac, and go to the land of Moriah, and offer him there as a burnt offering on one of the mountains of which I will tell you." (vs 3) So Abraham rose early in the morning and saddled his donkey, and took two of his young men with him and Isaac his son; and he split wood for the burnt offering, and arose and went to the place of which God had told him. (vs 9) Then they came to the place of which God had told him; and Abraham built the altar there and arranged the wood, and bound his son Isaac and laid him on the altar, on top of the wood. (vs 10) Abraham stretched out his hand and took the knife to slay his son. (vs 11) But the angel of the LORD called to him from heaven and said, "Abraham, Abraham!" And he said, "Here I am." (vs 12) He said, "Do not stretch out your hand against the lad, and do nothing to him; for now I know that you fear God, since you have not withheld your son, your only son, from Me." (vs 13) Then Abraham raised his eyes and looked, and behold, behind him a ram caught in the thicket by his horns; and Abraham went and took the ram and offered him up for a burnt offering in the place of his son.

I have read this passage many times over, and I still stand in awe of Abraham's willingness to do what God asked. Abraham **had to know that it was God speaking**. Abraham had to have complete respect and confidence in the God whom he loved, trusted and "Belongs"!!!

Can we even imagine our thoughts if God asked us to do this? My thoughts were and are, "I would have to know with every certainty that it was the Almighty God of the Heavens that was talking to me". Even then I don't know if I could have carried this out like Abraham was prepared to do. I know God ultimately provided the sacrifice and Isaac was spared. Nevertheless, before Abraham knew of God's ultimate plan, he got up early and prepared to do that which he was so confidently, certain God had instructed.

As a "father", Abraham's heart had to be tremendously heavy as he was asked to do this most difficult task. God the **"Father"** was testing Abraham while He was setting the stage for His own Son's sacrifice. Our **"Heavenly Father"** will deliver us for all of eternity if we will only listen to **"His Word"** and follow **"It"** with obedience. Our **"Heavenly Father"** has our best interest at heart in all matters.

The most beautiful thing in all of these discussions is the fact that **"God, our Father"** has provided the **"once-and-for-all, perfect sacrifice of His Son Jesus"**, and therefore He has spared all of "Those Who Belong To Him", for all of eternity!!! The **"FATHER'S** love, as demonstrated in these passages, is beyond measure and comparison.

2. The "father" and "mother" of Moses.

(Exodus 2:1-2 & 5-6 & 10)(vs 1) Now a man from the house of Levi went and married a daughter of Levi. (vs 2) The woman conceived and bore a son; and when she saw that he was beautiful, she hid him for three months. (vs 5) The daughter of Pharaoh came down to bathe at the Nile, with her maidens walking alongside the Nile; and she saw the basket among the reeds and sent her maid, and she brought it to her. (vs 6)
When she opened it, she saw the child, and behold, the boy was crying. And she had pity on him and said, "This is one of the Hebrews' children." (vs 10) The child grew, and she brought him to Pharaoh's daughter and he became her son. And she named him Moses, and said, "Because I drew him out of the water."
(Hebrews 11:23) By faith Moses, when he was born, was hidden for three months by his parents, because they saw

he was a beautiful child; and they were not afraid of the king's edict.

We all know the rest of the story. How Moses became a great leader and guided the Children of Israel from exile in Egypt to the Promised Land. Moses' earthly "father" and "mother" were directed by God to give up their child, because God had a greater plan for this son of theirs.

3. Jesse and David.

(1 Samuel 16:1 & 11-13)(vs 1) Now the LORD said to Samuel, "How long will you grieve over Saul, since I have rejected him from being king over Israel? Fill your horn with oil and go; I will send you to Jesse the Bethlehemite, for I have selected a king for Myself among his sons." (vs 11) And Samuel said to Jesse, "Are these all the children?" And he said, "There remains yet the youngest, and behold, he is tending the sheep." Then Samuel said to Jesse, "Send and bring him; for we will not sit down until he comes here." (vs 12) So he sent and brought him in. Now he was ruddy, with beautiful eyes and a handsome appearance. And the LORD said, "Arise, anoint him; for this is he." (vs 13) Then Samuel took the horn of oil and anointed him in the midst of his brothers; and the Spirit of the LORD came mightily upon David from that day forward.

Samuel the Prophet, who had been appointed directly by God, is now to select the new King for the Children of Israel. This process of selecting the successor to Saul is to be done as a directive by God, through His servant Samuel. Jesse has eight sons and paraded seven of these before Samuel. Samuel rejected these seven and requested of Jesse if he had any others. David was brought before Samuel and we know the rest of this story, even though it has many, many chapters.

David was a mighty man of God, called a "man after God's own heart". We see his victories before God, we see his frailties in sin, we see his repentance and we see God's forgiveness.

We can only assume that Jesse, the earthly "father" of King David, poured God's Word into this youthful son, through instruction and training.

4. Zacharias and John the Baptist.

(Luke 1:5-7 & 12-16)(vs 5) In the days of Herod, king of Judea, there was a priest named Zacharias, of the division of Abijah; and he had a wife from the daughters of Aaron, and her name was Elizabeth. (vs 6) They were both righteous in the sight of God, walking blamelessly in all the commandments and requirements of the Lord. (vs 7) But they had no child, because Elizabeth was barren, and they were both advanced in years. (vs 12) Zacharias was troubled when he saw the angel, and fear gripped him. (vs 13) But the angel said to him, "Do not be afraid, Zacharias, for your petition has been heard, and your wife Elizabeth will bear you a son, and you will give him the name John. (vs 14) "You will have joy and gladness, and many will rejoice at his birth. (vs 15) "For he will be great in the sight of the Lord; and he will drink no wine or liquor, and he will be filled with the Holy Spirit while yet in his mother's womb. (vs 16) "And he will turn many of the sons of Israel back to the Lord their God.

The earthly "father" Zacharias, was rewarded for his righteousness by our loving Heavenly Father. Having a son at Zacharias' age was truly an "Act of God". This son was a blessing and a crown of glory to his parents as he went on to *"turn many of the sons of Israel back to the Lord their God"*. The rest of the story is best summed up in the statement … *(Matthew 11:11) "Truly I say to you, among those born of women there has not arisen anyone greater than John the Baptist! Yet the one who is least in the kingdom of heaven is greater than he.*

As a "father", wouldn't you be proud if your son ended up as a starting quarterback in the NFL? Wouldn't you **REALLY** be proud in you had a son like John the Baptist?!!!

5. Joseph and Jesus.

(Matthew 1:18-21 & 24-25)(vs 18) Now the birth of Jesus Christ was as follows: when His mother Mary had been betrothed to Joseph, before they came together she was found to be with child by the Holy Spirit.

(vs 19) And Joseph her husband, being a righteous man and not wanting to disgrace her, planned to send her away secretly. (vs 20) But when he had considered this, behold, an angel of the Lord appeared to him in a dream, saying, "Joseph, son of David, do not be afraid to take Mary as your wife; for the Child who has been conceived in her is of the Holy Spirit. (vs 21) "She will bear a Son; and you shall call His name Jesus, for He will save His people from their sins." (vs 24) And Joseph awoke from his sleep and did as the angel of the Lord commanded him, and took Mary as his wife, (vs 25) but kept her a virgin until she gave birth to a Son; and he called His name Jesus.

Now Joseph was Jesus' earthly "father", he was not His biological "father". Joseph was a righteous man. The Lord God of the universe, choose Joseph and Mary for this most formidable task. They parented as God directed, and we as the general populace of the world have reaped or have available to us, this most unfathomable blessing. ... *(John 1:29) The next day he *saw Jesus coming to him and *said, "Behold, the Lamb of God who takes away the sin of the world! (John 12:46) "I have come as Light into the world, so that everyone who believes in Me will not remain in darkness. (1 John 2:1-2)(vs 1) My little children, I am writing these things to you so that you may not sin. And if anyone sins, we have an Advocate with the Father, Jesus Christ the righteous; (vs 2) and He Himself is the propitiation for our sins; and not for ours only, but also for those of the whole world.*

The Son in this case is the Only Begotten Son of God!!! He was both man and God. This is impossible to understand, and we can only marvel at this fact. Also in this case of God the Father and God the Son, we can only fall on our face and worship because of this Father/Son relationship and Their *"propitiation for our sins; and not for ours only, but also for those of the whole world"*.

6. God the "FATHER" and His adopted sons.
John 15:12-13)(vs 12) "This is My commandment, that you love one another, just as I have loved you. (vs 13) "Greater

love has no one than this, that one lay down his life for his friends.

(Romans 5:6-10)(vs 6) For while we were still helpless, at the right time Christ died for the ungodly. (vs 7) For one will hardly die for a righteous man; though perhaps for the good man someone would dare even to die. (vs 8) But God demonstrates His own love toward us, in that while we were yet sinners, Christ died for us. (vs 9) Much more then, having now been justified by His blood, we shall be saved from the wrath of God through Him. (vs 10) For if while we were enemies we were reconciled to God through the death of His Son, much more, having been reconciled, we shall be saved by His life.

God the Father, through God the Son, completed this most unselfish act, of taking on the sins of the world while we *"were yet sinners"*. This "Act of Love" in a "fatherly" role is without comparison. As "earthly fathers" it should be the desire of our hearts to "Teach" our children the Word of God. This would be one way to say "thank You" for the love we have learned and experienced from our **"Heavenly Father"**.

D. A NEGATIVE OR WARNING IF THERE IS NEGLECT BY "FATHERS":

(1 Timothy 5:8) But if anyone does not provide for his own, and especially for those of his household, he has denied the faith and is worse than an unbeliever. Other words here for describing *"unbeliever"* are infidel, heathen, or one without Christian faith. The statement here can be paraphrased, **YOU MUST PROVIDE FOR YOUR OWN.** The earthly, Christian "fathers" have no alternative. Now what we must decipher is, what does it mean when the verse says *"provide for his own"*? I am not going to get into what it means to provide the necessary shelter, clothes, food, transportation, secular education, etc. This would certainly be neglect if those things were not provided. What I want to dwell upon is the responsibility of teaching our young ones.

What I believe can be the more severe neglect by a Christian "father", is to disregard the teaching of God's Word to his offspring.

Any child that we have been given is not a possession, but is a gift from God, and therefore is a stewardship responsibility to us. A major part if this stewardship responsibility is to teach and train up this child. *(Proverbs 22:6) Train up a child in the way he should go, Even when he is old he will not depart from it.* Bear with me as I share some thoughts from my 68 years of having been on this earth, 47 of those years having been a "father".

Life is not about pleasing yourself at the expense of your family. The "father" is the head of his household and along with this comes responsibilities where he must put all others first. This same responsibility is required of and demonstrated by a Godly "mother". We are not alone in this parenting situation and should enjoy the cooperation and support of our mate. The Chapter is directed at the "father", and addresses that parent, but please don't think I have ignored the "mother" and her important involvement.

A warning is to not put the full responsibility of teaching your children in the hands of Sunday School teachers, Church youth pastors, or Christian Schools. These resources can and often are a supplement to our training up a child in the way he should go. I warn you of this because I have seen it happen and generally the results were not pleasant. You can use the Church and Christian Schools to support you, but they are not to be our primary source of education. The next warning is to not practice, "do as I say , not as I do". These are wasted words and are a green light for the youth to ignore any teachings that you have clearly demonstrated are of no value. "Fathers", examine your heart, for if you see yourself not living up to the Biblical standards you expect of your children, you need to first get right with God and then go to this next step of lovingly preparing your offspring with God's Word.

One of the major problems I personally witnessed while teaching Sunday School for over 20 years to 11th graders, was the hands off policy of many of the parents. The parent who relied upon the Sunday School teacher, the Church and/or some Christian School, but didn't teach God's principles, or live out God's principles, developed some very evil children. I have since concluded the parents in these situations were very often found to be evil themselves. It is my conclusion these parents were not believers and only attended Church for some personal selfish reason. I may sound harsh here, but the lives at stake are not only your own , but those of the precious child, entrusted to you by a Holy God. Christianity is lost in one generation by those who do not teach their children. I am not off base on this one! I have personally witnessed too many horrible family situations while serving these 20 years as a Sunday School teacher. "Fathers", if you "Belong To Him" seek to be found as described as follows ... *(Ephesians 6:4) Fathers, do not provoke your children to anger, but bring them up in the discipline and instruction of the Lord.* Please don't neglect this most high calling. If you give your kids all the love they can stand, a knowledge of God's Word and a "father" who lives that Word, they are prepared for anything this world can throw at them.

E. OTHER VERSES REGARDING BIBLICAL FATHERHOOD:

<u>1</u>. *(Proverbs 4:1-10)(vs 1) Hear, O sons, the instruction of a father, And give attention that you may gain understanding, (vs 2) For I give you sound teaching; Do not abandon my instruction. (vs 3) When I was a son to my father, Tender and the only son in the sight of my mother, (vs 4) Then he taught me and said to me, "Let your heart hold fast my words; Keep my commandments and live; (vs 5) Acquire wisdom! Acquire understanding! Do not forget nor turn away from the words of my mouth. (vs 6) "Do not forsake her, and she will guard you; Love her, and she will watch over you. (vs 7) "The beginning of wisdom is: Acquire wisdom; And with all your acquiring, get understanding. (vs 8) "Prize her, and she will exalt you; She will honor you if you embrace her. (vs 9) "She will place on your head a garland of grace; She will present you with a crown of beauty." (vs 10) Hear, my son, and accept my sayings And the years of your life will be many.*

Solomon in all his wisdom spends much print regarding wisdom. He learned from his "father" and is now teaching all of us to learn of God's wisdom and pass this on to our children. Wisdom and under-standing are supreme. Accept the words of a Godly "father". Solomon as a "father" taught us to teach His wisdom and understanding. It is our responsibility as the "father" of the current generation, to pass this on to our children. I can think of no higher calling as a "father", than to pass the Holy Word of God, as found in our "Owner's Manual", down to our children. Each generation is subject to being lost to God's Word if this is not diligently accomplished. What we have to offer to our offspring is better than precious jewels. ... *(Proverbs 2:6) For the LORD gives wisdom; From His mouth come knowledge and under-standing. (Proverbs 3:13-15)(vs 13) How blessed is the man who finds wisdom And the man who gains understanding. (vs 14) For her profit is better than the profit of silver And her gain better than fine gold. (vs 15) She is more precious than jewels; And nothing you desire compares with her.*

2. Youth are particularly vulnerable to deception and mis-con-ceptions. It is the responsibility of the "father" to prepare these young minds for the entire span of their life. *(Proverbs 5:1-2)(vs 1) My son, give attention to my wisdom, Incline your ear to my understanding; (vs 2) That you may observe discretion And your lips may reserve knowledge.*

These particular teachings, at this time of your youth's life, cannot be delegated to the Sunday School teacher or the Christian School. It is the responsibility of the "father" to teach his children. I personally have experienced many failures by "fathers", and can say it was often because the "father" had no personal knowledge of the things required by Gods for him to be teaching. Don't let this happen to you. Study God's Word and teach it to your kids!

3. *(Matthew 7:9-11)(vs 9) "Or what man is there among you who, when his son asks for a loaf, will give him a stone? (vs 10) "Or if he asks for a fish, he will not give him a snake, will he? (vs 11) "If you then, being evil, know how to give good gifts to your children, how much more will your Father who is in heaven give what is good to those who ask Him!*

The point here is we as earthly "fathers" will not give to our sons a useless or dangerous item when they request a necessity. How much greater is God the Father, as He has given the greatest gift of all time, His Son, Jesus Christ, for the salvation to all those who believe.

4. *(Matthew 10:37) "He who loves father or mother more than Me is not worthy of Me; and he who loves son or daughter more than Me is not worthy of Me.*

"Fathers" don't make your children into idols, children don't make your parents into idols either.

5. *(2 Corinthians 6:18) "And I will be a father to you, And you shall be sons and daughters to Me," Says the Lord Almighty.*

As a "father" it is comforting to know that God the Father is looking after us.

6. *(Titus 1:4) To Titus, my true child in a common faith: Grace and peace from God the Father and Christ Jesus our Savior.*

(Philemon 1:10) I appeal to you for my child Onesimus, whom I have begotten in my imprisonment,

The Apostle Paul, who had no earthly children, often referred to his children of the faith, in endearing terms as in a "father" son relationship.

F. CONCLUSION TO FATHERHOOD:

My conclusion is this. It is an awesome responsibility to be entrusted with the gift of children. They are truly a stewardship and not a possession. As a "born again believer", "Belonging To Him", I must confess I have often failed in this area. Any success is because of the mercy, grace and forgiveness of God. It is our overwhelming task to prepare and train the hearts of these gifts. It is a blessing to be chosen by God to be in His service. To God be the Glory for any and all success we find in nurturing these young hearts.

(Jude 1:25) to the only God our Savior, through Jesus Christ our Lord, be glory, majesty, dominion and authority, before all time and now and forever. Amen.

SPECIAL NOTE:

I know many of you may have a special verse or verses regarding this Chapter's subject matter. This special verse or these verses may not have been mentioned due to my ignorance or because of brevity. I apologize for either of these reasons. Please feel free to write any special verse or verses in the space below. This will add your personal touch, and will serve to call to each person's mind their individual "experience of trust", in God's Holy Word.

For to each of us "Who belong To Him", His Holy Word can be truly recognized and relied upon as our **"Owner's Manual"**!!!

_____

_____

_____

_____

_____

_____

_____

CHAPTER 15

MOTHERS (GODLY MOTHERS)

INTRODUCTORY VERSE:

(John 16:21) "Whenever a woman is in labor she has pain, because her hour has come; but when she gives birth to the child, she no longer remembers the anguish because of the joy that a child has been born into the world.

A Mother experiences pain during the labor of the birth of her child. After the birth she no longer remembers the anguish, but experiences a joy, which I believe is directly related to the acknowledgment of God's hand in this birth. This joy is because of the opportunity and responsibility to bring up this child in the nurture and admonishment of the Lord. Mothers who "Belong To God" are very special and have been given an enormous task!

INTRODUCTION:

Mothers all over the world have given birth in many conditions. These have varied from slaves in poor housing conditions, to the wealthy in mansions. The Savior of the world was born in a stable. Regardless of the conditions, whether good or bad, all Mothers were given a joy in their hearts as their child came into this world.

A Mother is someone that has given birth. A Godly Mother is one who has given birth and has followed that up with the nurturing, teaching and training of that child, as would be honoring to her Lord and Savior. There is a joy to be expressed to God for the birth of a child. That joy is even beyond expressing when given the opportunity to nurture that child for some eighteen years.

You are forever a Mother. Parenting is permanent. As a Godly Mother you are to pray for, do for and be concerned in a non-obstructive way, for many years. You will find yourself preparing that child, encouraging that child and showing concern for that child, until either you have died or that child has gone on. Every Mother should recognize her children will someday be "on their own" and rightfully so. The Godly Mother's responsibility is to train up their children in order that they become all that God wants them to be.

The responsibility of Motherhood is beyond comparison. The Godly Mother's task is not to be taken lightly and will be rewarded by God accordingly. Let's look at some Biblical examples and the God given tasks and responsibilities we find in these Biblical Moms.

A. MOTHERS—THEIR POSITION IN HISTORY:

We have all seen the national sports hero give credit to their Moms. This happens during all sports seasons and very often during a game or an event which is being nationally televised. Most often this is followed by the camera, going to the Mother and presenting her to the world in tribute to her being the one most closely related to this recognized son or daughter. The camera zooms in and captures her at an event, in the crowd, or in some cases, it even interviews her in her home. She is honored for her well deserving part in this athlete's life. This is all very kind and well deserving to those honored, but the real "HERO Mothers" are those found in the Bible. Their role and position, in the forming of history, is unquestionable.

Without going into a detailed commentary, let's look at some of these international "HEROS", these "Biblical Hall of Fame Women".

1. Sarah—Mother of Isaac: *(Genesis 17:15-16)(vs 15) Then God said to Abraham, "As for Sarai your wife, you shall not call her name Sarai, but Sarah shall be her name. (vs 16) "I will bless her, and indeed I will give you a son by her. Then I will bless her, and she shall be a mother of nations; kings of peoples will come from her."*

Sarah considered God to be faithful in His humanly impossible promise. Because of her faith, she was found to be mightily blessed by God.

(Genesis 21:1-3)(vs 1) Then the LORD took note of Sarah as He had said, and the LORD did for Sarah as He had promised. (vs 2) So Sarah conceived and bore a son to Abraham in his old age, at the appointed time of which God had spoken to him. (vs 3) Abraham called the name of his son who was born to him, whom Sarah bore to him, Isaac.

(Hebrews 11:11) By faith even Sarah herself received ability to conceive, even beyond the proper time of life, since she considered Him faithful who had promised.

Sarah and Abraham were so certain they couldn't have any children, they both laughed at God's promise. Isaac was truly a miracle by God. Sarah's faith allowed her to become a Mother of nations, and all the while God received .... all the Glory.

2. Jochebed—Mother of Moses: *(Exodus 2:1-3)(vs 1) Now a man from the house of Levi went and married a daughter of Levi. (vs 2) The woman conceived and bore a son; and when she saw that he was beautiful, she hid him for three months. (vs 3) But when she could hide him no longer, she got him a wicker basket and covered it over with tar and pitch. Then she put the child into it and set it among the reeds by the bank of the Nile.*

Moses was born to Jochebed and he became the Hero to the nation of Israel. This all took place at the time the Pharaoh of Egypt was killing all Jewish babies. God so protected Moses that He allowed him to be raised as the Pharaoh's daughter, while allowing his birth mother to nurse and nurture him.

(Exodus 2:8-10)(vs 8) Pharaoh's daughter said to her, "Go ahead." So the girl went and called the child's mother. (vs 9) Then Pharaoh's daughter said to her, "Take this child away and nurse him for me and I will give you your wages." So the woman took the child and nursed him. (vs 10) The child grew, and she brought him to Pharaoh's daughter and he became her son. And she named him Moses, and said, "Because I drew him out of the water."

(Hebrews 11:23) By faith Moses, when he was born, was hidden for three months by his parents, because they saw he was a beautiful child; and they were not afraid of the king's edict.

These events had to be unbelievably traumatic for Moses' mother. Can any of us imagine giving our child over to a godless household, to be raised in unknown and uncertain circumstances. This daughter of Levi was found faithful to God for His purpose. Jochebed's faith puts this Mom, in the Biblical "Hero's" Hall of Fame.

3. Elizabeth — Mother of John the Baptist: *(Luke 1:5-7)(vs 5) In the days of Herod, king of Judea, there was a priest named Zacharias, of the division of Abijah; and he had a wife from the daughters of Aaron, and her name was Elizabeth. (vs 6) They were both righteous in the sight of God, walking blamelessly in all the commandments and requirements of the Lord. (vs 7) But they had no child, because Elizabeth was barren, and they were both advanced in years. (Luke 1:13) But the angel said to him, "Do not be afraid, Zacharias, for your petition has been heard, and your wife Elizabeth will bear you a son, and you will give him the name John.*

Elizabeth became the Mother of John the Baptist. John the Baptist became one of the greatest preachers of all time. He was bold, thorough and insisted upon proclaiming the coming of The Messiah. Even though John preached nothing but Christ, he became somewhat idolized. Under these tempting circumstances John was humble and had nothing but Godly fear and respect for Jesus. ... *(Matthew 3:11) "As for me, I baptize you with water for repentance, but He who is coming after me is mightier than I, and I am not fit to remove His sandals; He will baptize you with the Holy Spirit and fire.* ... Elizabeth was John's Mother, she was *"righteous in the sight of God"* and belongs in this list of "HERO Mothers".

4. Unnamed Mother of Peter and Andrew — Salome, Mother of James and John:

(Matthew 4:18-22)(vs 18) Now as Jesus was walking by the Sea of Galilee, He saw two brothers, Simon who was

called Peter, and Andrew his brother, casting a net into the sea; for they were fishermen. (vs 19) And He *said to them, "Follow Me, and I will make you fishers of men." (vs 20) Immediately they left their nets and followed Him. (vs 21) Going on from there He saw two other brothers, James the son of Zebedee, and John his brother, in the boat with Zebedee their father, mending their nets; and He called them. (vs 22) Immediately they left the boat and their father, and followed Him.

We don't have the full story of Peter and Andrew and James and John regarding their early life. We do know each pair of brothers had a Mother. These two teams of brothers that Jesus called into His confidence, along with the rest of the Twelve Disciples, were obviously very special. The only conclusion that I can make, is that they each had a special Mother. These special Mothers did their job of nurturing these teams of brothers, and probably never knew their sons would be used to change the world. The Mothers reward here will be many thousands of times over more significant than being highlighted on some television screen for 15 seconds. These mothers will be thanked for all eternity, by all of those who "Belong To Him", for being faithful to God, as they have earned their place in Biblical History.

5. Mary—Mother of Jesus, our Savior: *(Matthew 1:16) Jacob was the father of Joseph the husband of Mary, by whom Jesus was born, who is called the Messiah.*

Many times we save the best for last, and that is so true here. The last Mother to be considered in this section on the Chapter of Godly Mothers, is the most significant as measured in importance of Biblical history. Mary, the earthly Mother of Jesus our Messiah, is truly to be commended for her obedience and her faithfulness. She is certainly one to be honored for her part in God's miraculous plan.

Even though the Bible calls Mary blessed, I feel it is important to make it clear, that nowhere in the Bible will you find that she is to be worshiped or considered in any way to be a Deity. Very simply put, she was a young Jewish girl, chosen by God, who was found to be obedient to God, to carry out the most miraculous plan that will ever be seen throughout all of the universe and throughout all of time. She has been found to be faithful, and is deserving of being at the top of the list of the "HERO Mother's" Biblical Hall of Fame.

As Mary was chosen to be the earthly Mother of our Lord and Savior, Jesus Christ, let's look at some of the background of this miraculous virgin birth and her obedience.

(Matthew 1:18-21)(vs 18) Now the birth of Jesus Christ was as follows: when His mother Mary had been betrothed to Joseph, before they came together she was found to be with child by the Holy Spirit. (vs 19) And Joseph her husband, being a righteous man and not wanting to disgrace her, planned to send her away secretly. (vs 20) But when he had considered this, behold, an angel of the Lord appeared to him in a dream, saying, "Joseph, son of David, do not be afraid to take Mary as your wife; for the Child who has been conceived in her is of the Holy Spirit. (vs 21) "She will bear a Son; and you shall call His name Jesus, for He will save His people from their sins."

God orchestrated His plan with obedient and righteous people. God's master plan was to bring His Son, Jesus Christ, to the earth as both God and man. His plan was, and always will be, to use the sacrifice of His Son on the Cross for the sake of all of us. Mary, as an ordinary Mother, gives each Mother since then, the encouragement to be a teacher, a trainer of the children given to them.

As a Mother who "Belongs To God", be ready and available for you never know how or when He may choose to use you. To God Be The Glory for all Mothers who teach and train up their children.

B. MOTHERS AND THEIR MARTYRED SONS:

I believe it to be important to mention the Godly Biblical Mothers, who had sons who were martyred for their faith. These Mothers were really special and worthy of much recognition. This is not intended to be hurtful or morbid, but to bring to light both the heights and depths of emotions that might have taken place back then and are still taking place in parts of the world today.

Because of the time that has passed since these tragic events took place, we may not feel the strong emotions that were felt by the Mothers of the Biblical martyrs, but be sure those tragedies were real. It takes a special relationship with God to be able to endure this type of hardship.

These Biblical accounts may become very real, and if you are a Mother who has personally witnessed the loss of your offspring due to any tragedy, my prayer is that God's special grace and comfort, will engulf you and be sufficient. My prayer is also that you will not experience pain, but will be blessed by the recalling of the Biblical stories of the faithfulness of those who have experienced death for the cause of Christ . These events are truly tragic and we must remember to put these in a Godly perspective. Our earthly circumstances and lives are but a vapor in God's eternal perspective, and we must have confidence that everyone "Who Belongs To Him" is in the steady and capable hands of our "Almighty God".

There is only room for a few of the "Martyrs" to be mentioned here. The purpose is to give God the Glory, for these as well as all of the "Hall of Fame", "Hero Mothers", who could praise God in light of tragic events.

Let's look at these Biblical accounts of Martyrdom, and let God speak to each of our hearts, as we meditate on His Word and consider the role of "Motherhood".

The Mother/The Martyred/Some Biblical Facts regarding each of these:

1. Samson:
a. The Mother: Wife of Manoah.
b. The Martyred: Samson—Sacrificed himself while delivering Israel against the Philistines.
c. Some Biblical Facts: *(Judges 13:2-5 & 24)(vs 2) There was a certain man of Zorah, of the family of the Danites, whose name was Manoah; and his wife was barren and had borne no children. (vs 3) Then the angel of the LORD appeared to the woman and said to her, "Behold now, you are barren and have borne no children, but you shall conceive and give birth to a son. (vs 4) "Now therefore, be careful not to drink wine or strong drink, nor eat any unclean thing. (vs 5) "For behold, you shall conceive and give birth to a son,*

and no razor shall come upon his head, for the boy shall be a Nazirite to God from the womb; and he shall begin to deliver Israel from the hands of the Philistines." (vs 24) Then the woman gave birth to a son and named him Samson; and the child grew up and the LORD blessed him.

(Judges 16:26-30)(vs 26) Then Samson said to the boy who was holding his hand, "Let me feel the pillars on which the house rests, that I may lean against them." (vs 27) Now the house was full of men and women, and all the lords of the Philistines were there. And about 3,000 men and women were on the roof looking on while Samson was amusing them. (vs 28) Then Samson called to the LORD and said, "O Lord GOD, please remember me and please strengthen me just this time, O God, that I may at once be avenged of the Philistines for my two eyes." (vs 29) Samson grasped the two middle pillars on which the house rested, and braced himself against them, the one with his right hand and the other with his left. (vs 30) And Samson said, "Let me die with the Philistines!" And he bent with all his might so that the house fell on the lords and all the people who were in it. So the dead whom he killed at his death were more than those whom he killed in his life.

Samson, who had super strength, was blessed by God and used for God's Glory during much of his life. We see in his death he was used by God in one final mighty way. His Mother must have been very proud to see Samson being used by God, even though the end was so tragic.

2. Stephen:
a. The Mother: Mothers Name Unknown.
b. The Martyred: Stephen—Reportedly the first Christian Martyr.
c. Some Biblical Facts: *(Acts 6:2-3 & 5 partial)(vs 2) So the twelve summoned the congregation of the disciples and said, "It is not desirable for us to neglect the word of God in order to serve tables. (vs 3) "Therefore, brethren, select from among you seven men of good reputation, full of the Spirit and of wisdom, whom we may put in charge of this task. (vs 5) The statement found approval with the whole*

congregation; and they chose Stephen, a man full of faith and of the Holy Spirit, ... (Acts 7:55 & 59-60)(vs 55) But being full of the Holy Spirit, he gazed intently into heaven and saw the glory of God, and Jesus standing at the right hand of God; (vs 59) They went on stoning Stephen as he called on the Lord and said, "Lord Jesus, receive my spirit!" (vs 60) Then falling on his knees, he cried out with a loud voice, "Lord, do not hold this sin against them!" Having said this, he fell asleep.

Stephen, a man characterized as *"a man full of faith and of the Holy Spirit"*, after a lengthy dissertation regarding his faith, was stoned for this faith. His last words were to plead with God to *"not hold this sin against them!* Again, his Mother should be in the Biblical "Hall of Fame for Mothers", for her part in the teaching of this young man.

3. John the Baptist:
a. The Mother: Elizabeth married to Zacharias.
b. The Martyred: John the Baptist.
c. Some Biblical Facts: *(Luke 1:13) But the angel said to him, "Do not be afraid, Zacharias, for your petition has been heard, and your wife Elizabeth will bear you a son, and you will give him the name John.*

(Matthew 11:11) "Truly I say to you, among those born of women there has not arisen anyone greater than John the Baptist! Yet the one who is least in the kingdom of heaven is greater than he.

(Mark 1:4) John the Baptist appeared in the wilderness preaching a baptism of repentance for the forgiveness of sins.

(Matthew 14:3-10)(vs 3) For when Herod had John arrested, he bound him and put him in prison because of Herodias, the wife of his brother Philip. (vs 4) For John had been saying to him, "It is not lawful for you to have her." (vs 5) Although Herod wanted to put him to death, he feared the crowd, because they regarded John as a prophet. (vs 6) But when Herod's birthday came, the daughter of Herodias

danced before them and pleased Herod, (vs 7) so much that he promised with an oath to give her whatever she asked. (vs 8) Having been prompted by her mother, she *said, "Give me here on a platter the head of John the Baptist." (vs 9) Although he was grieved, the king commanded it to be given because of his oaths, and because of his dinner guests. (vs 10) He sent and had John beheaded in the prison.

John the Baptist, having been the forerunner to Jesus Christ, was martyred for his faith which included his openly preaching against the sins of the day. Elizabeth (John's Mother) was found to be faithful and righteous before God and therefore was hand-picked by God to be his "Mother".

4. Jesus Christ the Son of God:
a. The Mother: Earthly Mother was Mary, the virgin betrothed to Joseph.
b. The Martyred: JESUS! You might consider He was both sacrificed as well as martyred.

The lengthy Biblical facts below tell of Jesus' birth, life, ministry, crucifixion, raised by God from the dead, and His return to the Father. The emphasis must be upon Jesus even in this Chapter on "Mothers". Mary did her part and is to be recognized for her faithfulness. I feel confident, as His earthly mother, she would in no way want to get in the way of Jesus' purpose here on earth.

c. Some Biblical Facts about Jesus:
i. Prophesy foretold about Jesus and His virgin birth:
(Isaiah 7:14) "Therefore the Lord Himself will give you a sign: Behold, a virgin will be with child and bear a son, and she will call His name Immanuel.

(Matthew 1:18-23)(vs 18) Now the birth of Jesus Christ was as follows: when His mother Mary had been betrothed to Joseph, before they came together she was found to be with child by the Holy Spirit. (vs 19) And Joseph her husband, being a righteous man and not wanting to disgrace her, planned to send her away secretly. (vs 20) But when he had considered this, behold, an angel of the Lord appeared to him in a dream, saying, "Joseph, son of David, do not be

afraid to take Mary as your wife; for the Child who has been conceived in her is of the Holy Spirit. (vs 21) "She will bear a Son; and you shall call His name Jesus, for He will save His people from their sins." (vs 22) Now all this took place to fulfill what was spoken by the Lord through the prophet: (vs 23) "BEHOLD, THE VIRGIN SHALL BE WITH CHILD AND SHALL BEAR A SON, AND THEY SHALL CALL HIS NAME IMMANUEL," which translated means, "GOD WITH US."

(Matthew 2:2 & 11)(vs 2) "Where is He who has been born King of the Jews? For we saw His star in the east and have come to worship Him." (vs 11) After coming into the house they saw the Child with Mary His mother; and they fell to the ground and worshiped Him. Then, opening their treasures, they presented to Him gifts of gold, frankincense, and myrrh.

ii. Jesus grew in wisdom and stature:

(Luke 2:52) And Jesus kept increasing in wisdom and stature, and in favor with God and men.

iii. Jesus' purpose here on earth:

(John 14:6) Jesus *said to him, "I am the way, and the truth, and the life; no one comes to the Father but through Me.

(1 John 2:1-2)(vs 1) My little children, I am writing these things to you so that you may not sin. And if anyone sins, we have an Advocate with the Father, Jesus Christ the righteous; (vs 2) and He Himself is the propitiation for our sins; and not for ours only, but also for those of the whole world.

iv. The prophesy of His crucifixion:

(Isaiah 53:5-7)(vs 5) But He was pierced through for our transgressions, He was crushed for our iniquities; The chastening for our well-being fell upon Him, And by His scourging we are healed. (vs 6) All of us like sheep have gone astray, Each of us has turned to his own way; But the LORD has caused the iniquity of us all To fall on Him. (vs 7) He was oppressed and He was afflicted, Yet He did not open His mouth; Like a lamb that is led to slaughter, And like a sheep that is silent before its shearers, So He did not open His mouth.

v. The fulfillment of His crucifixion:

(Matthew 16:21) From that time Jesus began to show His disciples that He must go to Jerusalem, and suffer many things from the elders and chief priests and scribes, and be killed, and be raised up on the third day.

(Matthew 26:2) "You know that after two days the Passover is coming, and the Son of Man is to be handed over for crucifixion."

(Matthew 27:33-35)(vs 33) And when they came to a place called Golgotha, which means Place of a Skull, (vs 34) they gave Him wine to drink mixed with gall; and after tasting it, He was unwilling to drink. (vs 35) And when they had crucified Him, they divided up His garments among themselves by casting lots.

(Matthew 27:50-54)(vs 50) And Jesus cried out again with a loud voice, and yielded up His spirit. (vs 51) And behold, the veil of the temple was torn in two from top to bottom; and the earth shook and the rocks were split. (vs 52) The tombs were opened, and many bodies of the saints who had fallen asleep were raised; (vs 53) and coming out of the tombs after His resurrection they entered the holy city and appeared to many. (vs 54) Now the centurion, and those who were with him keeping guard over Jesus, when they saw the earthquake and the things that were happening, became very frightened and said, "Truly this was the Son of God!"

vi. Jesus' eternal place with the Father:

*(Matthew 26:64) Jesus *said to him, "You have said it yourself; nevertheless I tell you, hereafter you will see THE SON OF MAN SITTING AT THE RIGHT HAND OF POWER, and COMING ON THE CLOUDS OF HEAVEN."*

(Mark 16:19) So then, when the Lord Jesus had spoken to them, He was received up into heaven and sat down at the right hand of God.

(Luke 22:69) "But from now on THE SON OF MAN WILL BE SEATED AT THE RIGHT HAND of the power OF GOD."

Stephen, just before he died, spoke these words, as a first hand witness of what he saw. *(Acts 7:55-56) But being full of the Holy Spirit, he gazed intently into heaven and saw the glory of God, and Jesus standing at the right hand of God; (vs 56) and he said, "Behold, I see the heavens opened up and the Son of Man standing at the right hand of God."*

(Romans 8:34-partial verse) Christ Jesus is He who died, yes, rather who was raised, who is at the right hand of God, who also intercedes for us.

(Colossians 3:1) Therefore if you have been raised up with Christ, keep seeking the things above, where Christ is, seated at the right hand of God.

(Hebrews 8:1-2)(vs 1) Now the main point in what has been said is this: we have such a high priest, who has taken His seat at the right hand of the throne of the Majesty in the heavens, (vs 2) a minister in the sanctuary and in the true tabernacle, which the Lord pitched, not man.

(Hebrews 10:12) but He, having offered one sacrifice for sins for all time, SAT DOWN AT THE RIGHT HAND OF GOD,

(Hebrews 12:2) fixing our eyes on Jesus, the author and perfecter of faith, who for the joy set before Him endured the cross, despising the shame, and has sat down at the right hand of the throne of God.

When talking about Mary, the earthly mother of Jesus, the emphasis has to be on Jesus even though this Chapter is about Mothers. That is why all the verses above are about our Lord and Savior, Jesus Christ. Mary honored God by giving her life to the earthly care of the Father's only Son. We can only think about the many and varied emotions she endured. Praise is due her for her Godly attitude, her acceptance of a most difficult task, and the completion of a job well done.

Martyrs were common in the Biblical days. Martyrs today are happening more often than we are aware of. Martyrdom will take place in the future. For every Martyr there is a "Mother". The lives of the martyred were given in tragic death. The "Mothers", of those martyred and to be martyred, are to be honored for their unwavering "Faith" in God's Almighty Plan.

C. ADDITIONAL VERSES REGARDING BIBLICAL MOTHERHOOD:

Please review the following verses and meditate upon these. God's Word is exposed in many different contexts regarding Motherhood and its varied responsibilities, opportunities, challenges and rewards. These verses have the potential to have a dramatic and lasting effect upon your life.

1. (Genesis 3:20) Now the man called his wife's name Eve, because she was the mother of all the living.

Eve in the original Hebrew means "lifegiver". Eve was the original "lifegiver" or the mother of all of mankind. I am sure there is much to be learned if we were to do a study on her life.

2. (Genesis 17:16) "I will bless her, and indeed I will give you a son by her. Then I will bless her, and she shall be a mother of nations; kings of peoples will come from her."

The Bible is speaking here of Sarah, Abraham's wife. She was found to be used by God for all of time, to be a mother of nations and of kings.

3. (Psalms 22:9-10)(vs 9) Yet You are He who brought me forth from the womb; You made me trust when upon my mother's breasts. (vs 10) Upon You I was cast from birth; You have been my God from my mother's womb.

(Psalms 71:6) By You I have been sustained from my birth; You are He who took me from my mother's womb; My praise is continually of You.

Many believe these words are a prelude of Jesus Christ's coming into this earth. His arrival was purposefully designed to culminate in the salvation of all those who would believe. While contemplating the significances of the weight of the world's sins upon the body of Christ while on the Cross, we can look back and give honor to the earthly mother's part. This, the most precious thing that God has ever done for man, began with a Godly Mother. God was brought down from Heaven to us, in the form of Jesus, through an "ordinary" Mother. The word "ordinary" is used sarcastically (facetiously) here to really say there are no "ordinary" mothers, but only special ones. Mothers of the world, if you "Belong To Him", you are **"SPECIAL"** indeed.

4. *(Psalms 127:3-5)(vs 3) Behold, children are a gift of the LORD, The fruit of the womb is a reward. (vs 4) Like arrows in the hand of a warrior, So are the children of one's youth. (vs 5) How blessed is the man whose quiver is full of them; They will not be ashamed When they speak with their enemies in the gate.*

Man in *(vs 5)* above, is defined simply as: "a person". Therefore we can boldly assert and be assured the Mother is also included in this passage and can apply all the statements found in *verses 3-5*. The children of all Mothers and fathers are a blessing by God, and are to be counted as a gift and a reward to those who have found God's favor. Think about this ... **blessed is the man whose quiver is full**. Mothers, if you are given a gift and rewarded with children, you need to be quick to give God the Glory and seek to honor Him with this life consuming task.

5. *(Psalms 139:13-14)(vs 13) For You formed my inward parts; You wove me in my mother's womb. (vs 14) I will give thanks to You, for I am fearfully and wonderfully made; Wonderful are Your works, And my soul knows it very well.*

God uses the womb of a Mother to form us and make each of us individuals. It is without comprehension of how wonderfully we are made, while incubating in that Mother's womb. It is also without envy by the fathers, that we leave this important task to the Mothers.

6. *(Proverbs 1:8-9)(8) Hear, my son, your father's instruction And do not forsake your mother's teaching; (vs 9) Indeed, they are a graceful wreath to your head And ornaments about your neck.*

It is the Wisdom of Solomon, that first tells you Godly Mothers to teach your children, Godly things. There are no substitutes for the teaching about God, as required from the father and the Mother. Don't be fooled into thinking that the church and/or schools should exclusively teach your kids. They can help, but you fathers and Mothers are the main teacher of the things of God.

I can't help but take this opportunity to emphasize that these parental teachings are absolutely necessary and are a responsibility that should be in both **word** and **example**. Our sons and daughters need to both **hear** our instructions, and witness through our lives, our **living examples**.

7. (Proverbs 6:20-22)(vs 20) My son, observe the commandment of your father And do not forsake the teaching of your mother; (vs 21) Bind them continually on your heart; Tie them around your neck. (vs 22) When you walk about, they will guide you; When you sleep, they will watch over you; And when you awake, they will talk to you.

This section of the scripture seems to be about the son (child) and his/her responsibility to adhere to and follow Godly teachings. Yes, this is correct, but the beginning is with the responsibility of the Mother and father. They are the ones who administer the Godly teachings. Without them the child has no basis for guidance or purpose. Without instruction the child has no set of standards or convictions whereby to live. They are wandering and their sense of right or wrong is nothing but a floating and moving set of "peer pressure" values. Their life could be properly described as "blowing in the wind".

The children of Godly Mothers are to fulfill the wisdom imparted by them. That Godly wisdom will continually surround their hearts and be as close to them as a necklace hanging about their neck. Godly teachings will guide them in all of their journeys, protect them while they sleep, be ever present while awake and literally speak to them each and every day. Because of the Mother's teachings, she has assigned to her children, by the adherence to God's Holy Word, the protection of His Holy Spirit. If Mothers didn't exist, we would all be absolutely without value. Mothers, you are truly the bread that becomes the staff of life.

8. (Proverbs 22:6) Train up a child in the way he should go, Even when he is old he will not depart from it.

We have already proven this "training-up" is one of the responsibilities of the Mother. This is one of the most notable and encouraging promises of the Bible. Mothers do your part and you can be assured God will be faithful to do His part.

9. (Proverbs 23:22 & 25)(vs 22) Listen to your father who begot you, And do not despise your mother when she is old. (vs 25) Let your father and your mother be glad, And let her rejoice who gave birth to you.

These verses appear to be giving instructions to our children, but do not overlook the source of our instructions. Mothers who have given physical birth to their children are to impart spiritual truths to these same children, and these truths are to be taught for all of their life. Physical birth is beneficial for 70 plus years, spiritual birth through the teachings of the Mother, is beneficial for an eternity.

10. *(Jeremiah 1:5 & 18-19)(vs 5) "Before I formed you in the womb I knew you, And before you were born I consecrated you; I have appointed you a prophet to the nations." (vs 18) "Now behold, I have made you today as a fortified city and as a pillar of iron and as walls of bronze against the whole land, to the kings of Judah, to its princes, to its priests and to the people of the land. (vs 19) "They will fight against you, but they will not overcome you, for I am with you to deliver you," declares the LORD.*

Jeremiah was a mighty prophet. There is much history and Biblical scholar's information regarding Jeremiah that I must confess is beyond my knowledge. The purpose here is to recognize his Mother and her part in his fulfilling the awesome purpose demanded of him by God. Jeremiah was called by God before he was conceived. He was consecrated before he was born and he was appointed to be a prophet to nations. We can only presume that his Mother was also used mightily by God to nurture and train-up this child until adulthood. Mothers are like the line in football's offense. They are unknown and don't get the headlines, but have you ever seen a running back set any records without them. In fact have you ever seen a running back even get beyond the line of scrimmage without them? Mothers are often the unsung "HEROS" of our Christian world.

11. *(Matthew 15:4) "For God said, 'HONOR YOUR FATHER AND MOTHER,' and, 'HE WHO SPEAKS EVIL OF FATHER OR MOTHER IS TO BE PUT TO DEATH.'*

This is a most severe and stern warning regarding the respect we must have towards our Mothers and fathers. God has ordained this respect for these parents and we need to be conscientious of this statement made by Jesus. I realize this passage was stated by Jesus in a discussion with the Pharisees and scribes, as they were breaking the laws and traditions of the Jewish past, but I believe it can stand alone as instruction to us today. Mothers are to be honored!!!

12. *(Luke 2:48-52)(vs 48) When they saw Him, they were astonished; and His mother said to Him, "Son, why* *have You treated us this way? Behold, Your father and I have been anxiously looking for You." (vs 49) And He said to them, "Why is it that you were looking for Me? Did you not know that I had to be in My Father's house?" (vs 50) But they did not understand the statement which He had made to them. (vs 51) And He went down with them and came to Nazareth, and He continued in subjection to them; and His mother treasured all these things in her heart. (vs 52) And Jesus kept increasing in wisdom and stature, and in favor with God and men.*

When Jesus was twelve years old he was found in the temple, listening and asking questions of the religious leaders of the day. These leaders were astonished by His understanding and His ability to answer. He was scolded by His Mother for being what appeared to be uncaring to His parents, yet He remained in subjection to these earthly parents for many years to come. As He continued to be prepared for His God ordained ministry, you would be correct if you believe His Mother was faithful with her part during these growth years. I am not saying she had anything to do with His Deity, but she did have a lot to do with His growth as a man. Mary was raising and nurturing God's Son. Even though her task is beyond our comprehension, Mothers today are called upon to be just as faithful.

13. *(Acts 1:14) These all with one mind were continually devoting themselves to prayer, along with the women, and Mary the mother of Jesus, and with His brothers.*

Prayer is to be a part of each Mother's life as we see by the example found in this verse. Upon Jesus' ascension into heaven the Apostles were left gathered together and were promised the presence of the Holy Spirit. In obedience to Jesus, they gathered daily to pray and contemplate their continued earthly ministry. This ministry was to drastically change and to include even the remotest parts of the earth. Mary, the earthly Mother of Jesus, was a part of these most important prayer meetings. All Mothers are special and are not to be overlooked in the value and significance they have to offer. Prayer is one of these valuable and significant ongoing tasks, called upon by God for all Godly Mothers.

14. *(Acts 3:2) And a man who had been lame from his mother's womb was being carried along, whom they used to* *set down every day at the gate of the temple which is called Beautiful, in order to beg alms of those who were entering the temple. (Acts 14:8) At Lystra a man was sitting who had no strength in his feet, lame from his mother's womb, who had never walked.*

Don't you know there are special Mothers who are called to raise a crippled child. We have these most precious Biblical examples, for the encouragement and benefit of all such special Mothers throughout all of history, to help them to realize they are not alone in raising a crippled or in some manner a handicapped child. These special Mothers who have had or presently have such a child are really to be honored, as they lovingly care for this special gift, given by God. Only in heaven will we know the full reasons for these difficult situations, and only in heaven will the treasures be waiting for all of these "Hall of Fame Mothers"! May God fully bless the Mother and child who have had to endure severe physical and/or mental difficulties all of their earthly days. Heaven will truly be a place of rejoicing for these.

15. *(Galatians 1:15-17)(vs 15) But when God, who had set me apart even from my mother's womb and called me through His grace, was pleased (vs 16) to reveal His Son in me so that I might preach Him among the Gentiles, I did not immediately consult with flesh and blood, (vs 17) nor did I go up to Jerusalem to those who were apostles before me; but I went away to Arabia, and returned once more to Damascus.*

The Apostle Paul, whom God used to write most of the New Testament, was set apart for something special, while still in his Mother's womb. Paul was trained-up in the Jewish religion, even though he didn't know Jesus until adulthood. We don't have available the detailed circumstances, but this much we can be sure of, that Paul was set aside while in his Mother's womb. She was used mightily by God.

16. *(Ephesians 6:4) Fathers, do not provoke your children to anger, but bring them up in the discipline and instruction of the Lord.*

Fathers as used here can also be interpreted as "parents", which includes the Mother. Therefore Mothers are specifically instructed to guard the hearts of their youth with Biblical instruction. This verse is as direct of a command as can be possible. Mothers you are to instruct and discipline your children with Godly principles and wisdom.

17. *(1 Thessalonians 2:5-8)(vs 5) For we never came with flattering speech, as you know, nor with a pretext for greed—God is witness—(vs 6) nor did we seek glory from men, either from you or from others, even though as apostles of Christ we might have asserted our authority. (vs 7) But we proved to be gentle among you, as a nursing mother tenderly cares for her own children. (vs 8) Having so fond an affection for you, we were well-pleased to impart to you not only the gospel of God but also our own lives, because you had become very dear to us.*

Paul, as he addresses the church at Thessalonica can come up with no greater example of tenderness than the Mother's care of a nursing child. The generic Mother here is called out to make a dramatic point of how Paul spent his life while giving the Gospel message to the Gentiles. Paul had such a fond affection and such a tender heart, he gladly expended his life for the spreading of the Gospel. The use of the Mother as his major example to communicate his affection, is a testimony to the value and the highly esteemed position of Godly Motherhood.

18. *(Titus 2:3-5)(vs 3) Older women likewise are to be reverent in their behavior, not malicious gossips nor enslaved to much wine, teaching what is good, (vs 4) so that they may encourage the young women to love their husbands, to love their children, (vs 5) to be sensible, pure, workers at home, kind, being subject to their own husbands, so that the word of God will not be dishonored.*

There are a lot of instructions here, but who am I to tell others what to do. It is the responsibility of the Holy Spirit to convict, instruct and teach each of us. Mothers, meditate upon this passage and let God be your instructor and teacher. As wise, Godly, older Mothers, you are to teach what is good to the younger Mothers, thus passing on the Word of God from generation to generation. I have personally witnessed what happens when one generation is not taught. This is difficult to witness as you see this generation become lost in the world's thoughts and practices.

D. CONCLUSION TO GODLY MOTHERS:

The conclusion here is "Mothers are "Called" to a specific task and they need to "Respond" to that calling:

All Mothers are called to give, or expend their lives while living each day, by giving of themselves, to do the most difficult and Christ honoring job imaginable. You as a modern day Mother may not feel like you have been chosen for a specific calling, but your calling is as real and as honorable as any job to be named upon the face of this earth. Your job cannot be exceeded in importance by any other profession; and As a "Mother" you are to respond to this most high calling. This calling is the preparation of your children to meet the physical and spiritual pressures and opportunities of life. In God's eyes your labors are equal to any and all callings by Him. You job of "teaching" is absolutely necessary if we are going to see the ongoing spread and belief of the Gospel.

The Mothers highlighted in the verses above are but a few of the Biblical "Hall of Fame Mothers". Since the writing of the Bible we have millions of Mothers who have honored their God by teaching and training-up their children. In the present day we have millions of Mothers who are currently honoring God with these same qualities.

These current Mothers don't have a book written about them and they haven't been mentioned in the press or on some televised production, but they are just as important in the eyes of God as any in the past. Millions of faithful Mothers have fulfilled God's calling of nurturing, teaching and training-up God's precious children. You may have a thought that, "I can't be like one of these", but "Oh you are wrong"! Each Mother has the opportunity, the responsibility and the charge by God to be just as faithful. The child in your trust, if he is one that is taught the Word of God, nurtured in a loving Biblical way, will put your name alongside all the others Mothers who were found faithful throughout history. Your name may not be on a billboard, or in neon lights in this life time, but you will be listed in God's eternal "Hall of Fame for Mothers". If your only claim to fame, or only accomplishment in this life, is to raise up a Godly child, then your are more successful than any billionaire, you are more to be praised than any King and are more **HIGHLY** seen in God's eyes than can be explained.

(Proverbs 22:6) Train up a child in the way he should go, Even when he is old he will not depart from it.

This is both a command and a promise, coming directly to us from our "Most High God", the One to "Whom We Belong"!!! If "You Belong To Him", you can be a spiritual "HERO", and will find your name written in the Biblical "Hall of Fame for Mothers".

SPECIAL NOTE:

I know many of you may have a special verse or verses regarding this Chapter's subject matter. This special verse or these verses may not have been mentioned due to my ignorance or because of brevity. I apologize for either of these reasons. Please feel free to write any special verse or verses in the space below. This will add your personal touch, and will serve to call to each person's mind their individual "experience of trust", in God's Holy Word.

For to each of us "Who belong To Him", His Holy Word can be truly recognized and relied upon as our **"Owner's Manual"**!!!

_____

_____

_____

_____

_____

_____

_____

CHAPTER 16

RICHES, MATERIAL WEALTH

INTRODUCTORY VERSES:

(Acts 17:24-27)(vs 24) "The God who made the world and all things in it, since He is Lord of heaven and earth, does not dwell in temples made with hands; (vs 25) nor is He served by human hands, as though He needed anything, since He Himself gives to all people life and breath and all things; (vs 26) and He made from one man every nation of mankind to live on all the face of the earth, having determined their appointed times and the boundaries of their habitation, (vs 27) that they would seek God, if perhaps they might grope for Him and find Him, though He is not far from each one of us;

God made all things by speaking them into being. He made you and I. He fashioned us in the womb. He gives life and breath to all people. He made from one man every nation on all the face of the earth. He has appointed our times and set the boundaries of our habitation. He is in control of all things. He owns the "Material Wealth" of this world. He could turn dust into Gold by simply speaking it into being. He has need of nothing.

It is this "Almighty God of the Universe", that will define for us, these terms of "Riches" and "Material Wealth".

**INTRODUCTION AND OVERVIEW TO RICHES/
MATERIAL WEALTH:**

Please bear with me as there are hundreds of verses regarding "Riches and "Material Wealth". If this seems rambling and disjointed it may be due to the fact there is so much material to cover. I will certainly not use all of the possible scriptures, and of those chosen I will try to break them down into understandable categories.

1. Of what does Life "Consist"?:

When considering of what our life consists, we need to address the "Material Wealth" aspect. Luke 12:15 should cause us to wonder, since it plainly states of what it does not consist. It is very apparent "Life" does not consist of "possessions", even when we have those in abundance. *(Luke 12:15) Then He said to them, "Beware, and be on your guard against every form of greed; for not even when one has an abundance does his life consist of his possessions."*

This verse is a clear warning about the thought that "Life" is about the quantity of our "Material Wealth". This will be certainly covered in more detail throughout the Chapter. Please note for future reference the respective definitions of "Beware" and "be on guard". "Beware is defined as: to discern clearly; to behold; to perceive; to see or to take heed. "Be on Guard" is defined as: to watch, obey, avoid, beware, and observe. These two warnings are definitive and strong in their context. We know "Life" doesn't consist of an abundance of possessions.

2. There is "Much" Biblical Content about our "Financial" aspect:

The Bible says so much about "Riches" and "Material Wealth" that it is impossible to fully consider this subject without reading His entire Holy Word. It is my hope that this Chapter will give you some of the key principles and responsibilities we have to "Our Maker and Savior", as we consider the "Financial" aspect of our "Earthly Life".

3. "Fleeting" is a word used to Explain both "Riches" and "Life":

Anyone, of an age to have senior discounts available, will tell you, "Earthly Life" is "fleeting". The Bible puts it in perspective by calling it a breath, an alien, a tenant, a shadow, water that evaporates, flesh that deteriorates into aches and pains, and as the wind that passes. All of these can be seen in the following verses:

(Ecclesiastes 11:10) So, remove grief and anger from your heart and put away pain from your body, because childhood and the prime of life are fleeting. ... fleeting being defined in the original Hebrew as: emptiness; vanity or something transitory;

Job 7:7) "Remember that my life is but breath; My eye will not again see good. ... Job stating his life is but air or wind, it has no lasting or traceable substance;

1 Chronicles 29:15) "For we are sojourners ... (guests or aliens) ***before You, and tenants*** ... (a dweller, a temporary inmate as distinguished from a native citizen), ***as all our fathers were; our days on the earth are like a shadow, and there is no hope.***;

Job 14:10-12)(vs 10) "But man dies and lies prostrate. Man expires, and where is he? (vs 11) "As water evaporates from the sea, And a river becomes parched and dried up, (vs 12) So man lies down and does not rise. Until the heavens are no longer, He will not awake nor be aroused out of his sleep. ... (man is mortal and his life span is definable);

Psalms 78:39) Thus He remembered that they were but flesh, A wind that passes and does not return.; and

(James 4:14) Yet you do not know what your life will be like tomorrow. You are just a vapor that appears for a little while and then vanishes away.

4. "Neutral", "Negative" and "Positive", are all words used in Connotation with "Material Wealth":

With the above establishment of our "mortality" and having also briefly addressed our "purpose", we must consider these and their inter-relationships with "Riches", "Monetary Values", "Money", "Net Worth", etc. While most of the terms used above will have a "neutral" connotation, some may carry a "negative" or a "positive" atmosphere. This Chapter will consider the neutral, the negative and the positive of "Material Wealth". Hopefully each verse emphasized will be considered in its proper Biblical context.

5. "Stewardship" of "Financial" Matters:

Some of the things to consider are: a) being financially responsible to pay our living expenses; b) serving in your workplace job as God has commanded each of us;

c) setting aside wealth in your financial storehouse for periods of famine (that may include retirement); and d) our giving to God's ministries.

This Chapter will not get into the detail of our personally spending on ourselves, but will concentrate on our being a, **"Steward"** **of** and therefore **to** God, for all that He has entrusted to us. The intent is to expose God's Word regarding riches and wealth in multiple Bible passages, while highlighting, in God's perspective, the importance of being a **"Steward"** of His blessings. This perspective should be made clear by His word, as it pertains to our trust and our ongoing development of a true and pure relationship with Him. It will be made clear that God wants our trust to be in Him. He will not tolerate anything less! We are a **"Steward"** of 100% of what He has given us!

(Matthew 6:19-21)(vs 19) "Do not store up for yourselves treasures on earth, where moth and rust destroy, and where thieves break in and steal. (vs 20) "But store up for yourselves treasures in heaven, where neither moth nor rust destroys, and where thieves do not break in or steal; (vs 21) for where your treasure is, there your heart will be also.

Look around you and take stock of your treasures and you will know exactly the measurement of your heart's desires. You will know where your true heart is located. Does the accounting of your earthly treasures help you answer the question of "To Whom Do I Belong?"!!! The above is not meant as an accusation, but it is God's examination of your heart's true condition. If you passed, then keep on trucking. If you failed, then read and consider again His wisdom and promises. Why would anyone trade a relationship with the "Only True God" for "rusted, rotten, moth eaten goods" that could all wind up being stolen by thieves?

Riches in this world are not to be "Feared" or to be "Worshiped". Man measures our value by "Net Worth" and "Position of Prominence". God measures the value of man by "Our Relationship to Him". We will now try to explore the "Wealth of Scriptures" found in God's Word regarding "Riches" and "Material Wealth".

In this brief overview of an "Introduction", I hope you have a taste of the subject matter regarding "Material Wealth". The balance of this Chapter will hopefully will be a full meal with many details.

A. WHAT IS "MATERIAL WEALTH" AND THE "ASSOCIATED WARNINGS"?:

I have listed some items that may be considered to be "Material Wealth". These items are not all inclusive, but are representative of what man considers measurements of wealth. They may consist of: 1. Cash/Currency/Bank Accounts; 2. Stocks and Bonds; 3. Clothes; 4. Automobiles; 5. Houses; 6. Land or Real Estate/Ranches; and

7. Investments/Businesses and All Other Possessions. All of the ones described are useful and have their purpose. These items are neutral and have no inherent good or evil. It is only in the "Love of" or "Trust in" these items by their owners, where we might see them used for evil. These items can be used for good to bless people and yet the same item may control someone's heart and cause a distrust of God.

We will look at the "Warnings" to be heeded and then look at each individual representative of "Material Wealth" as listed above.

1. "Warnings" to be Heeded:

In the following two passages we have two examples of "warnings" by God over the misuse or attitude towards these "Material Wealth" items. It may seem that it is the "warnings" that are being majored upon. It is, as always, God's Word that is being majored upon, and the exposure here is significant as to His "warnings" in order that we see the severe consequences. I would be remiss to go lightly regarding these "warnings".

(1 Timothy 6:10) For the love of money is a root of all sorts of evil, and some by longing for it have wandered away from the faith and pierced themselves with many griefs.

The words here in the original Greek for *"love of money"* have an avarice meaning and are associated with wickedness. In other words, this *"love of money"* becomes our god (little g) and we don't care about how we obtain it. The word *"evil"*: means wickedness, and finally the words "pierced" and "griefs" respectively mean to be completed penetrated through from one side and out the other with sorrow. Our wandering away from the faith and seeking an avarice affair with the love of money will impale us with countless sorrows.

(James 5:1-6)(vs 1) Come now, you rich, weep and howl for your miseries which are coming upon you. (vs 2) Your riches have rotted and your garments have become moth-eaten. (vs 3) Your gold and your silver have rusted; and their rust will be a witness against you and will consume your flesh like fire. It is in the last days that you have stored up your treasure! (vs 4) Behold, the pay of the laborers who

mowed your fields, and which has been withheld by you, cries out against you; and the outcry of those who did the harvesting has reached the ears of the Lord of Sabaoth. (vs 5) You have lived luxuriously on the earth and led a life of wanton pleasure; you have fattened your hearts in a day of slaughter. (vs 6) You have condemned and put to death the righteous man; he does not resist you.

These words of condemnation are for the godless rich person. It is clear this "warning" is for those who have mistreated those in their path, while living a life of *"wanton pleasure"*. It is those who have *"condemned"* and *"put to death the righteous man"* that will reap the above disasters.

Now, who in God's Kingdom wouldn't want to know about these verses?

The purpose is to expose these "warnings" and encourage those with wealth to consider its proper use. We can neither condemn wealth, nor those who have it; it is the trust in it and its uses, which are in question.

The following is God's Word as it pertains to examples of different items of wealth and there will be "warnings" for the improper attitude towards it, as well as examples of those who used it for God's Glory and never let it interfere with their relationship with God. Please read with no pre-conceived bias towards what God has to say.

2. CASH/COINS/CURRENCY/BANK ACCOUNTS:

The Bible doesn't really mention bank accounts, but it does contain a few examples of coins, currency and therefore cash. The following passage is a tremendous example of how God so clearly defines our allegiance to Him over any monetary thing of this world.

*(Matthew 22:15-21)(vs 15) Then the Pharisees went and plotted together how they might trap Him in what He said. (vs 16) And they *sent their disciples to Him, along with the Herodians, saying, "Teacher, we know that You are truthful and teach the way of God in truth, and defer to no one; for You are not partial to any. (vs 17) "Tell us then, what do You think? Is it lawful to give a poll-tax to Caesar, or not?" (vs 18) But Jesus perceived their malice, and said, "Why are you testing Me, you hypocrites? (vs 19) "Show Me the coin used for the poll-tax." And they brought Him a denarius. (vs 20)*

And He *said to them, "Whose likeness and inscription is this?" (vs 21) They *said to Him, "Caesar's." Then He *said to them, "Then render to Caesar the things that are Caesar's; and to God the things that are God's."

Jesus was being "set up" in an attempted trap to contradict His teachings. The Pharisees and Herodians had malice or wickedness in their hearts. Jesus perceived this malice and made a simple yet dramatic statement. We are to render to God our true allegiance which is our relationship to Him. We are to render the things of this world, such as the coins of "that day", to the ruler of "that day". The coins of "that day" had the likeness and inscription of Caesar. The coins and dollars of "this day" have the likeness of former respected US Presidents, which represents today's responsibility to our government and society. God's calling is to render unto Him the things that are of God. This calling unto Him is totally separate from the financial world we live in. Yes, we need the monetary system to live our life, and pay our bills and debts, but our calling to Him is far higher. It is eternal and not of the perishable kind we find in all other responsibilities. He calls us to "know Him" in a personal relationship and render "to Him" our "Fear" or "reverence" of His Holy being. This "reverence" of Him will be what counts, not the quantity of coins or dollars we might accumulate.

In this same ***Chapter 22 of Matthew***, Jesus makes it clear our "Most High Calling" is not in wealth accumulation, but to follow His two foremost commandments. Upon these two commandments will "hang" all our responsibilities to our fellow man and therefore to God.

(Matthew 22:36-40)(vs 36) "Teacher, which is the great commandment in the Law?" (vs 37) And He said to him, " 'YOU SHALL LOVE THE LORD YOUR GOD WITH ALL YOUR HEART, AND WITH ALL YOUR SOUL, AND WITH ALL YOUR MIND.' (vs 38) "This is the great and foremost commandment. (vs 39) "The second is like it, 'YOU SHALL LOVE YOUR NEIGHBOR AS YOURSELF.' (vs 40) "On these two commandments depend the whole Law and the Prophets."

These two commandments are a summation of all of the Old Testament Law. These two commandments are implanted in our hearts, and in our personal relationship with God through Jesus Christ. What will come out of us will be the fulfillment of all the Old Testament

Levitical Laws. We will be unselfishly minded and find ourselves sharing the personal testimony of our relationship with Jesus Christ as well as sharing our "Material Wealth" as needed. This will not result in "Marxist socialism", but will result in truly rendering unto God the things that are God's. Our coins, dollars and bank accounts are not evil, but are to be used for God's glory and are to be loosely held. Our trust is not in our wealth, but in the Living God, and our responsibility is to be a "good steward" of all He has put under our trust.

Commandment One: we are to love our God with all our Heart, Soul and Mind. Commandment Two: we are to love our neighbor as our selves. Our Stewardship is not only to love God, but in the act of loving Him we will love our neighbors while also being good responsible citizens. Yes, we are responsible to render to Caesar the things of Caesar's, but MOST importantly we are to render unto God the things that are God's.

3. STOCKS/BONDS:

These examples of "Material Wealth" might be most often thought of as Investments for future use. They could also be thought of as a way of expanding what God has entrusted us with for retirement years.

Even though "Stocks/Bonds" are not words used in the Bible, the Biblical principles of planning for the future and setting aside enough to provide for our family members can be related to by looking at some Old Testament passages.

(Genesis 41:25-31)(vs 25) Now Joseph said to Pharaoh, "Pharaoh's dreams are one and the same; God has told to Pharaoh what He is about to do. (vs 26) "The seven good cows are seven years; and the seven good ears are seven years; the dreams are one and the same. (vs 27) "The seven lean and ugly cows that came up after them are seven years, and the seven thin ears scorched by the east wind will be seven years of famine. (vs 28) "It is as I have spoken to Pharaoh: God has shown to Pharaoh what He is about to do. (vs 29) "Behold, seven years of great abundance are coming in all the land of Egypt; (vs 30) and after them seven years of famine will come, and all the abundance will be forgotten in the land of Egypt, and the famine will ravage the land. (vs 31) "So the abundance will be unknown in the land because

of that subsequent famine; for it will be very severe. (Genesis 41:35-36)(vs 35) "Then let them gather all the food of these good years that are coming, and store up the grain for food in the cities under Pharaoh's authority, and let them guard it. (vs 36) "Let the food become as a reserve for the land for the seven years of famine which will occur in the land of Egypt, so that the land will not perish during the famine."

We can learn from what took place during the times of the Pharaoh's. One of the lessons to be considered here is laying up excess for a future time of need. Pharaoh was warned in a dream. God may not make this as obvious in our life as he did with Pharaoh's. We can't always predict what a person's future needs might be. We can draw from this, and if God's so calls us, we need to be responsible to lay up excesses now for future needs. One important point is that God had a plan and it included seven good years and seven bad years. It included the emergency needs for a nation, not just one person, and it did not provide for anyone's trust to be placed in the excess grain. If you are certain of your calling in this manner, do it, but "beware" of where your trust lies.

I certainly don't mean to imply that Stocks and Bonds are your investment strategy, but have only used them here as an example. The real KEY here is to seek God's calling and be sure you … *(Matthew 6:19) "Do not store up for yourselves treasures on earth, where moth and rust destroy, and where thieves break in and steal.*

There is nothing wrong in planning for the future. The danger is in trusting in "Material Wealth" and not in our "Living God". There was a reason that God gave the Children of Israel manna each day and there was a reason it rotted if they tried to store it or save it for the future. There was a reason God gave the Pharaoh seven years of stored grain. The point here is, there is a fine line of trusting, that only you can make for your situation. To be sure you are correct in your decisions, always be found to be "trusting" in Him and not "trusting" in your "possessions".

4. CLOTHES:
Solomon in all of his glory, riches, and position as king, was clothed like no other man of his day. God says that we need to seek His kingdom and His righteous more than "all these things".

(Matthew 6:28-33)(vs 28) "And why are you worried about clothing? Observe how the lilies of the field grow; they do not toil nor do they spin, (vs 29) yet I say to you that not even Solomon in all his glory clothed himself like one of these. (vs 30) "But if God so clothes the grass of the field, which is alive today and tomorrow is thrown into the furnace, will He not much more clothe you? You of little faith! (vs 31) "Do not worry then, saying, 'What will we eat?' or 'What will we drink?' or 'What will we wear for clothing?' (vs 32) "For the Gentiles eagerly seek all these things; for your heavenly Father knows that you need all these things. (vs 33) "But seek first His kingdom and His righteousness, and all these things will be added to you.

God is warning all of us about worrying about the material things of this world, eating, drink and clothing. If we fall within this trap of seeking the things of this world, He compares us to the Gentiles, or those who by implication are heathen or pagan in their beliefs. He is not condemning wealth or fine clothing, but it is the importance we place upon these things that can cause us to trust Him less and therefore falsely rely upon perishable goods. A grand, Godly promise is that He will add "all these things to us" as needed. "These things" are needed while here on this earth, even though they are all perishable, but even more than these is our need to seek "His righteousness".

Many years ago while in the mountains of Colorado, I witnessed a most beautiful scene. This was burned into my mental memory bank and it will remain there for the rest of my life.

It was on one of our Trinity Trail Riders outings, (a Christian organization

that ministers to businessmen) while riding in the Flat Tops Wilderness Area, at about 11,000 foot elevation, that I came upon this dramatically beautiful scene. We had been blessed this August morning with about four inches of snow. The morning was one of being cooped up in tents and talking and drinking coffee, until the restless explorer decided to come out. Since I had never been in this particular area I decided to get on my horse and bring out my best memories of Jedediah Smith, the real life Mountain Man adventurer of the 1800's.

It was about noon, while riding alone, God blessed me with what I am about to describe. What I was privileged to witness was a clump of Columbine flowers, in full bloom, growing at the base of a very white and large rock. Around the flowers was green grass where this unseasonal August snow had recently melted. Another critical factor that must be pointed out was the sky contained thick gray clouds and was overcast from horizon to horizon, the ceiling being about two to three hundred feet above the ground. It was at this exact spot, with a circumference of about four feet, that the sun and it's distinct sun shafts, reaching from the heavens, right through a hole in the cloud cover, was found shining upon these flowers. There in the semi-circle of exposed green grass (actually tundra with the minute blue, white and pink forget-me-nots), with the surrounding ground covered with the white snow, these Columbines were being highlighted in full bloom. The direct sun magnificently brought out the colors. You could see the registration of the bright green stems and leaves, the brilliant yellows, the pastel blues, and the most whiter-than-snow whites.

This scene is truly beyond adequate description. I can only say that I was blessed to witness a real life, God-made diorama. This so vividly framed picture, with the most intricate design that only Columbine Flowers can have, was unbelievably highlighted by God Himself, with this shaft of sunlight. I accepted this as a specific act of God, and have always and will always, want to share this with others. God arrayed these flowers, which in a few days were to be wilted and dead, more magnificently than Solomon was ever clothed by all of his wealth.

I kick myself to this day for not recording this picture via camera. Who knows, maybe it was too "Glorious" to be captured upon man made film. This much I know, when I read about the lilies of the field, and God's care for them and their beauty, I recall this special memory and it puts in perspective the words ... *(vs 29) yet I say to you that not even Solomon in all his glory clothed himself like one of these. (vs 30) "But if God so clothes the grass of the field, which is alive today and tomorrow is thrown into the furnace, will He not much more clothe you? You of little faith!*

We are special and I find God's words here to be profound, reassuring and blessed, a resounding statement of promise from our Almighty God, the One "To Whom We Belong"!!! Our Life does not consist of our "Possessions" – Clothes.

5. AUTOMOBILES:

Obviously automobiles were not mentioned in the Bible, but we do have mention of, **a.** Camels and, **b.** Chariots. Both of these were a means of travel, also used for hauling things and were considered a sign of wealth and power if owned in quantity.

a. *(Job 1:1-3)(vs 1) There was a man in the land of Uz whose name was Job; and that man was blameless, upright, fearing God and turning away from evil. (vs 2) Seven sons and three daughters were born to him. (vs 3) His possessions also were 7,000 sheep, 3,000 camels, 500 yoke of oxen, 500 female donkeys, and very many servants; and that man was the greatest of all the men of the east.*

There are 42 Chapters in the Book of Job. We are not attempting to cover this by any means, but only point out that Job was considered the greatest of all the men of the east, and listed among his possessions was that he owned 3,000 camels. Camels were a source of transportation and a beast of burden. That is a lot of cars and trucks. Job had a lot of garages and they were full. The point here is if he wanted to brag about his cars, he had more than anyone I know. The real point is that Job was described as blameless, upright, fearing God and always turning away from evil. He was God's model of a believer. You can own 3,000 camels and still be a God fearing man! As Job found out, the responsibility and stewardship that came along with his wealth and his favor before God, was severe. Read the entire Book and you will find that Job, even in the most trying times, which the majority of us couldn't withstand, was ultimately found faithful. Job lost his wealth, his family, and his dignity, all as a test by Satan in order to get him to curse God and die. Job was faithful to the God "To Whom He Belonged" even though he didn't understand why all this was happening. Job in his faithfulness, when all was said and done, routed Satan. God in His kindness fully restored Job and his possessions.

You will note God even restored Job's possessions two-fold, thus giving Job twice his original responsibility. *(Job 42:12) The LORD blessed the latter days of Job more than his beginning; and he had 14,000 sheep and 6,000 camels and 1,000 yoke of*

oxen and 1,000 female donkeys. In all of this Job was blessed with more, only because he was found faithful in loving and "fearing" or "reverencing" the only true God. Can you imagine owning 6,000 BMW's? That is a lot of responsibility. We can be assured Job was found faithful in honoring God with his entire being, which included his massive possessions.

b. Chariots are mentioned here because they were a symbol of wealth and a source of transportation.

(1 Kings 10:26) Now Solomon gathered chariots and horsemen; and he had 1,400 chariots and 12,000 horsemen, and he stationed them in the chariot cities and with the king in Jerusalem.

Solomon certainly didn't need these Chariots personally, so we can only conclude he needed these to defend the land. He was blessed by God to have these numbers and we can only believe he used them for God's Glory.

Let us be found to be faithful with our automobiles, whether it be a Pinto or a Mercedes, whether it be one or ten in number. May we be found to be a righteous "steward" of all of God's blessings, because it is "To Him To Whom We Belong"!!!

6. HOUSES:

Houses made of sticks, straw or bricks, houses from A-frames to Mansions, any or all of these are not evil or good in and of themselves. A house is necessary to protect from weather and intrusion, provides comfort and a family setting, provides a place to cook, relax, recreate, fellowship with family and friends, as well as a place for numerous other things or events.

A house becomes a home when it serves the family who live in it. A house becomes a detriment when it controls our thoughts and becomes an "Idol". It can be part of what destroys us if it has become our god. The attachment to a house and it's place in our perspective can become "vanity and a striving after the wind". Let's look at some verses that will describe both the good and the bad.

(Ecclesiastes 2:4-6 & 11)(vs 4) I enlarged my works: I built houses for myself, I planted vineyards for myself; (vs 5) I made gardens and parks for myself and I planted in them all kinds of fruit trees; (vs 6) I made ponds of water for myself

from which to irrigate a forest of growing trees. (vs 11) Thus I considered all my activities which my hands had done and the labor which I had exerted, and behold all was vanity and striving after wind and there was no profit under the sun.

This appears to be quite a palatial palace, with the vineyards (that's plural), the gardens (plural again), parks, orchards, ponds/lakes, and an irrigated forest. We can only imagine with this immense landscaping, the mansion or houses in these settings would not be dwarfed by their grandeur. Solomon had the wealth and didn't spare any in this building endeavor. Solomon didn't spare any trimmings in the building of his house and gardens, yet by his own confession, it proved to be "vanity and striving after the wind". ... *(Ecclesiastes 2:11) Thus I considered all my activities which my hands had done and the labor which I had exerted, and behold all was vanity and striving after wind and there was no profit under the sun.*

A re-affirmation of Solomon's conclusion was that his efforts were "of no profit under the sun". Sure, he as we all do, needed a place to live, but in this case he did not gain any comfort with his extravagant dwelling. If Solomon in all of his wisdom concluded there must be more to life than this extravagant dwelling, we can conclude the same without firsthand experiencing his mistake.

(Matthew 19:29) "And everyone who has left houses or brothers or sisters or father or mother or children or farms for My name's sake, will receive many times as much, and will inherit eternal life.

Jesus' mention here of giving up houses in the same sentence with brothers, sisters, fathers, mothers and children, places a value upon our homes in the highest regard. Our willingness to give up our home to follow Him would be a major sacrifice. In this difficulty and with our heart's desire to serve and submit to Him, we will find a great reward. If we follow Jesus rather than the possessions of this world, there will be a sufficient and eternal reward. If your heart has been with Jesus, your life found "Belonging To Him", your life counting for *"My name's sake"*, you will have an abundant inheritance and it will include eternal life. Not everyone is called to do this because of the great sacrifice. That sacrifice must come as a result of absolutely hearing and subsequently heeding God's specific calling.

You may think you have a great home here, wait until you get to Heaven, it will make this home look like a cardboard/stick shack. You think you have been shorted here with your living accommodations, wait until you get to Heaven, it will be a mansion with streets of gold.

(John 14:2-3)(vs 2) "In My Father's house are many dwelling places; if it were not so, I would have told you; for I go to prepare a place for you. (vs 3) "If I go and prepare a place for you, I will come again and receive you to Myself, that where I am, there you may be also. (Revelation 21:21) And the street of the city was pure gold, like transparent glass.

These descriptions of Heaven are not precise and we certainly don't want to be caught up in following Jesus just because we want a house made of gold, but I believe all we experience in Heaven will make the best down here, look like absolute poverty.

(Acts 7:46-50)(vs 46) "David found favor in God's sight, and asked that he might find a dwelling place for the God of Jacob. (vs 47) "But it was Solomon who built a house for Him. (vs 48) "However, the Most High does not dwell in houses made by human hands; as the prophet says:

(vs 49) 'HEAVEN IS MY THRONE, AND EARTH IS THE FOOTSTOOL OF MY FEET; WHAT KIND OF HOUSE WILL YOU BUILD FOR ME?' says the Lord, 'OR WHAT PLACE IS THERE FOR MY REPOSE? (vs 50) 'WAS IT NOT MY HAND WHICH MADE ALL THESE THINGS?'

God who made all things is not in need of a house built by human hands. He uses the best we have as His footstool. Meditate on these words and determine how we can honor Him with our "Houses" (homes).

7. REAL ESTATE/LAND/RANCHES:

I am sure every man's dream is to own a ranch with all the attachments. We can all envision the ranch house, barns, cattle, horses, goats, sheep, hills, grass lands, lakes, ponds, wildlife, etc. I, along with many of you, have had those dreams of falling in love with that most wonderful, western Rocky Mountain spread. I am just as sure those owning ranches in Texas, or all other parts of our wonderful and beautiful country, love their land just as much.

It was once said that Ted Turner owned more ranch land than any other individual. Ted Turner has been quoted as saying "Christians are weak and need God as a crutch or as a security blanket". I wonder if his owning land was his security blanket. I wonder if when Ted Turner lies upon his "death bed" he will receive any joy from owning all of this ranch land?

Real Estate/Land/Ranches have been proven to be desired by the rich and famous. They are not alone, as we all seem to crave to own a piece of this country. Many have given their life to acquire such. Real Estate/Land has an attraction as a symbol of wealth. Ranches especially have a certain fascination and aura which we will look at a little more closely.

I have looked at or have been on ranches in Wyoming, Montana, Utah, Idaho, Colorado, South Dakota, New Mexico, and Texas. I was in a rancher's home just north of Casper, Wyoming and heard personally from his lips, he was about to sell his large ranch and move on to his little one. The one he was about to sell was 120,000 acres. The one he would be moving to was only 10,000 acres. I have reviewed sales brochures from many other parts of our great country. There is private ownership of ranches from the East to the West, from the South to the North. We all have our favorite locations, and all of these locations have merits and different qualities that satisfy many different preferences.

Owning a ranch is truly a sign of significant disposable wealth (I have yet to see the "gentleman's ranch" that produces a financial reason for ownership). There are million dollar homes that only get used once a year. There are air strips that can handle private jets. There are air strips used to maintain the ranch and its domestic cattle, sheep or other livestock. There are fishing lodges and hunting lodges that will take your breath away. With no cost being spared in the buildings and accessories, the luxuries we find on some of these ranches are indescribable. Yet, all of these possessions are still perishable, and will not satisfy the God shaped void in man's soul. All "land" and "possessions" are only temporary and they are all perishable. There is no eternal value in these possessions.

Ownership of Real Estate is great, but we must take a closer look at this ownership from the God of the universe's perspective. If real estate makes up a part of your "Material Wealth" or "Riches", these things should be held with a loose hand. Our mindset of ownership should be one of recognition as being a temporary "steward" of God's abundant, earthly wealth. As we hold wealth loosely and recognize our steward-ship responsibility to God, this all needs to mesh, to the Glory of God.

The following verses give us a glimpse of God's desire for our minds, our thoughts, our attitudes, and how His desires inter-relate with the resulting accumulations of the work of our hands.

(Genesis 1:26 & 28)(vs 26) Then God said, "Let Us make man in Our image, according to Our likeness; and let them rule over the fish of the sea and over the birds of the sky and over the cattle and over all the earth, and over every creeping thing that creeps on the earth." (vs 28) God blessed them; and God said to them, "Be fruitful and multiply, and fill the earth, and subdue it; and rule over the fish of the sea and over the birds of the sky and over every living thing that moves on the earth." God has given us a charge to *"rule over all the earth"* and to subdue the land, while at the same time to *"rule over every living thing that moves on the earth."* We are to be smart, not pollute ourselves, to conserve and be wise in our "rule". This is a clear statement of responsibility or "stewardship". God didn't bring us this far to "freeze us in the dark", He expects us to use wisdom in our rule and subduing.

(1 Chronicles 29:11) "Yours, O LORD, is the greatness and the power and the glory and the victory and the majesty, indeed everything that is in the heavens and the earth; Yours is the dominion, O LORD, and You exalt Yourself as head over all. God owns it all. He owns the entire earth. He allows us to use it wisely. That means He owns the Gold in Alaska, the Diamonds in Africa, the Oil in the Far East, the Forest of Lebanon. You may want to note He owns the heavens also!

(Psalms 145:13) Your kingdom is an everlasting kingdom, And Your dominion endures throughout all generations. God not only owns everything, but His kingdom is for all time.

(Daniel 4:34) "But at the end of that period, I, Nebuchadnezzar, raised my eyes toward heaven and my reason returned to me, and I blessed the Most High and praised and honored Him who lives forever; For His dominion is an everlasting dominion, And His kingdom

endures from generation to generation. Even the Kings of this earth, when they came to their senses, recognized our Most High God has dominion forever.

Many books could be and have been written to describe the real estate ownership world. Our perspective here is to consider what God's Holy Word says directly, or very certainly infers, regarding these matters. It is He that owns the cattle on a thousand hills as well as the hills! It is He who demands our relationship with Him! ... *(Psalms 50:10-12)(vs 10) "For every beast of the forest is Mine, The cattle on a thousand hills. (vs 11) "I know every bird of the mountains, And everything that moves in the field is Mine. (vs 12) "If I were hungry I would not tell you, For the world is Mine, and all it contains.* With this concluding verse, we must realize we are only "stewards" of anything earthly. God has spoken into being all that we have. The world and all its real estate is His. It is He that is to be reverenced and it is He who deserves our allegiance. It is to Him we give all praise, honor and glory. It is in Him we trust, not in our "Wealth". If you "Belong To Him", honor Him with all the talents and treasures that have been entrusted to you including your **"Real Estate"**.

8. INVESTMENTS/BUSINESSES AND ALL OTHER POSSESSIONS:

This category is broad and a catch-all for everything not specifically discussed above. It is not intended to be all inclusive, but to remind us that everything belongs to God.

(Psalms 24:1) A Psalm of David. The earth is the LORD'S, and all it contains, The world, and those who dwell in it.

It is with much comfort that we consider the following parable of the talents as found in the first New Testament Gospel according to Matthew. The comfort is in the knowing that we are responsible only for what God has entrusted to us, and it is He who brings the increase as we trade these talents. Be fully aware and understand that the talents and any increase from these talents all "Belong To Him".

(Matthew 25:14-30)(vs 14) "For it is just like a man about to go on a journey, who called his own slaves and entrusted his possessions to them. (vs 15) "To one he gave five talents, to another, two, and to another, one, each according to his own ability; and he went on his journey. (vs 16) "Immediately

the one who had received the five talents went and traded with them, and gained five more talents. (vs 17) "In the same manner the one who had received the two talents gained two more. (vs 18) "But he who received the one talent went away, and dug a hole in the ground and hid his master's money. (vs 19) "Now after a long time the master of those slaves *came and *settled accounts with them. (vs 20) "The one who had received the five talents came up and brought five more talents, saying, 'Master, you entrusted five talents to me. See, I have gained five more talents.' (vs 21) "His master said to him, 'Well done, good and faithful slave. You were faithful with a few things, I will put you in charge of many things; enter into the joy of your master.' (vs 22) "Also the one who had received the two talents came up and said, 'Master, you entrusted two talents to me. See, I have gained two more talents.' (vs 23) "His master said to him, 'Well done, good and faithful slave. You were faithful with a few things, I will put you in charge of many things; enter into the joy of your master.' (vs 24) "And the one also who had received the one talent came up and said, 'Master, I knew you to be a hard man, reaping where you did not sow and gathering where you scattered no seed. (vs 25) 'And I was afraid, and went away and hid your talent in the ground. See, you have what is yours.' (vs 26) "But his master answered and said to him, 'You wicked, lazy slave, you knew that I reap where I did not sow and gather where I scattered no seed. (vs 27) 'Then you ought to have put my money in the bank, and on my arrival I would have received my money back with interest. (vs 28) 'Therefore take away the talent from him, and give it to the one who has the ten talents.' (vs 29) "For to everyone who has, more shall be given, and he will have an abundance; but from the one who does not have, even what he does have shall be taken away. (vs 30) "Throw out the worthless slave into the outer darkness; in that place there will be weeping and gnashing of teeth.

There is a powerful lesson to be learned here. The first part of that lesson is that we are to use the talents God has given us, for his glory, by putting those talents into the market place and expecting and trusting that God will give the increase, all the time trusting that the increase will be in accordance with His will and desires. The second part of that lesson is that God expects us to trust Him regardless of whether He has given us one or ten talents. We are not to be afraid to lose. It is our job to expose our God-given talent(s) to the market place. It is God's job to multiply our talents, whether they be one or ten, all in accordance with His desires.

Now, the talents God has placed within our care can be more than "monetary wealth", but it is within the "monetary values" that we are talking about in this Chapter. The other "talents" granted to each of us is not being slighted here, but is reserved for another Book.

I believe these verses to be the premier example of our "stewardship" to God for everything He has entrusted us with. This "stewardship" is to be honored for all the "talents" and "treasures" He has given to each of us. In all of our "business ventures", "investments", use of our "personal intellect" and "physical abilities", we are to get in on what He is doing and give Him the Glory for all the increase. We are a "steward" not an owner.

The above parable is dealing with what is called slaves. This is defined as: ones who are in subjection or subserviency. As a slave to our God, and as one who "Belongs To Him", we can see how this parable fits our "stewardship" to God as intended in the portrayal here. While living on this earth we are not to lay up storehouses of wealth for our own personal, selfish gain and use. We have too many examples of those who have done this and their subsequent testimony of the emptiness and lack of satisfaction in their trust in wealth. These testimonies have gone from movie stars to businessmen, and are all the same. There is no happiness in "earthly riches" and on the contrary there is only emptiness, loneliness and depression.

We find a joy in the above parable in that when we "trade" our talents, it is God who makes the increase, because it is to Him we are responsible and it is back to Him we deliver the original talent as well as the increase. The only one condemned for not making a profit is the one who was afraid to trade his talent, and even with the knowledge of his master's expectations of a minimal increase in what was entrusted, this one was still a poor "steward". Don't be afraid to trust your talents to be used by "The One To Whom You Belong" and to be blessed accordingly. Our responsibility is to TRUST our Heavenly Father, it is His responsibility to bless that TRUST. He owns it all! It is our responsibility is to be faithful to Him, and one of these ways of faithfulness is in our financial stewardship in business ventures, investments and all other material possessions. Remember that it is our responsibility to "get in on what God is doing, rather than trying to get God in on what we are doing".

Even though we find in these verses a severe warning to not clutch or cling to "material wealth", we also find the opportunity to be found a good and faithful servant. We see a loving Father allowing us and trusting to us the responsibility to turn our talent(s) into multiple talents and being praised for being found faithful. Please notice that our Christianity is compared to the above parable, and make firm note that the talents, one, five or ten, were entrusted to servants who were in subjection to the one giving the talents. This is like our "Belonging To God", as a child adopted into His family, and given special characteristics to be used for His glory. It was clear these servants were expected to take the talents given them and produce an increase. The talents given us, which vary with each individual, are to be multiplied for God's glory. They are to be put to work, and with God's blessings, returned to our Master with an increase. They are never our possession, but are on loan or entrusted to us, to be returned with increase on that day of His return. He then takes the increase and does with it as He chooses.

To "God Be The Glory and Praise ...... For Everything", including "All Business Ventures and All Material Possessions"!!!.

B. "LIFE" AND "MATERIAL WEALTH" ARE BOTH "FLEETING"!!!:

In this section we will attempt to establish that, "Man's Life" and "Material Wealth" are both "Fleeting". There will be much discussion about how to "honor" God with our "Material Wealth" and what is being a good "steward" of our wealth and time, during these "Fleeting" years.

1. Man dies and his soul is accountable to God, then "to whom will all these things belong"? Who will own your many goods when you have died? Life is "fleeting" and each person will die.

(Luke 12:19-21)(vs 19) 'And I will say to my soul, "Soul, you have many goods laid up for many years to come; take your ease, eat, drink and be merry."' (vs 20) "But God said to him, 'You fool! This very night your soul is required of you; and now who will own what you have prepared?' (vs 21) "So is the man who stores up treasure for himself, and is not rich toward God."

It matters not what you own when you die, for all of those things you owned will belong to someone else upon your soul being taken in death. If you are "not rich toward God", and your trust is in your "many goods", your "fleeting" life will be over and your goods will be enjoyed by someone else and your life will have been a waste. If you are "rich toward God" then your treasures will be waiting in heaven and there will be no loss upon death. You literally didn't leave behind anything of any value.

2. "Fleeting" is a word that comes to mind when we watch clouds scurrying across the sky. Depending upon the winds and amount of moisture, the clouds can be here now and gone before we look back. A very wispy cloud, while we are watching it, can change into many shapes and just disappear. This is how God describes the life of man. It is as "a vapor that appears for a little while and then vanishes away".

(James 4:13-15)(vs 13) Come now, you who say, "Today or tomorrow we will go to such and such a city, and spend a year there and engage in business and make a profit." (vs 14) Yet you do not know what your life will be like tomorrow. You are just a vapor that appears for a little while and then vanishes away. (vs 15) Instead, you ought to say, "If the Lord wills, we will live and also do this or that."

The planning of our "fleeting" life, and it becomes more "fleeting" the older you get, is subject to God's permission. As "fleeting" as our life is, we don't have time to waste on "our" plans, but must truly seek to "get in on what God is doing" during this brief lifetime experience. A lifetime that is described by God as a vapor, surely can be described herein as "fleeting".

3. King David recognized the brevity of his days on this earth. He refers to his lifespan as "transient" (vacant, ceasing or frail), "hand-breadths" (equal to the width of your palm) "mere breath" (emptiness or figuratively something transitory) and "a phantom" (illusion, resemblance or image). All of these demonstrate his understanding of our mortality and therefore the brief and perishableness of our human life. He writes these thoughts in the book of Psalms as follows.

(Psalms 39:4-7)(vs 4) "LORD, make me to know my end And what is the extent of my days; Let me know how transient I am. (vs 5) "Behold, You have made my days as handbreadths, And my lifetime as nothing in Your sight; Surely every man at his best is a mere breath. Selah. (vs 6) "Surely every man walks about as a phantom; Surely they make an uproar for nothing; He amasses riches and does not know who will gather them. (vs 7) "And now, Lord, for what do I wait? My hope is in You.

King David concludes the knowledge of this "fleeting" life with the ultimate statement, "*My hope is in You*". His "*wait*" as found in *verse* 7, is defined as an <u>eagerness</u> for, <u>hopefully</u> trusting, and <u>patiently</u> expecting, the eternal life to come. He recognizes the frailty of our present bodies and adamantly states, his hope is in the Only True God. David is truly a "man after God's own heart" and if we could interview him today he would confess, "especially because of this fleeting life", "I Belong To Him"!!!

4. What will a man give in exchange for his soul? When talking about "wealth", when talking about the "short lifespan" of Man, and therefore when these two are considered together, it only makes sense to share the following from God's Word.

(Matthew 16:25-26)(vs 25) "For whoever wishes to save his life will lose it; but whoever loses his life for My sake will find it. (vs 26) "For what will it profit a man if he gains the whole world and forfeits his soul? Or what will a man give in exchange for his soul?

You may gain the entire world's wealth in this short life, yet what do you have of any eternal value? Knowing Jesus, makes anything in this world, rate on any scale, only as "poverty"! "Fleeting lifetime" and "earthly wealth", compared to "eternal life" and "having the riches provided by Jesus", are incomparable. Jim Elliott, of missionary fame, once said something to this effect. "Only a fool would not give up that which he cannot keep in order to gain that which he cannot lose". He was referring to the mortal, decaying things of this world, versus the immortal, eternal thing from God.

5. (Ecclesiastes 2:4-11)(vs 4) I enlarged my works: I built houses for myself, I planted vineyards for myself; (vs 5) I made gardens and parks for myself and I planted in them all kinds of fruit trees; (vs 6) I made ponds of water for myself from which to irrigate a forest of growing trees. (vs 7) I bought male and female slaves and I had homeborn slaves. Also I possessed flocks and herds larger than all who preceded me in Jerusalem. (vs 8) Also, I collected for myself silver and gold and the treasure of kings and provinces. I provided for myself male and female singers and the pleasures of men—many concubines. (vs 9) Then I became great and increased more than all who preceded me in Jerusalem. My wisdom also stood by me. (vs 10) All that my eyes desired I did not refuse them. I did not withhold my heart from any pleasure, for my heart was pleased because of all my labor and this was my reward for all my labor. (vs 11) Thus I considered all my activities which my hands had done and the labor which I had exerted, and behold all was vanity and striving after wind and there was no profit under the sun.

This is confirmation that "Material Wealth" is of no value when it's only purpose is to serve ourselves. It is striving after the wind, and there is no profit in this life. It only becomes valuable when we use it wisely for God's Kingdom. Solomon's wealth was of no significance to himself. It did not bring lasting contentment. It's use was "fleeting" and considered to be vanity, and it was like trying to catch the wind. You work so hard at it and all you wind up with is a hand full of air.

6. (James 5:1-6)(vs 1) Come now, you rich, weep and howl for your miseries which are coming upon you. (vs 2) Your riches have rotted and your garments have become moth-eaten. (vs 3) Your gold and your silver have rusted; and their rust will be a witness against you and will consume your flesh like fire. It is in the last days that you have stored up your treasure! (vs 4) Behold, the pay of the laborers who mowed your fields, and which has been withheld by you, cries out against you; and the outcry of those who did the

harvesting has reached the ears of the Lord of Sabaoth. (vs 5) You have lived luxuriously on the earth and led a life of wanton pleasure; you have fattened your hearts in a day of slaughter. (vs 6) You have condemned and put to death the righteous man; he does not resist you.

The above condemnation of the rich man is assured by God. If all your security is in riches, there will come a day when those will be rotten, moth-eaten and rusted, and you will weep and howl for your security is gone. If the above is your story, we can't leave you there in this hopeless despair. God's word doesn't leave you lying there with the bus wheel prints all over your chest. It is with great "Joy" He has provided these next verses to replace the "fleeting" and 'emptiness" of life without Him.

(James 5:19-20)(vs 19) My brethren, if any among you strays from the truth and one turns him back, (vs 20) let him know that he who turns a sinner from the error of his way will save his soul from death and will cover a multitude of sins.

Let's put our resources into sharing the Gospel with those in need, and when we see a soul saved from death we will together rejoice a thousand times over with this "new creation". "Life" and "Material Wealth" are both truly "fleeting", so don't miss out on "Belonging To Him" and rejoicing with others who have found out how "To Belong to Him"!!!

7. Our present surroundings are "fleeting". His future new heavens and new earth will be forever!

(2 Peter 3:8-10 & 13)(vs 8) But do not let this one fact escape your notice, beloved, that with the Lord one day is like a thousand years, and a thousand years like one day. (vs 9) The Lord is not slow about His promise, as some count slowness, but is patient toward you, not wishing for any to perish but for all to come to repentance. (vs 10) But the day of the Lord will come like a thief, in which the heavens will pass away with a roar and the elements will be destroyed with intense heat, and the earth and its works will be burned up. (vs 13) But according to His promise we are looking for new heavens and a new earth, in which righteousness dwells.

Peter is explaining to each of us that time is of no significance to God. He dwells in a "timeless society". We might think a thousand years is really long, but God says it is only like a day. After this earthly brevity, with all of the daily trials and tribulations, we will be experiencing a new heaven and a new earth, all of which will remain forever. Those "Who Belong To Him", will experience life that cannot be measured years, and will possess the "riches" that cannot be burned. (Please note in the above passage, even though it is not related to this Chapter's theme, Jesus will return as a thief in the night, and He wishes for all of us to be ready for this glorious return.)

8. In God's eyes it doesn't matter the extent of your wealth. King Solomon is a great example that massive wealth has no bearing upon eternal values. Both "Material Wealth" and "Life" are "fleeting". Our days are but a vapor, and when we are gone someone else will have all of our "earthly things".

(2 Chronicles 9:15-17)(vs 15) King Solomon made 200 large shields of beaten gold, using 600 shekels of beaten gold on each large shield. (vs 16) He made 300 shields of beaten gold, using three hundred shekels of gold on each shield, and the king put them in the house of the forest of Lebanon. (vs 17) Moreover, the king made a great throne of ivory and overlaid it with pure gold.

With all of his wealth, Solomon still went the way of all of mankind. He died and was buried like all, whether peasant or king. You could say he put his pants on one leg at a time just like everyone else.

(2 Chronicles 9:30-31)(vs 30) Solomon reigned forty years in Jerusalem over all Israel. (vs 31) And Solomon slept with his fathers and was buried in the city of his father David; and his son Rehoboam reigned in his place.

Like all of us will experience, Solomon served, died and was replaced by future generations. The important thing in Solomon's "fleeting" life was his choosing to serve God and his resulting relationship with Him. Solomon "Belonged To God"!!!

9. Flowers and grass have a short life even in our human standards. Can you imagine the brief life associated with grass or flowers as considered by God's standards? The God, who has no constraints by time, records His perspective on "material wealth" and its "fleeting" life.

(James 1:10-11)(vs 10) and the rich man is to glory in his humiliation, because like flowering grass he will pass away. (vs 11) For the sun rises with a scorching wind and withers the grass; and its flower falls off and the beauty of its appearance is destroyed; so too the rich man in the midst of his pursuits will fade away.

The term "humiliation" as recorded above, means: to be made low or low estate. The rich man is to glory in this condition as he recognizes the frailty or brevity of this condition, even though he has many barns full of goods. The only "non-fleeting" thing about our human life is our "relationship with God". Be a "steward of", not one who trusts in, "material wealth".

The only conclusions to be drawn from the above verses are: all "Material Wealth" will remain behind; all earthly pleasures are vanity; and only a "personal relationship" with The Most High God is of lasting value.

C. THE "WICKEDNESS OF LOVING MONEY" AND THE GOD GIVEN FREEDOM FROM "THE LOVE OF MONEY":

The following verses are all applicable to the above heading and are generally self-explanatory. In many cases they both: condemn the "wickedness of loving money"; and encourage the finding of "freedom from the bondage of loving money".

<u>1.</u> *(1 Timothy 3:2-3 & 8)(vs 2) An overseer, then, must be above reproach, the husband of one wife, temperate, prudent, respectable, hospitable, able to teach, (vs 3) not addicted to wine or pugnacious, but gentle, peaceable, free from the love of money. (vs 8) Deacons likewise must be men of dignity, not double-tongued, or addicted to much wine or fond of sordid gain,*

These verses are referring to the qualifications of our Elders and Deacons. If these qualifications are good for our overseers, they are good for all of us. We as "ordinary believers" can find in these verses, morsels of healthy food for our spiritual diet, including the requirement to be "*free from the love of money*".

2. (Hebrews 13:5-6)(vs 5) Make sure that your character is free from the love of money, being content with what you have; for He Himself has said, "I WILL NEVER DESERT YOU, NOR WILL I EVER FORSAKE YOU," (vs 6) so that we confidently say, "THE LORD IS MY HELPER, I WILL NOT BE AFRAID. WHAT WILL MAN DO TO ME?"

Set your sights on Jesus, put your full trust in Him, and He will never forsake you. Our instructions are to be content with what we have, never allowing the "love of money" to flaw our character.

3. (1 John 2:15-17)(vs 15) Do not love the world nor the things in the world. If anyone loves the world, the love of the Father is not in him. (vs 16) For all that is in the world, the lust of the flesh and the lust of the eyes and the boastful pride of life, is not from the Father, but is from the world. (vs 17) The world is passing away, and also its lusts; but the one who does the will of God lives forever.

The word "world", as used six times above, means the things that we find to be: adorning or decorating this world. These are the temporary or perishable things including the various lusts of the flesh as mentioned above. Since, we as "believers", are in this world but not of this world, the word "world" is not referring to us or our "brothers in Christ". We are to seek to do the will of God and the associated eternal values attached thereto, not to seek the temporal or perishable things of this world. The temporal things will pass away and this will happen sooner than you think. "Forever" is a term used in God's Word, reserved for those who choose to follow Him ... **"but the one who does the will of God lives forever".**

4. (Ecclesiastes 5:10) He who loves money will not be satisfied with money, nor he who loves abundance with its income. This too is vanity.

There is no lasting satisfaction in the "love of money", nor in the "abundance" of possessions. The God-shaped void in man's life will not be satisfied by the "earthly material things" we may accumulate.

5. (1 Timothy 6:6-12)(vs 6) But godliness actually is a means of great gain when accompanied by contentment. (vs 7) For we have brought nothing into the world, so we cannot take anything out of it either. (vs 8) If we have food

and covering, with these we shall be content. (vs 9) But those who want to get rich fall into temptation and a snare and many foolish and harmful desires which plunge men into ruin and destruction. (vs 10) For the love of money is a root of all sorts of evil, and some by longing for it have wandered away from the faith and pierced themselves with many griefs. (vs 11) But flee from these things, you man of God, and pursue righteousness, godliness, faith, love, perseverance and gentleness. (vs 12) Fight the good fight of faith; take hold of the eternal life to which you were called, and you made the good confession in the presence of many witnesses.

These verses are what prompted the famous old saying, "while observing a funeral precession, have you ever seen the hearse pulling a U-Haul"? No one has ever been able to "take it with them"!

We find here the potential evils or wickedness of loving money, which ultimately can pierce you through with many griefs, and we also find the contrary. Our most high command is to flee from the evils of discontent and the love of money, and search after a full, loving, pre-serving relationship with the One "To Which We Belong"!!! When all is summed up, the most valuable thing we can have, is a "full and right relationship with The Most High God". That relationship is worth more than all the "Material Wealth" to be found in this universe.

I do believe there is merit in dwelling upon ... *(1 Timothy 6:10) For the love of money is a root of all sorts of evil, and some by longing for it have wandered away from the faith and pierced themselves with many griefs.* ... for it is a severe warning, therefore with much reason to be considered in detail. I can't add anything to God's Word, but here are some of my thoughts as we delve into the individual words making up this verse and their original meanings.

This verse sets the stage for the study of "riches" as found throughout the Biblical passages. It clearly and absolutely states in its warning that our "love of money" can cause our wandering from the faith and pierce us through with many griefs. Let's look at the definitions and Greek meaning of several of the key words in this verse. This single verse, with its severe warning, is so critical to our abundant, happy and fulfilling life in Christ, that we must give it full consideration.

a. *"love of money"* – This means being actively fond (more than passive or mildly seeking) of silver (money) with an avarice connotation. Thus it is negative in meaning and associated with covetousness. Avarice is defined as: fraudulency, extortion and practices greediness. This sets the stage as all of the above definitions of "love of money" are negative and totally contrary to God's two most high commands. These are both found in the Book of Matthew and are as follows: ... *(Matthew 22:36-40)(vs 36) "Teacher, which is the great commandment in the Law?" (vs 37) And He said to him, " 'YOU SHALL LOVE THE LORD YOUR GOD WITH ALL YOUR HEART, AND WITH ALL YOUR SOUL, AND WITH ALL YOUR MIND.' (vs 38) "This is the great and foremost commandment. (vs 39) "The second is like it, 'YOU SHALL LOVE YOUR NEIGHBOR AS YOURSELF.' (vs 40) "On these two commandments depend the whole Law and the Prophets."*

Our Love is to be focused upon our God and our neighbors, not on the seeking of "silver".

b. *"a root"* – Literally and figuratively a root. This is the foundation and the source of all life for a plant. In our verse here we see the "all sorts of evil" are rooted or grounded to our source of life, which is the "love of money". How can we possibly have time for our Righteous God, when our source of life and our foundation is in love with something else.

c. *"all sorts of evil"* – **All** is defined as: every, the whole, any, whatsoever. This is plainly all inclusive. **Evil** is defined as: intrinsically worthless, depraved, bad, harm, ill, wicked. "**All** sorts of **Evil**", having thus been so vividly defined should cause us to run with terror from any association with these definitions.

d. *"longing for it"* – This is to: stretch oneself, reach out after, covet after, desire. This appears to be a conscientious effort on our part to actively and knowingly seek after something and in this case longing for something that will produce depravity, worthlessness, wickedness, or in other words death.

e. *"wandered away from the faith"* – Wandering is: to lead astray, err, seduce. We are wandering from what? We are wandering from the very thing that God has granted to us and that is our FAITH. Faith is our credence, moral conviction, the truthfulness of God, reliance upon Christ for our salvation, our assurance in Christ, our belief in Christ, our fidelity to Christ. How could anything be more apostate, unforgiving, or unfaithful than to leave our "love of God" for the "love of money"! How can we leave the very thing which is the root of our existence, to follow after another god?! How can we forsake our very life, and forsake everything of any lasting, worthwhile or real value, for the "fleeting and perishable" toys of this world.

f. *"pierced themselves"* – This is to: penetrate entirely, transfix or impale with a pointed weapon, pierce through. All of the above appears to be severe, if not fatal. The interesting fact about this part of the verse is that the impaling with a pointed weapon is being done by the person to himself. Who would consciously poke his own eye out with a pointed stick? If we abandon our "FAITH" by our "love of money" we are driving the sharp stick through our own heart. We need to harbor the following verse in our heart, write it upon our garments and place it upon a billboard, so that it is visible to us every day. ... *(Luke 12:15) Then He said to them, "Beware, and be on your guard against every form of greed; for not even when one has an abundance does his life consist of his possessions."* If you don't pierce yourself through, I guarantee the Devil can't! You will find your worth and what life really consists of, as you continue to develop your relationship with God Almighty.

g. *"griefs"* – The root word means: to go down or to sink, the direct word is sorrow. We should have enough self-preservation to not intentionally inflict ourselves with pre-meditated sorrow. This warning is explicit and very understandable. **We inflict ourselves with many sorrows** by lusting after the "love of money". A word to the wise is sufficient. ... *(Proverbs 9:9) Give instruction to a wise man and he will be still wiser, Teach a righteous man and he will increase his learning.* A "wise" man will not inflict himself with "sorrows".

h. *"The summation"*— to I Timothy 6:10. The real problem or conclusion of being fond or avaricely covetousness of money, is that our affection is not upon our Savior. It is not concentrated upon the thankfulness for our salvation because of Jesus and His victory for us upon the Cross. Our thoughts and deeds are selfishly minded rather than being found serving our Savior by loving our neighbors as ourselves.

Our direction will be for the things of this world, and not laying up for ourselves treasures in heaven.

Our worthless striving after this world's wealth will only cause our wandering away from the faith and cause abundant and plenteous griefs. These can come in various forms too numerous to describe or imagine. If our desire is to be fond of "silver", our rewards will be like day old manna. God provided manna each day to feed His Chosen People, but if they tried to store it or save it, because of worrying about provisions for tomorrow, it became rotten and full of worms.

We cripple ourselves if we seek "material wealth" for personal gain rather than seeking a sweet, trusting relationship with our Lord. There is nothing wrong with this world's wealth, it is your attitude towards its value that creates the problem. This world's wealth is not to be selfishly used or trusted in, but rather to be used as, a good "steward" would, for God's glory and His purpose.

God's Word, our "Owner's Manual", warns us to not wander away from the faith and be pierced through with many griefs (don't be a human pincushion full of sorrow!).

6. You will find in this paragraph both a warning and a promise regarding ill-gotten gain. Wealth is not precious if we obtain it through anything other than God's blessings. If our gain is at the expense of our fellow man, it will come back to condemn us, as it is obtained by wickedness.

(Proverbs 1:13-19)(vs 13) We will find all kinds of precious wealth, We will fill our houses with spoil; (vs 14) Throw in your lot with us, We shall all have one purse," (vs 15) My son, do not walk in the way with them. Keep your feet from their path, (vs 16) For their feet run to evil And they hasten to shed blood. (vs 17) Indeed, it is useless to spread the baited net In the sight of any bird; (vs 18) But they lie in wait for their own blood; They ambush their own lives. (vs 19) So are the ways of everyone who gains by violence; It takes away the life of its possessors.

The "warning" is to stay away from those who tempt us to pursue wealth, spoil, or anything obtained by a band of thieves. Thieves can be legal, so beware as to what you pursue and make sure you "are getting in on what God is doing" not just taking advantage of a legal opportunity. If you "are not in on what God is doing" then you are wasting your time and energy. The "promise" is, whatever you do unrighteously for gain, will only wind up in the taking of your life … ***"everyone who gains by violence; It takes away the life of its possessors"***. Wickedness for gain is the exact opposite of knowing and loving God. It causes you to die internally. Remember His Word is our "Owner's Manual"!!!

7. *(Proverbs 21:5) The plans of the diligent lead surely to advantage, But -everyone who is hasty comes surely to poverty. (Proverbs 28:20) A faithful man will abound with blessings, But he who makes haste to be rich will not go unpunished.*

Solomon in all of his renowned wisdom wrote the above. In each of the two verses we are given two Biblical, text book principles, of business dealings. The first "advises us" to diligently consider all plans, the second "warns us" to avoid all hasty decisions. Both of these, and individually either of these, are wisdom from God. The good results, earned from the use of the diligent plans, should be used to honor the one who blessed us. The results of hasty decisions which lead to poverty are to be learned from and not repeated. God's word cannot be violated. … ***(Isaiah 55:11) So will My word be which goes forth from My mouth; It will not return to Me empty, Without accomplishing what I desire, And without succeeding in the matter for which I sent it. … (Hebrews 4:12) For the word of God is living and active and sharper than any two-edged sword, and piercing as far as the division of soul and spirit, of both joints and marrow, and able to judge the thoughts and intentions of the heart.***

God's word is so complete and thorough. It covers all of our needs, our directions, our hopes, our desires. It is alive! Only a fool would ignore it!

D. MAN'S PERSPECTIVE OF MATERIAL WEALTH:

1. Found in the following is a very direct and negative perspective for the respecting of "Material Wealth".

(James 2:2-6 & 9)(vs 2) For if a man comes into your assembly with a gold ring and dressed in fine clothes, and there also comes in a poor man in dirty clothes, (vs 3) and you pay special attention to the one who is wearing the fine clothes, and say, "You sit here in a good place," and you say to the poor man, "You stand over there, or sit down by my footstool," (vs 4) have you not made distinctions among yourselves, and become judges with evil motives? (vs 5) Listen, my beloved brethren: did not God choose the poor of this world to be rich in faith and heirs of the kingdom which He promised to those who love Him? (vs 6) But you have dishonored the poor man. Is it not the rich who oppress you and personally drag you into court? (vs 9) But if you show partiality, you are committing sin and are convicted by the law as transgressors.

Here we find a classical example of our human nature. We find ourselves judging others around us, by respecting those solely because of their demonstration of "Material Wealth". These verses all speak for themselves, and as one who "Belongs To God" we must take heed and be aware of such tendencies. James, as he speaks to "his beloved brethren", is lovingly chastising us to correct these mistakes. James calls the above attitude sin, and calls us to conviction and therefore repentance for this sin. We need to respect everyone equally.

A demonstration of respect to only those of "fine clothes" will likely destroy our testimony, showing us to be a respecter of "Material Things" and speaks for us, as if those things are more important to us than the things of God. On the contrary, a respecter of only those in "dirty clothes" may say to the rich, you are not worthy of my time and I don't have time for you, as God has probably written you off long ago. Either of these testimonies can be an abomination before our loving Savior. In both of the above cases we should demonstrate from our heart, the Love of God. If the Love of God doesn't come out in all of the above situations, we need to examine our lives as James has so clearly directed.

2. Man's perspective can be also found in the book of Luke.

(Luke 16:14-15)(vs 14) Now the Pharisees, who were lovers of money, were listening to all these things and were scoffing at Him. (vs 15) And He said to them, "You are those

who justify yourselves in the sight of men, but God knows your hearts; for that which is highly esteemed among men is detestable in the sight of God.

These verses are a demonstration of the human perspective in a covetous position. These are Jesus' own words and are directed at the Pharisees of the day. This condemnation can be applied today and is an attitude of the heart. God isn't condemning wealth, but He is condemning the attitude of the heart and the attitude of the mind that sets it's love and trust in money, instead of upon the relationship and trust being in Him. When God says "that which is highly esteemed (thought of in a lofty manner) among men is detestable in the sight of God", we must take note and digest its full meaning and intent. What Jesus is saying is, what is very often thought to be right in the sight of man is "detestable" in the sight of God. God is not mocked and will not tolerate the ignoring of His warnings.

3. Here we find in the Psalms a dissertation for all of mankind. In this passage we hear God speaking to us, regarding the path of man. God speaks to our frailty and yet in His might we are covered by Him for eternity. It is explained that man, even though he might be rich in this world's "material wealth", is still subject to death and leaving those possessions to others. Man's thoughts are that their houses are forever, God's thoughts are that we must trust in Him not our "things".

(Psalms 49:1-12)(vs 1) Hear this, all peoples; Give ear, all inhabitants of the world, (vs 2) Both low and high, Rich and poor together. (vs 3) My mouth will speak wisdom, And the meditation of my heart will be understanding. (vs 4) I will incline my ear to a proverb; I will express my riddle on the harp. (vs 5) Why should I fear in days of adversity, When the iniquity of my foes surrounds me, (vs 6) Even those who trust in their wealth And boast in the abundance of their riches? (vs 7) No man can by any means redeem his brother Or give to God a ransom for him— (vs 8) For the redemption of his soul is costly, And he should cease trying forever— (vs 9) That he should live on eternally, That he should not undergo decay. (vs 10) For he sees that even wise men die; The stupid and the senseless alike perish And leave their wealth to others. (vs 11) Their inner thought is that their

houses are forever And their dwelling places to all genera-
tions; They have called their lands after their own names.
(vs 12) But man in his pomp will not endure; He is like the
beasts that perish.

With the above passage speaking of both man's perspective and
God's perspective, it is His perspective that overrides ours. It is His
Word that states all people need to trust in Him, including the "wealthy".
His Word is so rich in meeting all of our questions, thoughts or issues.
His Word is speaking to both, "low and high" and to the "rich and poor".

E. GOD'S PERSPECTIVE OF MATERIAL WEALTH:

1. *(Psalms 17:13-15)(vs 13) Arise, O LORD, confront him,*
bring him low; Deliver my soul from the wicked with Your
sword, (vs 14) From men with Your hand, O LORD, From
men of the world, whose portion is in this life, And whose
belly You fill with Your treasure; They are satisfied with
children, And leave their abundance to their babes. (vs 15)
As for me, I shall behold Your face in righteousness; I will be
satisfied with Your likeness when I awake.

People of the world gain much while alive, but leave their wealth to
their children. Their only life is what they have here on this earth. Godly
men awake from death to see the face of God and His righteousness for
eternity. God's perspective is that we have a righteous relationship with
Him. This is the most important thing a man can obtain while here on
this earth. The "Material Wealth" is not forbidden, but it is secondary
to our relationship to Him and it is not to be our security, it is to be our
responsibility to use wisely.

2. *(1 Timothy 6:17-19)(vs 17) Instruct those who are rich*
in this present world not to be conceited or to fix their hope
on the uncertainty of riches, but on God, who richly supplies
us with all things to enjoy. (vs 18) Instruct them to do good,
to be rich in good works, to be generous and ready to share,
(vs 19) storing up for themselves the treasure of a good
foundation for the future, so that they may take hold of that
which is life indeed.

This is God's charge or command to those who are "Materially Wealthy" in this world. <u>Do Not</u> fix your hope upon the uncertainty of riches, but fix your hope upon Him. He makes it clear you are to honor Him with generosity because it was He who supplied you with those blessings. His other command is to "***take hold of that which is life indeed***" meaning the foremost, eternally profitable thing you can do is to establish "your relationship with Him".

3. *(1 John 2:15-17)(vs 15) Do not love the world nor the things in the world. If anyone loves the world, the love of the Father is not in him. (vs 16) For all that is in the world, the lust of the flesh and the lust of the eyes and the boastful pride of life, is not from the Father, but is from the world. (vs 17) The world is passing away, and also its lusts; but the one who does the will of God lives forever.*

The love of God and the love of the world, cannot both exist within man at the same time. The love of God is eternally lasting, the love of the world and its related fleshly lusts, are soon to be passing away.

4. *(James 2:5-6)(vs 5) Listen, my beloved brethren: did not God choose the poor of this world to be rich in faith and heirs of the kingdom which He promised to those who love Him? (vs 6) But you have dishonored the poor man. Is it not the rich who oppress you and personally drag you into court?*

Ted Turner of today's fame is very wealthy. He claims that Christians are weak and in need of a crutch in order to get through life. I pray that he becomes rich in faith in addition to his wealth. Based upon God's perspective, rich in faith is the only thing of lasting value.

5. *(Proverbs 15:16) Better is a little with the fear of the LORD Than great treasure and turmoil with it.*

This is a brief statement that is packed with wisdom. The "fear" of the Lord part is more significant than great treasures.

6. *(Proverbs 23:4-5)(vs 4) Do not weary yourself to gain wealth, Cease from your consideration of it. (vs 5) When you set your eyes on it, it is gone. For wealth certainly makes itself wings Like an eagle that flies toward the heavens.*

The word "weary" means: to gasp, hence to be exhausted, to tire, to toil, or faint. These definitions all indicate to major on something. God says to cease from these efforts, for they are only like chasing an eagle, which will fly away towards the heavens, where it cannot be reached.

7. (Mark 8:36) "For what does it profit a man to gain the whole world, and forfeit his soul?

This is God's perspective not man's perspective. As one who "Belongs To Him" we need to know His perspective and respect that. There is no gain should you own the whole world, yet lose your own soul.

8. (Ecclesiastes 5:12-13)(vs 12) The sleep of the working man is pleasant, whether he eats little or much; but the full stomach of the rich man does not allow him to sleep. (vs 13) There is a grievous evil which I have seen under the sun: riches being hoarded by their owner to his hurt.

There is no peace for the man who is "trusting" in his wealth.

9. (Deuteronomy 8:3) "He humbled you and let you be hungry, and fed you with manna which you did not know, nor did your fathers know, that He might make you understand that man does not live by bread alone, but man lives by everything that proceeds out of the mouth of the LORD.

All men need "bread" for physical, earthly survival, but for that which is "eternal" we need His Word. His Word is that which was given to the great men of faith, who long ago recorded it, in order that today's world might have this "living bread". We call this "living bread", the Holy Bible, which is our "Owner's Manual". It is what ... **"proceeds out of the mouth of the LORD"** ... that is the only thing that can satisfy our spiritual nature and give us "eternal" value.

10. (James 1:9-11)(vs 9) But the brother of humble circumstances is to glory in his high position; (vs 10) and the rich man is to glory in his humiliation, because like flowering grass he will pass away. (vs 11) For the sun rises with a scorching wind and withers the grass; and its flower falls off and the beauty of its appearance is destroyed; so too the rich man in the midst of his pursuits will fade away.

God's perspective is that riches will fade as a flower or the grasses of the field. We have all had fresh flowers in our home. We have all come to the time when they were discarded. They dried up, wilted and the pedals fell to the table top. It was so nice to see them in their full glory, but they were of no value when they died. They became a part of the trash and are now in a "stinking land fill". All riches will fade away. We need to look at history and try to find anyone who has died and see if they are still enjoying their wealth. In God's perspective the rich man is no better than the flower in the field, and without God he will wind up in a "stinking land fill".

11. *(Luke 16:14-15)(vs 14) Now the Pharisees, who were lovers of money, were listening to all these things and were scoffing at Him. (vs 15) And He said to them, "You are those who justify yourselves in the sight of men, but God knows your hearts; for that which is highly esteemed among men is detestable in the sight of God.*

I know I used this scripture passage in the above discussion of a "man's perspective", but it applies also to "God's perspective". God sternly warns about our heart condition. He is more concerned about our heart's attitude toward Himself then any amount of money. God doesn't ever condemn money, but what He condemns is its place or its value in our lives. When he warns us about being "lovers" of money and says this is "detestable" in the sight of God, He is saying "lovers" is: covetous with a strong negative connotation, and He is saying "detestable" is: idolatry or an abomination. Both, or either of these, are worth our hearing and heeding.

12. *(Zephaniah 1:17-18)(vs 17) I will bring distress on men So that they will walk like the blind, Because they have sinned against the LORD; And their blood will be poured out like dust And their flesh like dung. (vs 18) Neither their silver nor their gold Will be able to deliver them On the day of the LORD'S wrath; And all the earth will be devoured In the fire of His jealousy, For He will make a complete end, Indeed a terrifying one, Of all the inhabitants of the earth.*

Those who have sinned against God and have not found repentance will be devoured by the Lord. Their silver and their gold will not deliver them from the terror at hand. There is no safety in "Material Wealth", it is only in the blood of Jesus Christ through "believing faith" that we will be saved.

13. *(1 Timothy 4:4-5)(vs 4) For everything created by God is good, and nothing is to be rejected if it is received with* *gratitude; (vs 5) for it is sanctified by means of the word of God and prayer.*

All good gifts to us are from our Heavenly Father. All things from Him are to be received with gratitude. The word "sanctified" means: purify or consecrate; the word "prayer" means: supplication which is our petition to God. As we ask for things, we ask with pure motivation from our heart's desire and as He supplies we see and benefit from His perspective regarding the "things of this world". "Material Wealth" is neutral! It can be used for God's good or it can be trusted in to the destruction of man. "Material Wealth" is neither active or passive, it is the value placed upon it, that creates its' good use or our downfall.

14. *(Acts 20:32-35)(vs 32) "And now I commend you to God and to the word of His grace, which is able to build you up and to give you the inheritance among all those who are sanctified. (vs 33) "I have coveted no one's silver or gold or clothes. (vs 34) "You yourselves know that these hands ministered to my own needs and to the men who were with me. (vs 35) "In everything I showed you that by working hard in this manner you must help the weak and remember the words of the Lord Jesus, that He Himself said, 'It is more blessed to give than to receive.'"*

Paul is instructing a group of followers of Christ in Asia, and is about to leave them to go to Macedonia. He states that it is God who will give us our inheritance, meaning that the inheritance is eternal life with Him in Heaven. Paul desired no one's silver, gold or clothes, the things representing wealth at that time. Paul worked for his sustenance and demonstrated this by working in a trade that sometimes lasted far into the night. He then reminded them of Christ's very own words, *'It is more blessed to give than to receive.'* The principle here is that we are not to selfishly covet the "things" of others. This principle when put into action, will result in "giving", rather than our sitting around wishing for "gifts".

15. Jesus summarized His perspective on "Material Wealth" as He taught the disciples.

(Luke 12:22-31)(vs 22) And He said to His disciples, "For this reason I say to you, do not worry about your life, as to what you will eat; nor for your body, as to what you will

put on. (vs 23) "For life is more than food, and the body more than clothing. (vs 24) "Consider the ravens, for they neither sow nor reap; they have no storeroom nor barn, and yet God feeds them; how much more valuable you are than the birds! (vs 25) "And which of you by worrying can add a single hour to his life's span? (vs 26) "If then you cannot do even a very little thing, why do you worry about other matters? (vs 27) "Consider the lilies, how they grow: they neither toil nor spin; but I tell you, not even Solomon in all his glory clothed himself like one of these. (vs 28) "But if God so clothes the grass in the field, which is alive today and tomorrow is thrown into the furnace, how much more will He clothe you? You men of little faith! (vs 29) "And do not seek what you will eat and what you will drink, and do not keep worrying. (vs 30) "For all these things the nations of the world eagerly seek; but your Father knows that you need these things. (vs 31) "But seek His kingdom, and these things will be added to you.

The pertinent concepts here are: a) we as "faith believers", need not concentrate on the things of necessity; b) God will provide all of our needs as we daily walk with Him; and c) He will bless with what we need as we carry out our daily work or job.

Yes, we must provide a living for our family, but our worry is to be left with God. He gives us the example of the birds of the air. They neither sow nor reap, yet God feeds them. You may find a bird dead on the highway, but I have never come across one that has starved to death.

Our direct command by God is to ... **"But seek His kingdom, and these things will be added to you"**. We fulfill our human responsibilities, but leave the worrying to our Heavenly Father. It is in He, who clothes the lilies of the field, wherein our "trust" must lie.

<u>16.</u> (Revelation 2:9) 'I know your tribulation and your poverty (but you are rich),

Jesus, in speaking to the apostle John, here in Revelations, has comforted those who may believe themselves to be in this world's poverty. He has empathy for us in our tribulation. Tribulation literally means: pressure; it can mean: afflicted, anguish, burdened, persecution or trouble. God has recognized our earthly poverty (poverty is literally interpreted to mean: indigence), but He has declared our **"true worth"** *(but you are rich)*. It is God Himself who declares His perspective on true riches. He doesn't mean we are rich in this world's goods, but we are literally abounding and wealthy in true richness, and that is in our relationship with Him. We have found favor with God and that is more valuable than anything this world has to offer. What a wonderful proclamation when we hear God speak to each of us personally, when we hear Him say *"(but you are rich)"*. Do you feel as I do (?); can you feel His arms of comfort wrapped around you?

F. POSSESSIONS — WISE USES:

1. We find in Genesis that Abraham was extremely wealthy. Abraham has always been looked upon as one of the founders of our faith. Abraham was called upon by God to set himself apart from his family as God was setting the stage to make Abraham the Father of a vast nation.

(Genesis 13:1-4)(vs 1) So Abram went up from Egypt to the Negev, he and his wife and all that belonged to him, and Lot with him. (vs 2) Now Abram was very rich in livestock, in silver and in gold. (vs 3) He went on his journeys from the Negev as far as Bethel, to the place where his tent had been at the beginning, between Bethel and Ai, (vs 4) to the place of the altar which he had made there formerly; and there Abram called on the name of the LORD.

When the Bible says Abraham was "very" rich it means he was exceedingly or utterly rich. Abraham didn't trust in his riches but constantly *"called on the name of the LORD"* for his directions and needs. It is with this "fear" or "reverence" of God that Abraham lived his life. He is truly a positive example of those who use their wealth for God's Glory.

(Genesis 13:14-18) The LORD said to Abram, after Lot had separated from him, "Now lift up your eyes and look from the place where you are, northward and southward and eastward and westward; (vs 15) for all the land which you see, I will give it to you and to your descendants forever. (vs 16) "I will make your descendants as the dust of the earth, so

that if anyone can number the dust of the earth, then your descendants can also be numbered. (vs 17) "Arise, walk about the land through its length and breadth; for I will give it to you." (vs 18) Then Abram moved his tent and came and dwelt by the oaks of Mamre, which are in Hebron, and there he built an altar to the LORD.

Abraham, after giving Lot his choice of lands and after separating from him, was given a great deal of land. So extensive was this land, it encompassed as far as the eye could see. Abraham used this for God's Glory and was continually being found in favor by God, while building an altar to the Lord on these possessions. Abraham was faithful to God for he knew to "Whom He Belonged"!!!

2. Joseph, the one who was left to die in a pit, the one who was sold by his brothers to a traveling band of Midianites traders for twenty shekels of silver, and was re-sold as a slave to Potiphar, Pharaoh's captain of the bodyguard, is now given the Pharaoh's wealth and a position of authority and prominence, second only to Pharaoh himself. Joseph was put in a position of great wealth and authority. His lifelong faithfulness to God is to be admired as we see his "trust" in God never wavered.

He falls into the category of "Wise Uses" of a life lived to honor God. In both of his new found abundances of "authority" and "riches", he was an honorable "steward".

(Genesis 41:41-44)(vs 41) Pharaoh said to Joseph, "See, I have set you over all the land of Egypt." (vs 42) Then Pharaoh took off his signet ring from his hand and put it on Joseph's hand, and clothed him in garments of fine linen and put the gold necklace around his neck. (vs 43) He had him ride in his second chariot; and they proclaimed before him, "Bow the knee!" And he set him over all the land of Egypt. (vs 44) Moreover, Pharaoh said to Joseph, "Though I am Pharaoh, yet without your permission no one shall raise his hand or foot in all the land of Egypt."

We find that Joseph did not selfishly use his power and wealth, but used it to glorify God and save the entire Jewish Nation from starvation. He was found to be faithfully serving and continually "trusting" in, the God "To Whom he Belonged"!!!

G. MAN'S RESPONSIBILITIES OR STEWARDSHIP OF HAVING "FINANCIAL WEALTH":

1. Our "Trust" is to be in the Living Lord, not in the "riches" he has given us.

(Deuteronomy 8:6-20)(vs 6) "Therefore, you shall keep the commandments of the LORD your God, to walk in His ways and to fear Him. (vs 7) "For the LORD your God is bringing you into a good land, a land of brooks of water, of fountains and springs, flowing forth in valleys and hills; (vs 8) a land of wheat and barley, of vines and fig trees and pomegranates, a land of olive oil and honey; (vs 9) a land where you will eat food without scarcity, in which you will not lack anything; a land whose stones are iron, and out of whose hills you can dig copper. (vs 10) "When you have eaten and are satisfied, you shall bless the LORD your God for the good land which He has given you. (vs 11) "Beware that you do not forget the LORD your God by not keeping His commandments and His ordinances and His statutes which I am commanding you today; (vs 12) otherwise, when you have eaten and are satisfied, and have built good houses and lived in them, (vs13) and when your herds and your flocks multiply, and your silver and gold multiply, and all that you have multiplies, (vs 14) then your heart will become proud and you will forget the LORD your God who brought you out from the land of Egypt, out of the house of slavery. (vs 15) "He led you through the great and terrible wilderness, with its fiery serpents and scorpions and thirsty ground where there was no water; He brought water for you out of the rock of flint. (vs 16) "In the wilderness He fed you manna which your fathers did not know, that He might humble you and that He might test you, to do good for you in the end. (vs 17) "Otherwise, you may say in your heart, 'My power and the strength of my hand made me this wealth.' (vs 18) "But you shall remember the LORD your God, for it is He who is giving you power to make wealth, that He may confirm His covenant which He swore to your fathers, as it

is this day. (vs 19) "It shall come about if you ever forget the LORD your God and go after other gods and serve them and worship them, I testify against you today that you will surely perish. (vs 20) "Like the nations that the LORD makes to perish before you, so you shall perish; because you would not listen to the voice of the LORD your God.

I know this is a long passage, but no other place in the Bible is it any more clear that our "Material Wealth" comes from God and we are never to forget His blessings. We are never to forget His power or His provisions in all that we have. We need to be "Humble" before our Lord and beware of becoming "Proud" for He supplies all of our needs ... *"for it is He who is giving you power to make wealth".* It will be fatal for anyone who turns their back upon the Lord, seeing that He has so abundantly provided for them.

Continue your trust in the Lord God, because it is to Him you are indebted for all things.

2. (Deuteronomy 24:15) "You shall give him his wages on his day before the sun sets, for he is poor and sets his heart on it; so that he will not cry against you to the LORD and it become sin in you.

This is a short verse, but far reaching. God's Word is concise and not to be neglected even when we consider it to be a minor passage. What might be insignificant in value to us, may be the life blood to someone else. It is our responsibility before God to not withhold the wages of those who have earned them. This may be due to "financial" negligence or indifference, but either way, don't bring sin into your life because of this action.

3. (Romans 13:7-8)(vs 7) Render to all what is due them: tax to whom tax is due; custom to whom custom; fear to whom fear; honor to whom honor. (vs 8) Owe nothing to anyone except to love one another; for he who loves his neighbor has fulfilled the law.

To "Owe" means to be under obligation, or from a moral standpoint it is to fail in duty. We are commanded to "owe nothing". We must not be in obligation to someone for something which is impossible to pay back. We must not fail to keep our word. I am aware there has been much discussion regarding this verse as it pertains to money and I can only say, apply the principal taught in this passage. Don't commit to something you can't or you are unwilling to finish.

4. *(Proverbs 24:3-4)(vs 3) By wisdom a house is built, And by understanding it is established; (vs 4) And by knowledge the rooms are filled With all precious and pleasant riches.*

It is wisdom, understanding and knowledge from God that builds our houses and fills them with precious and pleasant riches. It is "TO GOD BE THE GLORY .... FOR EVERYTHING".

For everything we have, we must be thankful to God and give praise to His Holy Name. We must be found a faithful and a proper "steward" of the possessions to which we have been entrusted. We, and all of our "wealth", truly "Belong To Him"!!! Being "wealthy" in this world's goods doesn't make us any better than a "poor" man, but only heightens our responsibility for that which God has entrusted to us.

5. The following passages explain to us the principle of faithfulness to our Savior. We cannot serve God and "wealth", defined as: greed; greediness; materialism; covetousness; the opposite of generosity.

To fully understand the true deep meaning of these words, one must decide, "Do I Belong to God or Not"? It is our commitment to our Savior and therefore the resulting service which is being discussed here. We cannot serve more than one master. If God is not our master, we are serving mammon or wealth. With this in mind the words in Luke should come alive.

(Luke 16:10-14) (vs 10) "He who is faithful in a very little thing is faithful also in much; and he who is unrighteous in a very little thing is unrighteous also in much. (vs 11) "Therefore if you have not been faithful in the use of unrighteous wealth, who will entrust the true riches to you? (vs 12) "And if you have not been faithful in the use of that which is another's, who will give you that which is your own? (vs 13) "No servant can serve two masters; for either he will hate the one and love the other, or else he will be devoted to one and despise the other. You cannot serve God and wealth." (vs 14) Now the Pharisees, who were lovers of money, were listening to all these things and were scoffing at Him.

If we are one "Who belongs To Him"!!!, these words of Jesus will clearly demonstrate our "responsibility" and "stewardship" in having wealth and the burden it becomes. We are to be faithfully using those things which God has entrusted to us, and if we demonstrate this faithfulness in little things, we will be entrusted with much. The more we are entrusted with, the more we must exercise "stewardship" responsibilities. "Material Wealth" isn't inherently bad, but it can become a temptation that can lead us away from depending upon our Savior.

H. BIBLICAL ACCOUNTS OF RICH MEN:

1. JESUS — The following verse is one of the most beautiful accounts of a "Rich" man found in the Bible. *(2 Corinthians 8:9)* *For you know the grace of our Lord Jesus Christ, that though He was rich, yet for your sake He became poor, so that you through His poverty might become rich.*

I believe what God is saying to us is that God the Son, Jesus Christ, in the form of man, gave up His heavenly home (true riches) and place of prominence, for His stay and purpose here on this earth (poverty at best). Jesus, who describes Heaven as a place where He was "rich", exchanged that for a place where He was "poor" (earth). The best earth has to offer, no matter if we have the Wal-Mart wealth, the wealth of the top 100 billionaires, is **"poverty"**. We are poor in comparison to being in God's heavenly company. The best this earth has to offer is "poverty". Yes, I know God is referring to our "wealth" of being "Born Again" believers, but I believe this can also be likened to "Material Wealth". All the "wealth" in this world is considered "poverty" in comparison to becoming "rich" in coming to know Jesus Christ. "Riches" is to know Jesus, not having or owning BMW's, Mansions, and/or Gold.

Beyond Heaven's Gates are contained the glorious presence of the Almighty God. The "riches" there are beyond explanation: Cherubims, Angels, Thrones, Streets of Gold, Praises, Righteousness; all are a part of the experience we lack. We know nothing of these riches and can't even describe this unknown. Jesus left this to come to earth in the form of a man. He stepped out of heavenly riches into our world of poverty. The best this world has to offer; money, houses, cars, clothes, property, businesses, etc. is poverty in the eyes of God. We must seek His "true riches" and we will be found to be "A Child Of A King"!!!

2. RICH YOUNG RULER — An extremely (exceedingly, greatly) rich young ruler (one being first in rank or power, a chief, a magistrate or a prince) approached Jesus. He, like so many others with wealth, had a "VOID" in his heart. There was something lacking and he felt that Jesus might know what it was.

(Luke 18:18-23)(vs 18) A ruler questioned Him, saying, "Good Teacher, what shall I do to inherit eternal life?" (vs 19) And Jesus said to him, "Why do you call Me good? No one is good except God alone. (vs 20) "You know the command- ments, 'DO NOT COMMIT ADULTERY, DO NOT MURDER, DO NOT STEAL, DO NOT BEAR FALSE WITNESS, HONOR YOUR FATHER AND MOTHER.'" (vs 21) And he said, "All these things I have kept from my youth." (vs 22) When Jesus heard this, He said to him, "One thing you still lack; sell all that you possess and distribute it to the poor, and you shall have treasure in heaven; and come, follow Me." (vs 23) But when he had heard these things, he became very sad, for he was extremely rich.

This man claimed to have kept all of the commandments mentioned by Jesus. As we well know, keeping these commandments is not the criteria for salvation. Jesus already knew this gentleman's heart and got right to the point. Do you desire to follow Me or will you continue to cling to the things of the world. We don't have the answer to this man's decision, but we have a hint. This man became very sad, for he was extremely rich. The rich young ruler appears to be torn between the two choices and all indications were he rejected God because of his extreme wealth.

This doesn't have to happen as Jesus said ... *(Luke 18:25-27)(vs 25) "For it is easier for a camel to go through the eye of a needle than for a rich man to enter the kingdom of God." (vs 26) They who heard it said, "Then who can be saved?" (vs 27) But He said, "The things that are impossible with people are possible with God."* . ... With this concisely and clearly worded statement from Jesus, we understand that all things are possible with God. In the case of a rich man coming to Christ, it will happen as with all other people, and that will be as a miracle of God's Grace. I would

345

beg anyone to "give up that which you cannot keep in order to get that which you cannot lose".

3. PRODIGAL SON — An inheritance was given and an inheritance was lost, yet the father still loved his son. Even though this parable is about a rich family, it is even more about forgiveness. The God of the universe, whose riches are without measure, is willing to forgive our sins and adopt us as sons.

(Luke 15:11-24)(vs 11) And He said, "A man had two sons. (vs 12) "The younger of them said to his father, 'Father, give me the share of the estate that falls to me.' So he divided his wealth between them. (vs 13) "And not many days later, the younger son gathered everything together and went on a journey into a distant country, and there he squandered his estate with loose living. (vs 14) "Now when he had spent everything, a severe famine occurred in that country, and he began to be impoverished. (vs 15) "So he went and hired himself out to one of the citizens of that country, and he sent him into his fields to feed swine. (vs 16) "And he would have gladly filled his stomach with the pods that the swine were eating, and no one was giving anything to him. (vs 17) "But when he came to his senses, he said, 'How many of my father's hired men have more than enough bread, but I am dying here with hunger! (vs 18) 'I will get up and go to my father, and will say to him, "Father, I have sinned against heaven, and in your sight; (vs 19) I am no longer worthy to be called your son; make me as one of your hired men."' (vs 20) "So he got up and came to his father. But while he was still a long way off, his father saw him and felt compassion for him, and ran and embraced him and kissed him. (vs 21) "And the son said to him, 'Father, I have sinned against heaven and in your sight; I am no longer worthy to be called your son.' (vs 22) "But the father said to his slaves, 'Quickly bring out the best robe and put it on him, and put a ring on his hand and sandals on his feet; (vs 23) and bring the fattened calf, kill it, and let us eat and celebrate; (vs 24) for this son of mine was dead and has come to life again; he was lost and has been found.' And they began to celebrate.

This parable makes a comparison of how God's forgiveness is offered to us even though we have sinned against Him. Our rejection of God is compared to the Prodigal Son's squandering his father's wealth. The forgiveness by the earthly father when his son repented and returned to his father's estate is likened to our repenting of our sins and coming to the Heavenly Father for forgiveness. In both cases there were acts of wrong doing(s), acts of repentance, followed by the subsequent forgiveness. True "Wealth" here is clearly "knowing God" and our ongoing "relationship with Him".

4. A MAN AND HIS BARNS — We find in the following parable: **a)** a "stern warning"; **b)** the "folly of riches" as these riches pertain to our ability to trust in them; and **c)** a "tremendous principle of our faith". This passage in Luke encompasses all of the above.

(Luke 12:15-21)(vs 15) Then He said to them, "Beware, and be on your guard against every form of greed; for not even when one has an abundance does his life consist of his possessions." (vs 16) And He told them a parable, saying, "The land of a rich man was very productive. (vs 17) "And he began reasoning to himself, saying, 'What shall I do, since I have no place to store my crops?' (vs 18) "Then he said, 'This is what I will do: I will tear down my barns and build larger ones, and there I will store all my grain and my goods. (vs 19) 'And I will say to my soul, "Soul, you have many goods laid up for many years to come; take your ease, eat, drink and be merry."' (vs 20) "But God said to him, 'You fool! This very night your soul is required of you; and now who will own what you have prepared?' (vs 21) "So is the man who stores up treasure for himself, and is not rich toward God."

a) The "stern warning" is that "true life" does not consist of our possessions. "True Life" is only found if we are rich toward God. We are warned to "beware" and "be on guard" against every form of greed. "Greed" as found in *(vs 15)* has the following meanings: avarice; fraudulency; extortion; and a practice of covetousness or greediness. Each of these expanded meanings of "Greed", as seen in the above definitions, implies a connotation of actively practicing such. Since all have a negative sense about them, and fully indicate less than honorable practices, we are to conscientiously remove ourselves from these vices. This "warning" is not from me, but is directly from the words of Jesus.

b) The "folly of riches" is your trust in them. If you really fill your barns full and say "now I'm set", "I can eat, drink and be merry for the rest of my life", this is where God addresses you as a "fool". The consequences of these types of actions are that your trust in possessions will end up by your being determined to be a "fool" by God. Your possessions, which will endure beyond your existence, will wind up belonging to someone else and therefore have no eternal value to you. The other part of this being called a "fool" is that your soul is required of you, meaning your eternal being, is being judged by God, and no amount of "material possessions" will be of any value or significance in this day of judgment. … *(James 5:1-3)(vs 1) Come now, you rich, weep and howl for your miseries which are coming upon you. (vs 2) Your riches have rotted and your garments have become moth-eaten. (vs 3) Your gold and your silver have rusted; and their rust will be a witness against you and will consume your flesh like fire. It is in the last days that you have stored up your treasure!* … If the "material treasures" which we have stored up are our "security blankets" these will be the very things that stand up and condemn us. Harsh words to accept? YES!!!, But not from any man, these words are from God's Holy Bible.

c) Fortunately, as always, the "warning" has a solution, and the position of being a "fool" is alleviated by the following "tremendous principle of our faith". If we are to be rich, **WE** "must be "***rich toward God***". … *(1 Timothy 6:17) Instruct those who are rich in this present world not to be conceited or to fix their hope on the uncertainty of riches, but on God, who richly supplies us with all things to enjoy.* … You cannot trust in "wealth", you can only trust in God and regardless of your mountains of possessions, your life is not measured by "material/perishable" things. This parable doesn't condemn "riches", but it severely condemns our "trust in them"! *(Proverbs 3:5-6)(vs 5) Trust in the LORD with all your heart And do not lean on your own understanding. (vs 6) In all your ways acknowledge Him, And He will make your paths straight.*

God's Holy Word was written some 2,000 years ago, but it is still active. Don't be a "fool" and allow "riches" that have rotted and "garments" that have become moth-eaten to be you prize, when you could have had **"JESUS"**!!!

5. LAZARUS AND A RICH MAN — In the selection of "Rich Men" of the Bible, this section would not be complete without this one. This account is so **"RICH"** in the Gospel presentation that it begs to be included. It dramatically demonstrates God's true eternal values.

(Luke 16:19-31)(vs 19) "Now there was a rich man, and he habitually dressed in purple and fine linen, joyously living in splendor every day. (vs 20) "And a poor man named Lazarus was laid at his gate, covered with sores, (vs 21) and longing to be fed with the crumbs which were falling from the rich man's table; besides, even the dogs were coming and licking his sores. (vs 22) "Now the poor man died and was carried away by the angels to Abraham's bosom; and the rich man also died and was buried. (vs 23) "In Hades he lifted up his eyes, being in torment, and *saw Abraham far away and Lazarus in his bosom. (vs 24) "And he cried out and said, 'Father Abraham, have mercy on me, and send Lazarus so that he may dip the tip of his finger in water and cool off my tongue, for I am in agony in this flame.' (vs 25) "But Abraham said, 'Child, remember that during your life you received your good things, and likewise Lazarus bad things; but now he is being comforted here, and you are in agony. (vs 26) 'And besides all this, between us and you there is a great chasm fixed, so that those who wish to come over from here to you will not be able, and that none may cross over from there to us.' (vs 27) "And he said, 'Then I beg you, father, that you send him to my father's house— (vs 28) for I have five brothers—in order that he may warn them, so that they will not also come to this place of torment.' (vs 29) "But Abraham *said, 'They have Moses and the Prophets; let them hear them.' (vs 30) "But he said, 'No, father Abraham, but if someone goes to them from the dead, they will repent!' (vs 31) "But he said to him, 'If they do not listen to Moses and

the Prophets, they will not be persuaded even if someone rises from the dead.'"

After re-reading the above, all I can do is to plead with anyone that doesn't have "believing faith" to listen to the modern day Moses and the solid, gospel teaching preachers of our day, and come to a trust in Jesus Christ. "Riches" will not last forever. Your relationship with Christ will!

6. MOSES AND PHARAOH'S WEALTH — **(Hebrews 11:24-26)(vs 24) By faith Moses, when he had grown up, refused to be called the son of Pharaoh's daughter, (vs 25) choosing rather to endure ill-treatment with the people of God than to enjoy the passing pleasures of sin, (vs 26) considering the reproach of Christ greater riches than the treasures of Egypt; for he was looking to the reward.**

Moses considered his faith in God more valuable than the passing pleasures of sin and the great riches found in the treasures of Egypt. It was the rewards of "knowing" God that Moses choose. Moses "Belongs To God"!!!

7. KING SOLOMON AND HIS KINGDOM OF WEALTH — **(1 Kings 10:23-29)(vs 23) So King Solomon became greater than all the kings of the earth in riches and in wisdom. (vs 24) All the earth was seeking the presence of Solomon, to hear his wisdom which God had put in his heart. (vs 25) They brought every man his gift, articles of silver and gold, garments, weapons, spices, horses, and mules, so much year by year. (vs 26) Now Solomon gathered chariots and horsemen; and he had 1,400 chariots and 12,000 horsemen, and he stationed them in the chariot cities and with the king in Jerusalem. (vs 27) The king made silver as common as stones in Jerusalem, and he made cedars as plentiful as sycamore trees that are in the lowland. (vs 28) Also Solomon's import of horses was from Egypt and Kue, and the king's merchants procured them from Kue for a price. (vs 29) A chariot was imported from Egypt for 600 shekels of silver, and a horse for 150; and by the same means they exported them to all the kings of the Hittites and to the kings of the Arameans.**

(2 Chronicles 1:11-12)(vs 11) God said to Solomon, "Because you had this in mind, and did not ask for riches, wealth or honor, or the life of those who hate you, nor have you even asked for long life, but you have asked for yourself wisdom and knowledge that you may rule My people over whom I have made you king, (vs 12) wisdom and knowledge have been granted to you. And I will give you riches and wealth and honor, such as none of the kings who were before you has possessed nor those who will come after you."

Solomon with all of his silver, gold, imported chariots and horses, mansions, and cities made of Lebanon Cedars, found no peace in the world's "material wealth". His only peace was in doing the will of God. Solomon chose wisdom and knowledge. He used submission, and delighting in serving "The Only True God", as his stronghold. Yes, he was made a "steward" of "material wealth", but his real purpose was to be found carrying out God's calling of ruling over God's people of the day. He was found faithful in this calling and arrived at the ultimate conclusion for all of mankind: ... *(Ecclesiastes 12:8,13 & 14)(vs 8) "Vanity of vanities," says the Preacher, "all is vanity!" (vs 13) The conclusion, when all has been heard, is: fear God and keep His commandments, because this applies to every person. (vs 14) For God will bring every act to judgment, everything which is hidden, whether it is good or evil.*

Solomon with all of his wealth and worldly pleasures could only arrive at one conclusion—*"fear God and keep His commandments"*. Our "fleeting" life, which will be over like the vapor of a cloud, needs to be saturated and grounded by God's Word, our "Owner's Manual". Fear ("reverence") God and keep His commandments. You will have difficulty obeying this unless you know his commandments. If you "Belong To Him", learn of His ways.

8. SIMON THE SORCERER—ASSUMED TO BE ACCUSTOMED TO MONEY — *(Acts 8:9-13 & 18-24)(vs 9) Now there was a man named Simon, who formerly was practicing magic in the city and astonishing the people of Samaria, claiming to be someone great; (vs 10) and they all, from smallest to greatest, were giving attention to him, saying, "This man is what is called the Great Power of God."*

(vs 11) And they were giving him attention because he had for a long time astonished them with his magic arts. (vs 12) But when they believed Philip preaching the good news about the kingdom of God and the name of Jesus Christ, they were being baptized, men and women alike. (vs 13) Even Simon himself believed; and after being baptized, he continued on with Philip, and as he observed signs and great miracles taking place, he was constantly amazed. (vs 18) Now when Simon saw that the Spirit was bestowed through the laying on of the apostles' hands, he offered them money, (vs 19) saying, "Give this authority to me as well, so that everyone on whom I lay my hands may receive the Holy Spirit." (vs 20) But Peter said to him, "May your silver perish with you, because you thought you could obtain the gift of God with money! (vs 21) "You have no part or portion in this matter, for your heart is not right before God. (vs 22) "Therefore repent of this wickedness of yours, and pray the Lord that, if possible, the intention of your heart may be forgiven you. (vs 23) "For I see that you are in the gall of bitterness and in the bondage of iniquity." (vs 24) But Simon answered and said, "Pray to the Lord for me yourselves, so that nothing of what you have said may come upon me."

This passage has been included because we have all seen the "Charlatans" on TV, raising money in the name of God and Jesus. It is despicable, and only if these turn to God as Simon did in the above verses, will they be saved. Let us not major on the "Charlatans" of this world, but rather major on the Word of God and its message to us.

We see a man in Simon the Sorcerer who had "believing faith" in Jesus. Then in his exuberance, immaturity in Christ and his humanness, after witnessing Philip doing great miracles in the name of Jesus, tried to purchase the Holy Spirit. We can only presume that Simon wanted to profit from this. Philip pointed out the error of trying to buy God's blessings by calling this "wickedness" and the need for repentance (which was immediately sought by Simon). We can gather from this that money is not to be used to buy God's blessings. We are not to try to manipulate God in any way with "Material Wealth" or to try to make money by using God's Holy name.

I. WHAT IS IMPORTANT! — "JESUS" OR "GOLD"?:

There are many examples of what is important in this life and the life to come. We are to sort out the important things and choose to honor our Lord and Savior with this wisdom. The following are a few examples of the **"important things"**.

1. (Acts 3:1-9 & 16)(vs 1) Now Peter and John were going up to the temple at the ninth hour, the hour of prayer. (vs 2) And a man who had been lame from his mother's womb was being carried along, whom they used to set down every day at the gate of the temple which is called Beautiful, in order to beg alms of those who were entering the temple. (vs 3) When he saw Peter and John about to go into the temple, he began asking to receive alms. (vs 4) But Peter, along with John, fixed his gaze on him and said, "Look at us!" (vs 5) And he began to give them his attention, expecting to receive something from them. (vs 6) But Peter said, "I do not possess silver and gold, but what I do have I give to you: In the name of Jesus Christ the Nazarene—walk!" (vs 7) And seizing him by the right hand, he raised him up; and immediately his feet and his ankles were strengthened. (vs 8) With a leap he stood upright and began to walk; and he entered the temple with them, walking and leaping and praising God. (vs 9) And all the people saw him walking and praising God; (vs 16) "And on the basis of faith in His name, it is the name of Jesus which has strengthened this man whom you see and know; and the faith which comes through Him has given him this perfect health in the presence of you all.

Peter and John had only one choice. They had no silver or gold, but even if they did have silver and gold they **STILL** would have offered the lame man the most precious gift this world has ever known. They offered Jesus, and it was the lame man's "believing faith" that made him whole, both in physical strength and more importantly in a spiritual "New Birth". This man was praising God for his being able to walk, but more than that he was **PRAISING** God for his "New Life In Jesus Christ", the One "To Whom he Now Belongs"!!!

2. (Joshua 24:13-15 & 18)(vs 13) 'I gave you a land on which you had not labored, and cities which you had not built, and you have lived in them; you are eating of vineyards and olive groves which you did not plant.' (vs 14) "Now, therefore, fear the LORD and serve Him in sincerity and truth; and put away the gods which your fathers served beyond the River and in Egypt, and serve the LORD. (vs 15) "If it is disagreeable in your sight to serve the LORD, choose for yourselves today whom you will serve: whether the gods which your fathers served which were beyond the River, or the gods of the Amorites in whose land you are living; but as for me and my house, we will serve the LORD." (vs 18) "The LORD drove out from before us all the peoples, even the Amorites who lived in the land. We also will serve the LORD, for He is our God."

God gave the children of Israel land, cities, vineyards and olive groves. They were spoiled. Joshua called these people to attention and said **"choose for yourselves today whom you will serve", as for me and my house, we will serve the LORD."** Joshua chose the "important things" above the "material wealth" of this world. We see in **(vs 18)** these people followed his leadership and declared the "LORD to be their God".

3. (Proverbs 17:3) The refining pot is for silver and the furnace for gold, But the LORD tests hearts.

The world refines silver and gold and tosses aside the "dross". God refines the heart and put our sins as far away as the East is from the West. He remembers our sins "no more".

4. (Proverbs 22:1-2)(vs 1) A good name is to be more desired than great wealth, Favor is better than silver and gold. (vs 2) The rich and the poor have a common bond, The LORD is the maker of them all.

When God comes into a person's life, that person is no longer "rich" or "poor" as the world defines such, but he is now a Child of the Living God, a brother to all other "believers", and is an heir to the One who "owns the cattle on a thousand hills".

J. OTHER SCRIPTURES REGARDING "RICHES"/SOME INCLUDE THE "FOLLY OF RICHES"!!!

There are many scriptures found in the Bible regarding "Material Wealth" and "Riches". The following are a few and are fairly self-explanatory. We can all benefit from these.

<u>1</u>. *(Jeremiah 9:23-24)(vs 23) Thus says the LORD, "Let not a wise man boast of his wisdom, and let not the mighty man boast of his might, let not a rich man boast of his riches; (vs 24) but let him who boasts boast of this, that he understands and knows Me, that I am the LORD who exercises lovingkindness, justice and righteousness on earth; for I delight in these things," declares the LORD.*

You want to delight yourself in the Lord, then boast in understanding and "knowing the Lord". There is no value in boasting in wisdom, might or riches. All of these give God no delight, but in "knowing Him", He delights. "Knowing Him" or "Understanding Him" is to have a delightful relationship with Him, this is true "Riches".

<u>2a</u>. *(Psalms 49:1-12)(vs 1) Hear this, all peoples; Give ear, all inhabitants of the world, (vs 2) Both low and high, Rich and poor together. (vs 3) My mouth will speak wisdom, And the meditation of my heart will be understanding. (vs 5) Why should I fear in days of adversity, When the iniquity of my foes surrounds me, (vs 6) Even those who trust in their wealth And boast in the abundance of their riches? (vs 7) No man can by any means redeem his brother Or give to God a ransom for him—(vs 8) For the redemption of his soul is costly, And he should cease trying forever—(vs 9) That he should live on eternally, That he should not undergo decay. (vs 10) For he sees that even wise men die; The stupid and the senseless alike perish And leave their wealth to others. (vs 11) Their inner thought is that their houses are forever And their dwelling places to all generations; They have called their lands after their own names. (vs 12) But man in his pomp will not endure; He is like the beasts that perish.*

This scripture puts "Material Wealth" in its perspective. It is so descriptive to see that God in the Old Testament knew the heart of man.

He knew that man would even name their houses after themselves, a form of idolizing their possessions. Again it is not evil in and of itself, but the foolishness or evil is in the trusting in such. All men will die, and all "possessions" will belong to someone else.

2b. *(Psalms 49:16-20)(vs 16) Do not be afraid when a man becomes rich, When the glory of his house is increased; (vs 17) For when he dies he will carry nothing away; His glory will not descend after him. (vs 18) Though while he lives he congratulates himself— And though men praise you when you do well for yourself— (vs 19) He shall go to the generation of his fathers; They will never see the light. (vs20) Man in his pomp, yet without understanding, Is like the beasts that perish.*

Man without God is relegated to and described as a "beast", which perishes in the wild, while no one looks on.

A word to the wise is sufficient, ... *(Proverbs 9:8-9)(vs 8) Do not reprove a scoffer, or he will hate you, Reprove a wise man and he will love you.*

(vs 9) Give instruction to a wise man and he will be still wiser, Teach a righteous man and he will increase his learning. ... but when God repeats Himself, we better have our ears perk up. Look at **verses 12 and 20** above. See the similarity. Man in his owning wealth or precious things, by his considering his status or value being related to these things, is like the cattle or a dumb beast, which will be cut down and destroyed, because of this poor discernment. That is what it says, twice!

"Riches" or "Material Wealth" are not bad unless we place our value or trust in them. We need to "Belong To God" not our "earthly things".

3. The parable of the four soils has several warnings, including the three warnings that are found in the third soil. *(Mark 4:18-19)(vs 18) "And others are the ones on whom seed was sown among the thorns; these are the ones who have heard the word, (vs 19) but the worries of the world, and the deceitfulness of riches, and the desires for other things enter in and choke the word, and it becomes unfruitful.* It is the ... *"worries of the world, and the deceitfulness of riches, and the desires for other things"* ... that can destroy us.

Within these three warnings are specifically two "material things" that can take our affection away from God. These two are "***deceitfulness of riches***" and "***desires for other things***". "Other things" is defined in this case as: having no relationship to anything Godly, but only of physical things, remnants, or residue. "Riches" is defined as: wealth, money, possessions, abundance. In both cases they refer to "material" things of this world. The warning is not against the having of these things, but in the deceitfulness and desires that can take control and choke our love for God. These "things" can control our being, therefore taking away our trust in God and placing our trust in perishable possessions and self-worth. It is absolutely certain the warnings are, "to not be choked by a desire for the things of this world". "We Belong To Him"!!! We are not to be controlled by the "financial net worth principle" found as this world's measurement of success and value.

4. The dangers of both "riches" and "poverty".

(Proverbs 30:7-9)(vs 7) Two things I asked of You, Do not refuse me before I die: (vs 8) Keep deception and lies far from me, Give me neither poverty nor riches; Feed me with the food that is my portion, (vs 9) That I not be full and deny You and say, "Who is the LORD?" Or that I not be in want and steal, And profane the name of my God.

These verses are so neat in that they give us powerful, yet gentle warnings about the potential weaknesses of our human nature or our human character. We don't want to be so wealthy and "full" that we forget our relationship with God, and forget that it is He who provides even the food for the birds of the air. Neither do we want to be found in poverty to the point we are tempted to do wrong to gain our necessities.

In other words we need to be found trusting God. We have, by all certainty, many verses of scripture found in our "Owner's Manual", that promise His provisions as needed. Please note the critical keys to the above verses, ... "***Keep deception and lies far from me, Give me neither poverty nor riches***". The plea here is that God will protect us from all deception and lies. This trust relationship with our God is the most important thing we have and needs to be cultivated. Since "We Belong To Him", and as we study our "Owner's Manual", we will find peace and balance in the midst of this earthly turmoil.

5. *(Psalms 62:10) Do not trust in oppression And do not vainly hope in robbery; If riches increase, do not set your heart upon them.*

Certainly we are not to seek to gain by oppression or robbery, this is universally recognized in all societies as being wrong. If your "riches" seem to come naturally and the word "riches" in this verse means: wealth; with the association of valor; worthy; and virtuously gained, we are given a warning to ***"not set your heart upon them"***. Be thankful to God for all His blessings, and do not be tempted to trust in one of those God-given blessings, rather than "trusting" in the "giver" of the blessings.

6. *(Proverbs 11:4) Riches do not profit in the day of wrath, But righteousness delivers from death.*

"Temporal things" will not be a source of confidence when God judges the entire population of the world. This judgment will come for all who have ever lived upon the face of this earth, from day one to present. ... ***(Isaiah 45:23) "I have sworn by Myself, The word has gone forth from My mouth in righteousness And will not turn back, That to Me every knee will bow, every tongue will swear allegiance. ... (Romans 14:10-11)(vs 10)But you, why do you judge your brother? Or you again, why do you regard your brother with contempt? For we will all stand before the judgment seat of God. (vs 11) For it is written, "AS I LIVE, SAYS THE LORD, EVERY KNEE SHALL BOW TO ME, AND EVERY TONGUE SHALL GIVE PRAISE TO GOD."***

If you "Belong To Him", the righteousness as imputed through Jesus, will be your salvation in that day of death or judgment. Jesus will return, and even if we die before His return, upon our death we will experience our day of judgment. In the Day of Judgment, "riches" will hold "**NO VALUE OR RESPECT**"!!!

7. God owns it all! ***(Psalms 50:10-12)(vs 10) "For every beast of the forest is Mine, The cattle on a thousand hills. (vs 11) "I know every bird of the mountains, And everything that moves in the field is Mine. (vs 12) "If I were hungry I would not tell you, For the world is Mine, and all it contains.***

(Psalms 24:1) A Psalm of David. The earth is the LORD'S, and all it contains, The world, and those who dwell in it.

After reading these verses, is there anyone out there that thinks God is impressed with our "Material Wealth"? The forests are His, the cattle on a thousand hills. If He is hungry(?), He doesn't need to tell us, He owns every pizza house in the world.

Can we imagine or visualize the largest ranch in Texas? It is a speck from outer space compared to what God owns. If He owns the cattle on a thousand hills, I guarantee you He owns the hills also. If He owns it all, and we are a Child of His through His grace, then we are a "Child and an Heir" of a "King". We "Belong To Him"!!!

Isn't it beautiful how God's Word all ties together, from Genesis through Revelations. His Word is truly magnificent, and it is our "Owner's Manual".

K. CONCLUSION TO "MATERIAL WEALTH" OR "RICHES":

1. An Introduction To The Conclusion:

Can you believe this, an Introduction to a Conclusion. *(Jeremiah 9:23-24)(vs 23) Thus says the LORD, "Let not a wise man boast of his wisdom, and let not the mighty man boast of his might, let not a rich man boast of his riches; (vs 24) but let him who boasts boast of this, that he understands and knows Me, that I am the LORD who exercises lovingkindness, justice and righteousness on earth; for I delight in these things," declares the LORD.*

True riches are "Knowing God". He has many mysteries. He will reveal many things that we now see dimly or as looking through a dark glass. He is "just" and "righteous". He will judge the hearts of all mankind. Our only "boast" is in understanding and knowing Him, therefore, our only "boast" is in "Belonging To Him"!!!

What has been documented by many sources as the most wealthy family and business in the world, are the Walton heirs and the Wal-Mart Corporation. This Company, according to their own Web Site started in 1962. From a single discount store, this Company has grown through 2009, into the largest retailer in the World. It has 1.4 million U. S. employees, operates more than 4,000 U. S. stores and adds an additional 30,000 employees to their domestic staff each year.

With all of this being counted on their financial statements in the Billions of dollars, the one who "KNOWS" Jesus in a personal way is wealthier, beyond measure, than Wal-Mart and its heirs.

Knowing Jesus gives us a "peace that surpasses all understanding". *(Philippians 4:6-7)(vs 6) Be anxious for nothing, but in everything by prayer and supplication with thanksgiving let your requests be made known to God. (vs 7) And the peace of God, which surpasses all comprehension, will guard your hearts and your minds in Christ Jesus.*
Knowing Jesus, by simple childlike faith, is far more "riches" than all the money in the world.

2. Some Additional Thoughts In Conclusion:

A very good friend of mine once told me to "never own anything that eats while you sleep". Fine wisdom for sure, but this thought can be taken one step further and that is, "don't own anything that cannot be used for God's Glory"!!! Unless what we own can bring Glory to God, we should consider its value, why do we have it, and is it a detriment to my "Belonging To Him"!

This spiritual assessment of owning or accumulating "material wealth" or "possessions" should be exercised frequently and those items which don't or can't bring "Glory To God" should be "exorcised" out of our life. Each person that "gets in on what God is doing", rather than trying to "get God in on what we are doing", will want to "Exorcise" those items of uselessness from their possessions.

Assuming these items have monetary value, you can always con-tribute the items, or the money from the sale of such items, to Missions, Missionary work, feed the poor, etc. You and God be the judge where it goes. There are so many places that can become a blessing to others.
... *(Acts 20:35) "In everything I showed you that by working hard in this manner you must help the weak and remember the words of the Lord Jesus, that He Himself said, 'It is more blessed to give than to receive.'"*

3. Miscellaneous Thoughts To Conclude this Chapter on 'Material Wealth", "Riches":

a. *(Proverbs 2:1-5 & 21-22)(vs 1) My son, if you will receive my words And treasure my commandments within you, (vs 2) Make your ear attentive to wisdom, Incline your heart to understanding; (vs 3) For if you cry for discernment, Lift your voice for understanding; (vs 4) If you seek her as silver And search for her as for hidden treasures; (vs 5) Then you will discern the fear of the LORD And discover the knowledge of God. (vs 21) For the upright will live in the land And the blameless will remain in it; (vs 22) But the wicked will be cut off from the land And the treacherous will be uprooted from it.*

If you "Belong To Him", surely you listen to Him. He says, *"receive my words And treasure my commandments"*, *"cry for discernment, Lift your voice for understanding"*. The conclusion is found in verse four. If we will seek and search to know God as much as we seek and search for silver and hidden treasures, then we ... *"will discern the fear of the LORD And discover the knowledge of God"* ... and we will be found to be *"upright"* and *"blameless"*.;

b. *(Proverbs 3:13-17)(vs 13) How blessed is the man who finds wisdom And the man who gains understanding. (vs 14) For her profit is better than the profit of silver And her gain better than fine gold. (vs 15) She is more precious than jewels; And nothing you desire compares with her. (vs 16) Long life is in her right hand; In her left hand are riches and honor. (vs 17) Her ways are pleasant ways And all her paths are peace.*

The Bible has a way of perfectly stating and reinforcing itself. It does this here, in a classical manner, for everything found in this Chapter.;

c. *(Job 22:21-27)(vs 21) "Yield now and be at peace with Him; Thereby good will come to you. (vs 22) "Please receive instruction from His mouth And establish His words in your heart. (vs 23) "If you return to the Almighty, you will be restored; If you remove unrighteousness far from your tent, (vs 24) And place your gold in the dust, And the gold of Ophir among the stones of the brooks, (vs 25) Then the Almighty will be your gold And choice silver to you. (vs 26) "For then you will delight in the Almighty And lift up your face to God. (vs 27) "You will pray to Him, and He will hear you; And you will pay your vows.*

God does not condemn "material wealth" or "riches", He simply says place your trust in Him, not in the things of this world. He even says in doing so, one of the blessings will be riches and honor.; and

d. (Psalms 19:7-10)(vs 7) The law of the LORD is perfect, restoring the soul; The testimony of the LORD is sure, making wise the simple. (vs 8) The precepts of the LORD are right, rejoicing the heart; The commandment of the LORD is pure, enlightening the eyes. (vs 9) The fear of the LORD is clean, enduring forever; The judgments of the LORD are true; they are righteous altogether. (vs 10) They are more desirable than gold, yes, than much fine gold; Sweeter also than honey and the drippings of the honeycomb.

The precepts of the LORD, the Word of God and His Instructions, are more desirable than "pure refined gold". Yes, they are more blessed than anything we can imagine. His Word, our "Owner's Manual", teaches these truths to all who "Belong To Him"!!!

4. A Conclusion To The Conclusion:

Can you believe this, a Conclusion to the Conclusion. I did mention there were a lot of scriptures regarding "material wealth" and "riches", didn't I?

We are going to look at one last verse, it contains the "unfathomable" riches of Christ. There could no better conclusion to "riches" then to expose you to ... _"**the unfathomable riches of Christ**"._

(Ephesians 3:8-12)(vs 8) To me, the very least of all saints, this grace was given, to preach to the Gentiles the unfathomable riches of Christ,

(vs 9) and to bring to light what is the administration of the mystery which for ages has been hidden in God who created all things; (vs 10) so that the manifold wisdom of God might now be made known through the church to the rulers and the authorities in the heavenly places. (vs 11) This was in accordance with the eternal purpose which He carried out in Christ Jesus our Lord, (vs 12) in whom we have boldness and confident access through faith in Him.

These words, written by the hand of Paul, the least of all of God's saints, fully enlighten us to God's miraculous and glorious plan of salvation, to both the Gentiles and the Jews. "Riches" or "Material

Wealth" are indescribably usurped by "True Unfathomable Riches" in "Knowing" Jesus. We have access to this "eternal purpose" of God, this plan before the beginning of time, which was to bring "salvation" to man through "believing faith" in Him. What beautiful and impacting words, and just to think it is all found in His Holy Word!!!

These "unfathomable" riches are defined in the original Greek to be: not tracked out; by implication—untraceable; past finding out; inscrutable; incomprehensible; and unsearchable. These "unfathomable" riches in Christ are, "knowing" Christ in a personal way and not at all talking about or pointing to, "material wealth".

As we think about this, we cannot even comprehend these "unfathomable" riches in Christ. If we think about or discuss the wealth of this world, and we define or reduce to print a description of earthly riches as compiled into one person's financial statement, or one place such as the gold in Fort Knox, we are only highlighting a poor example of His "real" riches.

Sam Walton founded the Wal-Mart stores. He started small, and now if his wealth was put back into his hands alone, he is the wealthiest person in the USA if not the world. His wealth can and is measured daily in the Billions and grows by multiple Billions each year. This is defined and measured, yet it is NOTHING compared to each person who is a Child of The Living God.

We as adopted members of His family, have all the rights as full heirs to His kingdom. As an heir of God the Father, we have these "immeasurable", "indescribable", "inscrutable", **"unfathomable"** riches of Christ Jesus. With our "unfathomable" riches in Christ, we will only know in glory the true meaning of this verse. We truly live by faith, as taught throughout the Bible, and as the Holy Spirit gives this faith and hope, we trust in things presently unseen. Someday it will all be gloriously revealed to us.

The "UNFATHOMABLE" riches in Christ are our hope , our conviction, our reason for living, our reason for placing our lives in the hands of the Almighty God, and our reason for desiring to and truly "Belonging To Him"!!! Our reason is not for earthly "wealth", which rots, rusts or is stolen, but it is in the "KNOWING HIM" that matters.

We will never be able to define "UNFATHOMABLE". It is like trying to put a numerical value on the word infinity. "UNFATHOMABLE" riches in Christ are the "best", the only true "riches' and the only ones that are "imperishable". .... *(Psalms 4:2)...How **long will you love what is worthless and aim at deception? Selah.***

"Material Wealth" is neutral, it is neither good nor bad, it has its place.

"KNOWING JESUS" is the true **"UNFATHOMABLE RICHES"**!!!

SPECIAL NOTE:
I know many of you may have a special verse or verses regarding this Chapter's subject matter. This special verse or these verses may not have been mentioned due to my ignorance or because of brevity. I apologize for either of these reasons. Please feel free to write any special verse or verses in the space below. This will add your personal touch, and will serve to call to each person's mind their individual "experience of trust", in God's Holy Word.

For to each of us "Who belong To Him", His Holy Word can be truly recognized and relied upon as our **"Owner's Manual"**!!!

_____

_____

_____

_____

_____

_____

_____

CHAPTER 17

GOD'S CONCLUSION (TO ALL MATTERS)

INTRODUCTORY VERSE:

(Ecclesiastes 12:13-14)(vs 13) The conclusion, when all has been heard, is: fear God and keep His commandments, because this applies to every person. (vs 14) For God will bring every act to judgment, everything which is hidden, whether it is good or evil.

A breakdown of the above verse will be the conclusion of all matters. Our instructions are to live with a fear or reverence of the Almighty Heavenly Father. We are to know His commands and keep them. To know His commandments we must get into His Word and learn of His mind and His ways. If we "Belong To Him" we will trust His "Owner's Manual" to give us direction. God is the final judge. He will bring to light everything which is hidden.

A. CONCLUSION DEFINED ... *(vs 13) The conclusion, when all has been heard,:*

Conclusion in the Hebrew definition means: a termination, end, conclusion, hinder part. It is the final word when all has been heard and done. As Solomon has so appropriately stated in Chapter 14 of Ecclesiastes, the true evaluation of all of life is measured by our reverence and respect for God and His Word. Solomon had spent 13 previous Chapters in Ecclesiastes explaining in detail how all things in this world will not satisfy our human desires. He explains that every human pleasure that is sought after is "vanity" and "blowing in the wind". Neither of these, the descriptive noun nor the descriptive phrase, are of any eternal value.

It is only God who delivers peace and sanity as we come to understand and know Him. Conclusion in the Hebrew means the last word, the end of all matters. It is God's final Word on all matters!!!

B. WHAT IS THE BIBLICAL CONCLUSION TO ALL MATTERS ... *(vs 13) The conclusion is: fear God and keep His commandments, :*

The first part of our command is to *"fear God"* or to be afraid, awesomely terrified or in reverence of the Only Supreme God (Yahweh). Our second command is to *"keep His commandments"*. My thoughts, when thinking about keeping His commandments, keep coming back to one major necessity. If we are to keep His commandments, and we have certainly concluded we must do so, we are to know His Word. Successful living on this earth is to reverence God, know His Word and keep these God given principles, keeping His Word as found in our "Owner's Manual" – The Holy Bible. To know His Word, we must put time into the study of It!!!

C. TO WHOM DOES THIS APPLY ... *(vs 13), because this applies to every person.:*

The Hebrew definition for "every" means: whole, any, all and every, with the attachment of one, place or thing. Thus the definition includes any, all and every person that has or will have walked the surface of the earth. We are all to hear and heed His Holy Word!!!

D. CONSEQUENSES OF HEEDING OR IGNORING GOD'S CONCLUSION:

(vs 14) For God will bring every act to judgment, everything which is hidden, whether it is good or evil.

It matters not what our pursuits were while on this earth, for God will bring them all to judgment. His final Word and Judgment is **just**, and will cover all human endeavors whether *"good or evil"*. His omnipotence, as exercised in His judgments, will be final!!!

E. SUMMARY OF GOD'S CONCLUSION:

1. It is God's desire that we place Him and reverence Him above all earthly things!!!

2. It is His desire that we know His Word and so love Him, that we keep His commandments!!!

3. It is His desire, that this Most Holy Relationship with Him, be required of **all** "faith believers"!!!

4. It is His desire that we know that His judgment will be fair and final for all of our endeavors!!!

5. It is His desire that along with His judgment, there is **forgiveness** available for all of our sins, … *(John 3:16) "For God so loved the world, that He gave His only begotten Son, that whoever believes in Him shall not perish, but have eternal life.* … for without this **forgiveness** all would perish!!!

6. It is His desire that we become Father and adopted son, with all the rights of His Son, Jesus!

(Revelation 21:6-7)(vs 6) Then He said to me, "It is done. I am the Alpha and the Omega, the beginning and the end. I will give to the one who thirsts from the spring of the water of life without cost. (vs 7) "He who overcomes will inherit these things, and I will be his God and he will be My son.

7. It is His desire that we come to Him, but if we choose to remain in our "unbelieving" state, it is His judgment that we must face.

(Revelation 21:8) "But for the cowardly and unbelieving and abominable and murderers and immoral persons and sorcerers and idolaters and all liars, their part will be in the lake that burns with fire and brimstone, which is the second death."

The "Conclusion" of man upon his death is One of Two things. Either an acceptance of the Gift from God, and that is the completed work of Jesus Christ upon the Cross of Calvary, or to face eternal separation from God, facing eternity in the lake of fire and brimstone. The "Conclusion" of "man" can be only One or the Other. I plead with **YOU** to search your heart and search the Scriptures until **YOU** are certain that **YOU** "Belong To Him"!!!

F. MY PERSONAL TESTIMONY REGARDING THE CONCLUSION OF MAN:

I, for one, in all humility, make my declaration that I "Belong To God the Father and Jesus Christ the Son, with the indwelling of the Holy Spirit"!!! This statement of "believing faith" is based upon ... *(Ephesians 2:8-9)(vs 8) For by grace you have been saved through faith; and that not of yourselves, it is the gift of God; (vs 9) not as a result of works, so that no one may boast.* Because of this "personal relationship" with the Only True and Almighty God, I can absolutely state without a quiver or a doubt, I know "To Whom I Belong". I equally know His Holy Word is my "Owner's Manual".

There is a much Truth and Wisdom found in this Book, but it is only real because it is the Living Word of God. His Scripture contains all Truth and Wisdom and is the only thing that can be found to be eternal. Anything else will rust, rot or turn to dust. The Word of God is the only "True Wisdom" to be found anywhere, and it will be found to be Imperishable. If we "Belong to Him", the Word of God is our "Owner's Manual". He designed us, He built or created us, He knows every detail of our being (including the number of hairs on our head)! The Conclusion is simple, yet so extraordinarily complete ... *"The conclusion, when all has been heard, is: fear God and keep His commandments, because this applies to every person".*

(Genesis 1:27) God created man in His own image, in the image of God He created him; male and female He created them. Unfortunately, ever since Creation, man has been trying to re-create God in man's image.

(Matthew 5:48) "Therefore you are to be perfect, as your heavenly Father is perfect. Let each of us "Who Belong To Him", attempt to be perfect. We all know we will fail, for that is why God has provided for repentance and forgiveness, but I pray that as we each ramble through this earthly life, that we do not **PLAN** to fail.

His Holy Book, our "Owner's Manual", will set all things straight as we ... *"fear God and keep His commandments".*

SPECIAL NOTE:

I know many of you may have a special verse or verses regarding this Chapter's subject matter. This special verse or these verses may not have been mentioned due to my ignorance or because of brevity. I apologize for either of these reasons. Please feel free to write any special verse or verses in the space below. This will add your personal touch, and will serve to call to each person's mind their individual "experience of trust", in God's Holy Word.

For to each of us "Who belong To Him", His Holy Word can be truly recognized and relied upon as our **"Owner's Manual"**!!!

_____

_____

_____

_____

_____

_____

_____